WORDS MATTER.
Elections and Consequences in American Politics

by: S.J. Helgesen

Introduction

Groucho Marx was one of my boyhood heroes, and now that I'm older, he's become one of my superheroes. His unique brand of wisecracking, disdain for authority and slightly off-kilter views of life continue to appeal to me. Take this quote: "Outside of a dog, a book is a man's best friend. Inside of a dog, it's too dark to read." In a roundabout way that quote points to one of the thorniest political problems we face today...how to find common ground that is built on mutually accepted truths (*inside of a dog it's too dark to read*). This book is not about Julius (Groucho) Marx nor any comic or political satirist for that matter. Instead, it's my take on what our national politics has become since I returned to the USA after spending 20 years abroad in the U.S. Foreign Service. I came back just in time to see George W. Bush re-elected.

As a U.S. diplomat serving abroad, I observed American politics from a vantage point *way outside* the Beltway: in Europe, the Caribbean Basin and the Pacific Rim. Living and working in over 30 countries, I was expected to be a spokesman for the 'American way of life.' I did my best to explain our country, its political system and culture to people who had never been to the U.S. and to many who had but were confused about what they experienced. As a stand-in for America, I was often the target of pointed criticism, some praise and occasional gratitude. One time a man came up to me in St. George's, Grenada in the West Indies and thanked me for the U.S.' intervention in that island country in 1983 that threw out the Communists. I simply said, "You're welcome" and went on my way.

Why you should read this book

There are two reasons: The first is that we should not forget what got us to this point in our political history. By remembering the last eight years, we are more likely to avoid the same mistakes in the next eight years. The second is that I believe we have chosen a new path - a third way - in how we conduct ourselves, politically, and it's probably time we did some soul-searching and self-analysis. Also, there's a slew of *Trump books* popping up over the last few months. Seems like anybody that can spell Trump feels they can write a book about him - with authority. I'm not one of them, though my co-author of "Breaking Republican" and "How Republicans can win in a changing America" (Lance Tarrance, a renowned and roundly respected pollster) and I spoke of the likelihood of a non-traditional *third way* candidate winning the presidency in 2016. I'm proud to say that we were right on target.

I even predicted Trump's win on live Danish television on election eve from a studio overlooking Times Square long before the State of Pennsylvania was called. (In the end, my prediction came within one electoral vote of the actual outcome.) Near the end of the program, the Danish moderator asked me what I thought Trump's chances of winning were. I said, "80%." At that point, the other panelists sort of chuckled to themselves feeling certain that a Hillary Clinton victory was in the bag. We closed down the set at midnight and a few hours later I was awakened by a phone call telling me that Trump had, indeed, pulled it off.

I decided to stay up and begin preparation for my next interview which was to be held bright and early on November 9th on Times Square. I remember walking there from my hotel past throngs of people with their heads bowed, looking like zombies. An antediluvian pall had descended on New Yorkers who realized that 'their' gal had been cast out from the political Garden of Eden by a Philistine who had little or no regard for the art of politics, and they were in a profound state of shock. Some were still wearing their Hillary buttons, but nothing even remotely resembling a smile passed their lips. It was at that moment that I knew we had crossed the political Rubicon and that life wouldn't be the same...at least for the next four years.

We were about to enter the age of a *third way* presidency and I was determined to chronicle it as I did with the eight-year long *winter of discontent* for conservatives during Barack Obama's reign.

What follows are about 300 articles on the new politics of America, starting with the Obama Presidency extending into the first few months of Donald J. Trump's administration. They are presented in alphabetical order by chapter. For me, the political clock of our new millennium really started ticking with the entry of businessman Ross Perot into the Presidential race in 1992. But that's another story for a whole other book. In the meantime, enjoy this one.

CONTENTS

Chapter I
The giant sucking sound

Who would have thought way back in 1992 that a wiry plain-talking businessman from Texarkana, Texas would be cast as a spoiler for President George H.W. Bush in his bid for a second term in the White House? And who would have guessed that Mr. Perot (now 87 years old) would garner 18.9% of the popular vote to do it? Not many. Certainly not Mr. Bush himself. But spoil his chances he did and managed to usher in a new paradigm in American politics...for good.

For those too young to remember, or for those who've already forgotten, Mr. Perot began his business life as a salesman for IBM. Later, not feeling terribly appreciated, he formed his own company, Electronic Data Systems (EDS) in Dallas (the company offered data processing services). After beating the pavement, Perot finally landed some lucrative U.S. government contracts in 1960 computerizing Medicare records.

Eight years later, Mr. Perot took the company public, and the stock price went from $16/share to $160 within mere days, making him a very rich Texan, indeed. Sixteen years later, General Motors bought controlling interest in EDS for a cool $2.4 billion. Unfortunately, in April of 1970, the company's shares plummeted and the loss of $450 million in a single day earned him the distinction of being "the biggest individual loser ever" on the NYSE.

Perot has always been a firm believer in technology, so it was natural that he decided to invest $20 million in Apple founder, Steve Job's venture, NeXT (he missed out investing in Microsoft when he had the opportunity). Ross Perot's political ambitions go way back. He was involved in the Vietnam POW/MIA cause believing that many American servicemen were left behind after America's exit from that country. He was active behind the scenes (much to the consternation of the Reagan and George H.W. Bush administrations) and actually reached an agreement in 1990 with Vietnam's Foreign Ministry to become its business agent should relations with the U.S. Government become normalized.

Perot's stance on social issues like abortion and homosexual rights put him at odds with mainstream Republicans though he rarely discussed them, openly. It is reported that he now supports a 'right to life' platform, but it is on the issues of fiscal responsibility that Perot's star shone most brightly. He announced his intention to run as an Independent on the

'Larry King Live' show in February of 1992. His main themes were: a balanced Federal budget with deficit reduction, a softening of gun control and the cessation of outsourced jobs to foreign countries, mainly to Mexico.

Amazingly, in June, a Gallup poll gave him 39% of the likely vote which shocked both the Republican and Democratic camps. A month later, he mirrored the actions of America's now 45th President by 'going his own way' and refusing to listen to his political advisors who were encouraging him to be more specific about his policies.

Preferring the populist route, Perot tapped into a growing dissatisfaction with the Washington establishment and the policies of President Bush who favored a multi-lateral trade agreement with Canada and Mexico (something his successor, Bill Clinton, would successfully sign after winning the Presidency).

The political marker was laid down, but Perot's troubles lay in steadily dropping polling numbers. When he got to 20% he briefly suspended his campaign only to revive it in October after qualifying on all 50 states' ballots. The campaign was fraught with resignations, but Perot soldiered on and spent a little over $12 million of his own money and participated in a now famous Presidential debate with Bush and Clinton in which he predicted that there would be "a giant sucking sound" of jobs leaving the U.S. unless something was done fast to stem the flow of outsourcing. A day of reckoning, he said, would be coming for the American economy.

Perot did receive the largest number of votes ever cast for a U.S. third party candidate, 19,741,065, though he didn't capture a single electoral vote. For most people that would have been the end of the story, but quitting wasn't in his DNA. In 1995, he formed the Reform Party and won the nomination to be its standard-bearer in the 1996 Presidential election, but because of ballot access laws he was forced to run as an independent. The result was disappointing. He managed to get only 8% of the vote, a significant drop from his 18.9% in 1992.

Mr. Perot receded into the political bleachers for many years until he made news by coming out against Republican Presidential candidate, Senator John McCain, and instead supported former Massachusetts Governor Mitt Romney. In 2012, he again endorsed Governor Romney for President. The issues that Ross Perot championed back in 1992, especially those affecting the outsourcing of jobs and the subsequent passage of NAFTA (which by most accounts led to the loss of over 600,000 American jobs) are still relevant today. Mr. Perot lifted the veil on a stubborn problem. It is now up to current and future presidents and the Congress to tackle it. Perhaps Perot's most lasting political achievement was his clearing of a path for the emergence of third party movements like the Tea Party AND for a *Third-way* Presidency, something for which we should all thank him.

Chapter II
Eight years in the desert

For many Americans, William Jefferson Clinton's eight years in office were just a warm-up exercise for the main event - the Democrats' permanent control of the levers of power in Washington, DC. Unfortunately for them, George W. Bush interrupted their plans, but not for long.

The 'right man' was waiting in the wings, one with Bill Clinton's charisma and charm and a gift for oratory. But this man was different. He wasn't going to move to the center like Clinton unless it was on the basketball court for a layup. He was on a mission to radically change the way America thought, the way it acted AND the way it voted...forever.

His presidency was one of the most divisive in history and served to widen the gap between the two political parties in a way heretofore unseen in modern history. That division and the underlying anger which fueled it motivated many on the Right to head to the polls. It would ultimately seal his party's loss in 2016 to a man of charm and wealth...but his political polar opposite. What follows are articles (in alphabetical not chronological order) written at various times during those tumultuous years, 2009-2017.

Adios amigo numero uno

Barack Hussein Obama will be ratcheting down his tenure as our 44th president tonight from his hometown of Chicago, Illinois. Given the *Windy City's* escalating crime rate, I'm hoping the Pres doesn't decide to take a detour into some of that city's neighborhoods that managed to gin up 762 murders in 2016 before his nationwide farewell address. Mr. Obama's decision to hold his address in Chicago's McCormick Place trade show venue is proof positive that he has not outgrown his unparalleled need for attention.

In doing so, he has broken with tradition (again) that previous presidents set by holding theirs in the Oval Office. Given the Democrats' thumping at the polls, this venue choice is probably Mr. Obama's way of resurrecting some of his party's enthusiasm that turned from hope for a Hillary Clinton win into a Trump malaise on November 8th. I doubt, seriously, if there are many of us - on the Left or the Right - that expect Mr. Obama to retire or recede into the background in the same way that his predecessors did...with dignity and humility. It is not in his narcissistic nature to do so, and it is his nature that rules him, and not respecting the time-honored role of being a subdued President emeritus is proof of that.

From a marketing standpoint, I understand his need to stay in the game, for his party is in serious disarray and searching for leadership. The Democrats cannot look to Hillary Clinton nor to Bernie Sanders to lead them forward. They are fading images, not beacons of hope and excitement. In short, there is no one else other than Barack Obama to remind the Party that it is still viable and has a mandate to stand for Progressivism and Liberal thought.

While Barack Obama's approval rating is high at around 56%, it proves one thing...that under his Presidency, Americans focused more on the man and his rhetoric than on his accomplishments. Many genuinely liked him and his laid-back style. They laughed with him and they swooned when he went off Presidential script and sang and danced. For many of America's youth he was Mr. Cool, like the third Blues Brother. Unfortunately, like the Blues Brothers, he was more *showman* than show manager. To many thinking people who compared his lofty speeches to his ineffective and often misguided actions, his Presidency will go down in history as one of missed opportunities.

~

Active and passive scandals

The President's advisor, Valerie Jarrett, was recently heard boasting of the absence of scandals in his administration. To those of us that remember 'fast and furious', the IRS persecution of conservative non-profits, his illegal Executive Orders on immigration, his lies regarding Obamacare and the half-billion dollar website fiasco, the squandered millions to companies like Solyndra to say nothing of his foreign policy failures like his 'red line' in Syria and Benghazi, can only conclude that we have had a chief executive in a profound sense of denial.

He even had the audacity to claim as recently as last week that America's race relations are better today than they were when he took office. Surely he must have forgotten his own racial meddling from the outset of his Presidency in the unprecedented 'Cambridge, Massachusetts intervention' on through his censured Attorney General, Eric Holder's attacks on policing, right down to his reluctance to condemn the 'Black Lives Matter' movement. Whites and Blacks are more polarized now than in recent memory and no closer to understanding each other's views on race relations.

This is, perhaps, his most glaring failure as America's first mixed race President. It is ironic that ex-President, William Jefferson Clinton, is still more revered as 'America's first Black President' than Mr. Obama, having done more to bring the races together. On domestic issues, Mr. Obama's socialist intentions led him to focus on getting a national healthcare system passed (without a single Republican vote) that would up-end the entire country instead of helping the 30 million uninsured.

The result? A system that effectively threw an industry that was already on life support into chaos and instead created a system that was a financial house of cards. He will, no doubt, trumpet this as a victory, though millions who are suffering with unconscionably high premiums and exorbitantly high co-pays will certainly disagree.

The Presidency ought not become a cult of personality, but this is what Barack Obama has made it. His numerous failures, both domestically and internationally, are undeniable, but deny them he will and try to convince us all that we are stronger and more resilient because of his attempts to re-engineer our democracy. What Mr. Obama cannot escape is that his policies (which he said were on the ballot) were roundly repudiated in the 2016 Presidential election.

Barack Obama did prove one thing for certain...that Leftist ideology cannot replace a system of governance that was not built on pure collectivism. He was not deterred by that reality, however, and he pushed relentlessly to remake America into something it was not.

Finally, his legacy will be that of Walter Mitty, a man who saw himself in grandiose ways and as a hero in make-believe situations that proved he was superior to other men. His 'bubble' was almost impervious to reality and will continue to enclose him as he takes the long walk towards a new brand of Presidential activist retirement. Adios amigo numero uno.

~

America's anger: Recipe for change or chaos?

I was overseas when our Presidential Election of 2000 took place, but I saw the whole messy thing play out through the eyes of the international media. The hanging *chads*, the recounts, the Supreme Court's weigh-in on Florida's outcome. Looking back, this may have been the birth of our new national anger at our political system and politicians. Many Liberals were convinced of a Republican conspiracy and mourned Al Gore's loss while the Republicans spiked the football in celebration of George Bush' win. America was seriously split along ideological lines. Half the country was fit to be tied and showed it until the tragedy of 9/11 when we came together for a brief period. Detractors of Bush' policies intensified their anger towards his prosecution of the Iraq War and redoubled it when it was discovered that Saddam Hussein's cache of weapons of mass destruction were his incendiary words.

Democrats continued their angry opposition throughout the rest of "W's" Presidency, and chants of "Bush lied, people died" became their mantra until the election of their man, Barack Obama, made them put down their placards which he replaced with promises of hope and change. It then became the Republicans' turn to declare the *sky was falling* as the new administration thumbed its nose at them. Senate and House Republicans soon joined forces to vigorously oppose the new President and his policies, but there was little time for heightened Democrat anger as the first order of business was to save our economy from what was described as the worst recession since the Great Depression.

Mr. Obama got his stimulus package passed. The so-called rescue of the big banks and then General Motors touched off a firestorm of discontent from all sides. Both hardcore proponents and opponents of free market Capitalism were angry that the President would use taxpayer money to support an encroachment into the private sector by propping up private assets with government financial guarantees. While anger crossed party lines, Republicans in particular were furious when it became clear that stimulus money wasn't being used to create jobs but was used, instead, by States to *save jobs* by paying the salaries of existing workers. It was an FDR-style 'public works program' - minus the works.

Republicans' anger was then directed at the Obama Administration's binge-investment into companies like Solyndra that took a half-billion dollars of taxpayers' money and then squandered it on a financially shaky company and technology. By now it was clear to all that Barack Obama's agenda was to radically transform America away from the successful free enterprise model to one that would empower the Federal Government to pick winners and losers. Predictably, this didn't set well with free-traders and Republicans that wanted less government influence over corporate America and less ideologically-directed government spending.

Just when it seemed that the anger curve was flattening out, along came Senate rules changes and a sharp poke in the eye with the passage of the largest government entitlement program of modern times...Obamacare. This Federal Ponzi scheme touched off an inferno of anger and poisoned the shallow well of comity where both House and Senate Republicans and Democrats went to drink. The gloves were officially off and the muzzle that held back the worst vitriol was discarded.

What little bi-partisanship that existed was destroyed by an avalanche of Executive Orders, IRS persecution of Conservative non-profit organizations, immigration slow-walking, Justice Department gun-running and intervention in local community policing, mismanaged military operations, the Benghazi debacle and the Administration's stubborn refusal to recognize the seriousness of radical Islamic terrorism. Republican anger escalated steadily until 2015 when Hillary Clinton announced her intention to run for President. This single event expanded the target-rich environment for the GOP from the President and his Leftist agenda and the new Left-leaning Supreme Court to include the Democrats' nominee which reminded the Rs of their long-held animosity towards the Clintons. It reminded the rest of us that anger doesn't take vacations.

The Democrats' anger is also palpable and it's directed (no surprise) at all the Republicans that somehow don't 'get it' and have unfairly and consistently opposed their man in the White House and have kept him from achieving his goals for a more 'equal' America.

They're also mightily angry at the Republicans' Presidential candidate, Donald Trump, for having the temerity to criticize Barack Obama and his policies and for his aggressive pursuit of their heir apparent to the White House, "crooked Hillary Clinton."

It seems that the American anger well is bottomless and that American voters, especially Conservative ones, have felt their own personal rage building stronger and stronger with every passing year of Barack Obama's Presidency. This anger changed the makeup of the Senate in 2014, and many political pundits wonder now if it can last another three months. Several polls and focus groups indicate that anger is still a powerful motivating factor among voters and that it will, indeed, propel many of us to head for the voting booths in November.

There are three questions we need to ask ourselves before we do. The first is, "Is anger-based voting good for America's political process?" The second is, "What does our anger say about us as a people?" And finally, "Has our anger showed us that we've lost our way or does it tell us that we've actually found it?"

~

And the winner is....

Love that phrase, "and the winner is." It takes me back to a time when winning really was winning and not just showing up to collect a trophy for participation. Political correctness has changed all that and has wormed its way into nearly every aspect of our lives, making it almost impossible for OWGs (old White guys) like me to even open our mouths lest we be accused of saying something unsympathetic. Like you, I'm getting tired of even talking about political correctness, but if we're going to fight these pagan hordes that would take away our right to speak plainly then we have to keep calling them out every time they try to twist our words into something that doesn't remotely resemble what we mean.

The political campaigns are rich fodder for the PC crowd. Words like 'misremembered' has taken the place of 'lied,' and I can't help connecting it with one of the Democratic Party's candidates who has suffered from convenient and creative memory for decades. One of the first 'misrememberings' of this candidate was her assertion that her mother named her after Sir Edmund Hillary who climbed Mt. Everest. The only problem with that was that she was born five years before old Sir Ed climbed it. I also remember that the candidate said that she landed in Bosnia (with her daughter) under sniper fire.

13

Trouble was there wasn't any. I would be remiss if I didn't say that misremembering isn't confined to America's political class. Our old friend Brian Williams of NBC was called on the carpet for misremembering that he wasn't under fire by a rocket propelled grenade shot at his helicopter during the invasion of Iraq. Sorry, Brian, soldiers from the U.S. Army Third Infantry begged to differ with America's newsman by saying that the helicopter shot down was theirs not his! Williams' credibility soon started to unravel and people began to question other stories he had reported on, like Hurricane Katrina for example, when he said that he saw dead bodies floating down the street.

According to a story on PBS, Dr. Ford Vox, a physician that specializes in brain injuries, says that Williams' *misrememberingness* (my word) is actually a naturally occurring thing in our memories and that an <u>emotional memory</u> is even more susceptible to embellishment or 'modification.' Before you jump out of your chair and yell, "Quack, quack, that sort of thing is impossible!" just listen to New York University psychologist Elizabeth Phelps who said, "While the memory of the event itself is enhanced, the vividness of the memory of the central event tends to come at the expense of the details.

We experience a sort of tunnel vision, discarding all the details that seem incidental to the central event." If I understand what she's saying, all of us can experience these emotional memories and we can forget or 'misremember' the details. That's got to be the biggest *get out of jail free card* I have ever heard and richly deserving of a blue ribbon in the annals of 'World's Best Creative Excuses.'

Let me give you a practical example of that: Cousin Ralph has been having an affair with his sister-in-law, Rita. Ralph comes home very late after an amorous encounter with Rita. His wife Eunice confronts him at the front door with the accusation of infidelity. Flustered and emotional Ralph says he was over at Rita's watching her dog. Not buying it, Eunice says, "Then what's that lipstick doing on your cheek?" Not missing a beat, Ralph says he was "just fooling around with 'Buford' (Rita's dog) and some of *his* lipstick came off when *he* kissed me goodnight."

You tell me, should Eunice: a) believe Ralph and ask for forgiveness for doubting him, b) not believe Ralph and look for a sharp object, or c) call Hillary Clinton for advice? No question for me; she should believe the poor guy. After all, there can't be that many dogs around wearing lipstick anymore, and to know one is a rare privilege, indeed.

~

Better to ask for forgiveness than permission?

Contrary to popular opinion, this Presidential election is not all about choosing nominees; it is also about choosing a workable political philosophy AND a transparent and constitutionally-defensible governance style. If we use the current administration as an example, its operating philosophy is one of: "It's far better to do what we want rather than ask for permission when legislation stands in the way of our objectives."

Translating that into actual daily operating management means that this President has decided that whenever he doesn't like an existing law he will try his utmost to circumvent it with an Executive Order (EO) and *run out the clock* until the Congress or an 'injured party' takes his decision up the judicial ladder to the Supreme Court for a ruling on its constitutionality. This strategy can be very effective because it gives the President time to substantially alter existing policy and procedures and re-direct resources away from the area he is attacking (think the 'Dreamers' deportation cessation for example). By doing so, he makes it more difficult and expensive to direct resources back after a negative court decision has come down. In short, the damage has been done and cannot be undone, quickly.

In sports, that's like intentionally fouling someone to stop the clock or better yet falling on the ball. This is not a new strategy, however. Every President except one (William Henry Harrison with zero EOs) has issued Executive Orders in both peacetime and war. The top five of all time were: Franklin Roosevelt (3,522), Woodrow Wilson (1,803), Calvin Coolidge (1,203), Theodore Roosevelt (1,081) and Herbert Hoover (968). Of the most current Presidents, the top five were: Ronald Reagan (381), Bill Clinton (364), George W. Bush (291), Barack Obama (224 and still going strong) and George H.W. Bush (166).

Of the top five EO-issuing Presidents, two were Democrats and three were Republicans. Of the newest five, two were Democrats and three were Republicans. That would lead many to believe that Republicans are the biggest users/abusers of the Executive Order privilege, but not all EOs are created equal. Some are useful and help streamline and clarify existing regulations. Others, however, stand out like a carbuncle on Lady Liberty's smooth alabaster face. For example, there was FDR's EO 6102 forbidding the hoarding of gold and EO 9066 which sent Japanese-Americans and German-Americans into internment camps.

A more benign but nonetheless controversial EO was Bill Clinton's EO 13155 which mandated that when federal benefits were provided they had to be done in foreign languages (this was later overturned). Though issuing relative few EOs when compared to his predecessors, our current President has issued more *sweeping* EOs than many other Presidents and has taken the EO to a higher more dangerous level as they now affect nearly the entire U.S. population! Immigration, health care and freedom of religion are just three areas where Barack Obama has shown that he is unwilling to ask or wait for permission (Congressional legislative action) but would rather risk crossing the constitutional line and let the lawsuits catch up with him.

Given past history, recent history and many statements made by <u>all the candidates on both sides in this Presidential race</u>, there is every reason to believe and especially worry that the next President will continue on the hazardous path of interpreting, writing and re-writing existing legislation as a means to satisfy his/her ideological objectives, and THAT could throw us into a judicial and constitutional tailspin and hamstring the orderly process of governing our country. The last thing we need at this critical juncture is to make adherence to the law a victim of internecine governmental warfare.

~

Blueprint for America: Dr. Obama's Amazing Elixir

The fight for America's soul and the debate on socialism is not new in America. It's just entered our orbit of consciousness with a vengeance since the election of a president who, in his own words in October of 2008, said, "We are five days from fundamentally transforming America." Pundits and parsers will probably say that was just a candidate being political, but those of us on terra firma will recognize it as a prophetic statement about a radical transformation of our economic and political system that would soon be made by a committed ideologue who was days away from doing it! Either way, it was a clear marketing victory.

Those who say Mr. Obama didn't live up to his central campaign promises weren't paying attention. He told us, repeatedly, that he was a change agent. Knowing that, why wouldn't we believe that he would change his positions once he was elected? Americans weren't listening with their ears. They were in a shopping trance, wanting to buy something new that reflected their own self-image. They were searching for a product that would cure all their ills.

16

What they wanted was actually a miracle wonder product from an earlier century, routinely sold on street corners and at carnivals all over this land. It was commonly known as, 'snake oil.' They found exactly what they were looking for in *Dr. Obama's Amazing American Elixir*. By voting for him, they cleansed their consciences about America's past racial transgressions. Younger voters got their *cool guy* who was slim, played basketball, had smoked cocaine and was only slightly removed from their generation.

The Black and Hispanic communities elected a man seemingly sympathetic to them. Barack Obama made the presidency attractive to first-time voters who were looking for transformational change. The only problem was that many in these groups knew little about how America actually *worked* let alone how to transform it. They only knew how it *looked* to them and hadn't a clue how Wall Street, Main Street and Capitol Hill fit together. Ideologies have always needed memorable images, words, songs and symbols to sell their message, and secularism and socialism are no different. Secularism sells itself on a simple premise: society is better served, more fair and easier to manage without all this religious nonsense. Socialism is not far behind with: the needs of the many outweigh the inconvenience of the few.

The truth is we've always had a dollop of secularism and socialism in America and seen its ebb and flow, especially during times of crisis when standing together made for a solid defense (in the Great Depression, during WWII, and now in the Age of Obama and the Great Recession). The danger now is that we'll jettison our traditional capitalistic system and adopt an unworkable government-managed economic model out of fear.

Pushing a social justice theme and espousing income redistribution with a "you didn't build that" mantra, the 44th president continues to ride a populist wave of support on a surfboard of pointed rhetoric, rhetoric that has worked up until now. Americans have always been suckers for a good slogan whether it's *where's the beef* or *the pause that refreshes*. We bought big cars with shark fins, hula hoops and pet rocks, spiked our hair, wore dog collars and suffered high colonics. With all that consumer history, why would anyone think that we couldn't be sold and re-sold a president and that he would ride in on a messianic message of hope?

Ad men were proud of candidate Barack Obama's 2008 presidential campaign. It was masterful, right down to the use of the new social media which became the message. Young people self-identified with the media Mr. Obama used and the bond was forged.

They bought the T-shirt, the *new world* decals for their back packs AND the message. It was change we could believe in...at first sight and any thinking person had to be thinking Obama. The others were just unenlightened.

It wasn't a hostile takeover that America experienced on January 20, 2009. We got a taste of the classic leveraged buy-out. The financial sponsor (the candidate) acquired the controlling interest (our votes) in our equity (the running of the country) and then financed his operation through leveraged borrowing (increased national debt), trillions of dollars of it, in record time. That was then, but in eleven short weeks Americans will have a choice: sign on to four more years of the same or to turn around, go back to the place where we left our values and start anew. We may have to face facts, however... that we have become mere consumers of promises and have lost our taste for critical thought. If that is the case, we should all be investing our money in the media, because that is where the battle for the hearts, minds, pocketbooks and votes of Americans will be fought, at least until November. Caveat emptor.

~

Breaking up (the party) is hard to do

A number of articles have recently addressed the likely breakup in the Republican Party, but very few speak of the breakup in the Democratic party. Perhaps that's because many in the media are liberal and prefer to focus on the 'demise' of the Republicans. While there is no question that Republicans have been at loggerheads with each other since the loss of John McCain in 2008 and Mitt Romney in 2012, the ensuing years have pushed the party farther away from the center and moved it solidly to the right. Few would argue with that assessment, but the question is, "What is the *right*?"

The right of the Republican Party today is not the right of 2008 nor 2012. If anything, it is the right of 2000 but strengthened and intensified <u>because of 2008 and 2012.</u> Depending on your point of view, it is either an elephants' graveyard where old attitudes and opinions go to die or it is the wellspring of a re-birth for the Republicans. Because the establishment's *no-discussion perimeter* has been breached by the straight talk of non-PC candidates like Donald Trump, the new right is willing to confront third-rail social issues like religious freedom, (especially as it relates to the new Supreme Court-approved legality of homosexual marriage) and illegal immigration, to name just two.

18

It is also ready to take a principled stand on issues like the sanctity of life, drug abuse, illiteracy, government overreach and abuse of power, states' rights, national healthcare and foreign policy. On the financial and economic side, the new right is an unabashed born-again supporter of capitalism and the inherent right of the individual to generate and keep wealth.

It demands reduced federal spending and accountability for government's actions along with a call for safeguarding our currency and the creation of a fiscally prudent environment. Most of these issues are non-negotiable for right of center Republicans. For example, they have stepped up their defense of states' rights and support for the Constitution's enumeration of powers. It's an incredibly simple argument, but one that comes up all the time in interactions between Republicans and Democrats.

The reason is simple...Democrats wish to create a new social order in America by usurping power from the states and transferring it to the Executive Branch and then rubber-stamping it by a liberal judiciary of their making. Roe versus Wade is an example, so are the Patient's Affordable Healthcare Act and the recent ruling on universal homosexual marriage (striking down existing state laws). Far right Republicans will continue to push back against any Democratic Party attempt to weaken or eliminate more states' rights.

Regardless of a Republican presidential win or loss, the party will be comprised of largely working-class, non-college educated, Caucasian males and females 40 and older. Though small in number, the youth component will remain stable. The Party will open its arms to minorities, but they will not represent more than 10-15% of its members. It will continue to attract small-business owners and large companies, alike. It will include 'right-to-work' advocates, the moneyed classes of Wall Street and the 1%. In addition, it will have garnered the support of a large number of special interest or single interest voters (largely 'traditional' Americans) who eschew fundamental societal change.

The party will also retain its Tea Party members, evangelical Christians and other true believers. Its numbers will be positively affected by the nomination of either Donald Trump or Ted Cruz and will be significantly strengthened (after a period of re-building and reconciliation) should either one win the presidency. Moderates and centrist independents will be in limbo, with no place to go that reflects their beliefs should those beliefs be liberal on social issues or flexible on states' rights issues.

19

Those with strong, fiscally-conservative leanings will probably stay with the party unless they can no longer abide by its new 'social covenant.'

The end result could well be a smaller (but stronger), more focused Republican Party, one that is better able to mobilize its base when needed. The Democratic Party has been undergoing its own metamorphosis since the 2008 presidential election when it split into two halves: an activist *Progressive* wing that seeks to redefine the social and economic status quo and a *Traditional* wing that includes large financial contributors, labor unions, minorities and committed more moderate ideologues. This division in the Party was most visible by an intensification of support for the 'Elizabeth Warren/Bernie Sanders Progressives.' So far, this hasn't caused any irreparable harm. It does, however, present a challenge for re-unification around a set of core principles that can appease the growing *socialist-light* thought within the Party.

Gone are the days of the Clinton moderates and centrists. The party moved farther left with the election of Barack Obama and is now on a steady trajectory for an even greater leftward swing in 2016, largely because of the growth of a vocal youth movement that has embraced the *Black Lives Matter* racial message and the 1% *Occupy Wall Street* ideology of a divided America.

The evidence of this lies in the turnout of hundreds of thousands of college-age students and their support for an avowed socialist candidate, Senator Bernie Sanders and their rejection of the Democratic Party's establishment candidate, former Secretary of State, Hillary Clinton. This schism was inevitable due to a number of factors, among them: the impact of the recession of 2008, the resultant high unemployment among America's youth, escalating college costs, the unfinished business of environmental issues and the perception that the establishment didn't move fast enough (under Barack Obama) to create the Ideal America for millennials.

The current conflict within the Democratic Party has also revealed some potential ideological disagreements with the party establishment on a host of issues such as the future role of labor unions in the American economy, multi-lateral trade agreements, America's foreign policy, drug legalization, immigration regulations, the role of the family in society and religion in the 'marketplace.' While breaking up is hard to do for any political party, let alone two powerful parties at the same time, it is often necessary in order to put the pieces back together in a way that reflects the prevailing philosophy of its members.

Let's hope, that by the end of the summer, both Republicans and Democrats will figure out who they are and what they stand for in time to choose a nominee that truly represents their ideology and one that we, the electorate, can get behind.

~

Carrots and sticks, honey and vinegar

We are a nation of laws, but we're also a nation built on incentives. The problem is that our elected representatives do not seem to understand basic human nature. That may explain why they mostly focus on the *sticks* (law-making) and don't consider the *carrots* (incentives) as a way to influence American behavior. Both political parties are guilty of excessive and bone-headed law-making from time to time, but both parties are not always equal in their distrust of their fellow citizens which has led to the passage of hundreds of unwieldy laws and thousands of onerous regulations.

Yes, there is a distinction between laws and regulations. Laws beget regulations. Regulations are the bureaucratic flotsam and jetsam that ultimately wash up on the shores of the unwitting average citizen, and which demand their full and immediate attention. When we realize that a law has spawned a multitude of regulations we're surprised, confused and angry. We feel betrayed and don't understand how very different the regulations are from the original law.

At this point, my father would have said, "Son, the devil is in the details," and he would have been right. That's where the devil always resides, and he's not picky about his roommates, either. Here I speak of the thousands of bureaucrats who view themselves as *shadow law-makers* – ideologically-driven green eye shade types who see regulation-writing as their way of interpreting and influencing the law. Before I do a number on bureaucrats (which they so richly deserve), let me call out the House and Senate Committees and staffers AND THE GENERAL PUBLIC for either not thoroughly reading the proposed laws and the resultant regulations or for not objecting to them during the review/comment process.

Fortunately, (yes I said *fortunately*), we have lobbyists and non-government organizations (NGOs) that religiously take on that task. Because their mission is to protect their special interest constituents, they pour over regulations to make sure that the regulators are not *pulling a fast one* that would disadvantage their bosses.

21

The public should want the same involvement BEFORE the laws were passed as well as during the comment period, but that's another story. It would seem that many Americans are blasé about the impact that legislation and the ensuing regulations have on their lives. Case in point is the three-year old 3,256-page *Patient Protection and Affordable Care Act* (aka. Obamacare). If law professors and political science/civics teachers needed a textbook case for earlier citizen involvement in the political process, this is it.

Many credible critics have spoken eloquently on this subject, but Dr. Barbara Bellar (a licensed physician and lawyer in Illinois) stated the bureaucratics and ham-handedness of it succinctly in one (albeit long) sentence: "We're going to be gifted with a healthcare plan we are forced to purchase and fined if we don't which purportedly covers at least ten million more people without adding a single new doctor but provides for 16,000 new IRS agents, written by a committee whose chairman says he doesn't understand it, passed by a Congress that didn't read it, but exempted themselves from it and signed by a President who smokes with funding administered by a Treasury chief who didn't pay his taxes for which we will be taxed for four years before any benefits take effect by a government which has already bankrupted social security and Medicare, all to be overseen by a Surgeon General who is obese and financed by a country that is broke."

The act created 159 new bureaucracies and boards and thousands of new regulations, and to add insult to injury, the government is now contemplating shortening the public comment time on its proposed regulations from the normal 60 days to 15!

President Theodore Roosevelt (the original Progressive) said, "Walk softly and carry a big stick." It's probably time for the Progressives to channel some really big brains like Bugs Bunny, or at the very least, Elmer Fudd. Maybe they can locate some of the carrots they will need to make their makeover plan for America more palatable to the average citizen. Otherwise, they'll wind up with a very unfunny cartoon parody of a once-great country.

~

Dealing with Scandals 101

The Obama Administration hit the trifecta in May 2013 with three massive scandals that knocked it off its axis and put it squarely on the defensive. Congressional investigative committees smelled blood in the water and went into high gear. Though there were no bets wagered, even the casual observer could have predicted that an administration that couldn't keep its ducks in a row would end up defending an indefensible lack of management of the machinery of government. Getting grilled on Benghazi-gate, the AP surveillance scandal and the IRS targeting of conservative groups, the Obama Administration learned all too well that that which can go wrong will go wrong as the atmosphere on Capitol Hill turned uber nasty.

For the Republicans, there are many lessons to be learned from this experience some of which can be applied to dealing with scandals in general. Let's take a look at the investigative committee hearings on Benghazi to see how they conducted themselves and what might be learned, in hindsight, from the experience.

Congressional hearings offer something for everybody: salacious media sound bites, damning testimony, grandstanding, face time for Congressional Representatives and sometimes redemption for the accused. Knowing all that's riding on hearings and the damage that can be done to the reputations of companies, government agencies and individuals, it's surprising how poorly both the interrogators and the interrogated perform when the house lights go on! As far as Congressional Committee Representatives go, they are blessed (and sometimes cursed) by staffers who gather information, do research and prep them before the mikes go live.

When the Chairman hits the gavel calling the meeting to order and the cameras start whirring, the mood always becomes tense. Republicans and Democrats go to their respective corners, and come out swinging when the bell sounds. Within the first few minutes it becomes abundantly clear to the audience without even seeing a name or party designation on a tent card which representative will go on the attack and which one will defend an Administration; it usually breaks along party lines but not always with equal ferocity.

The group dynamic of the Benghazi hearings was a perfect case in point. While the Republicans aggressively interrogated each and every witness, they didn't all use the same tactics. Theirs was an eerie combination of bad cop interrogation and the not-so-friendly country lawyer approach used by the late Senator Sam Ervin of North Carolina when he participated in the McCarthy and Watergate hearings.

23

Some gave long opening statements (specifically targeted for the record) and others sought the *afterlife repetitiousness* of the media with short, dramatically delivered questions designed to be played and replayed for wider and wider audiences on TV and the internet. The latter represent the new young lions of the party who used the hearings to burnish their party credentials with their colleagues and the folks back home. Procedure dictates that the Chair moves from Republican to Democrat. Each revealed from the outset the tone their party decided to adopt: from attacker to defender or from predator to protector.

The Benghazi hearings were steeped in emotion and intrigue as were the IRS hearings. Both shared one thing: an effort to uncover in detail the astounding breach of confidence that the government created through its actions. In Benghazi, the players were the top decision-makers of the federal government, the CIA, DOD and STATE, and none were terribly interested in being put on the Congressional hot seat.

One of those was then Secretary of State, Hillary Clinton, who lost her cool. Exasperated after questioning by a Republican committee member she curtly stated, "With all due respect, the fact is we had four dead Americans. Was it because of a protest or was it because of guys out for a walk one night decided to go kill some Americans? What difference at this point does it make?"

Republicans should all thank Mrs. Clinton for these remarks; they are a valuable lesson which is *always maintain your composure especially when you're being videotaped for posterity.* Under normal circumstances, Republicans have a strong kinship or at least understanding with both the CIA and the military and would probably have been willing to moderate their questioning, but Benghazi was different and everyone knew it.

These hearings weren't looking at a philandering President or a real estate transaction gone awry. The subject was the abuse of power and the death of four Americans...and a cover-up of the real reasons behind the attack on our Consulate and annex in Libya.

On balance, Republicans acquitted themselves well apart from a few thespian-like utterances. They maintained their composure and left their diatribes in the drawer. Seeing that, the Democrats were forced to retrieve the *partisan card* from their vest pocket and play it shamelessly, accusing the Republicans of grandstanding and using the seriousness and sanctity of the hearing environment for their own political purposes.

As more facts about the twelve iterations of the Benghazi talking points and the video blaming came out, the White House became more and more defensive to the point where the President added more fuel to the fire by calling the hearings a *sideshow*. This was a tactical error and a very poor choice of words that most Americans would find repugnant even if they were supporters of the President.

To the Republicans' credit, they stayed on message and redoubled their efforts to peel back the onion and seek the truth about Benghazi, and because the Administration (and the mainstream media) had downplayed the scandal for months, the public's attention span was still very fresh. This enabled the Republicans to maintain their appearance as truth-seekers and helped them to deflect the Administration's attempts to paint them as bald-faced partisans on a "witch hunt" (an epithet used by White House spokesman Jay Carney to describe the hearings). Scandals are part and parcel of American political life. Every administration must expect them AND have a plan to deal with them. That goes for their political parties, too. The fallout from scandals can often taint political parties for many years and adversely affect future candidates' chances for election. While the odd individual scandal can sometimes end with an administration's term, it is not, however, deleted from the hard drive of the collective American consciousness.

~

Duck and cover generation rides again

Fear of nuclear annihilation was rampant when I was in grade school, and the *Russkies* were responsible. Every so often there was a surprise A-bomb drill in our school. Wherever we were, our teacher instructed us to walk swiftly to a safe area in the school. If we were in the classroom, it was duck under our desks and cover our heads with our hands. Looking back, it sounds (and is) ludicrous to think that somehow we were going to be spared the ravages of man's most horrific weapon simply by putting a wooden school desk between us and a few megatons of killing force. What is even more ludicrous is the fact that a team of U.S. negotiators of my generation who've had more than a half-century to wake up to certain facts of life after *duck and cover* thought it possible to do a nuclear deal with a bunch of malicious thugs in Iran!

I managed to slog through selected sections of the 159-page document...It is a stunning tribute to naiveté on the part of the U.S. team who deserve a rousing Bronx cheer for placing their trust in a untrustworthy adversary.

It is also supreme confirmation that our government's negotiators are actually capable of suspending reality for extended periods of time without succumbing to truth withdrawal.

Believe me. I get the whole point of negotiating with one's adversaries to avoid armed conflict. I support it. I just don't buy the argument of President Obama who essentially said that either the Congress approves this agreement or the alternative is war. War, really? Apparently, he doesn't remember that it was international sanctions that forced Iran to the negotiating table in the first place.

We made them cry uncle (*amu* in Farsi), and all we had to do was stall THEM for a few more years while the sanctions cut even deeper into the muscle of their economy. Instead, they played us. Their negotiators (who obviously read Donald Trump's, "The Art of the Deal") hemmed and hawed and shucked and jived their way through two years of stalling tactics while they presumably continued to enrich uranium and presumably continued to put the final touches on their clandestine off-the-grid installations, free from the prying eyes of the international community.

The deeper point is the negotiations themselves. What in heaven's name made our government think that an international sponsor of terrorism, a state that has vowed to "wipe Israel off the map," that held 52 American diplomats hostage for 444 days thirty some years ago and that still holds three Americans hostage now was trustworthy enough to even sit down with in the first place? There is so much in this agreement that defies explanation, but I'm confident that the Administration will spin its approval as vital to world security. I'm somehow not sure that Prime Minister Netanyahu and Iran's neighbors will see it the same way.

The Administration's coup de grace and ultimate slap in the face of the American public is its intention to walk the agreement to the United Nations before the Congress even takes off the wrapper. Next thing you know, the *Deal* will spawn a made-for-TV movie. If it does, Ed Wood of 'Planet 9 from Outer Space' better step aside. The Iranian Nuclear Deal or 'Pollyanna does shuffleboard diplomacy on the Good Ship Lollypop' will be hot on his heels for recognition as the worst movie of all time.

~

Erasing history

Recently, the State Department came under criticism for erasing 8½ minutes of one of its press briefings. On the surface, that doesn't seem to rise to the level of impeachable or jailable offenses, but it does concern me as a person that was always taught to be truthful and honest that my government has now gone rogue.

It seems someone in the Department felt that Fox News reporter, James Rosen, asked a particularly embarrassing question – one the fellows in striped pants didn't want on the public record. He asked, quite innocently, if anyone in the State Department was ever engaged in secret discussions with the Iranians to which the press spokeswoman Jen Psaki replied that sometimes diplomacy needs to work behind the scenes, out of the public eye – an obvious pivot away from a definitive answer.

Even that oblique admission was obviously too truthful for her superiors who proceeded to erase it from the final archived recording. When asked about that erasure, State quickly said that it was due to a technical *glitch*. Unfortunately, that, too, was a lie, and they later came under pressure and had to admit that it was a purposeful erasure, BUT they couldn't identify who actually gave the order. Really? And we're supposed to believe that?

To be fair, this is not the first erasure (or theft) of public information nor will it be the last. President Richard Nixon is famous for his 18½ minutes of dead air on a Presidential taped recording in 1972 and for his non-explanation of how it happened. More recently, there was former National Security Advisor under President Bill Clinton, Sandy Berger, who decided he would visit the National Archives and proceeded to lift a few highly classified documents relating to terror threats during the 2000 Millennium celebration. He then stuffed them into his pants and socks and later destroyed some of them.

Fast-forwarding to the present, there is Presidential candidate and former Secretary of State, Hilary Clinton, who unilaterally decided that she would circumvent her own Department's regulations and a Presidential directive to set up her own private email server (complete with over two dozen private email addresses) and then routinely communicated sensitive and occasionally classified U.S. Government information to the outside world without benefit of adequate data protection.

Add to that her abdication of her responsibility in the tragic deaths of four Americans in Benghazi and the subsequent lies she told to grieving family members of the victims (and the American public), and it's obvious to me, at least, that subterfuge and obfuscation have now become the new coin of the realm of government activity.

What is it that prompts government employees or elected officials to engage in and/or condone this type of behavior? Do they feel that the rules don't apply to them because of their own perceived and often exaggerated self-worth? Is it possible there is a more sinister ideological or political reason behind their actions or do they break rules and laws out of loyalty to their bosses? Whatever motives are behind their actions, it's their actions that must come under our scrutiny. A thief is a thief, regardless of the reasons for his thievery. And when it comes to stealing from or lying to an entire nation, the penalties must be severe, swift and consistently applied. Once stolen, the public trust cannot easily be replaced.

~

Fowling Opponents of Free Speech

Who would have thought that a few comments on traditional marriage by a usually quiet COO would have lit the fuse on a feud between proponents and opponents of homosexual marriage and between free-speechers and limited speechers?

And who would have thought that this battle would be waged on the politically non-partisan floors of fast food restaurants around the USA? In case you've been deep-sea diving in Fiji or backpacking up the Blue Mountains of Australia and haven't been near a TV, the family-owned Chick fil-A company has become the new ground zero for American free speech. After expressing his opinion, complete with a few Bible references, COO Dan Cathy unleashed what might be the first salvo in a new economic range war pitting the American public against its own businesses!

If this were not so potentially dangerous for an already fragile economy (think of millions of consumers protesting in front of businesses intimidating customers or organized boycotts that could bankrupt companies) it would be comical, but it's not. While many are classifying this as a free speech issue - the right of a business owner to speak his mind – it may actually be the next logical step following the *Citizens United* case that redefines corporations as individuals. The Citizens United case was adjudicated in the Supreme Court in 2010.

The Court ruled that corporations had the right to exercise their free speech under the First Amendment on a par with individuals when it came to making political contributions. In a recent ruling in June, the Court refused a request to revisit the initial ruling, saying: "Political speech does not lose First Amendment protection simply because its source is a corporation." Political speech or politically correct speech does not come without risk, however.

For businesses, this may be a further redefinition of their status and it could get a bit uncomfortable if people really start focusing on businesses as people. Think about this way. It's a little like a man giving up his bachelor status when he gets married. There are certain advantages, but certain disadvantages, too. No more Wednesday nights with the guys hanging around Hooters. No more drying your clothes in the microwave. No more expletives filling the air, either, especially when the in-laws are visiting. Like our bachelor friend, corporations can't have it both ways. If the CEOs, COOs, CFOs or anybody in positions of corporate power want to spout off on social issues, they have to be ready to reap the whirlwind and pay the price for it. That's the double edged sword of free speech, but to deny them their right to do so is unacceptable and illegal.

The mayors of Chicago, Boston and Washington, DC might want to read their job descriptions more carefully. I doubt if their mayoral rights include creating a single overarching value system for their cities. That's what their constituents do, individually. If mayors get into the moralizing business, they may find fewer companies beating their way to their borders, and if they choose to go that route, they, too, must pay the price for THEIR free speech with dwindling tax bases and fewer jobs for the people who voted them into office!

As for Chick fil-A, I drove to their restaurant the other day (the same day of the proposed *kiss-out* or *kiss-off*) only to find the place mobbed with ordinary folks chowing down on delicious chicken sandwiches. I looked everywhere for kissing couples but without success. All I saw was a successful company doing a land office business with order takers going from car to car in the drive-in lane smiling and having a good time enjoying their 15 minutes of fame. I'm sure that if *Finger lickin' good* Colonel Sanders and Frank *it takes a tough man to make a tender chicken* Perdue were alive today they would have been dancing the chicken polka in the parking lot, excited to see so many people supporting free speech while downing heaping portions of the food that made them both famous. It's amazing what a little free speech and a few chicken nuggets will do to soothe the savage beast in all of us.

Has devil's advocacy gone to the devil?

I can't recall a time in the last decade where critical thinking, constructive criticism and devil's advocacy have been under such heavy fire all over the USA than right now. Those who are willing to step outside their comfort zone and speak truth to power or question the conventional (or prevailing) wisdom in a straightforward way are quickly labeled as nay-sayers or provocateurs to keep them from de-railing whatever train the few at the top want to stay on track.

Take our elections for example. The last Presidential election was a 52-48% win (3 million vote difference), but no sooner had the President taken the oath of office than he declared that "You lost. We won." His administration had a mandate to govern, but their attitude was that they had an <u>overwhelming</u> number of Americans behind them (the margin of support was equivalent to the population of Chicago). They sought no real negotiation with the 48% nor did they want any criticism, constructive or otherwise.

In situations where solid majorities exist, it's easier to accept an unwillingness to listen to criticism on the part of those who hold power. After all, 'most' rules, but what *most* often don't understand is that the best way to hold on to that power is to maintain open channels of communication with the opposition. That would mean that those who hold the cards would need to be good listeners and must not demean, degrade or dismiss the sincerely-held views of others. Granted, no emperor likes to be told that he has no clothes just as no proponent of a controversial project or gate-keeper of a revolutionary idea relishes the prospect of being told he's guarding a faulty premise, but to succeed he must listen.

Supporters of the 'devil's advocacy approach' to confronting the status quo can sometimes be their own worst enemies, too. Occasionally, their arguments or complaints aren't grounded in fact, but are rooted in emotion instead. Ferguson, Missouri is a recent example where the devil was definitely in the details. As America's leaders become more afraid to lift the lid from Pandora's Box of racial, economic and other problems, they will become even <u>less</u> tolerant of any criticism of their leadership for fear of losing control.

This will make it increasingly more difficult for reasonable critics to be heard above the din of America's protestors. And it will have a catastrophic effect on rational decision-making. When your house is burning around you, your first thought isn't why you put the candles so close to the drapes. The same is true of protecting America's communities.

Firemen put out fires first and then look for their causes and correct them. America's in for some tough times. Violent dissent is on the rise, along with a growing attitude that the way to achieve social justice is to ignore opinions that are based on reason, facts and verifiable cause and effect. If we are to manage the expectations of our citizens and keep moving forward towards achieving a fair and balanced society where opportunities exist for everybody (especially in America's inner cities) then we must be ready to confront certain inconvenient and uncomfortable truths about our society and its flawed governance.

Americans on both a national and local level need to stand up and challenge their leaders' ideas and proposals before decisions are made that cannot be reversed. This goes for international agreements and local investments, strategies and courses of action that commit us years down the road and that will have a profound effect on the decisions we make in our own careers and where and how we live our lives.

The devil's advocacy issue isn't so much one of the free exercise of speech as it is about getting our free speech noticed and registered by those in positions of authority. It's about the growing tendency of our society to limit honest brokers' critical opinions by making it difficult to get their voices heard in public meetings and in the traditional media. If the only voices being heard are midnight bloggers, social media junkies and those that rail the loudest, then the logical next step is for critical-thinkers to self-censor their comments, give up or join the protestors on the barricades. We needn't look back any further than the 60s and 70s to see how that worked out.

Finally, as much as it pains me to say, it doesn't do much good to bemoan the loss of civility. What's gone is gone. The only way forward is to find a way to truly listen to each other while rejecting the impulse to defeat the argument by destroying the arguer.

~

Has the paradigm shift begun?

When any armchair economist, amateur psychologist or novice market-watcher looks at the last five years of America's recession and the 30 years leading up to it and then takes the trouble to lay out all the facts and stats on the kitchen table, it's not difficult to conclude that maybe the great American economic model has finally entered its otium cum dignitate.

Granted, the rest of the world lives in the same *neighborhood* of rising social demands, shrinking tax bases, eroding economies of scale, ultra-competitive markets, balance of payments pressures and burgeoning debt, but they are not the USA. We are. We do things differently, or do we? There are two economic belief systems at work in Washington DC and around the country. Both are attached at the hip to the two political parties. The Republicans believe we should cut government spending, get lean and mean and save our way out of the recession and preserve the current wealth distribution levels.

On the other side of the aisle, Democrats are convinced that if we will only spend more taxpayer dollars, create more government jobs, conjure up more 'stimulus packages,' redistribute more of America's wealth by taxing the rich and have the Treasury pump billions more into our economy that everything will be hunky dory. Both are missing the point.

Prosperity is hiding, but it's not in some out of the way alcove in America's boardrooms or in a secret memo in a Wall Street hedge fund office. It's certainly not sequestered in the halls of Congress or in the White House, either. No, it is hiding in all of us, masquerading as the fear of change and cloaked in the mantle of intractable tradition. Let me explain. Millions of Americans have been brought up to believe that our country rests on a solid, impenetrable foundation that never moves, never changes and never should change. Some would say that that foundation is the Constitution. Others will tell you it's our values, and a third group would point to the heavens and say that it's God's will, as "He has ordained the democratic capitalist system for us to follow."

The truth is, America, like every other country, grows up and grows older and changes along the way. In its youth, America was rebellious. In adolescence, it swam upstream a bit, and now that it's approaching middle age it's gotten a little soft, a little tired, a little nostalgic and more than a tad unwilling to change.

I can't fault all Americans, maybe just those who, like myself, grew up without a Depression, a World War or a massive natural disaster to contend with.

This article is not about assigning blame. It's about *getting real,* waking up and manning up to the reality that in order for us to move forward we may have to move backward a few steps so that we can review our attitudes, realign our economy and expectations and re-think what America is really <u>meant</u> to be. If we are religious, we believe that God meant for our country to be an example of compassion, openness and inclusion for the rest of the world to emulate. If we're non-believers, the Divine Providence argument can be easily replaced with one based on the preservation of individual rights and freedom.

The status quo has been kind to many in our society, that is until the *bubbles* of Wall Street, housing, and Dot com burst, leaving millions with emaciated portfolios and then, later, when the great downsizing of American business began, eliminating millions of jobs leaving middle-aged, near retirement-age workers to fend for themselves. There's no shortage of villains in today's America. Take your pick. There's government, business outsourcers, China, Congress, the Administration, closed-shop states, but there's one uber villain that controls all of them...intransigence and intractability. Times have indeed changed, but many of us are unwilling to acknowledge that simple fact. There are more Americans to be fed, housed, clothed, educated and employed than we care to think about. "Ten pounds of potatoes won't go into a five-pound sack," my grandmother always used to say, and she was right.

An immigrant from a country that experienced enormous poverty in the last few decade of the 19th century, her measurement of success was having enough to eat and a place to stay dry...and that attitude stuck with her until she died.

Her generation was accustomed to change and viewed it as natural (if not uncomfortable and frustrating). They adapted to circumstances and made the best of what they had. Some today would say that their expectations were okay for them but not for us. They are simply too LOW! "Our jumping off point is higher, therefore our expectations should be higher," say the young among us, "Why should we tighten our belts when you did nothing but loosen yours for decades!"

That remark reflects one of our biggest problems, perception. Our planet is not expanding to accommodate the millions of people added to its surface every year. Our resources are not increasing, commensurately. Our construction sprawl is threatening our natural world and disturbing the natural balance. On a business level, the markets for new goods and services <u>are</u> expanding, thereby creating the prospect of potential prosperity, until you realize that many former markets for our exports have now become domestic producers of the same goods <u>and are exporting them back to us!</u>

The world economic order is held together by international trade agreements and a complex body of regulations AND by the market forces of supply, demand and the profit motive. Traditional thinking has kept them all going in the same direction in the 20th century until Communism came along. Tested in practice, the experiment failed and 'free marketeers' shifted into higher gear and traveled the predictable path of strengthening their own hands while championing free trade for all. The aggregation principal - of capital or other resources – creates larger wholes, but it also creates greater vulnerabilities. We saw this in the banking crisis in 2008/9 when a new, more dangerous principle took over – too big to fail (TBTF). TBTF was never meant for the private sector; it was always reserved as a last resort solution for cash-strapped countries. America's mistake was allowing it to be used, privately.

Today, fear (of the unknown) and distrust (of institutions) rank high as considerations in corporate decision-making and may just be precipitating the *death roll* for America's great economic paradigm. Ironically, this could be a positive thing for our country. In fact, some of the changes are already occurring, perhaps in no small part to the lack of adequate financing and massive corporate downsizing.

Take *crowdfunding* or *co-working*. Each is built on the concept of smaller groups coming together with a collective (but open) mindset to accomplish common tasks, unencumbered by an oppressive bureaucratic hierarchy. Knowing <u>when</u> to change is every bit as important as knowing <u>how</u> to change. America needs to create a new business structure that's built on our innovativeness, creativity, productivity, flexibility and pluck. It needn't be rooted in manufacturing, but it must have a strong manufacturing component to it. We must be able to control the manufacturing apparatus instead of being at the mercy of foreign production lines. It can't be solely rooted in services, either, because we cannot develop a diverse economy simply by providing services to one another.

34

While my generation has been pretty good at recognizing opportunities, it's time to join up with the young entrepreneurs of today and build a new foundation that can grow and prosper using new methods and by setting realistic short, medium and long term goals that fit within a nationally-beneficial framework designed to empower the American people to think and do for themselves. This will take leadership, commitment and cooperation. That's why we need to encourage our political, business and cultural leaders to engage in a national dialogue on what we want America to be in the 22nd century. Maybe a good starting point would be a motto like: "Size matters: bigger is just bigger, but smaller can be smarter."

~

Horse-trading the Presidency and the low-information voter

Our 2012 Presidential election distinguished itself as having had the third largest participation rate since the election of John Kennedy in 1960, and that reminds me of a phrase I heard about history. It goes something like this, "a person's historical frame of reference begins with their own birth." I guess it's only natural to focus on one's self when looking at something as personal as history, but there's also something very dangerous about it. Take Presidential elections, for example. Most of us remember how contentious the Bush versus Gore election was, but I'll bet we don't remember the contentiousness of the 1876 election between Rutherford B. Hayes and Samuel Tilden, do we?

Let me refresh your memory. Rutherford B. Hayes was the Republican candidate and Samuel J. Tilden was the Democrat. After the first vote, Tilden had won 184 electoral votes to Hayes' 165, but there were 20 electoral votes that were unresolved and in dispute in four states: Florida, Louisiana, South Carolina and Oregon. *By the way, Tilden won the popular vote with 4,284,020 votes (50.9%) to Rutherford's 47.9%.*

It was the first Presidential election in 20 years that a Democrat had won the majority of the popular vote. The election was notable for other statistics as well, but historians look at this election for one REALLY INTERESTING twist of fate. It seemed that neither party was able to get the other to concede the outstanding 20 electoral votes, so a very unique compromise was made. Basically, the Democrats gave the election to the Republicans in return for the end of *Reconstruction!* So, Midwesterner Hayes became President and Yankee Tilden became a near hero to southerners who saw Federal troops withdraw from old Dixie.

35

Since no one from that time is around to give us a first-hand interview, we can only speculate as to how the electorate dealt with the trade. They may have been upset, but I doubt they were as outraged as Americans during the election of 2000 when both parties went to legal war over *hanging and dimpled chads* AND used Federal election law and Florida State law to decide who would inhabit the White House.

When the 2000 election was finally decided by the Supreme Court, a new political Mason-Dixon Line was drawn in the sand, effectively reinforcing a *Red-Blue* ideological divide akin to the *Blue-Grey* mentality of 1876. I suspect that it also created a boomlet of low (or no) information voters who cared less about the policies of the opposition than they did about bringing them down and replacing them with their own team. No or low-information voters are the worst kind of voter imaginable, and a few of the founding fathers warned against them because they had no *skin in the game*. They owned no property but would be allowed to decide how the property of others could be treated.

They had no education but could influence the workings of the educational system. They didn't understand how government functioned but would be able to tell it how to do its job. Americans have always been proud of the *one man, one vote* form of Democracy, but many, I suspect, have secretly wished that those with no real interest in the issues nor any real understanding of them would just stay home and let the rest of us who care enough to learn about those things choose the right people to represent all of us. It's a thorny situation alright.

It's also not talked about openly, precisely because we steadfastly protect our *right* to be ignorant, out of touch or uninformed. Maybe we should start discussing how to better inform our electorate before any more no/low-information votes are cast, unless of course we want another disputable election like the one in 2000 or God forbid, the one of 1876.

~

Introducing the Non-recession recession

The Hope and Change Newswire Service (HCNS) reported today that the White House announced that the Administration has just solved the financial crisis. The solution was unveiled at a signing ceremony held in the work-out room of the White House in which the President signed an Omnibus Executive Order (OEO) giving him the power to override any law that Congress passes despite their 2/3 majority.

The OEO allows the President to forbid the use of words like *recession* or phrases like *economic downturn* and replace them with what Press Secretary Jay Carney calls, 'hope words' like *Economic Adjustment Period (EAP)*, formerly called the recession (permission granted for use of this phrase for this article).

Carney continued, "There's absolutely no reason for anyone to worry about job or stock losses, defaults, bankruptcies or foreclosures as those words will be outlawed too. Pointing to the President's leadership on the entire range of economic issues, Carney revealed that the President signed the OEO now affectionately dubbed, *New Hope and New Change: WINNING* after thinking about it for, "a whole day, something no other President in history has done."

In addition to forbidding the use of 117 words that the administration calls, 'downer words,' it is resetting the unemployment percentage to zero and renaming all currently unemployed Americans as *Employment Ready Workers*. Sweeping changes in several departments of government will also result as a consequence of the new OEO. In the Department of Education, a new Czar for *Textbook Harmonization* will be named and who will be empowered to review every history book now in use in the USA with a view towards correcting *inconsistencies*.

In the Department of Health and Human Services, a new program for *Citizen Health Modeling* will be implemented that will require all Americans to submit to an extensive *wellness check*. The check will be done by government doctors who will classify them as either 'preferred' or 'common' citizens.

The President has also instructed the Department of Energy to immediately shut down 90% of all gas stations around the country using right of eminent domain. The DOE will also be converting those stations to 'Stop and Juice' electric power relay stations that will sell electricity to the new all-electric *O-Cars*. The government will also be requiring owners of gas-powered vehicles not getting 200 miles to the gallon to buy the new vehicles from government-operated dealerships owned by Government Motors (the new GM). Answering a reporter's question on the legality of the mandated purchasing of vehicles, Carney had a two-word response, "Remember Obamacare?" Finally, the Obama Administration unveiled its bold strategy for eliminating the worldwide economic downturn. Pressing a reset button on his podium, curtains parted behind Mr. Obama revealing a life-size image of the President on the wall. Underneath were the words 'Si, se puede' proudly drawn in graffiti-like style.

37

Both were centered on a facsimile of the U.S. dollar bill. Thus the new "O Dollar" currency was born. According to Carney, the room was bursting at the seams with the White House Press Corps and ordinary onlookers (carefully vetted by the White House to be sure they were *average Americans*). Sitting on the edge of their seats, the Press Corps saw the President's jaw jut forward and his face ark upwards with his eyes half-closed as if he were seeing way into the future.

With a drum roll from a lone Marine Corps drummer, the voice of James Earl Jones rumbled out of the twin speakers beside the President's podium, "And now, ladies and gentlemen, the President of the United States proudly introduces to the world, for the very first time ever the new 'O Dollar.' The One world currency that will end poverty and despair as we know it and that will replace the old outmoded U.S. dollar. Starting immediately, Secretary Timothy Geithner will be buying back your old dollars at the new rate of 25¢ for one new, improved O Dollar before its use becomes mandatory in 30 days."

~

Is Barack Obama really Punxsutawney Phil?

Just when we thought Barack Obama was out of our collective hair for good, he re-appears like that famous groundhog, Punxsutawney Phil. Unlike Phil, who would sensibly retreat to the warmth of his burrow for a few weeks of peace and quiet after seeing his shadow, Mr. Obama is happily out in the open basking in the glow of his fellow liberals, receiving accolades like the 'Profiles in Courage' award given him last week from the Kennedy Family Foundation. From that podium he made it abundantly clear to anyone who would listen that he alone is the only true, real President.

At that same venue, he lectured Congress about needing to summon up the *courage* to come together and become less partisan - and presumably help him save his major legislative achievement, the 'Patients' Affordable Health Care Act'. I'm curious as to how he will attempt to re-write history on all the outright lies he told about "keeping your doctor if you like him, keeping your insurance plan if you like it and the reduction of $2500/yearly cost of health insurance to the average family." We needn't worry too much about that, however, because the *Fourth Estate* will be right beside him, carrying his water and a bushel basket full of 'White-Out.'

The hypocrisy about finding courage and coming together is stunning, considering Mr. Obama presided over - and perhaps bore primary responsibility for - the greatest political division America has seen since the Johnson years! Those of us who had Mr. Obama's number and knew his modus operandi were well aware that this early return to the limelight was going to happen. A man of his oversized ego could not be silent nor remain in the background for long. And sure enough, after just 100 days into his successor's administration, '44' took off his self-imposed, disposable muzzle and grabbed the spotlight at the expense of the Kennedy Foundation award in Boston. A real Profile in Courage.

After eight years of organizing the largest community (the United States of America), Mr. Obama has attempted to reclaim his *street cred* and grab the moral high ground with both hands, reverting back to his old narcissistic self. This was expected, but it is not welcomed by those of us who were dearly looking forward to his retirement from public life. If the past is prologue, Mr. Obama will be constantly in our face as the political action committee he is associated with gathers speed and shifts into high gear, positioning itself at the vanguard of the new Resistance (aka 'No-Trump') Movement. Soon, all of America will again be subjected to more lofty and empty rhetoric that is Mr. Obama's signature style.

Look for him to accept more $400,000 speeches and personal appearances on America's airwaves as he ramps up his new campaign to take America back...for the Democrats! We can also expect to see dueling Presidents and dueling surrogates who will be spreading out like a virus in the mainstream media's ecosystem where they will be posturing, pontificating and preaching their bosses' gospels, driving an even bigger wedge between the right and left. If this comes to pass, it will delay or make impossible a healing of our nation's polarization. It will be interesting, however, to watch the bonanza of TV coverage of the two Presidents as they vie for widespread national 'ink'. I doubt seriously if this particular groundhog will ever go back into his burrow, shadow or not.

~

Julius Caesar's posthumous lament

"I have come to bury Caesar, not to praise him. The evil that men do lives after them; the good is oft interred with their bones." So said the Bard of Stratford-upon-Avon, William Shakespeare, through his character Marc Antony who was a friend of Caesar's in his play, *Julius Caesar*, written around 1599. It may be a stretch to compare Julius Caesar with outgoing U.S. President Barack Obama, but the desire for a lasting legacy that accentuates the accomplishments and minimizes the failures is part and parcel of being a powerful leader. It's also one that the centuries do not diminish. During these past eight years, I have often pictured Mr. Obama dressed in a toga with a laurel wreath crown on his head sitting on an imperial throne as he signed his many Executive Orders, surrounded by a throng of sycophant 'yes men.' That may be a bit harsh, but this *imperial tendency* is what I think will be the burr under Mr. Obama's legacy saddle for years to come.

I am one of the countless millions that will be glad to see the back of Barack Obama on January 20, 2017 as he metamorphoses from the present into the past. In my opinion, he has been an abject failure as a President, a leader, a manager and a role model for future leaders. In 2008, America was clamoring for change, and a 'savior like' figure emerged to knock the heir apparent to the Democratic Party's presidential nomination, Mrs. Hillary Clinton, off her perch. The Democrats being what they are quickly herded Mrs. Clinton under Mr. Obama's wing in the belief that it was better to have her as part of the Administration than opposing it and planning a run in 2012. The plan worked and she took the job on Nov. 14, 2008 and the President announced it on December 1st.

Six weeks later, the Senate Foreign Relations Committee voted 16-1 to approve her, and Mrs. Clinton played the 'good soldier' for four years until stepping down in 2013 to make her run for the top job.

Legacy grade for appointing Hillary Clinton to a cabinet position: A+
Reason: According to Sun Tzu, it's better to keep your enemies closer to you than your friends (in Mrs. Clinton's case where she could do less harm and be constantly watched).

Legacy grade for the country's benefit: D
Reason: Because she created too many problems for the White House and the Democratic Party with her various scandals (Benghazi, Libya and e-mail server) and her lackluster diplomatic performance (Russian reset, etc.).

It was clear from the outset that Mr. Obama had come to Washington to re-make it into his image, but he also came to use it for his own purposes - to consolidate power for the Democrats and create a larger more dedicated voter base that would carry him easily to a second term. He had no use for Republican help and basically thumbed his nose at them in a meeting on the economic stimulus package in the White House on January 23, 2009, when he said, "I won, so I think on that one I trump you...and that debate is over" to Representative Eric Cantor and Senator John McCain. If not the shot heard round the world, it was a clear shot across the bow to the Republicans that they should save their ammunition as this was not the Rocky and Bullwinkle Show; it was the Rocky show and Obama was Rocky.

Legacy grade for respecting the Republicans: F
Reason: If you aren't nice to people on the way up the ladder you may regret it because you may meet them on the way down.
Legacy grade for the country: F
Reason: It wasted time, energy and money and made compromise impossible with John Boehner, Mitch McConnell and others.

It's hard to say whether the President failed more with the economy or with foreign policy. On foreign policy, as it affected the Afghanistan and Iraq wars, the President refused to listen to his military advisors time and time again, on deployments, troop levels, status of forces agreements and more. His public announcements on troop withdrawal timelines shocked the Pentagon that believed that military strategy was not something you go public with, especially when the enemy is listening. His decision to suspend talks on reaching a status of forces agreement (SOFA) with the Iraqis basically left them vulnerable and resulted in the deaths of thousands of innocent civilians as ISIS filled the void.

Legacy grade: F
Reason: His unwillingness to listen to those with superior experience cost lives.
Legacy for the country: F
Reason: It made many military leaders unwilling to go up against the President, therefore the country lost the benefit of their opinions on strategy and tactics. And thousands of people were put in harm's way because of his ego and mistrust of his advisors.

"We are not the blue states or the red states. We are the United States of America." Those words were the pap that was fed to the American electorate in 2008, and many believed Mr. Obama and voted for him. However, there were greater divisions than just the political, and they had been building for decades. One of them was America's worsening race relations. Instead of using his position and 'bully pulpit' to take on America's racial divide, he did the opposite.

On July 16, 2009, when Harvard professor Henry Gates was arrested for acting suspiciously near his home after a 911 call had been placed alerting the Cambridge police that men had been breaking and entering his residence, Mr. Obama immediately intervened into a local law enforcement situation and deemed it wrong for the Cambridge Police to have detained Professor Gates.

He was also AWOL when his own Attorney General, Eric Holder, said, on February 19, 2009 that, "Though this nation has proudly thought of itself as an ethnic melting pot, in things racial we have always been and continue to be, in too many ways, essentially a nation of cowards." This would have been the perfect time to begin the conversation on race, but Obama remained silent. There were other instances in which the President made attempts to insert himself in local racial matters, but the bottom line was that he neither said nor did anything to improve the racial dialogue between Whites and Blacks. In short, he squandered an exceptional opportunity for the first half-Black President in the whole of America's history to make a meaningful difference in the lives of Whites and Blacks, together, as one group.

Legacy grade for missing his best opportunity to heal the racial divide: F
Reason: He felt it was an issue that was too politically charged and would be detrimental to Democrats and his next run for office. Also, it would remind Black voters that their lives were actually worse off than they were led to believe (inner city Black youth unemployment is over 20%, for example).

Legacy grade for the country: F
Reason: Racial tensions were steadily building and nothing was being done on a national level, leaving many to believe that Mr. Obama was oblivious to the problems of the Black community.

The appellation associated with the Patients Affordable Health Care Act, 'Obamacare' won't be the jewel in Mr. Obama's crown as millions of people have been adversely affected by a poorly-designed and managed program for over 300 million when it should have focused on the 30 million without insurance. After spending roughly $834 million on marketplace-related (information technology/website) contracts (sixty contracts to be specific) and inter-agency agreements (according to HHS Secretary designate Sylvia Burwell's testimony to lawmakers on February 24, 2014) the website was a shambles.

The healthcare program, itself, was not much better as premiums soared, patients' deductibles skyrocketed and doctors and other healthcare professionals were leaving their professions in record numbers, leaving fewer workers behind to serve the growing pool of patients. If that wasn't bad enough, many state-based health exchanges were losing money and in danger of disappearing. A total FUBAR situation.

Legacy grade for constructing a workable and affordable system: D
Reason: It totally ignored human nature (the resistance of young people to sign up) and was financially unsound. Additionally, it did nothing to fulfill Mr. Obama's promises that the average family would save $2500/year and that they could keep their insurance plan and their doctor. None of these was possible. The President just lied about them.

Legacy grade for the country: D+
Reason: Obamacare did bring a few million people into the health exchanges and did enable young people to stay on their parents' policies as well as guarantee that nobody with a pre-existing condition could be refused.

It is doubtful that President-elect Donald Trump would have hit the immigration issue so hard had it not been for Barack Obama's unyielding position on making America's southern border a massive immigration turn-style. The President ordered the border patrol to count 'turnarounds' - the dispatching of illegal border-crossers immediately back to Mexico after their arrival - as *deportations* thereby making him look tough on illegal immigration to the right. For the illegal immigrant community he needed to look compassionate so he signed an illegal Executive Order to protect the children of illegal immigrants from deportation (the Supreme Court nullified that order in 2016).

Add to that his unwillingness to support tougher restrictions on 'sanctuary cities' so that repeat illegal aliens were quickly located and deported before they could commit class II felony crimes and you have an Administration and a chief executive that clearly did not value border or citizen security.

Legacy grade for lawful executive branch behavior: F
Reason: By ignoring his responsibility to secure America's borders and to apply the law as it is written, he abrogated his charge to uphold and defend the Constitution (and therefore the laws duly enacted by the Congress).

Legacy grade for the country: F
Reason: His actions made it more difficult to find common ground as he poisoned the well of comity that both the Executive and Legislative Branches must share.

While much more can be said about Mr. Obama's legacy in the areas of religious freedom and states' rights issues, it is fair to say that his 57% approval rating on exiting his office is a conundrum and may portend an early 'rehabilitation' from his critics. There might just be another reason for his high rating, however, and that is that many voters (at least the 62 million that voted for Mr. Trump) are just plain happy to see him go. Don't let it hit you on the way out, Mr. President.

~

Kindergarten government

My suspicions are confirmed. Before watching an interview of the former National Security Council spokesman, Tommy Vietor, by Fox's Brett Baier, I had a hunch that kids were turning the dials and pulling the levers of our government. Now, after that five-minute interview I'm sure of it. In case you didn't catch it, Baier was questioning the 32-year old Vietor about his role in the Benghazi scandal. Yes, I said scandal, because when four Americans are killed and it's blamed on a video that most of the Middle East had never seen or heard of and when no military assets were sent to the area to try to save an American Ambassador and three colleagues who were fighting for their lives during a seven-hour attack and it takes nearly 18 months to get documents like simple emails from the White House, it's a scandal.

So Baier asks Vietor where he was at the time of the attack. Vietor says he was in the 'Situation Room.' You remember the Situation Room don't you? It's that place in the White House where everybody goes to be photographed by the White House photographer while brave special ops teams are killing Osama bin Laden thousands of miles away. Baier then asks if the President was there. Vietor says, no, he wasn't. So Baier asks where he was. Vietor responds snidely. I don't know. He was in the White House somewhere. *"I didn't have a tracking device on him."*

Baier takes the beanball pitch of sarcasm to his head in stride and comes back with, "Did you change the word *attacks* to *demonstrations* in the CIA's talking points?" To which Tommy V. says, "Maybe. I don't really remember." Baier: "You don't remember?" Then Vietor shows his age with, *"Dude,* this was like two years ago. We're still talking about the most mundane process...we're talking about editing talking points. That's what bureaucrats do all day long!" At this point, I half-expected Vietor to rip off his coat and tie and reveal his Bevis and Butthead t-shirt and give the inane three-fingers up 'homeboy' sign to the camera or at least *moon* Baier.

My mind started to wander, back to another controversial boychick, Ben Rhodes. (*Rhodes' Sept. 14th 2012 email to 12 highly-placed White House officials in which he stressed that all should "Underscore that these protests*

44

are rooted in an internet video; and not a broader failure of policy" preceded Tommy V's appearance on Baier's program.)

Vietor's allusion to a 'long time ago' is typical of how the pee wee gang of 30-something spokespeople, advisors and assorted hangers-on in the White House (Burton, Rhodes and others) and the State Department (Jen Psaki) feel about time. It either began the moment they were born or it's something that only older people concern themselves with. They act as if no history book will ever be written again or that the Internet will not entomb them in an endless loop for all eternity.

Their actions could be chalked up to youthful naiveté, but I think it goes deeper, into the pit of hubris and arrogance that characterize power-hungry people. They're like Frodo with Tolkien's ring in their pocket, and we are Gollum. We're desperately trying to make some sense out of their power mania as they stymie and stonewall our every attempt to look behind their blind ambition and understand what is really happening with our government. Maybe the youngsters who've been entrusted with important jobs in our government should stop spinning or obfuscating so much because they've completely lost sight of the truth. They need to grow up and stop living in the 'Twilight Zone' reality show of inside the Beltway and the rarified atmosphere of their own words. Can we please hire some adults next time?

~

Last Tango in Argentina: the optical dance of politics

How important is style or optics to governance? Our memories only allow us to reach back to Franklin Delano Roosevelt's presidency, but his presidency is a great starting point for reflection, especially considering his affliction with polio. At that time, Roosevelt and his handlers went to great lengths to avoid showing American citizens his inability to walk, normally. This was probably a good decision, considering Americans' penchant for tough, resolute leaders at a time of war. Many presidents since have discovered the importance of optics to shaping their image and political campaigns. Television viewers and radio listeners of the Kennedy-Nixon debates in 1960 may have been split in their opinions of who won, but no one watching could deny the stark visual contrast between the two candidates.

Those debates altered optical politics forever. So did the Kennedy presidency that was carefully managed by his image-makers to continually place the President in the best possible light. It helped that Kennedy was a media natural because of his easy-going under-stated style, his sense of humor and his good looks. A beautiful, well-educated, soft-spoken wife was also an asset to his campaign and his presidency.

The optics of Kennedy's successor's presidency were the polar opposite. Lyndon Johnson didn't share Kennedy's looks or lightness. He was lank and taciturn and had a proclivity for the unorthodox like allowing reporters to interview him in the bathroom, for pulling up his dog by the ears and for lifting up his shirt and showing his operation scars.

It's hard to believe that that kind of optics would endear anyone to a President today. Despite the fact that the majority of his public appearances were stilted and stiff, Johnson's consummate skills as a politician behind the scenes were legendary, and had they been visible, it might have made him more likable among American voters. We all know that the camera doesn't like certain people, but the camera's lens has changed over time along with America's electorate. Arkansas Governor, Bill Clinton, is a case in point.

A ready smile and a crackling disarming voice helped him seduce his way, optically, into the Presidency and kept his popularity going until the very thing that brought him there eventually brought him down. The optics of a bony finger and a full-throated denial of sexual misconduct on camera served to erode his popularity and believability and eventually get him impeached. Optically, he was finished, no matter his wife's attempts at 'standing by her man.' The hook was set. Optics can buoy or destroy. It can reinforce or repudiate, but most of all it can be manipulated. We needn't go back any farther than the election of Barack Obama in 2008 to see how optics, demographics and a mastery of oratory can combine to make a would-be President into a real one.

What has happened in the ensuing 7.2 years of Mr. Obama's presidency will keep media types, sociologists, historians, political strategists and image-makers busy writing books and lecturing on the circuit. They will try to explain something that, to me, is self-evident. That is, that anyone can be President if they have the determination, the political savvy, the financial support, the right style and charisma AND if they enter a race at the right time when the electorate wants their particular brand of leadership.

Michael J. Fox, who played the President's Assistant for Domestic Policy in the film, 'The American President,' said the following lines: "The American people want leadership. And in the absence of genuine leadership, they will listen to anyone that steps up to the microphone. They're so thirsty for it, they'll crawl through the desert toward a mirage, and when they discover there's no water, they'll drink the sand." To which the President responded, "People don't drink the sand because they're thirsty; they drink the sand because they don't know the difference."

Optics can change the political landscape in a heartbeat, but the optics of a situation should never be THE decisive factor in how or who we elect as our leaders. Candidates and leaders must be evaluated by a number of other factors that are not accidental media missteps like a Tango in Argentina. They should, instead, be judged on whether the optics of their actions were contrived or deliberately stage-managed to mislead, misdirect or manipulate.

~

Litmus Testing the Fence-Sitters

I'm proud of the fact that I'm politically engaged and fairly politically astute. Frankly, I don't understand those who don't care about politics or its effects on their lives. Don't they know that the only innocent thing about bystanders is their naiveté? Do they really think that by not taking sides they'll exempt themselves from the consequences of other people's actions?

Ever seen the TV cameraman on the sidelines at a football game get mowed down by a wide receiver running dangerously close to the out-of-bounds line? Everything's going fine. He's capturing some great footage until he realizes that a mano a mano collision is about to take place and HE'S one of the manos! Because he's spent all of his time looking through somebody else's lens he's missed an opportunity to positively affect his own situation and get the heck out of the way before this oncoming freight train of a man turns him into tapioca pudding.

Anyone who stands at the sidelines of politics with his arms folded, dispassionately watching cataclysmic events take place deserves to be hit by that wide receiver, and I for one have no sympathy for them. I guess it's because my skin has been toughened these last 20 years of the Clinton, Bush and Obama Administrations (not to mention the many Congresses that have come and gone and the really pathetic laws they've turned out). I could no longer stand idly by and say, Hmm, isn't that an interesting piece of legislation (like the Affordable Healthcare Act). I wonder how that will affect me? Then I could say to the tax man, Could you please take a little more of my money? I was only going to leave it to my children anyway. Ya, right.

A good friend of mine lives in Texas, and I was talking with him about these fence-sitters. He remonstrated against them in a typically Texan way. He said that, "Suppose you're watchin' two big Texas bulls fightin' in a corral. They've been at it for an hour, knockin' themselves out with their repeated attacks, but now they've kicked the fence boards loose, are tearin' up the corral and puttin' the rest of the herd in danger. What do you do? Ignore 'em and hope they'll come to their senses before they destroy the place or do you step in and get involved'? Brother, that's what we call a Texas no-brainer." True fence-sitters and real non-committals aren't the only casualties on the political battlefield nor are they the only ones giving *freedom* a bad case of indigestion by their lack of participation.

Political correctness seems to be pushing us and our opinions so far underground that we may need to start applying a litmus test to everybody so that their ideologies are visible to the naked eye and so that we know who we're talking to.

For those of you who haven't thought about it for awhile, litmus is a coloring matter that comes from lichens and the litmus test helps identify two solutions. When litmus is added to acids it turns red and when it's added to alkaline solutions it turns blue. (*That is not a political comment, my friends though it is an interesting thought). It's just chemistry.* Our litmus test could be my friend's bull-in-the-corral situation. Here's what you do, when you're with someone whose political philosophy you're unsure of...

You repeat that situation and wait for your conversation partner's answer. If he says he'd wait until the bulls get tired so they fall over from exhaustion, he's probably a very doctrinaire, laissez-faire type who won't intervene no matter how serious the situation is (maybe a Libertarian). If he says he'll get a couple of the boys to jump over the fence and try to lasso the bulls and pull them apart, he's probably an academic and has never done this before. So, basically, he has no clue of the danger he would put himself and his pals in.

If he says he'll pull out his Winchester and kill one of the bulls, chances are he's a doer not a talker, *but not necessarily a long-term thinker* as he clearly hasn't thought about how the shot might stampede the rest of the herd AND send one of his best 'producers' to the big stockyard in the sky (possibly a Liberal). If you find someone who says he'll fix the fence boards first, sequester the exposed herd and saddle up his ranch hands on their horses so they can guide one of the bulls into an open chute, then you've found a person (definitely a Conservative) who understands *human* nature as well as animal nature. My advice is, get him to run for public office. We must start pulling people off the fences and making them aware that their voices count and that none of us can afford to just vote 'present' while bad things happen to our blessed land.

This high-pitched disagreement about what kind of America we want and the demonization of the opposition is eventually going to tear down the fence the undecideds are sitting on. They had better get ready and choose for themselves which side to come down on. Let's hope for all our sakes that it's the side of common sense, conversation and the Constitution.

~

Moderation is not the solution

All my life I've been told that *all things in moderation* was the way to happiness and contentment. And for a long time I bought the argument, except when I played sports when the coach said, "Go out there and annihilate them;" or building my small businesses (when it was critical that I bested the competition); or raising my children (when I told them, "Don't play in traffic").

Now, as the deadlines for re-opening the Government and raising the debt ceiling are upon us, there is an intensified call for *moderation*. Mind you, there are vastly different definitions of moderation depending on whether you're a Republican or Democrat, but a call for it has nevertheless been made. Before we go any further, let's strip away politics for a minute and get down to brass tacks.

First, it is the responsibility of The House of Representatives and the Senate to protect the people of the United States from bad legislation by not enacting it. Second, it is the responsibility of the House to regulate appropriations of our tax dollars to pay for legislation (Sections 7 and 8 of Article I. of the Constitution). Herein lies the conflict on extending the Continuing Resolution ('CR') to pay America's bills. Many House (and Senate) Republicans believe that Obamacare is a bad law and shouldn't be funded and were willing to go to the mat to exercise their Constitutional right to deny or delay such funding.

Their justification for doing so was reinforced by the President's own intervention with 19 changes made by his Executive Branch to the law without Congressional approval, effectively overstepping his bounds and acting as a legislator instead of an implementer! Republicans found this unbelievable and ample reason to make the demands they did like granting the same one-year exemption of the individual mandate for Obamacare to ordinary people that the President gave to large businesses. There are other political motivations from both sides, but that was the principal rationale and public case made by the Rs who considered their actions, *moderate*, given their view of the basic inequality of the situation (i.e. preferential treatment).

Now to the Democrats who were standing on the legal argument of, "the law was passed (albeit without a single Republican vote in either the House or Senate); it was adjudicated by the Supreme Court (actually the Court focused largely on the penalty for not buying insurance - the mandate - which was the law's lynchpin); now it should be implemented without further ado, and anything that would delay its implementation or deny its funding is against the law."

Not quite. The costs for implementing the regulations that flow from laws are routinely funded or not funded every time a budget is approved, and there's the rub. We haven't had a real budget which has been agreed to by the House, the Senate and the President for over four years! Instead, we've been limping along with an unending series of CRs that fund our Government without taking a hard look at what really fiscally ails us (the 'Sequester' was the exception though that didn't get into the 'weeds' where the real waste lies). Like Congressional Representatives, budgets and laws come and go, but sometimes it takes awhile before we admit the truth about them. Prohibition was one such law. Enacted on January 16, 1919 by the 18th Amendment to the Constitution, this cockamamy law continued for nearly 15 years before being nullified by the 21st Amendment on December 5, 1933.

While most of us are appalled at how our legislators are acting these days, maybe we shouldn't be so hard on them. After all, they've never had to sneak away to a speakeasy for a drink of bad whiskey.
Maybe it will take a stealth visit to a black market doctor to get good healthcare before they understand real moderation and fix what now appears to be unfixable...that is if there is anything left to fix by then.

~

One-worlder at 1600 Pennsylvania Ave.?

It was a lot easier to be a one-worlder (*def. A person who believes in a single-world order or government that joins all nations under one flag for the purpose of promoting the common good*) back in the time of the Holy Roman Empire than it is today. That is unless you're a true believer of the world according to Obama.

Having now alienated all of the Democrat readers who have just cursed me under their breath and perhaps even ripped out my column and consigned it to the dustbin, let me just say that I do not come to this conclusion lightly. Back in the day, the Romans ruled a fair amount of the world and their one-world view was one of empire where they held the top jobs. Stay with me, now.

Judging by many of Mr. Obama's decisions he seems to hold a classical one world order view AND that the USA should be part of the 'B' team. The U.S. should not be the coach or the quarterback or certainly not the team's owners. No, we must first go through a process of social, financial, cultural and ethnic homogenization where all our differences are blowtorched away and we become truly equal, indistinguishable from one another.

I must say that he's been pretty clever at how he's gone about trying to 'right-size' America into his image of a second-string one-worlder country. He's painted with the whole palette of human emotions at one time or another to make Americans feel guilty for actions of the past like slavery, for example. Then he tied the past to the present to convince us that we still bear the 'original sin' of our forefathers and used strawmen like the 'power-mad police' or 'vigilante justice' to convince us that America is racist.

This after the President's Attorney General told us we were cowards because we didn't talk about race! Then when we were ready to have that conversation, the President and the AG changed the topic from race to *racism* by unleashing government lawyers and a full-blown investigation on the actions of the Ferguson, Missouri police because the AG (and presumably the President) couldn't believe that actual justice could be had in the wake of the Michael Brown killing. After all, we couldn't move on towards a one-world view without an appropriate amount of self-flagellation and recrimination.

51

On the economic front, the Koch brothers, Wall Street and the 1% moneyed class were all conspiring against ordinary Americans to rob them of their birthright of 'income equality.' Curiously, the Koch Brothers became the bad guys while the billionaire Warren Buffet became the good guy. To add to the flattening of the argument, the President's constant drum beat of "You didn't build that" or words to that effect were heard on the stump. It wasn't sinister. It was just an attempt to bring everybody down to the same level (no matter how low), something his entire administration has tried to do from day one.

'Obamacare' proves that point. Then there's what some would call the reluctance to lead or to 'lead from behind' in foreign affairs. Again, this is in line with an ideology that many one-worlders share...that no one country should lead, and Mr. Obama adds, <u>least of all</u> **us**.

While there's no law against believing that the Earth would be better governed by a group of countries that shared each other's values, we have a few things working against that inevitability. One of those is human nature. As long as there are humans, there will be greed, theft, injustice, discrimination, incivility and megalomania.

Here's the rub, when we elect a President we expect him to be in America's corner first and foremost and not subordinate our views and actions to those of the world community. Our framers made sure that foreign law could not trump our laws, but they didn't count on presidents like Barack Obama to end-run the process through unparalleled executive power grabs. Mr. Obama has shown his contempt for our Constitution and our legislators on more than one occasion.

His most recent action was this last fall when he unilaterally declared that HE would not deport nearly five million illegal aliens but instead would 'regularize' their status and allow them to stay here AND get work permits and social security cards! My prediction is that he will continue along this path until his last day in office, because many of our laws do not reflect his essential beliefs in a one-world society AND because he's keeping his eye on the prize...the Secretary Generalship of the United Nations when he leaves office.

~

Our beleaguered Second Amendment

The recent massacre of innocent children in Newtown, Connecticut got me to thinking about the Second Amendment to the Constitution and the

52

controversy that swirls around it. It is probably fair to say that this amendment is the most contentious among the 27 in that great document, though there have been instances where acts of violence have occurred after citizens have exercised their First Amendment rights, among others.

"The right to keep and bear arms" means different things to different people, but the innocent victims of crimes committed with guns haven't the luxury of parsing that amendment. They are the tragic reminder that the criminal and the mentally disturbed in our society have both the means and the opportunity to break (with any type of weapon) the sacred covenant of peaceful coexistence that the framers of the Constitution wanted for us. Each generation of Americans wrestles with the evil that is inherent in human beings, trying to understand what motivates people to take another person's life, especially the lives of children.

For all our introspection, however, it hasn't brought us much clarity. Maybe the only conclusion we can draw is that evil exists and mental illness exists, and when these factors come together we're all in peril, especially when <u>any</u> weapon can be obtained by these people. So, knowing we cannot eliminate evil or are seemingly powerless to seriously treat the disturbed in our society, we cast about trying to do something, anything, that will give us some consolation and maybe close the circle of grief. This time we're focusing on a new 'gun bill' that will shortly be introduced by California Senator Diane Feinstein that will focus on limiting the *tools* that the perpetrators use to commit their heinous crimes.

It would seem obvious, that by eliminating the spread of high-powered multiple-round capable semi-automatic weapons that we will stop crimes committed with those weapons. While I commend Senator Feinstein or any person who is passionate about saving lives, I do not believe that her bill will work.

There are just too many of that particular type of weapon in circulation already (millions to be exact). Her bill would probably stop the further spread of those weapons, but it will do absolutely nothing to cure the mental illness that plagues far too many Americans who would use them or any weapon to wreak havoc on the rest of us. We must be realistic about our gun laws. With over 300 million weapons currently in the hands of Americans (most of them law-abiding) we must do a better job in the screening process and on other fronts. Here are a few areas we might focus on first knowing that the confiscation of guns is illegal or impossible to achieve.

Suggestion #1: Tighten up the licensing process as it refers to background checks. Each state must have a foolproof means of eliminating persons with mental illness, illegal aliens, underage buyers or felons from getting a license to purchase a firearm, period.

Suggestion #2: Make Federal Firearm License holders (dealers) the first line of defense in insuring gun safety by requiring that first-time gun purchasers who qualify to buy a gun take a short on-site gun safety course and then have the Federal Government pay the dealers to administer it.

Suggestion #3: Allow purchasers of gun safes, gun locks and those who choose to de-commission firearms to get a federal income tax deduction (their choice to take it or not) for purchasing or de-commissioning them.

Suggestion #4: Require background checks of gun purchases at bona fide gun shows. If the seller is not a FFL holder then the seller and purchaser must go to a seller at the show who does have one to do the background check for them (a token reimbursement for that service should be given the FFL holder by the prospective seller and purchaser).

Suggestion #5: Encourage all states to issue certificates of reciprocity to other states for concealed carry permit holders.

Suggestion #6: Bring outlying states like Illinois and New York and the District of Colombia into compliance with other states' regulations for gun ownership. It is simply not right to disadvantage law-abiding citizens in those states.

Suggestion #7: Encourage all schools to hire professional armed security guards or police officers to guard their students or allow specific school personnel to carry a concealed weapon (the criteria for this would be up to the individual school district). Strengthen other security procedures as well such as CCTV.

Suggestion #8: Offer a free annual firearm safety course to those persons already possessing a firearm. Funding for these courses would come from the individual states' budgets, perhaps from the fees charged concealed carry permit holders or from voluntary financial support from gun manufacturers and gun dealers.

Suggestion #9: Develop a Federal public awareness program about firearms and firearm safety.

<u>Suggestion #10:</u> Encourage gun-owner groups like the NRA to support the above-mentioned suggestions.

Finally, our mental healthcare professionals must be given more resources to help identify, early on, and on a continuing basis, those among us whose mental or emotional state puts them and the rest of us at risk should they gain access to a firearm. Gun safety and responsible gun use is just as important to our communities as the regulation and safe operation of a motor vehicle and should be treated with the same level of seriousness.

~

Our eight years with Barack Obama

The last eight years under President Obama have seemed like a lifetime to this Conservative. We've learned much and yet not much of what we've learned is new, like America is hopelessly divided along ideological, racial, economic, generational, gender, ethnic and geographical lines. There are some things, however, that did come as a surprise to us since 2008 such as when given an opportunity to effect change in our race relations with the Black community, Mr. Obama failed miserably.

He set the tone for his presidency in July 2009 when he involved himself in a municipal dispute in Cambridge, Massachusetts by defending Prof. Henry Louis Gates against the Cambridge Police by saying, "I don't know, not having been there and not seeing all the facts, what role race played in that. But I think it's fair to say, number one, any of us would be pretty angry; number two, that the Cambridge police acted stupidly in arresting somebody when there was already proof that they were in their own home, and, number three, what I think we know separate and apart from this incident is that there's a long history in this country of African Americans and Latinos being stopped by law enforcement, disproportionately."

This was the first salvo in what would be several more instances where the President jumped to conclusions in support of Black citizens' involvement with law enforcement officers. We should have expected this attitude about who America's real victims and perpetrators are given the President's academic history, his time as a community organizer in Chicago and his left-leaning philosophy about America's inequality as it applies to our justice system <u>and</u> concentration of wealth.

It would have been easier for all of us had we realized that he laid it all out before he became President. If his oath of office had included the computer description: "WYSIWYG" (What you see is what you get) it might have been a smoother transition for us to make from his lofty rhetoric to his actions. We learned not to believe him early on when he told us that the Stimulus Plan was critical and we should pass it so we could create or save jobs (and that it only would cost us nearly a trillion dollars).

While some jobs were, indeed, created, they were short-lived and popped up when the smell of government money was in the air and then quickly disappeared or became part-time jobs after the money had run out. In the State of New Mexico, much of the money was used to pay current salaries, hardly an exemplary job-creating enterprise. We saw how Federal dollars were wasted on projects or companies in the alternative energy sector like the Silicon Valley startup, Solyndra, which left us, the taxpayers, holding the bag for $535 million in losses.

Obama was out of the starting gate too early with plans that had no connection to reality such as an ill-conceived $80 billion energy investment scheme. His loyalties to his brothers and sisters in the labor movement were evident during his first term as he prioritized payments of $23 billion to the GM and Chrysler auto workers' Voluntary Employee Beneficiary Association (to assure the solvency of their health benefits) which were unsecured obligations instead of paying suppliers and bond-holders first, totally contrary to normal bankruptcy proceedings.

At the time of bankruptcy, GM owed these unsecured creditors $29.9 billion, for which they received 10% of the stock of "new" GM, which went public in November 2010 along with warrants to purchase 15% more at preferred prices. The handwriting was clearly on the wall for what was to come, a flight towards an ideological utopia that took America on a 180 degree turn towards, dare I say it, socialism. Mr. Obama routinely ignored the Congress and its committees and chose, instead, to sail his own ship (of State) relying on a core of sycophant underlings to leave the reservation whenever necessary to accomplish his goals of "fundamentally transforming America."

Scandals quickly followed as staffers and *Schedule C* appointees took it upon themselves to drive the wagon as fast as they could until the wheels came off. One of the first to do it was the GSA that spent $823K on a Las Vegas conference featuring clowns and mind readers. The GSA Administrator resigned shortly thereafter. Then there was the 'Fast and

Furious' gun-selling/walking controversy that resulted in the death of Border Patrol Agent, Brian Terry. Mr. Obama's Attorney General, Eric Holder, claimed to have no prior knowledge of the scheme, and the President blamed George Bush.

Then, just after the 2012 elections, it came to light that the IRS was targeting Tea Party or conservative-leaning groups to exclude them from tax-exempt status and actively denying or slow-walking their 501(c)(3) applications while swiftly approving those of left-leaning organizations. After extensive investigations, it was found to be true, but nobody lost their jobs because of the actions of IRS employees and managers. Mr. Obama said that he first heard about it in press reports.

Mr. Obama pushed through the Patients Affordable Health Care Act (aka 'Obamacare') with the help of a budget rule from 1974 called, 'The Reconciliation Act.' It passed without a single Republican vote in the dead of night, making it the largest entitlement program in U.S.' history since the introduction of Social Security. Before passage, then House Speaker Nancy Pelosi said that, "We would have to pass the bill so that you can find out what is in it."

Had former Wisconsin Senator William Proxmire been alive he would have surely given Ms. Pelosi his "Golden Fleece Award" for her history-making comments that reflected the true obfuscatory nature of Washington politics.

Before the bill was steam-rolled through, President Obama promised the American public that we could keep our doctor if we liked him and that the average insured family would save up to $2500/year on premiums. Both were lies, designed to sell the program, according to Jonathan Gruber, one of the architects of the legislation who admitted as much in 2014, "I mean, this bill was written in a tortured way to make sure CBO did not score the mandate as taxes. If CBO scored the mandate as taxes the bill dies. Okay? So it's written to do that. In terms of risk rated subsidies, if you had a law which said that healthy people are going to pay in, you made explicit healthy people pay in and sick people get money, it would not have passed. Lack of transparency is a huge political advantage. And basically, call it the stupidity of the American voter or whatever, but basically that was really, really critical to get for the thing to pass."

The result? Only 11.3 million people have signed up for a program that was supposed to insure 30 million. Obamacare has caused premiums, co-pays and hospital/medicine costs to rise for nearly everybody and has been the chief motivator for doctors' retirements across the country. It is expected to self-implode because the cost projections (younger people are not signing up, causing the expenses of the system to strangle itself) can't support its existence without a massive injection of more taxpayer money.

There is no question that we have learned much from the entire Obamacare experience. We've learned not to trust our President, not to trust his surrogates, not to trust so-called experts, and that if something looks too good to be true, it probably is. The next President will have a white elephant on his hands with few buyers as most of the insurance companies have already bailed out of the many state exchanges, leaving, in some cases, only one private insurer in a state.

Staying with the domestic achievements, Mr. Obama successfully upended a centuries' old American tradition of marriage between one man and one woman as an accepted institution. This delighted the homosexual community and insured him a place in their hall of heroes. It did little to ingratiate him with the millions of religious voters, however. In the same vein, he was able to get "Don't ask. Don't tell" removed from the military. What was personal before is now public, and if not directly promoted within the military, is ensconced in regulation.

On immigration, we learned that a President can unilaterally decide to suspend the law and accord protections to special groups that he deems worthy. By issuing Executive Orders (DACA) for the "Dreamers" and suspending their deportation, he effectively end-ran the House and Senate and set himself up as judge and jury, disregarding the "Immigration and Naturalization Act" by giving protection to whole *groups* instead of individuals (which was his right). He showed us that he wasn't afraid of the House or the Supreme Court and basically said, "Sue me!" He delayed judgment day and ran out the clock. It was only during the latter part of his second administration did he get his Executive Orders nullified by the Court.

We've discovered, by Mr. Obama's preference for EOs, that Presidents can take on the persona of a king and issue edicts at their will, and because of the time it takes to move a disputed EO through our legal system, those edicts can have a deleterious effect on the very muscle of our laws.

The legacy of Barack Obama is one of delaying justice not upholding it. On violence in America, Mr. Obama has tried repeatedly to blame the inanimate gun instead of the animus of the shooter. His efforts to link the 'gun show loophole' and 'military-styled weapons' to crazed killers failed as many of the perpetrators had obtained their firearms, legally. We learned that he didn't understand the arguments of millions of law-abiding gun owners nor did he really support the Second Amendment that gave them their rights.

One of his statements during his run for office in 2008 exemplified his disconnect with - and disdain for - the American people, "And it's not surprising then they get bitter, they cling to guns or religion or antipathy toward people who aren't like them or anti-immigrant sentiment or anti-trade sentiment as a way to explain their frustrations."

On race relations, Mr. Obama has failed miserably to help get young Blacks off the unemployment rolls or to provide them with even a modicum of hope for a future outside the inner cities' cloak of fear. No substantive efforts were made to have a discussion on race in America these past eight years. The President showed himself to be an opportunist, preferring to let events dictate his actions instead of actions dictating events. No outstretched hands were offered.

Shortly after Barack Obama became President, one of his first 'international' acts was to give the bust of Winston Churchill back to the Brits. (It had occupied a prominent spot in the White House for years.) He then proceeded to tell the world that our relationship with Great Britain was not 'special' and that every nation thinks of itself as exceptional. I believe he did this in an attempt to destroy the long-held belief that America was exceptional because of her freedoms and liberty.

We learned that Obama loved to travel and loved to diminish America's standing in the eyes of foreign leaders as when he bowed deeply before the Saudi King in 2009. In Mr. Obama's eyes, America needs to repent for its history of abuse of Native Americans, slavery of the African, for capitalism, America's wealth and its consumption of the world's resources.

This has influenced his push for lower greenhouse gas emissions, the Paris Climate Change Agreement and even the recently-concluded Iran Nuclear Deal. Mr. Obama is a believer in global cooperation through a wholesale transfer of America's sovereignty rather than establishing a strong America at home. I believe that he believes this to be his unique role as chief executive of the most powerful nation on earth. Unfortunately, this is not part of his principal job description.

He believes that <u>by not making war you are making peace</u> and has tried to prove it by delaying important decisions in the Middle East (though he was able to locate and kill Osama bin Laden), on ISIS, Iran, Syria and others. By publicizing our departure dates from Afghanistan, Mr. Obama emboldened America's enemies. His naiveté cost American lives and seriously hampered our efforts to contain international terrorism. We learned that his stubbornness knows no bounds. He is still unable to label the current wave of terrorism as having roots in Islamic Extremism. And he also refuses to call the Islamic State, in Iraq and Syria, ISIS. He prefers to use the term, 'ISIL' which stands for the Islamic State of Iraq and the Levant (*Levant* encompasses several geographical areas like the west part of Syria and Lebanon, the west part of Jordan and Palestine (West Bank and Gaza Strip), Israel and Sinai (Egypt).

We've learned that he believes that the current terrorist attacks in Europe and the U.S. are not related to a fundamentally perverted form of Islam but are somehow more directly related to conditions of poverty and ignorance than religious ideology. This has been Mr. Obama's blind spot all along. His world view is that of a 1960s radical rather than that of a practitioner of *realpolitik* and is driven by a belief that America's wealth is too concentrated in the hands of a few and, that if only it were redistributed, our enemies would recognize our good intentions and leave us alone.

We've seen Mr. Obama's disdain for his military advisers play out by not acting on their best counsel on troop levels in the Middle East or on exit strategies. We've seen his determination on wanting to close our prison in Guantanamo Bay without a plan for re-locating enemy combatants, and we've watched him trade five high-level terrorists for one deserter. If the military needed proof that their Commander-in-Chief was not 'all in' they need only look to these decisions.

Perhaps the single most egregious error was Obama's failure to negotiate a status of forces agreement (SOFA) with the government of Iraq so that our troops could remain and withdraw in an orderly fashion, over a period of time, consistent with the improvement of the security situation on the ground. As previously stated, Mr. Obama broadcast his strategies in the Middle East to terrorist groups and others who would use this information to stage their force deployment or retreat. No commander allows his subordinates to reveal their strategies or timetable, lest the enemy seize upon them and adjust <u>their</u> strategies, accordingly. Yet, Mr. Obama felt comfortable in not only telling the enemy <u>when</u> we would withdraw but <u>how</u> we would do it.

We have also seen the President meddle in the affairs of other nations like when the U.K. was debating whether to stay inside the European Union. He stated, before the vote, that "Great Britain would have to stand in the back of the queue (with respect to trade) with the USA." So much for the special relationship. We have learned from Mr. Obama's tenure as President that compromise is a thing of the past and that cooperation across the aisle is dead at least as far as the Democrats are concerned. We have learned that it's the *Chicago Way* from now on, a scorched Earth policy that takes no prisoners.

We now know what our President meant when he said that he would fundamentally transform America, and we know that his red lines in the sand are mirages and that tough talk seldom precedes tough actions from his office. We have learned that while words matter, they don't matter enough for him to spend even the tiniest political capital to get things done that would require a rapprochement with Republicans. He has kept his gaze fixed firmly on his legacy or on the stars as if the latter would show him the way forward. He has been a curious mix of elitist and regular guy, opting for appearances on popular television shows or impromptu singing at fund raisers.

Every powerful person wants to be adored, and our 44th President is no different, except that he seems to crave it more than many of his predecessors. What we've learned from eight years of Barack Obama is that Americans should always eat a meal before buying groceries and that choosing a President must never be done on the basis of their speeches, especially those that tug at our heartstrings. We need to climb into their skin, look at their track record, listen to their enemies as well as their friends and never, ever, fall in love with them (like so many millennials and Blacks did in 2008 and 2012).

We've learned from his tenure that there are also incompetent Black leaders as well as incompetent White leaders, that unlike the Pope, our Presidents are fallible, able to make bad decisions on matters of State, and the sooner we do something with that knowledge, the better. The job of president has a very specific set of requirements, but the American electorate doesn't necessarily focus on those qualifications when electing a chief executive. Instead, it looks into the mirror and tries to see its candidate side by side with its own reflection. Unfortunately, the looking glass can be deceiving and America doesn't have eight more years to spare. The process of self-destruction has already begun. Thanks to Mr. Obama's failed Presidency it is a now a runaway train, careening out of control and bound for a head-on collision with reality.

~

Own Up

Today, President Obama signed an executive order banning government 'giveaway' items like notepads, special pens, coffee mugs, etc. that Departments have customarily used at conferences and other official gatherings. I don't object to this specific EO because it spotlights the drip, drip, drip of 'budget creep' that is an integral part of Federal Washington, evidenced by the now famous $16 muffins. A reduction of USG travel is also a part of the new EO.

I hope that one of the consequences of this action will be the President staying home with his wife and family more often AND leaving Air force One in the hangar and the phalanx of black SUVs in the garage. I'm sure he could also find some work to do once somebody shows him where his office is. (OK, I admit that was unkind, but maybe warranted given all the politicking the President has done in the past few months.) During the signing ceremony of the 'giveaway EO', the President reiterated his mantra of blaming our current financial crisis on other people and inanimate objects.

His words "...I suppose this is, (because of) the deficits we've inherited and those that have grown as a consequence of the recession..." are remarkable for what they *don't* say. The right response might have been some variation on the following theme: "Admittedly, this is a small step to reduce government spending and our burgeoning deficit, part of which I inherited from the previous administration and part of which was exacerbated by my policies, aided by a partisan Congress." Good luck on getting *that one into the teleprompter*. Congratulations go to the word-spinners at the White House who have succeeded in creating a language that enables the President to absolve himself, his advisors and his Party of any blame for anything that has been done since January 20, 2008.

It is truly remarkable language, and it has been adopted by Cabinet Secretaries as well. It was observed at Congressional Hearings yesterday where Attorney General, Eric Holder was on the hot seat. While Holder was being questioned about his role in the 'Fast and Furious' gun-walking debacle, Sen. John Cornyn asked the AG if he had contacted the family of slain Border Patrol Agent Brian Terry. Holder looked surprised at the question and said, "no." Then he was asked if he had apologized for the death of Agent Terry or would like to now. Rising to the occasion, Holder adopted the newspeak of responsibility avoidance and ducked the question by saying that he "regretted" Terry's death.

This is a sterling example of the non-apology apology that has become so popular: "If I have offended anyone with this statement or actions, I regret it." While these weasel-worded statements may protect people from responsibility, culpability or civil suits, they are simply <u>cowardly</u>. Americans want their government populated by people with moral courage and conviction, individuals who can answer questions in short declarative sentences. What they <u>don't want</u> is a bunch of mealy-mouthed bureaucrat lawyers whose specialty is truth avoidance.

I would bet my prized copy of William Safire's 'Political Dictionary' that the current crew of politicos in DC were pretty good at getting out of jams as teenagers. I'm sure that more than a couple of them used these two: "My dog ate my homework" and "The tree came out of nowhere and struck the car, Dad." After three years of obfuscation and the verbal two-step around the truth, many of us are hungry for accountability.

Unfortunately, there is another group of us that has been de-sensitized to the truth having embraced the version that passes for it these days. The coming Presidential contest will test our patience and our alertness. We must stay awake and be critical of what we hear...from both sides of the podium.

~

Re-imagining a leader

The airwaves and blogposts are full of rants and complaints about our President. I'm determined not to add even a few lines to those millions of words that take Mr. Obama to task for everything that's wrong with our country. At this point, with only a year to go before he leaves office, it's probably an empty exercise, anyway. It is what it is, and he is what he is. What might be valuable to explore, however, are the types of Chief Executives we the American public might want to choose to lead us into the future. Without passing judgment on any President past or current, let's talk about four types of Presidential leadership: the *rhetorical motivator*, the *straight talker*, the *integrator* and the *manager*.

No. 1, the rhetorical motivator, attempts to lead through inspirational words and manages behind the scenes, sometimes micro-managing. Number 2, the straight talker, says little but takes action. Number 3, the integrator, uses political capital to find common ground and brings people together. Number 4, the manager, identifies problems and finds solutions through consultation and then delegates authority. Applying these to past Presidents without giving them a pass or fail grade - I would say that FDR was a solid No. 1. Truman was a No. 2. Eisenhower was a combination of Nos. 2 and 4. Kennedy was a combination of Nos. 1 and 4. Johnson was a combination of Nos. 3 and 4. Nixon was a clear No. 4. Ford was a combination of Nos. 3 and 4. Carter was a combination of Nos. 1 and 3. Reagan was a combination of Nos. 1 and 4. George H.W. Bush was a pure No. 4. Clinton was a combination of Nos. 1 and 3. George W. Bush was a solid No. 2 and Obama was a pure No. 1.

If you accept my analysis as accurate and look at the times these Presidents were in power you will see that FDR presided over a country in dire economic straits and at a World War. Truman had the awesome responsibility for ending WWII and moving us toward peace. Eisenhower rebuilt our economy and dealt with the first stages of the Cold War. Kennedy was faced with the escalation of that Cold War while trying to keep the peace and prosperity of the nation, intact.

Johnson was caught up in a divisive foreign war and spent most of his time trying to keep our society from unraveling. Nixon was bogged down in 'LBJ's war,' was preoccupied with his own image and with creeping paranoia about the press. Ford was the *janitor* that had to deal with cleaning up Nixon's mess and with a divided country.

Carter was faced with a worsening economy and a nation that wanted moral clarity in the face of international turmoil. Reagan had to find a solution to a three-decades long Cold War and heal the wounds of a divided culture that was experiencing great generational challenges. Bush '41' had to make good on Reagan's promises for a 'shining city on a hill' while dealing with increasing governmental mistrust.

Clinton had to be the bridge between the 'old America' and the emerging new country of America's youth's aspirations, and he had to rebuild our economy that had been through two serious recessions by the time he entered office. G.W. Bush dealt with the changing paradigm of terror and desperately tried to return to America's 'core values' through a paradoxical entry into yet another foreign war.

Obama took the reins of Presidential power during the most significant economic crisis since the Great Depression and attempted to create a new America out of whole cloth by fashioning a kinder, gentler country that eschewed war and tried to deal with society's growing wealth schism.

The political pendulum continues to swing wildly. At this stage, we could well get a President that is either a combination of Nos. 2 and 4 (Trump, Cruz, or Rubio) or we could get one (Clinton) that is another No. 1 with a touch of No. 3. In my mind, we cannot afford <u>any</u> President that ignores the reality of our country's moral, international and economic challenges nor one that shies away from the task of building intersecting pathways of understanding between competing generations, the impoverished and our minorities. The task is monumental, and our choice next November must not be based on empty rhetoric, unrealistic promises, jingoism, sleight of hand or divisiveness. America needs a leader that will inspire us, help us re-imagine and re-shape the American Dream <u>and</u> make the decisions that will keep us on the path to greatness. We neither deserve nor should we settle for anything less.

~

SCOTUS 2, Tradition 0

This has been a bad week for lovers of tradition in America, and we have our Supreme Court to thank for it. For some, SCOTUS' decisions on Obamacare and homosexual marriage may signal the end of our way of life as we know it. For others, it may herald the opening of a new chapter in the ever-evolving idea we call America. Pundits will be quick to call this a win for the Democrats while others will say that it is a harbinger of the Republicans' defeat in November of 2016.

While an appealing binary choice, it would be a simplistic view of things, a sellout to the temptation to characterize everything in political terms. The truth is, these two decisions are neither Republican defeats nor Democrat victories. They are what happens in a Democracy when people with strong traditional beliefs remain passive and don't engage their elected representatives. It's also what happens when we are open-minded and are willing to accept change.

Maybe we are growing up and learning to live with diversity instead of fearing the disparate groups in our society. What worries me now, on healthcare, is that we will continue down a path towards a total breakdown of our entire healthcare system. Subsidies are not the problem with Obamacare. What's wrong is the way the law was passed and the lack of serious debate and discussion before its passage. That was downright un-American and a slap in the face of Lady Liberty. The Supreme Court's ruling is also a wake-up call to the Congress to read what they write before they vote on it in the future.

I have no doubt that we will climb many more mountains before we can re-make the law so that it truly accomplishes the twin goals of better insuring our population and providing truly affordable healthcare to every citizen.

As for the other Supreme Court ruling on homosexuals' rights, true acceptance of homosexuality will not come through legislation. That can only happen when people find it morally right to drop their prejudices and view their non-mainstream neighbors as equals under God. Most of our churches preach tolerance and forgiveness, and I believe that most parishioners know in their hearts that that message not only demands their attention but also their fidelity to it.

Personally, I don't see why two people who love each other shouldn't be able to be joined together in a bond that is recognized by society at large. I just stop short of saying that it should be called *marriage*, that's all. On that score, I'm a traditionalist, not a bigot nor a homophobe though I'm afraid the latter appellations will be bandied about with great regularity as the Administration pushes even harder to force private businesses to provide services that may infringe on their religious beliefs. We have an example of that in Albuquerque, New Mexico, with a local photographer that declined to photograph a homosexual wedding, causing a lawsuit by the prospective customers.

Judging by the Obama Administration's track record on ignoring the Constitution, we will probably see an attempt to end-run the Commerce Clause of the Tenth Amendment and force private businesses by executive order to provide services to anybody regardless of the business owners' strongly-held religious convictions. To refresh everyone's memory, this early 1791 provision of the Articles of Confederation said, "Each state retains its sovereignty, freedom, and independence, and every power, jurisdiction, and right, which is not by this Confederation expressly delegated to the United States, in Congress assembled." The Tenth Amendment is definitely the next target.

The question that must be debated is not a civil rights one. It is a religious rights question that has to do with declining to participate in ceremonies that can be contrary to a service provider's strongly-held beliefs. This is really a thorny dilemma. While the temptation might be great to amend the Constitution or write an Executive Order to solve the problem, it might be better dealt with between the individual buyer and seller, themselves. In the case of the Albuquerque photographer and the homosexual wedding, if I had heard a sincere objection to photographing my wedding on religious grounds I would have just moved on to another service provider that wanted my business.

The issue is also a commercial one: "Does a private business legally operating in a state have the right to serve whomever they please?" I would submit that if a business can demand that a person entering their establishment be properly clad with shirt and shoes, then surely it can refuse service based on a sincere and pre-existing moral or religious conviction. While we move through this new maze of rights, privileges and responsibilities, some guaranteed by law and others relying on our basic humanity and goodness, we must try to put ourselves in our neighbor's shoes. We all want respect, but no law can guarantee that from our fellow citizens. It is something we must give to each other, freely and without reservation. That's a tradition worth observing.

~

SCOTUS Drives Stake through the Heart of America

Just when I thought it was safe to turn to the news channels to escape *True Blood* or *Vampires Suck*, I'm hit with the latest salvo in the vampire wars in the form of a surprise ruling from none other than the Supreme Court. On Thursday last, the Supreme Court upheld the controversial Patients' Affordable Health Care Act (aka Obamacare). Writing the majority opinion, Chief Justice John Roberts gave all Americans and especially America's small business sector the bad news with a stiff punch to the solar plexus.

The ruling was a 'major withdrawal' from America's already anemic small business sector. By siding with the liberals on the court in a 5-4 ruling upholding one of America's most despised pieces of legislation EVER, Chief Justice Roberts may have shown himself to be the consummate non-partisan, but he certainly didn't boost his stock with the average Constitutionalist, Independent, Libertarian or Conservative, not to mention the typical small business owner that was counting on an outcome that would keep the Federal Rottweilers away from the meager scraps in his feeding bowl.

Bram Stoker would have been impressed with the stealth and secrecy of the 9Js by not revealing their positions. Only the blood-sucking flying rodents of his novel, "Dracula," did it better, laying in wait for the poor victim to fall asleep before relieving them of a pint of their life's blood. Vampire hunters didn't have to brave the uppermost regions of the Capitol Rotunda to find a web-winged specimen either. There were plenty of them on the senate floor two years ago when Democrats used arcane tactics like 'reconciliation' to get their way and coupled it with epic deal-making to get the deciding votes in what has now become known as the 'Cornhusker Kickback' and the 'Louisiana Purchase,' etc.

At the end of the day, when the votes were counted not a single Republican had said 'yea.' The most comprehensive, most all-encompassing piece of legislation that would affect the lives of every single American passed without a single Republican vote.

We should have seen the bloody handwriting on the wall when then House Speaker Nancy Pelosi said, "We're just going to have to pass this bill so that we can know what's in it." And when we did find out what was in the 3,200 pages of gobbledegook like the mandate, the thousands of new IRS agents who would be hired to monitor our insurance policy-holder status, it was enough to turn even the most battle-hardened vampire's blood-shot eyes white with fear.

Yes, we should have seen it coming, but nobody on the left or right anticipated that rock-solid, pragmatic, constitutionalist, Chief Justice John Roberts, would succumb to the siren song of the Obama legal team's arguments. No, the CJ effectively cast the tie vote and thus drove a stake through the heart of our healthcare industry, our small business sector and our indebtedness while moving us one step closer to one nation of the government for the government and by the government with some liberty and a little justice for a few.

First it was the Congress who fell from our grace. Now it's the Supreme Court. There's only one branch left, and the opportunity to hold its feet to the fire will come November 6th. Maybe, just maybe, we can roll back Justicia Cunctator est Justicia Denego ("justice delayed is justice denied"). There is one thing that the 9Js forgot amid their deliberations and that is the other court that is even more powerful than themselves. It is the court of public opinion, and its sentences are rarely plea bargained down, and its collective memory is long.

~

Selling Obamacare

Forgive me for mentioning Obamacare again. But what better time is there to do so than when the whole country is sick? Sick of hearing about it, that is. You've heard from the supporters and you've heard from the detractors. You've heard from the vested interests and from the would-be vested interests. You've listened to the doctors, the insurance companies, the hospitals, the healthcare products industry, the moneyed class, the NGOs (non-government organizations) and the politicians. But you haven't heard from the unborn as yet – the millions of babies who are going to grow up needing all sorts of post-natal to geriatric care. They're the *Newcon* (new consumers) *Generation.*

This new demographic won't know about the battles that were waged by their parents or grandparents back in the early part of the 21st century over healthcare. They're not going to feel our pain as we moved from a personal to an impersonal healthcare insurance system which morphed into a new impersonal government-based healthcare delivery system. They're going to feel their own pain which will be rooted in new diseases, maladies, syndromes and disorders that cross the boundaries of a physical, emotional and mental nature. The causes may be attributed to obesity, poor nutrition, environmental changes, stress, the economy, addictions caused by new permissive drug policies or from sources unknown to us now.

The Newcon Generation will be the ones standing in line or sitting for hours in overcrowded clinics' waiting rooms to receive 'care by the numbers' – treatment that is based on the actuarial tables or by government studies. Theirs will be the brave new world of GWL (Genetic Wellness Legislation) that will require individual genetic testing of every American with a view towards 'flattening out the cost curve' through early identification of those who would become *overusers* of a healthcare system that cannot sustain itself if used too often by too many people.

In short, the Newcon Generation will become the most watched, the most investigated, the most analyzed and the most surveyed of any generation in American history. What happens with their healthcare experience will invariably influence where America invests its healthcare dollars. The other major healthcare demographic and potential financial drain, the Baby Boomers, will be watching, carefully, to see if America's new healthcare budget has room enough for them as they head into the home stretch of their lives that will be fraught with increased healthcare demands and accelerated healthcare costs.

If a government-dominated healthcare system is what everybody wants, okay, but before those decisions are made we need to think of *the children* and what kind of world we want to pass on to them. And then there's the selling job to be done. If we want this thing to work, let's not adopt the methods and message of the current Administration as a blueprint for an 'Obamacare 2.0'. I still maintain that if dental care (Americans spend nearly $100 billion on dental care, annually) had been a part of Obamacare we wouldn't have such a high number of *dissatisfieds* with the legislation.

~

Smorgasbord of weak tea and leftovers

Last week I felt like a waiter at a soup kitchen. It's because I watched the President's State of the Union address and couldn't help feeling that I was tasting an unappetizing meal made from last week's leftovers.

After one hour and five minutes of this cuisine and 85 interruptions for applause, I still felt hungry. Maybe it was my anticipation after hearing so many of this President's previous speeches in which he was able to lift us all up to the rhetorical stratosphere. Be that as it may, the items on Obama's political menu offered something for every one of his voter groups. Education got a 'high quality pre-K' shout out. Just exactly what 'high quality pre-K' means I don't know.

Maybe it involves guest lectures by Nobel Prize winners to excited four-year olds or pop quizzes on the origin of crayolas or paper-mâché. College students (a big voter group in 2012) were told they would have their college loan repayments capped at 10% of their income. The only trouble with that is that most of them can't find a job because of the recession (which was supposed to be over four years ago).

Healthcare and the Patients' Affordable Healthcare Act was highlighted as working for Americans (though no mention was made of the millions that have already been thrown off their plans or the multitude of new policy-holders who have been saddled with exorbitant co-pays, deductibles or unaffordable premiums). I was surprised that HHS Secretary, Kathleen Sebelius didn't show up with her dunce cap on after the miserable roll-out of the ACA website!

Predictably, the economy, which according to the President, was rebounding (citing the *evil* Wall Street gains) had center stage as he bragged about all the CEOs that would soon descend on WASHDC to give him their promises to intensify their efforts to *seriously consider* unemployed people for jobs in their organizations. What? After he has spent an inordinate amount of time criticizing the captains of industry (and taking their campaign donations) he has now discovered they can be used for something else! It's about time. One of the principal entrees on the menu was the minimum wage, and the President portrayed raising the minimum wage as a panacea for elevating the poor up the 'ladder of opportunity' while underscoring that the majority of those in minimum-wage jobs were WOMEN.

At times, the Master Chef in Chief sounded like he was cooking up a brand new dish, witness the introduction of the 'MyRA,' presumably a reincarnation of the good old U.S. Savings Bonds (or War Bonds for the older reader).

How this new old idea will make any appreciable difference when most of those without a 401K can barely pay their bills now, I just don't know. Small business owners like a pizza parlor CEO were recognized for bellying up to the bar and volunteering to give their employees a raise to the new magic $10.10/hour level, and the President exhorted all business owners to follow his lead. Imagine the fallout if all pizza franchisees followed suit...deep dish pizza would become deep dish pizza lite as the new costs would have to be offset by cuts in their offerings.

While no mention was made of the workers still jobless and the increasing number who've given up looking for work, one unemployed single mother was profiled for her plight. I wonder how she felt having her tragic story plastered all over the TV screens of America.

Who knows, maybe she'll be offered the job of *Unemployed Single Mother Job Searching Czar* in the Administration for bravely sitting among 535 members of the privileged political class and being humiliated. In stark contrast, the President then acknowledged the new female CEO of General Motors who sat in the gallery and whose salary could buy and sell hundreds of unemployed single mothers. Good old 'Uncle Joe Biden' was thrown a bone to chew on and was named to head up a task force on education and training. One wonders how the Education Secretary feels about that one!

Unlike his attack on the Supremes in a previous SOTU address for their decision on the Citizens United case, the President spared them this time around. Perhaps it was because the right-leaning justices weren't all there and he felt that it would be unfair to criticize the left-leaning justices in attendance. No jus de justice was spilled on their long black robes. The Blue Plate Special was a tribute to the First and Second Ladies for their work in denying America's youngsters their Ding Dongs and Twinkies. Apparently, they have succeeded in getting our children to push themselves away from the fat kids table. Finally, obesity is a thing of the past! Even America's proud military men and women were served up on a silver platter for their selfless service in wars that the President was proud to state would soon be a thing of the past.

No more troops were in Iraq and soon only a handful would be left in Afghanistan thanks to a President who went out of his way to say he wants Guantanamo Bay closed again while he continues to use it. No Obama State of the Union address would be complete without multiple digs at the Congress, and the President's mantra of blaming that august body for his failures was only eclipsed by his urging of them to work with him. Some critics would call this the height of hypocrisy, but as we all know, those heights are constantly being ratcheted upwards.

The table was cleared this evening of any and all Presidential fault for America's problems and the napkin thrown down like a gauntlet in the face of the ungrateful and glutinous Republicans. The President expects them to eat crow and like it as he uses his pen and his telephone to end run them while he gins up a new concoction of Executive Orders. All that's left is to clean up the mess that he's made, and as usual he expects others to do it for him. So endeth the fifth Obama State of the Union address.

~

That old Nature vs. Nurture

Many of my friends are baffled over our government's (read: the President, his press spokesman and the State Department's) inability to come out and call a spade a spade when that spade is Islamic extremism. They don't understand that when the terrorists identify themselves as followers of Islam and that state that their actions are justified and indeed required under the Koran that WE can't take them at their word and insert the word 'Islamic' in between 'fundamentalist' and 'terrorists.'

When Mr. Obama became President there were many people on both sides of the political aisle that had high hopes that he would make good on promises to heal the divide between the Blue states and the Red states. His words then were uplifting, optimistic, the kind that made you believe that bridging that political divide was not only possible but was just around the corner.

Six years later we know better. The reality is: those divides are unbridgeable because the ideologies of both parties are so radically different. There are similarities, however, like the current crises in the Middle East. An example: many right-wing fundamentalists would like to blame our troubles with terrorists in the Middle East on President Obama for his laissez faire attitude, but just as many if not more on the far left blame the same troubles on his predecessor, President George W. Bush. Who's right? I believe the answer lies in the old *Nature versus Nurture* argument. Essentially, the argument goes like this...Republicans believe that Nature (human nature that is) is the foundation for everything Man does.

Man has a free will, given to him by God, and he is capable of doing good or evil, but when he is tempted by the 'seven deadly sins' (wrath, greed, sloth, pride, lust envy and gluttony) he will choose the path that suits his personal needs, best.

For the Republicans this explains, but does not justify, what happens around the world. It explains war and genocide, thievery, lies, oppression and excesses of power. They believe that the way to combat them is to confront them and label them for what they are and then attack the problem and bring the perpetrators to justice. That's how we won WWII and how the world handled terrorists in the seventies and eighties like the Khmer Rouge in Cambodia, the Baader-Meinhof gang in Germany and the Red Brigades in Italy. This approach may explain why these groups were eradicated.

Democrats, on the other hand, believe that the Nurture part of the argument is the one that rules. Yes, Man is capable of good and evil, but through the proper conditioning (nurturing) and behavioral modification that includes appropriate incentives/inducements and continual reinforcing rhetoric he will reject his more base instincts and instead choose the left's version of sensibility and reasonableness. Labeling is undesirable as it limits the unfettered mobility of the individual to move towards the light, free of society's negative opinions of him.

This may explain why the Administration is unwilling to 'stigmatize' the Islamic State of Iraq and Syria (ISIS) and prefers to use softer language like *degrade* instead of *destroy* and to speak of the root causes of terrorism rather than focus on preventing more brutal killings of innocent men, women and children.

Both my Democratic and Republican friends pushed back on my theory. The Republicans told me that they were not so one-dimensional and weren't a flock of 'black and white' absolutists. The Democrats said that they were not so Pollyanna-ish or so illogically optimistic about Mankind's basic instincts. I guess the debate will go on.

The Great Depression 2.0

I know it's election season and that anything politically said will be taken with a nano-grain of salt, but I ask you to stop and think about the state of our country before you cast your ballot. Those old enough to remember THE Great Depression will tell you that I'm talking through my hat by trying to compare the America of 2014 with the dustbowl Depression America of the thirties. While I might concede the point about the severity of Depression 1.0 which was characterized by a massive loss of wealth and equally massive unemployment, I do think that our current state of affairs has much in common with those times and that we need to be super critical of the people we send to Washington this January and beyond.

America is suffering a massive depression of spirit and a gargantuan lack of self-confidence. Add to that our growing political, gender, ethnic, religious and racial polarization (most of which has been drummed up by hustlers and partisan fanatics) and you have a sizable number of folks at odds with each other. At the top of that layer cake of emotional and psychological trauma there's abject fear - fear for our children's future, fear for our health under a Byzantine national health care insurance system, fear for job security, fear of terrorism, fear of Ebola. Add to that a growing deeply-rooted distrust of our government due to a number of nasty scandals and you have the recipe for social upheaval and conflict.

Depression 1.0 hit us all at once. On October 24, 1929 the stock market lost 11% of its value. The following Monday, the market lost 13%. The next day it lost another 12%. The market lost $30 billion ($14 billion in just two days)! America's companies' share values hemorrhaged and many were forced to close or drastically reduce their workforces causing the financial ruin of many families. Breadlines and soup kitchens appeared.

In 1932, with unemployment at 20%, FDR was elected. For the next three years he ushered in a 'New Deal' for America that, thankfully, worked. I would contend that a new Depression descended on America in the waning days of the Bush Administration. The 'chickens' of our financial sector's bad mortgage-bundling came home to roost and was remedied by a behind-the-scenes generated solution that left the picking of winners and loser banks up to a handful of powerful men. It was followed by a flawed recovery program that basically helped to create a paucity of new 'shovel-ready' jobs which the Administration had promised.

Half the country, comprised of dejected Republicans whose candidate lost by a few percentage points, bade farewell to hope of maintaining the status quo of 'traditional American values' while hundreds of thousands of other Americans got pink slips. The costs of two wars had severely impacted our indebtedness (which now stands at $17.9 trillion) and the side effects of a divisive gender and ethnic-centric campaign served to split us farther apart as a nation. In short, we were on our way to Depression 2.0. Today, we have more families on Food Stamps than ever before.

Our labor participation rate is the lowest since the days of the Carter Administration. Food prices and energy costs have risen by 25-35% over the last six years. While our unemployment rate has dropped to 6.3%, many Americans have given up looking for work entirely as the work that's out there is only part-time. Our consumer credit card debt is increasing at over 3% per year and stands at an average of $15,607 per family.

Hundreds of thousands of Americans have lost their homes and have been forced to radically downsize their lifestyles and seek financial help for their sons and daughters attending college. Thankfully, many of our brave veterans have returned from Iraq and Afghanistan, but way too many are being shut out of the labor market and offered sub-standard medical care while they attempt to heal severe physical and emotional wounds.

We've disintegrated as a homogeneous people and re-formed along gender, age, ethnic, racial and ideological lines so much so that there aren't enough hyphens to put in between all our identifiers. So don't tell me there's no cause for alarm. And don't tell me that we're not in a depression of mind and spirit, for we are. More of us may be working and still own our homes than our grandfathers did in the thirties, but we're still every bit as fearful about the future as they were.

And while we aren't on street corners rattling a tin cup saying, "Brother, can you spare a dime?" we're worried that the American Dream was just a fairy tale told to us to keep us quiet while bureaucrats and our legislators spend their time tinkering and dithering. Vote this November like your life depends on it because it does.

~

The Hidden Costs of Campaigning

There are four Republican candidates for President and it's pretty easy to figure out what they spend on campaigning as they must regularly identify and report those expenditures along with their campaign contributions. It's a very different kettle of greenbacks when it comes to figuring out what the real costs of Presidential campaigns are.

Here's something to think about. The Hatch Act (passed in 1939) says that an incumbent/candidate like a sitting President must not campaign from federally-owned facilities and must keep his campaign costs separate from his official costs. That should mean having two of most things like Blackberries, email accounts, cars, etc. For example, you can't make campaign calls from U.S. Government offices and you can't travel to campaign speeches/dinners in a Government vehicle. There are plenty of ways to get around that, however. Meetings, speeches and dinners can be *dual-purpose* events – events where the President's presence is desirable to advocate for, or speak on, national policy issues or give interviews to the media.

The thinking is: since he's at the venue anyway, he might as well hold a fund-raising dinner at $35,800/plate (the maximum allowable contribution an individual may give to a political party in a given year – see Federal Election Commission regulations at www.fec.gov). Later, the party can openly support his campaign with all that money raised.

At this point in their respective campaigns, President Obama has held 100 fund-raisers compared with former President George W. Bush's 56. To me, that says that George Bush was either: a) not motivated, b) too confident or c) was too busy focusing on the country's business. It could be said that Barack Obama is either: a) a more active campaigner, b) is worried that he won't have enough money to beat the Republican nominee, or c) just likes the limelight. While firewalls must be set up between the campaign and the office staff, it's really hard to identify which of the hidden costs associated with campaigning are paid by the taxpayers. Let's pretend you are the Pres for a moment.

You wake up in the morning, review your secret CIA and DOD briefings, have your breakfast, read the papers and speak with your Chief-of-Staff and Press Secretary to see 'what's shaking' out there in America. Your mind is not firewalled, however, and during the conversations, you spot a few events that present opportunities for making a campaign pitch. You spend a fair amount of time discussing the venue, the speech, the possible pre- and post event interviews, the local and national spin, the travel and how this event might benefit *the country* and in the back of your mind...how it will help your campaign.

You call your campaign liaison to speak with him about the event. He suggests that you hold a fund-raising luncheon and dinner built into the Presidential Event (after all, the President has to eat, doesn't he?). You agree and go over the potential donors list, making sure that you haven't overlooked any high-rollers. The event goes on the official schedule and is communicated to the Secret Service which sets a massive operation into motion involving visits to the site, interviews and liaison with law enforcement, local security and venue managers, all costing the taxpayers a considerable chunk of change.

It's a few days from the actual event, and you decide it would be nice to bring your family along, so a few more seats on Air Force One are booked for your children and the First Lady (and her Chief-of Staff and Protocol Assistant which are added to the passenger manifest that already includes your top staffers, speech-writers, personal physician, Secret Service contingent, selected media from the White House Press Pool, the White House Photographer and that nice military man who holds the launch codes to our missiles).

In case you're wondering, you won't have to take the mid-town bus to the event. Your limousine and 4-6 other official vehicles depart WASHDC ahead of you in a C-130 transport so that they're all gassed up and ready for you when you land at your destination. It's 'wheels down' time. So far, the cost of your trip is way up in the six-figure or more range. And since this is mostly a *Presidential Event*, your re-election campaign won't be writing a big check to the Treasury for the costs. Instead, you'll be depositing a thick wad of $35,800 checks from eager supporters, proving once again that Americans are world leaders when it comes to multi-tasking... and using other people's money.

~

The Invalid Economy?

It's time to stop pretending that we are preeminent whether it be in design, manufacturing or marketing, and it's high time that our economy and job market find its elasticity and mojo and re-capture the fundamentals necessary to return us to the world's top spot in any one or all of those three areas. In some circles, that statement would be interpreted as unpatriotic, but for those who study the world's economies and markets, it's probably regarded as reasonable when considering the state of our exports and the anemic investment in manufacturing in the USA. We must stop viewing ourselves as a dowager nation searching for a comfortable chair, limping along with a bad case of economic gout from living too high on the hog, the victim of spending our wealth before it's earned. Our public sector has grown way too fast in the last decade and especially during the past three years of the Obama administration which has added nearly five trillion dollars of debt and over 100,000 government jobs while losing 13 million private sector ones.

Our unemployment rate has stayed above 8.0% (and even hit the terrible 10% mark) for over 30 months while the number of workers that have given up searching for employment soars from month to month and is now thought to be around 20 million. Our export growth rate (which <u>should</u> be analyzed in terms of volume and diversity of goods produced/sold and not solely as a dollar figure relative to GDP) has lagged behind many of our competitors' while our companies steadily contract for more manufactured goods (originally designed or developed in the USA) to be made overseas.

Our economy has been robbed of its vitality and jobs by sins of commission as well as omission, but the blame cannot be placed on outsourcing alone. We need to drill down into the fundamental structure of our economy for the real reasons. Labor unions and right-of-center talk shows and certain cable news channels were, up until the President's recent manufacturing charm offensive, the lone voices crying in the wilderness about job losses, especially those due to off-shoring. Off-shoring, however, is a fig leaf covering our unwillingness to tackle the BIG problems (over-regulation, government intrusion into the free marketplace, a Gordian Knot tax system, etc.).

We're living on borrowed time, and the clock is rapidly ticking while we attempt quick government fixes like 'Stimulus Packages' that are only postponing the inevitable day of reckoning when we could see whole industries fall by the wayside and new small business start-ups stop dead in their tracks. Job-creating foreign investment has slowed to a trickle in an America that was once thought of as 'Treasure Island,' the place where fortunes were made and where real estate turned freely and often.

America's factories, office buildings and now homes lay empty waiting for the day when the *For Sale* sign is replaced by the *Repo* sign. Real corporate values have plummeted, and while some would say that these are market corrections or periodic adjustments, others offer a more dire explanation and posit that they are the harbinger of a serious flight from risk-taking and a wholesale desertion of confidence in the American engine of growth. To many, we're looking more like the "Little Engine That Could" as we chug along, trying our best to get up the hill towards prosperity, buoyed by our own cheerleading.

Our country is a dike that has sprung many leaks from neglect. Our infrastructure is crumbling. Apart from the obvious roads and bridges that desperately need repair throughout the USA, we need a massive investment in our energy grid that could cost upwards of $1.5 trillion. Our broadband coverage in some parts of the country is truly third-world. We have no coherent short-term or long-term workable energy plan that will assure us the energy we need to jump-start energy-intensive industries and provide for the general public's mobility. If the President is looking for a 'Sputnik moment' to galvanize the country and move us out of our economic morass, he's going to need to make it himself with sound leadership by addressing some of the problems I've described.

Incurring more government debt won't cut it. Pouring money helter skelter into fledgling industries or companies like recent billion dollar plus investments in solar energy companies or electric cars won't cut it, either. That will get you a temporary bump in the polls among academicians, scientists and special interest groups, but the general public knows that these fixes aren't easy ones.

The Wall Street Journal recently published an article ("Manufacturing Decline," Feb. 17, 2012). In it they propose that we should take heart, because our manufacturing sector is not as bad off as we think, pointing to advances in productivity as one of the main reasons that we should not despair. But everybody knows that worker productivity has grown because fewer workers are doing more work due to retrenchments in the workplace AND because of a steady adoption of automation.

None of us should be against new technology or technology-spurred innovation in America's workplaces, but all of us should be concerned that a country our size cannot live by selling services to one another (the service sector, as a percentage of GDP in 2010, grew by 24% while manufacturing grew by only 11.7%). While the problem of right-sizing the American economy is enormous, we have no choice but to tackle it both as virus that's attacking our immune system and as a debilitating illness. Antibiotics and short-term measures may kill what's immediately assaulting our system, but we also need a lifestyle change which includes going offline for awhile and thinking through the impact of all of the decisions we make that will ultimately affect our economic lives.

~

79

The Obamacare Healthcare Fiasco: Turning *a silk purse into a sow's ear*

I admit it. I haven't read the whole Patient Protection and Affordable Care Act (aka 'Obamacare'). It's not because the law isn't important. There are just too many great books gathering dust on my shelf that would accuse me of cheating on them if I dove into a Leaning Tower of Pisa-like stack of pages written by a flock of bureaucrats about a law that nearly nobody completely understands. (If you search the Internet you will see that the number of pages attributable to the Act are in the tens of thousands because they include the numerous regulations that have been written to implement the Act, making the tower an imposing structure.) Before you invest any more time in this Op Ed, let me say that you will be able to get through it without bursting a blood vessel.

Here are my top two points: 1. our law-makers have taken complete leave of their senses and ignored basic human nature in constructing and passing this legislation and 2. they have seriously misjudged the anger of the people, now that the impact of the law is being felt in their personal lives. On point number one, Americans' pre-Obama human nature dictated that, *if I have something that you want, you must first persuade me that your right to take it from me supersedes my right to keep it.*

The modern-day Obama-era version of that is evidenced in the passage of Obamacare that is an assault on property rights (by exercising control over insurance plans and the freedom of selecting coverage that fits an individual or family), money (low or reasonable premiums) and profits (earned by insurers or healthcare providers) which are deemed by Government to be in the wrong hands can be seized, re-valued, re-assigned or re-located by Government as it sees fit.

Every monarch, dictator or elected body makes an occasional stupid, unfair or unworkable law, and Obamacare is one of those because instead of working together to reform our healthcare system with enforceable, realistic regulations that ended up insuring the uninsured, the Democrats decided to 'scrap the vehicle' (the entire health insurance system) instead of pinpointing the source of the 'knocking noise' (the 30 million or so underinsured or uninsured) and fixing THAT!

Knowing what we know now about the law and the unintended or intended consequences of it, I half-hoped that the Obamacare Congressional hearings today, which featured the leading lady of this bureaucratic passion play, HHS Secretary Kathleen Sebelius, would somehow be the venue for an announcement of a waiver of the individual mandate for purchasing health insurance. I fantasized that Secretary Sebelius would reach into her purse for a crumpled nurse's cap and unfold it, place it on her coiffed gray hair and then look straight into the camera and say, "My fellow Americans, we made a mistake. We misjudged the severity of the healthcare crisis in America. Instead of insuring the few, we decided to de-insure everybody and re-build a new system that adversely impacted one-sixth of our economy and brought everyone down to the same level of healthcare, thinking that you wouldn't mind paying three or four times more for coverage as long as your neighbor paid three or four times less."

Then she replaced the nurse's cap with an accountant's visor and said, "We also misread the economic needs of our young citizens. We thought that because they voted for the President, and even though they might be unemployed, that they would be happy to pony up thousands of dollars a year for something they had little immediate need for, despite the fact that we mandated every plan contain 'reproductive rights' items like free contraception and the morning-after pill. We thought, too, that by creating a snappy website that they'd fire up their ipads and sign up in droves, just for the sheer fun of it. We were wrong."

Then Sebelius removes the visor and wraps herself in a shawl made of an American flag and makes an impassioned plea to the entire Republican side of the Congressional Committee.

"Friends, fellow Federal workers, comrades in arms, join with the President and me. Forget our past mistakes. Let's bury the hatchet. It's always the first cut that hurts the most. This is not a double-edged sword if we do not want it to be. Let's beat them into plowshares and share a future that guarantees its citizens true quality healthcare. Today, I am proud to announce that my Department has negotiated a brand new contract with the Canadian Government to provide all U.S. citizens with healthcare.

Tomorrow, my department will be turning over the ownership and re-building of the website to Canadian Prime Minister Harper's government and I will be stepping down from my post as Cabinet Secretary to become the CEO of CGI Canada. Good luck and bon chance."

~

The Obama melodrama

Let's see a show of hands. How many of you were shocked at the President's newest adventure into the exotic land of executive orders, this time on immigration? OK, how many of you were emotionally moved by his little vignettes about a couple of innocent illegal immigrants as he proceeded to lay waste to the separation of powers? For me, I always tune in to watch the President no matter what subject he's speaking about, but I always remove my pointy tin foil hat before I do. You know, the one that helps me suspend disbelief and lets me uplink to any extra-terrestrials that might be circling over area 51.

I've come full circle from head-shaking in horror on his pronouncements to head-nodding. I'm now nodding the same way I used to do when I watched 'Peyton Place' back in the early 60s. Whenever Dorothy Malone (Constance MacKenzie) would step into camera view my pupils began to dilate and my interest intensified, not because I believed anything that was going on with that decadent crew in that make-believe town but because I became lost in the web of entertainment and intrigue they created. The same is true of Barack Obama.

I'm convinced he's a cross between Franz Mesmer (the German physician who believed there was an energetic transference between all animate and inanimate objects, referred to as 'mesmerism') and Buffalo Bill of the Wild West Show of the same name. Yup, our President is really a showman at heart and he uses all the tools of the showbiz trade to entertain us.
He has a unique ability to throw Republicans into catatonic fits and salivate at the prospect of dressing him down while they're busy flopping on the ship's deck like flounders gasping for air.

I'm fascinated by the man, by how he can create his own reality. After all, how else would you explain his comments on the recent mid-term election results when he referred to the 2/3 that didn't vote as those who *would have voted* for his Democrat candidates if they had voted? I'm impressed at how he can go down for the third time and re-surface only to blame the water for being too deep instead of taking responsibility for throwing himself in the pool!

Yes, he's an ideologue, and everyone should have taken him seriously when he said that he would fundamentally transform America. He has walked the walk, and for that I give him high marks on staying his course, though it's not a course many of us would have chosen for our beloved America. I'm not a psychologist and can only guess at his deeper motivations. Neither am I prescient and can predict what he'll do next. Only he knows what's up his Presidential sleeve, but one thing's for certain...we're all in for a roller coaster ride for the next two years and I'm addicted to the Obama soap opera. I'll stay glued to my TV and radio, waiting for the next size 12 shoe to drop and hope that it doesn't drop on the head of Lady Liberty, knocking the old gal out.

With his new executive order delaying deportation of five million plus illegal aliens, giving them social security numbers, a work permit, access to many of the same benefits that millions of legal Americans enjoy and a temporary 'get out of jail' card, he has re-written the instruction manual on the Presidency and maybe on the Constitution. For his followers, he's just delivering on his promises. For those of us who don't wear tin foil hats, it's as if he's trying to mesmerize us and re-direct our attention away from the recent election. While that may be good politics for the Democrats, it can't be good for unifying America. It's time that our President woke up to the reality that not everybody thinks he's the *chosen one* with a golden crown of invisible protection. Like all Presidents he must answer for his actions, hopefully before he's re-written from the script.

~

The politics of passing

A giant of jurisprudence and juris practice died yesterday. Supreme Court Justice, Antonin Scalia, 79 years old and father of nine children, had spent nearly 30 years on the bench of the highest court in our nation. Those who knew him thought him to be a brilliant legal mind and a warm and engaging human being.

His opinions, and especially his dissents, were the stuff of intense discussions among law students and their professors. There is no question that his family, friends and the legal community will miss him, but his absence will also be felt by all Americans who love the integrity of the U.S. Constitution. Justice Scalia was an originalist and defended the intent of the framers of this, our country's guiding document, at every turn, so his death will leave the U.S. without a critical reasoned voice and protector of our guaranteed rights under the law.

The passing of any individual that defends freedom and equality is to be mourned, but in the USA, the period of such mourning has now become reduced to nano time. Justice Scalia's body wasn't even cold nor been returned from Texas to his family in Washington when the political crosswinds starting whipping up around the question of who would replace him. In America, nothing or no one is immune from the politicization of their words, their deeds or even their demise. In the death (or resignation) of a Supreme Court Justice, it is the President's right to put forth a nominee to replace him or her, and this President will be no different from his predecessors.

What will be different is the speed and intensity with which President Obama will push the Senate to accept and vote on his nominee. In Obama's case, it's all about getting another liberal activist justice appointed, one that believes that the Constitution is a 'living, breathing document' and that should be interpreted in today's language and today's time instead of observing the intent of the framers at the time of the Constitution's inception. Many arguments have been heard on issues that will affect President Obama's legacy (something he is understandably obsessed with), but many have not been decided and will need to be re-heard because of Justice Scalia's death.

Most observers dealing with the Supreme Court describe it as a 4-4 court, evenly split along ideological lines. This means, that without a ninth member, the court is as deadlocked as the legislative branch was before the 2014 election, leaving America with judicial gridlock. Democrats will surely push for a speedy vote to insure that a liberal appointment is assured, thereby guaranteeing a left-leaning, ideologically pure court for decades to come.

Senate Republicans, on the other hand, will push for a delay of a vote until the next President is elected, something that is in keeping with an 80-year long precedent of not filling a Supreme Court vacancy during a Presidential election year. Either way, Americans can expect a no-holds barred ideological and procedural fight in the coming months, timed perfectly to coincide with a bare-knuckle fight for party nominations and ultimately the BIG fight in the general election. Lookers-on from outside the U.S. will be shaking their heads in disbelief and confusion about our society and our political system and asking themselves, "Is there nothing that Americans hold sacred, that they are not willing to make political?" I'm afraid that the answer to that is "no." Not even death is a 'politics-free zone.' Rest in peace, Mr. Justice Scalia, though I have no doubt that you are chuckling to yourself, up there, as you look down on us.

~

The real gun control argument

It's about time we took off our politically correct muzzle, removed our rose-colored glasses and talked about the real reason many Second Amendment supporters are pushing back at the anti-gun forces with extreme prejudice. The reason is simply many don't trust their government and have lost faith in that government's willingness to protect its citizens' basic freedoms as guaranteed in the Bill of Rights.

These low-trust citizens are really *fall-away Americans* who are now viewing many of their government's decisions with extreme skepticism. They have come to this conclusion over a number of years and over several political administrations. I believe their distrust has deepened and grown enormously over the last four years but that it started in earnest under President George W. Bush with the enactment of the Patriot Act, which was for many an infringement of their privacy rights.

To be sure, the Patriot Act became law during a period of intense terrorism and was designed, according to the Administration, to protect our liberties rather than prevent us from pursuing them, but the result was a considerable increase in the government's ability to surveil us, thus limiting our basic rights to privacy. (Don't forget, fall-away Americans guard their privacy and their right to be left alone as passionately as any other freedom.)

Low-trust Americans and critics point to real decisions the current Administration has taken to bolster their case for withholding their confidence. Some of those decisions were rendered by the President himself like the one that totally ignored the Immigration and Naturalization Act by *slow-walking* and then down-prioritizing the deportation of certain immigrant groups rather than adhering to the regulations which only permit this act for individuals.

Then there were those ignored by America's chief law enforcement officer and the Justice Department like Operation Fast and Furious, the nose-thumbing of Congress on this issue and the refusal to prosecute voter intimidation cases like that of the Black Panthers' in Philadelphia.

Others were made by Administration surrogates (like the Democrat dominated Congress that imposed the Patients' Affordable Healthcare Act on us) and the recent Vice-President led task force on gun control. For many *fall-away Americans* this task force, along with several pending gun bills and the media's mobilization of anti-gun activists is viewed as the Battle of the Bulge for the Second Amendment – but the Right has dug in

85

and is not going to give up without a fight. That's why Liberals should not chuckle when they see bumper stickers the likes of: "You can have my gun when you pry it from my cold dead fingers." These people mean business and will not go quietly into the dark night as they have checked out of the third person and checked into the active voice.

A quick look at booming NRA membership and skyrocketing gun and ammunition sales will tell even the most naive observer that something's up and it's not support for omnibus gun legislation spearheaded by Presidential Executive Order. Fall-away Americans are also looking at the media and seeing the handwriting on the wall. Here I speak of the Journal News newspaper in Westchester County that recently revealed the names and addresses and interactive Google map of all gun owners in that county - an action that has put gun-owners and non gun-owners alike at risk from an escalation in home burglaries.

A loss of Second Amendment rights is often preceded by a loss of First Amendment rights. Just ask the peoples of Poland about their occupation in 1939 by the Nazis under trumped-up charges they were persecuting Sudeten Germans living there. How many weapons were confiscated from the Poles? Answer: All of them. This falling domino method of losing rights has been used by many oppressors, but the West Germans learned their lesson after WWII. They banned the gathering of unnecessary information on German citizens and the sharing of it with other government agencies in contrast to what the Nazis and the Stasi did.

The law is called the 'Datenschutz' (data protection), and it enshrines the right of German citizens' privacy. Fall-away Americans believe that by creating a federal registry of guns and gun-owners and then sharing this information with any/all government agencies will perfectly position an unethical or rogue government to keep tabs on its citizens and enable it to tax, regulate and eventually confiscate America's weapons. Even trusting citizens should be worried about this possibility, because once set in motion, the domino could fall backwards or forwards taking other rights down with it.

We must not trifle with our Bill of Rights nor should we believe as many progressives and liberals do that it is a *work in progress*. No. It is like the Ten Commandments. After all, God didn't tell Moses these were the 'Ten Suggestions,' and our founding fathers didn't call the Bill of Rights the 'Bill of Possible Options,' either.

~

There's no hyphen in America

I couldn't be more adamant about it. We've got to stop hyphenating ourselves. Just when I thought we had moved beyond the urge to further separate ourselves from one another, here comes the old hyphen back to wreak havoc on all of us, just in time for the political season.

In November of 2008, hyphenated-Americans were vindicated at the polling place. African-Americans turned out with over 92% of the vote for then Senator Obama, and his campaign won over Hispanic-Americans, Jewish-Americans, female-Americans and college-Americans. Democrats were ecstatic. They had defanged the conservative Republicans and spiked the ball in the cultural end zone. Their tactics of laser-guided campaigning worked. By splitting us up into four demographic groups (race, ethnicity, age and gender) they messaged differently to each one and succeeded in cobbling together a patchwork quilt of Americans for hope and change.

There is a problem with this strategy, however. It is, quite simply this: once you dissect, classify and separate people into groups and sub-groups, how do you re-combine them when you want them to act in unison? What is the unifying element that can make the proudest most vocal sub-group think and act like a truly homogenized American? And why would they want to give up their unique status once they've created special interest organizations to promote their cause? It's not easy to put the ethnic genie back in the bottle.

It appears that the Administration has a solution. They've created a common enemy... those nasty, money-grubbing rich people. You know, the ones who already pay a disproportionate share of taxes to our government, the same government that can't get enough $16 muffins and never met a bail-out it didn't like. Class warfare is a strategy that will backfire because our great middle class aspires to be those rich capitalists! Have we forgotten the dot com bubble of the 90s when hoards of middle class software nerds were catapulted to the upper ranks of the tax rolls? Or the housing bubble of the 2000s when other middle class families bought houses and used them as piggy banks to leverage their way to wealth?

It wasn't so many generations ago that newly-minted immigrant Americans were willing to subordinate their differences (not give up their cultures or their history) to become part of a truly exceptional society - the American society. Immigrant fathers and mothers told their children, "We're in America now. Let's speak English." Most didn't advocate wearing their ethnicity on their sleeves or worse yet blame it for their inability to move up in the world. On the contrary, they encouraged their children to get educated and assimilate so they could <u>earn</u> their way to the American Dream.

Make no mistake, our society has greatly benefited from the diversity of its people. Those cultural and ethnic differences have provided the spice to our great American stewpot, but there comes a time when those differences must take a back seat to the intrinsic value of the *melting pot*. If we spend an inordinate amount of time focusing on our differences we will miss the opportunities that lie in pulling together as one nation. We have been the 'Assimilation Nation,' and that desire to assimilate has been our greatest strength - the true specialness of America. Millions of opportunity hungry immigrants didn't come to our shores to become hyphenated; they came to be joined together as Americans.

If we fail to live up to America's promise to provide equal opportunity to all we will be punished by a reversal of our fortunes. We will become the countries that our immigrant grandparents left, societies that gave preferential treatment to one group over the others. The price we will pay will be a disintegration of our collective values, of our laws and our attitudes. The advantage will then be in the hands of the group that shouts the loudest and uses its hyphenated status to further its own special agenda. E pluribus unum (out of many, one) is proudly emblazoned on our money. It's too bad it hasn't become part of our social currency.

~

The State of the (dis)Union

I'm looking forward with great anticipation to see how our President will spin the miserable state of our American union into a message of hope for the future. If he is somehow able to turn this massive sow's ear of abject administrative failure into a silk purse of success he will undoubtedly go down in history as one of the greatest prestidigitators of all time.

Even the most skilled sleight-of-hand artists will have to applaud him if he convinces the American public that they are better off today than they were even one year ago let alone seven years ago. The laundry list of items that Mr. Obama will have to check off are legion. On the economy, he'll have to tell us why his administration has failed to loosen numerous regulations that hamstring business' progress. A case in point is his stubborn opposition to the Keystone Pipeline that would have created thousands of high-paying jobs for American workers. Why, too, has he not worked with business and the Congress to right-size our tax code to allow for more job creation and capital repatriation?

On energy, why has he not allowed more oil and gas exploration on Federal lands and at the same time taken credit for the increase of exploration on PRIVATE lands? On the minimum wage issue, why did he not think through the problem and create a two or three-tiered minimum wage system that would help entry-level employment for young people instead of establishing a profit-punishing single rate for all workers in small businesses? His Obamacare healthcare system has failed miserably and created chaos.

Instead of insuring the 30 million uninsured, his plan helped to upend many of the insured causing their premiums and deductibles to rise beyond the point of affordability. Healthcare professionals like doctors, nurses and nurse practitioners are quitting in droves, leaving Americans without adequate care. Add to that, the half-billion dollars spent on an amateurish website that failed to entice adequate numbers of the uninsured, and it will be a tough slog for the Commander-in-Chief of optimism to say that America is healthier today. On race relations, Mr. Obama has reversed or at least halted many of the gains made by the White and Black community over the last fifty years. His 'jump to conclusions' side-taking has severely diminished his credibility, not to mention his Justice Department's capricious intrusion into police practices America's towns and cities. His schizophrenic foreign policy has been misguided at best and dangerous at worst.

By substituting passivity and weakness for strength and resolve he has put America in peril, an example of which is his characterization of ISIS as the JV (junior varsity), the precipitous pullout from Iraq, his 'Mulligan strategy' in Afghanistan and the release of five top Taliban leaders in exchange for one mentally troubled American traitor. His flaunting of the Constitution on immigration matters (cessation of deportation of a whole group of illegal immigrants) was a slap in every American's face and should have prompted a reprisal from the Congress. Instead, he amped up his vilification of any opponent to his Presidential edicts.

His most recent attempts to *make new law* through executive actions on background checks for firearms purchases reveal a headlong dash to the finish line to check off the final boxes of his Presidential promises, as was also demonstrated by his support for an international 'climate change' agreement in Paris not one month ago that disadvantaged American industry.

If it were in my power to compel the President to do anything in his last State of the Union speech, it would be to make him stand before Congress and the rest of us and explain how his *divide Americans and conquer* philosophy has been good for our country. More than likely, he will <u>not</u> do that and instead pivot to his preferred posture of gazing upwards towards Mount Olympus and with great hauteur tell us that the state of the union is sound and then direct our attention to the Republican elephant on the stage...and attempt to make it disappear. Such is the mark of the master of legerdemain.

~

The war between the states...of theory and practicality

It came to me in a flash while watching the President deliver the commencement address at Liberty University in Lynchburg, Virginia. I wasn't struck by his eloquence because he isn't eloquent. Nor was I bowled over by his speech, which was good but predictable. What did strike me was that the current political war being waged in America is not between Republicans and Democrats, nor is it between conservatives and liberals. It is really a conflict between two competing ideological life choices: theory (idealism) or practicality (realism).

The battle lines were drawn a long time ago during the first part of the FDR years, before the start of WWII, when we were digging our way out of the Great Depression and experimenting with a uniquely American type of socialist *theory*. Then, in 1941, we found our way of life and country under siege. Enter *practicality*. America couldn't afford to go in two directions at once, so it chose pragmatism to win the war. We reverted to protective mode, and this always happens when survival is threatened, whether it's a country or a species. It's what humans do. We exit the larger thought (idealism) and enter the less ethereal one (realism).

When we are under stress, we take a vacation from our everyday lives. We set aside our activities, realizing we need rest and relaxation. This is often the only sensible way to recharge our batteries and re-dedicate ourselves to our larger mission. To get there, we don't overdraw our checking accounts or hop into make-believe cars to get on pretend airplanes to take us to imaginary destinations.

Americans are a pretty level-headed people whose feet are usually planted on terra firma but whose heads are sometimes in the clouds. Over the course of our lifetimes, we are encouraged to reach for the stars, to be all that we can be and to never give up on our dreams. That means we are always looking for a *special spot* where we can live in both those worlds: the world of our own philosophies and aspirations and the one where practicality rules. This presents problems when we choose our political paths, however.

The path of *hope and change* wrapped in a *one world* philosophy is appealing on many levels, not the least of which is a religious one. An integral part of this philosophy is a belief in the inherent goodness of man and in his willingness to join hands, link arms and work towards achieving common goals like: safeguarding the planet's environment, promoting democracy and leveling the economic playing field. I have no argument with the goals. My problem is the starting point - the belief that all men are willing to subordinate their self-interests in favor of the common good. That is a bridge of faith too far for me to cross and is precisely the place where the political idealists (usually the liberal Democrats) collide with the political realists (usually the conservative Republicans). Both groups are skeptical of the other while some in them despise the other. The rest actively oppose the other.

A national or international catastrophe is the only thing that could unite Americans again. Our political polarization is too deeply-rooted to be healed by one leader. We saw the Right's opposition to a idealistic one-world President for eight years and we are now seeing the Left resist a reality-grounded *America first* President. No, I'm afraid that only a crisis of national or international proportions will unite the idealists and the realists. We saw it happen before on December 7, 1941 and on September 11, 2001, but we haven't seen it since.

As one who believes in man's better angels and in his ability to tell the difference between hope and reality and act accordingly, I think we have underestimated the importance of the election of a President that sees the world with all its flaws and self-interests. If there are those among us that want to follow their dreams of building a more peaceful and prosperous world, then let them join with the pragmatists that elected our current leaders to realize those dreams here, first. There is a reason the flight attendants say, "Put your own oxygen mask on, first, and then help the person next to you."

~

"We are not amused."

Queen Victoria, now THERE was one tough lady at a time when toughness was considered the sole province of men. I suppose that Hillary Rosen

91

could have said that Queen V hadn't worked a day in her life either, and she might have been right if she was talking about a 9-5 hourly wage job, but Queen Victoria ruled the British Empire for 63 years, and few doubted her qualifications or energy.

It amazes me that political strategists and pollsters think they can strip away all the accoutrements that make up the outward face of women, isolate and then label them like an entomologist pinning butterflies to a board. If these 'professionals' think that women are nothing more than the sum of disparate parts or can be re-assembled like a Mrs. Potato Head (and messaged to accordingly), they have never met a real woman let alone lived with one.

Ms. Rosen must have made her now famous comment as a result of an acute case of *talkingpointitus* or she suffered a momentary gender lapse, otherwise she wouldn't have coughed up such a hairball, especially at the time when her party's chieftains were mobilizing their troops to ratchet up the *War on Women* and take it to the barbarian Republican camp and their front-runner, Mitt Romney. We shouldn't punish people for speaking their minds on national TV. We should just precede their appearances with a couple of their famous quotes thrown up on the screen for the viewers to see in case they've forgotten them.

To quote Shakespeare, "The evil men do lives after them; the good is oft interred with their bones," but with so much drivel to sort through in any given day, we need to be reminded occasionally of that *evil*. We don't judge books by their covers, so why should we pigeonhole women voters into stereotypical boxes to fit a political narrative or target group? Are all college-age single women alike? Do all working women (those that have out-of-the-home paying jobs) have the same aspirations or share the same ideologies? Are all wealthy women protected from hardships or immune from life-changing personal challenges?

Do all women want their contraception devices or pills paid for and regulated by the government? Is the *sisterhood* of NOW and other female organizations only comprised of liberal East Coast academic women? Do middle-aged married Mid-Western women only vote for Republican candidates? Are women more persuadable than men when it comes to education and healthcare issues? Are all women pacifists?

Do women love their children more and their jobs less (and men the reverse)? Are they all driven by their protective nurturing nature? I swear, sometimes these political strategists are nothing more than vultures perched on the hill, intimidating the most vulnerable of the herd, waiting for them show their weakness. Preying on their fears they wear down their subjects with incessant rhetoric until they succumb. One hundred and fifty-four years ago, Abraham Lincoln gave a famous speech in Illinois in which he said that, "A house divided against itself cannot stand."

That speech didn't win him the Senate seat he sought, but it did remind a deeply divided nation that it was teetering on the brink of its own dissolution. I am not an expert on women, but I see no virtue in pitting American women of any party, race, age, social status or ethnic group against each other, nor do I see any gains to be made from using our differences as a weapon to bloody the opposition. What we do to others we do to ourselves, and that inescapable truth ought to be enough to make us want to lower our voices and moderate our tone.

~

Wins, losses and draws

A little over 48% of American voters are licking their wounds while about 52% are licking their chops now that the *greatest show on earth* has finally come to an end. I'm speaking of course about the Presidential election – the one that cost campaign contributors nearly a billion smackeroos.

In its wake, I've struggled to understand how 95% of all Blacks, 71% of all Hispanics and 55% of all women (who have all suffered the most since 2008) voted for the man who has presided over the biggest economic catastrophe since the 30s (I know, I know, 'Bush did it all and left the President with a mess.'). That mantra's been heard more often than *Hail to the Chief* – and you really have to have some high numbers to outdo the times the President's triumphal entry music is played, believe me. Seems that voters were not as concerned about rising unemployment, escalating poverty, widespread food stamp use, falling house values, a burgeoning national debt and the coming fiscal cliff as I thought.

That's where the Republicans were wrong, too. They thought the American electorate was singularly focused on America's pocketbook. After all, previous generations have voted with their wallet, why should this one have been any different? The answers were right in front of the Republicans all along, and had they looked, they would have recognized the telltale signs of a coming Democratic victory.

The President's party kept people on the ground in key parts of the U.S. after the 2008 election as a kind of motivational 'mod squad.' They steadily organized *get out the vote* campaigns, and they were deeply immersed into fund raising – with the President holding out the biggest tin cup man ever before seen! They also devised a masterful and winning strategy that included destroying the opposition by playing the 'old white men' race card on candidates, labeling them as against women's reproductive rights because they didn't support government-provided birth control or abortions. They cozied up to the media and celebritydom full-well knowing that Hollywood actors occupy choice real estate on America's Mount Olympus.

Then they used the social media to shotgun their message of *coolness, progressivism,* and *inclusivity* to the mind-numbed living in earshot of this new American jungle drum of mediocrity.

Admittedly, the Republicans willingly shot themselves in their own feet from time to time or hung themselves with rope happily supplied by the DNC. For example, I would really like to know which boneheaded consultant told Governor Romney that he should use a phrase like *self-deport* when talking about his immigration reform ideas. Personally, I believe the Governor lost all or most of the Hispanic vote that night on the strength of that one, hyphenated word. The huge African-American/Black vote came as no surprise, as most political analysts believed that that community would readily support their man for another four. What was shocking was the size of the percentage AND the fact that the Republicans hadn't bothered to cultivate that vote or at least conservative Black voters long before the final months of the campaign.

Military tacticians and corporate strategists would do well to study the Obama re-election campaign. It was both successful and revelatory. Not only did it help a President remain in the White House but it also unveiled the *real America* for all to see. We know more about our electorate now than ever before. We know it listens to NPR, the Daily Show and Bill Maher. We know it is easily persuaded by ethnic or gender-charged messages delivered by specialty haranguers.

We know it values smart phones, Facebook and YouTube over church on Sunday, and we know that it is perpetually hungry for something <u>new</u>. I have no doubt that the new (old) Administration will definitely give them that in spades. It remains to be seen what they'll do with it. I think I know what the other 48% will do.

~

Work is life

Ask the average person about their jobs and you'll probably hear a stream of consciousness explanation of what they do, how they do it and what motivates them. If they're unemployed, they'll probably say they're 'between jobs,' that is if they haven't given up searching, altogether. Many of us identify closely with our chosen fields, and it's often hard to separate the person from the career as we tend to 'become' what we do, especially if we're highly motivated. Without work, we cease to exist in the eyes of just about everybody except the Department of Labor whose Bureau of Labor Statistics will faithfully track us until the end of our days. For example, the Bureau just announced that our unemployment rate dropped from 4.9% in October to 4.6% for November and that 178,000 new jobs were added.

The press proudly reported this today as if the nearly 93 million work-capable but unemployed people who are part of the chronically unemployed category (see the 'U6' unemployment statistics) don't exist anymore, like they all got jobs and just forgot to tell someone about it. Depending on whose numbers you look at, it takes the creation of around 142,000 new jobs each month just to keep up with the new people entering the workforce!

Then there's the underemployed, people who are working at part-time jobs because they can't find full-time work. There are also seasonal workers (in the agricultural sector, for example). They're another category. The Census Bureau (part of the U.S. Department of Commerce) also tracks the unemployed and regularly surveys 60,000 households on their employment status. So you see, our U.S. government does keep a watchful eye on us and dutifully prepares reports on who's working where and for what wages.

In essence, their model for compiling data is simple: people with jobs are employed; people who are jobless or looking for a job and are available for work are unemployed; the labor force is made up of the employed and the unemployed; people who are neither employed nor unemployed are not in the labor force. It's all pretty straightforward, actually, but these reports don't tell the story of the unbreakable nexus of work to life and its importance for our self-preservation, our self-image and self-esteem, our health and our financial security.

Most people work for someone else, but millions are self-employed with no employees. When THEY are unemployed, they have nowhere to go to

95

get unemployment benefits, unlike those who have lost their jobs from a company. They're plumb out of luck. It's no secret that our manufacturing jobs have disappeared at a rapid pace. In the 70s, the oil crisis was a wake-up call to industry that quickly realized it needed to reduce costs in order to offset the additional pressure on their bottom line from higher energy prices. And what was on the chopping block? Wages and jobs.

While some labor unions were successful in achieving short-term small wage and/or benefit gains, the majority of them tightened their belts and prayed that the storm would blow over. That wake-up call saw corporations take a closer look at worker benefit packages, productivity and automation. "Say hello to the assembly line, R2D2. This your new home. You have now replaced a whole crew of welders and assembly personnel!"

Now, all corporations needed was a cost-benefit analysis on moving their whole production offshore or across the border. Enter U.S. bi-national and multi-national trade agreements and the granddaddy agreement of them all, NAFTA. The North American Free Trade Agreement was signed by President Clinton in 1993 and became law on Jan. 1, 1994.

Initially designed to make the North American continent one huge trading bloc and low tariff trade zone, it also had two other purposes: 1. to provide a cheap manufacturing platform for U.S. companies wanting to move their operations to Mexico for its low wages; and 2. to act as a bulwark against large-scale illegal Mexican emigration to the USA. In his 1992 Presidential campaign, businessman Ross Perot uttered probably the most famous words on NAFTA, "We have got to stop sending jobs overseas. It's pretty simple: If you're paying $12, $13, $14 an hour for factory workers and you can move your factory South of the border, pay a dollar an hour for labor,...have no health care—that's the most expensive single element in making a car— have no environmental controls, no pollution controls and no retirement, and you don't care about anything but making money, there will be a giant sucking sound going south."

In 2015/16 then candidate for President, Donald Trump, used similar rhetoric to assign blame for America's job losses. Labor unions opposed NAFTA (and still do) for one simple reason - U.S. job loss - and for a few others like allowing sub-standard overseas working conditions to exist and permitting off-shoring to place a downward wage pressure on domestic U.S. wages. Now that we have a 20-plus year history with NAFTA, we actually have a reasonable period of time in which to assess its success...or lack thereof. In point of fact, NAFTA actually succeeded TOO WELL, as many Blue Chip American companies have re-located operations across our southern border. In so doing, they have improved their profitability by significantly reducing labor costs.

They have also avoided paying heavy duties on products bound for the USA from Mexico. The main unintended consequence has been that too many jobs have left our shores, but NAFTA did something else. It showed potential re-locating companies that they could duplicate the maquiladora experience on the other side of the Pacific and manufacture or assemble in the Far East and China for a fraction of their U.S.-based costs. Most of America's electronic goods and nearly all of our televisions are now made in foreign countries. The last TV manufacturer hold-out was Zenith. In 1995, it sold its controlling interest to South Korean 'LG Electronics' (the Lucky Goldstar Group). Goodbye hundreds of jobs. This steady hemorrhaging of U.S. contract manufacturers' business to Chinese and Mexican companies was of growing concern to America's labor leaders who saw companies and their union jobs move offshore, presumably, forever.

The Clinton, Bush and Obama administrations fell in love with globalization and supported keeping NAFTA in place if only to help Mexico move away from becoming a failed nation after its 'Tequila Crisis' of 1994-95. According to many experts, NAFTA helped lower costs for basic necessities in Mexico by 50% (source: Tufts University). It also helped raise income in the maquiladora sector by 15.5% since its start (source: Institute for International Economics). NAFTA has recently come under fire in the Presidential Election of 2016 for its ability to 'kill U.S. jobs' and lay waste to the American manufacturing sector. Many opponents of the agreement have cited job loss numbers that range from 600K to 800K and indicate that new 'NAFTA-like' trade agreements like the TPP and the TTIP should never see the light of day.

Democratic strategist, James Carville, said that there was only one real campaign issue that President Bill Clinton needed to be concerned with back in 1992. He was right then to talk about the economy and the structure of our regulatory system and pocketbook issues, but the focus now is not on some system-tweaking but job creation. The Trump campaign built its success on appealing to the millions of under- or unemployed American voters. It also knew that work is life, and without a reason to get up in the morning and pull on work clothes and pack lunchboxes, Americans will unplug from their own society and become passive non-participants in the political process; we need more voters, not fewer.

Finally, trade agreements are not the only bogeymen to blame for our unemployment ills. When corporate tax rates and the cost of doing business are too high, businesses will always look for other ways to bend back their cost curve.

These may include re-location, downsizing, automation or other solutions. Either way, we must understand that job creation is not only the business of business, but also that of communities and consumers. I'm convinced that American consumers would be willing to spend a dollar more to save an American job if they could see the direct cause and effect of their actions. I believe, too, that American businesses are willing to create jobs if they can be assured that their government will pass some job-friendly legislation and not pull the financial rug out from underneath them once they've decided to remain in the USA or return from foreign markets. Now is the time to support a nationwide drive to make America *work* again.

~

Wrestle Mania Political Style

I remember when political conventions used to be a hoot. I got a kick out of watching the *Ridiculous Meter* go off the charts when TV cameras spied delegates wearing elephant hats, Uncle Sam outfits and other outrageous getups, some straight from Ringling Brothers' wardrobe wagon. Seemed, too, that the conventions of old weren't scripted down to the minutest detail. Thankfully, there were no teleprompters back then to steer the speakers' every word.

This year there was one genuine moment from the Democrats' convention that will go down in the annals of convention history. It was when the Democrat delegates were asked for a voice vote on re-inserting the words *God* and *Jerusalem* back into the party platform (seems somebody had left them out and the President surprisingly wanted them back in, thus requiring a vote from the delegates).

Dem Convention Chairman and Los Angeles Mayor Antonio Villaraigosa called for a voice vote three times before showing *real* democracy by adopting the platform change with less than the 2/3 majority required to do so. I guess he was going for a version of the old Flip Wilson, 'the Devil made me do it' rule here and say that he had to call it that way because it was on his teleprompter! For my money, this one event was worth sitting through the full three days of the convention - not just for the deer in the headlights look on Villaraigosa's face - but for the departure from the rigid programming that now characterizes these conventions.

Over in Tampa, the previous week, the Republicans had their own magical moment when *Dirty Harry* Clint Eastwood decided he'd go off-script and talked to an empty chair that supposedly held the President. I cringed watching the great actor and director reduce himself to a comedic role for which he clearly wasn't prepared.

It was like seeing Richard Nixon doing stand-up, telling jokes about Spiro Agnew. Conventions have become Petri dishes into which are added all manner of speakers designed to address every conceivable voter demographic or special interest group. I counted the following: celebrities, working mothers and single women, the handicapped, Black Americans, Latinos, labor unions, athletes, pro-abortion groups, the military, small business owners, teachers, conservationists, anti-big energy advocates and seniors. I kept waiting for them to get really specific, bringing on speakers representing New England ball-bearing manufacturers, blind ATV off-roaders, transsexual spelling bee winners and maybe disgraced dead politicians, but it never happened.

There were no great surprises for the Republicans. They didn't exhume Ronald Reagan and prop him up in front of an American flag near the podium. They just had "workmanlike" (quote from the media) speeches by the candidates. The Democrats on the other hand did recycle former President Bill Clinton (the Dem commentators and surrogates called him "former President Clinton" I think to remind their faithful that *Bubba* wasn't on the ballot).

Clinton proceeded to give a lecture on domestic realpolitik that focused largely on himself and his eight years in office and a father/son talk on the birds and the bees. I stopped counting the, "Listen to this; it's important" lines as I was transfixed by his crooked index finger that was busy doing an intricate dance of the sugar plum fairies while he droned on, effectively keeping the real President waiting behind the curtain.

Then the President spoke, and my mind went back to FDR and his Fireside Chats, John Wayne in any war movie, Knut Rockne at half-time, and finally Davy Crockett. The Beatles crept in there too, with the 'Long and Winding Road.' It was heady. I'm sure glad I didn't have go anywhere afterwards because I couldn't have driven my car for fear I would have been cited for driving under the influence of hyperbole. Words and exceptional speakers will do that to you, and I've found I need to decompress after the conventions to regain my equilibrium. Thank goodness the debates are a month away so I'll have plenty of time to prepare for my next political rush.

Chapter III
2016 Presidential Election

Regardless of your political persuasion, most ardent political observers would have to agree that the 2016 presidential primaries and general election were probably the most exciting we've seen in decades. The only possible exception is the Gore vs. Bush contest.

That said, it seems that the election turned an important corner in American politics and moved us squarely into what could be termed a new 'third way' campaign paradigm where traditional rules of engagement (especially in the primaries) are now neither desirable nor viable to win the presidency - all thanks to Donald J. Trump.

With a field of sixteen candidates, Republicans had an 'embarrassment of riches' of men (and one woman) that represented every wing and feather of the party on important issues. By using a consistent and unmercifully applied combination of 'in your face' punches, demeaning personal epithets and schoolboy taunts, Trump dispatched his opponents, one-by-one, until the field narrowed to a few. The gentlemanly gave way to bare-fisted, no holds barred, street fighting, until one man was left standing. Trump managed to wrestle his way to victory by calling out the 'demons' of the mainstream *fake news* media and by targeting Americans' fears of joblessness, illegal immigration, escalating crime and a failing healthcare system, harkening back to Ross Perot's platform of 1992.

He gave no quarter and took no prisoners in his fight for the nomination and then simply replaced his attacks on Republican opponents with his Democratic contender, Hillary Clinton. His lack of *appropriate decorum* and *respect* for the normal rules of political fisticuffs was exactly what Republican and disgruntled independent voters wanted, and they rewarded him with their support.

His choice to campaign in traditional Democratic strongholds -'blue' states like Wisconsin and Michigan - gave him the boost he needed to offset large popular votes elsewhere. He won the hearts of many in the Midwest, in Pennsylvania and in blue collar America where voters had seen their jobs and futures disappear under eight years of the Obama presidency. As for Hillary Clinton, her message was vague and short on substance. It lacked detailed policy suggestions and was delivered, unconvincingly.

Statements like the "basket of deplorables" made about Trump supporters did nothing to win over fence-sitters or independents. Truth be told, Trump's messages also lacked substance, but his strength lay in his tenacity, his consistency, his energy AND his populist style.

It must also be said that one of his greatest assets was that he wasn't Hillary Clinton, a candidate that failed to tap into Americans' anger and mistrust of career politicians (like herself). Instead, the absence of that message stuck out like a sore thumb for Mrs. Clinton. She was the WYSIWYG candidate, and the baggage she carried from her time as Secretary of State (Benghazi, the 'Russian Reset,' etc.) and as the First Lady when she accused Republicans of a "vast right-wing conspiracy" to do her husband in, was simply too heavy to carry across the finish line.

The James Comey statements about the FBI not being completely done with the Hillary investigation which came two weeks before election day effectively cast enough doubt in the minds of the undecided for them to move their vote Trump's way. The handwriting was on the wall and became visible for all to see on the evening of November 8, 2016.

A few universal laws

We're in a law and order phase of life in America right now. We elected a new President that promises to crack down on lawbreakers and send them packing to prisons or detention centers. We're seeing an outcry for deporting more illegal criminal aliens along with threats to Sanctuary Cities from the Feds to take away funds for not cooperating with ICE. There's an increasing drum beat from the Right for more protection for conservative speakers at public universities and from the Left, a clamoring for more 'safe spaces' from un-PC like speech. Death is spreading in the form of dangerous drug cartels and gangs, both on the border and deep within the interior of the USA.

Our senior citizens are being preyed upon by unscrupulous scam artists and organized rings of so-called 'home companions' that steal from them after gaining entry to their homes. Phony email 'phishing' for our identities and bank account info is on the rise as are all other forms of telephone schemes to steal our money or our personal data. We're warned to cover our PIN number on the touchpad at the supermarket or the gas station and to secure ourselves with identity protection plans and our property with elaborate electronic police monitoring home alarm systems. Our children cannot walk home from school, unaccompanied, anymore. Our cars must have steering wheel locks or tracking devices because car theft is reaching alarming proportions. Even our pets are being stolen right from under our noses.

I'm convinced that most Americans have had enough and demanding more law and more order and their old way of life back. This brings me to a few modern 'laws of the universe' that may be in play. See if you agree.

The First Law of Law-making: Laws are created by lawyers for their benefit not yours. While that sounds ominous, there is some good news here. Since the 1960s, the number of Congressional Representatives and Senators that are lawyers has been declining. It's now around 40% of all 535 of them. I'm afraid that when it comes to law-making in general we have the wrong idea. We shouldn't be creating new laws at the rate most rabbits multiply. Instead, we should be eliminating as many as we can, certainly those that constrict our personal freedom. We should reward the law-makers that share that philosophy by re-electing them and rejecting those that feel that everything must be regulated.

The First Law of Materialism: That which can be acquired will wear out before the warranty expires (planned obsolescence). Manufacturers are clever. They wear-test their products and will guarantee them just until the warranty ends. Unfortunately for us, the products generally fail a few months later. Fortunately for us, most of them are made in China or Mexico and don't cost an arm and a leg.

The First Law of the Marketplace: Things must never remain the same. It seems that the longer a product remains unchanged it becomes more vulnerable to failure. Think of the products of your youth and then look for them on your supermarket or drug store's shelves. There's a reason that you won't find them. The primary one is that we're fixated on the *new* and led to believe that version 7.0 is vastly better than version 6.0 or that a new size or a new design is going to make life infinitely easier for us. On the digital front, it seems that there's a new start-up company formed every week and headed by thirty-something entrepreneurs offering a "revolutionary new" smart phone application. They all have one thing in common...separating you from the paltry sum of $4 to download it. That's the marketplace. Love it or hate it, but you can't ignore it.

The First Law of True Love (perhaps the most important of all): True love is not a question of who, but more of how. We are the only creatures capable of loving without protecting and protecting without loving. Animals fiercely protect their young and so do we, but we continue to do so even after our children are grown. That's not Nature's way, but it is our way. We romanticize love to the tune of hundreds of billions of dollars every year with books, television shows, movies, and we desperately search for it through online dating services and other electronic means. We compete for it among our peers and pray to God for it on Sunday. Truth is, love is a force like electricity - unseen but real - all we have to do is believe in it and release ourselves from our own self-absorption and it will come to us.

There are many more universally accepted laws out there and I would invite you to read them, but there is another law (more a maxim really) especially worth mentioning in these overly cynical times. I call it the *Forever Optimist Law* and it is, "A dream is a wish your heart makes when you're fast asleep. In dreams you lose your heartaches; whatever you wish for you keep. Have faith in your dreams and someday your rainbow will come smiling through. No matter how your heart is grieving, if you keep on believing, the dream that you wish will come true." Thanks, uncle Walt Disney and Cinderella.

~

Alice in political land

This year's Presidential candidates have been described (by each other and by others) as *dangerous, liar, crooked, megalomaniac, bigot, racist, misogynist, incompetent, bully, anti-immigrant, insensitive, unfeeling, naive, elitist, power-hungry, calculating, hypocritical, unprincipled, unpatriotic, out-of-touch, cold,* and many other adjectives, too numerous to mention.

Most Republicans despise Hillary Clinton and most Democrats wouldn't help Donald Trump out of a burning building. Sure there are those that love each one but still wouldn't dream of crossing over to the other side and voting for the 'enemy,' but there is a third, even larger group. This group dislikes <u>both</u> candidates and is very conflicted about who to vote for. These are what I call the *crisis of conscience voters.* They are reasonable people - generally older - who've been brought up to believe that a President of the United States ought to act and speak in a very specific way, and that goes for campaigning as well. Unfortunately, many of these people are stuck in the past where the lines of demarcation of good taste, appropriateness and courtesy were clear for all to see but are now blurred by time. Battles were fought on the middle-to-high ground, not in the mud of uber-nastiness.

Those folks desperately want the clock turned back to 'their America,' but they are spitting in the wind, for gone are the days of the 'Gipper,' Ronald Reagan and "morning in America" and his "shining city on a hill." There are no more George H.W. Bush' "thousand points of light." Irrelevant are Lincoln's "better angels of our nature" that he mentioned in his inaugural address in 1861 - angels which would trigger the "mystic chords of memory" and "swell the chorus of the Union."

So much for the better angels; the Civil War followed soon thereafter and took over 620,000 American lives. We've been moving steadily down the path of total annihilation politics. This path has given us roadside attractions like: opposition research, Super PACs, character assassination, fear mongering and identity politics. There are no rules of engagement here as there are on modern battlefields. It's a 'Mad Max' world where it's every man (or woman) for himself or herself. To make this political tragedy on the Potomac even more bizarre, there are also uninvited guests that have crashed the party.

Enter Wikileaks and (maybe) the Russians and you have a whole different game, one where you don't have to suit up or be in the lineup to play on the field. This was the case when Wikileaks' founder, Julian Assange, decided to release 20,000 emails that were obtained from the Democratic National Committee's server that proved, conclusively, that that venerable protector of party neutrality, the DNC, had actively sabotaged Bernie Sanders' campaign for the Dems' nomination. Assange vowed that more emails would follow, assuring himself of a pivotal role in our Presidential election from his current residence in the Ecuadoran Embassy in London.

This year's campaigns remind me of Tom Lehrer's song, "They're rioting in Africa" - a brilliant piece of satire from the Eisenhower years of 1958. Lehrer's lyrics betray his real feelings that the world doesn't like itself or each other very much and THAT is how the bulk of the electorate is feeling today in 2016. <u>We don't like anybody very much</u>, the least of whom are Mrs. Clinton and Mr. Trump, and that dislike is forcing us to make a 'Sophie's choice' between the least reprehensible of the two.

The real choice, however, is an existential one and is embarrassingly simple. Do we choose Hillary Clinton and assure ourselves a 'third Obama term" of four more years of the same flat-lining economy, high unemployment, out-of-control debt, diminished world influence, increased racial strife and domestic intranquility (and/or a movement even farther Left to the electrified fence of Socialism) OR do we cast a ballot for a political novice who relishes tweaking the nose of the establishment, is self-indulgent, says exactly what comes to his mind at virtually any gathering and is regarded as far right of center of everything that the opposition party stands for? Which *devil* do we want? The one we know or the one we don't?

Lewis Carroll (actually Charles Dodgson, author of 'Alice's Adventures in Wonderland') said, "If you don't know where you're going, any road will get you there." Unfortunately for all of us, America is still not sure which path it wants to follow. Do we take the *red pill* which represents the painful truth of reality or choose the *blue pill*, blissful ignorance and illusion?

~

America chooses, but who really decides?

We do a fair amount of chest thumping here in the USA -some justified and some not. Take our pride in being the world's leading democracy, for example. When we look at how we nominate our candidates, I'm afraid that our boast of being the place where one man-one vote reigns falls short of our rhetoric. I've tried to explain the U.S. political candidate nomination system to my friends in Europe for some time now, and while I can't always see the expressions on their faces, I sense that my descriptions of how the individual states choose their candidates confuses more than clarifies.

Admittedly, most Americans probably don't understand our system either, but that doesn't make the task of explaining it to foreigners any easier. Matter of fact, most Americans probably think that our primaries are very democratic in their structure and that they are representative of the one man-one vote myth of choosing a nominee. We have some states with real primary voting contests. Depending on the state, delegates are apportioned by a simple and transparent system.

There are others that have chosen caucuses as their way of nominating a candidate and then there's a third which is more like a coffee klatch than an election. I'm speaking, of course, of the most recent such hybrid gathering in the State of Colorado. If someone can explain to me in a few well-chosen words how Colorado's method of choosing a candidate is anything close to a one man-one vote democracy, I'd be eternally grateful.

On the surface, most of it seems pretty straightforward. We hold elections and the votes are tabulated and then delegates are given to the candidates, but it is how the delegates are actually apportioned that presents the problem. Some states apportion delegates by how a candidate has fared in a congressional district, and some award by 'winner takes all' or by simple proportional means. Others have more Byzantine ways of allocating delegates. Speaking of those, you might have heard Republican candidate Donald Trump complain about the "unfairness" of the process.

With several million more votes than the second place challenger, Senator Ted Cruz, Trump feels that "a win is a win," and that win should entitle him to all the delegates in a 'winner take all' situation. Mr. Trump seems to be echoing the complaints of many candidates in the past who have entered the race thinking that all they needed to do was get the majority of votes in a given state to win its delegates. How wrong they all were.

Before we explore the history or the evolution of primaries, let's look at the real abuse of the system, the Super Delegates. The Republican Party has 162 Super Delegates (roughly three from each state). All are chosen by the party faithful. They are pledged to vote for the nominee that won their state's primary or caucus, on the first ballot at the convention. After the first ballot, the Super Delegates are free to vote their conscience, and are, essentially, unbound from any pledge they may have made as a result of their state's primary vote.

Democrats on the other hand, have 712 Super Delegates that <u>may vote any way they choose, irrespective of the way the votes were cast in their individual states.</u> For example, if a Super Delegate, which could be a Democrat Mayor, Governor, Congressional Representative, Senator or just a party bigwig, pledges to support Hillary Clinton (even before the states' primaries), that delegate will be in Mrs. Clinton's column and be counted on the first ballot at the Democrats' convention. That is not to say that the individual delegates, themselves, cannot be wooed away from Mrs. Clinton at any time before the vote is taken at the convention. They can, but the real question is, will they? Probably not, considering she is the establishment's preferred candidate and that many of the Super Delegates are dyed-in-the-wool 'Clinton Democrats.'

After the 1968 Democratic national convention, the Party made some changes in its selection process. By creating Super Delegates, the idea was to return some of the power to the people from the party leadership. However, not everyone was happy with the changes, and in 1982, the Hunt commission that was set up to analyze the delegate selection process, recommended that up to 30% of all delegates should be Super Delegates. When the 1984 Election took place, however, that number was only 14%.

Today, the number is around 20%. Several changes have also been made since that time, but the end result has been that the party faithful have not been able to choose the Super Delegates because in 1996, the Democratic Party decided that all elected Democrat Congressional Representatives and Senators (along with mayors, governors and other party VIPs) would be given Super Delegate status. On its face, that's not all bad, inasmuch as most of those Super Delegates are people that were elected by the one man-one vote process, by the people of their state. Unfortunately, it doesn't change the personal side of the equation - the likely pre-disposition of those representatives to vote for the person they *like* the best or the person that will give them the best deal after January 20th.

The 2008 election saw Barack Obama handily win the majority of the pledged delegates and the Super Delegates. Today, in 2016, the Democratic National Committee Chairwoman, Debbie Wasserman Schultz, is quoted as saying, "Unpledged delegates really exist to make sure that party leaders and elected officials don't have to be in a position where they are running against grass roots activists. We are, as a Democratic Party, really highlight and emphasize inclusiveness and diversity at our convention, and so we want to give every opportunity to grass roots activists and diverse committed Democrats to be able to participate, attend and be a delegate at the convention. And so we separate out those unpledged delegates to make sure that there isn't a competition between them."

That is Washington speak at its obfuscatory best. The Democrats have come under considerable criticism for creating a system that is 'rigged' and that clearly advantages the establishment over the rank and file membership.

Even hard core party members like Susan Estrich have argued that these Super Delegates would have more power over the other delegates because of their freedom to vote as they wish. The bottom line on the subject of Super Delegates is that the Democratic Party's preference for delegate loading stands in stark contrast to the Republican Party's bound Super Delegates and serves to reinforce the belief that the cards are stacked in favor of the Democratic Party establishment's candidate.

The other aspect of the American political election system which contradicts Americans' steadfast belief that the ordinary man chooses his own leaders in a democratic one man-one vote fashion is the Electoral College (EC). It is not a college but a group of electors chosen by each state "in such Manner as the Legislature thereof may direct" (U.S. Constitution, Article II, section 1). Each state has a number of electors that are equal to the combined total of the states' Senate and House of Representatives delegations. At present, the number of electors per state ranges from 3 to 54, for a total of 538. (The winner must get at least 270 of those electoral votes).

Here's the tricky part...even if the candidate wins the popular votes in low electoral vote, low population states, he may not win the election. Why? Because he must win the popular vote in states with large numbers of electoral votes in order to get to the magic number of 270. The 12th amendment of the Constitution, ratified in 1804, changed the way the EC elects our presidents. The Electors now have separate ballots for president and vice president and only cast a single vote for each office (prior to 1804 they cast two votes each for president and no votes for vice-president).

After the presidential election has taken place, Electors are convened in each state to ratify the vote, and they are expected to vote for the candidate that won in their states. There have been instances in which individual Electors have not honored their commitment, however, and have voted for a different candidate. They are called, 'faithless' or 'unfaithful' Electors. Obviously, this can complicate matters, considerably. (Many constitutional scholars consider the Electors to be Constitutional 'free agents' that are able to vote for any candidate who meets the requirements of president or vice president.) Fortunately, there have been few instances of these 'faithless' Electors switching sides, and none of them have actually influenced the outcome of a presidential election. Knowing all this, is it any wonder, that the outside world finds America's elections to be both arcane and slightly undemocratic?

In an ideal world, the perfect scenario would be for each person to cast one vote for one candidate in one election. Then, the votes would be tabulated and the winner of a popular vote majority would be elected president and vice president. Finito. We are a long way from that scenario and may never really come close, so what are we to do? Given the cumbersome and complicated method of changing America's election process, I'm afraid that we must accept incremental change and try to persuade the states to eliminate caucuses and other hybrid means of choosing nominees. It would be a formidable task, but it's definitely worth trying if it will move us one step closer to the Holy Grail of American politics...one man-one vote.

~

Americans' love affair with 'new'

Americans love the idea of being in love with anything *new* which probably explains why political candidates of the recent past that kept repeating a 'return to yesteryear' message came up short. The reasons for failure are simple and many. A sobering thought: over 225 million Americans don't remember the Vietnam War or our race struggles of the sixties.

Only 25 million people are old enough to remember WWII and slightly over 5 million Americans can remember the Great Depression. Add to that the fact that Americans have a short attention span and don't know their own history and you have a nation that's firmly rooted in the present with little or no respect for - or connection with - the past. When the majority of Americans recall prosperous times, they think back to two administrations: that of Ronald Reagan and/or Bill Clinton, each for

109

different reasons. Reagan's was new in the sense that while older than President Jimmy Carter he offered something new to voters that they hadn't had in a long time...hope.

Reagan's appeal to the 'morning in America' in all of us was right out of the human nature playbook. He comforted us as only a strong father figure could do and told us that 'America's best days were ahead of us.' He gave us permission to throw off our pessimism and usher in optimism with a benevolent authority figure (himself) at the helm, and he connected the generations, albeit tentatively and temporarily.

After two terms, we were ready to leave Reagan's nest, but not quite. We chose to extend the 'buyer protection plan' for four more years to make sure we were strong enough to set out on our own while we searched for something even newer. In 1992, our pent-up desire for change and our nation's demographics merged, and we chose a sibling instead of a father to lead us. Our 'new' was a safe 'new' - generationally rooted in our present. Not JFK, but JFK light. Not 'New Deal' nor 'Great Society,' but new great expectations in the form of William Jefferson Clinton.

Our new choices today, in Presidential campaign year 2016, consist of a 74-year old socialist, a 70-year old real estate wheeler-dealer and a 68-year old political retread. If we are to put a face on the two front-runners, we have another Reagan (though untested in the political world) and another Clinton (literally). If we look at the issues facing us we can see some striking similarities to both previous administrations.

They are: high unemployment, war weariness, racial tension, gender conflict, ideological battles, income disparity, international tension and a profound lack of faith and trust in government. Seen demographically, many of the issues are common to both young and old, but some are specific. For the older folks, it's worsening and increasingly unaffordable healthcare, the steadily rising cost of retirement and a creeping disenfranchisement from society, created in part by a lack of respect for their generations' contributions and sacrifices.

For the young, the issues are high unemployment with a bleak outlook for improvement, college tuition indebtedness, a lack of identity and a sense of impermanence. These are conditions that have made change a foregone conclusion or inevitable in our past, and there's every reason to believe that Americans will choose something 'new' again this year. Whether it's a father or mother figure (or an uncle or cousin figure like Senator Cruz or Rubio) is anybody's guess.

What is certain is that voters will tap a strong, confident authority figure to lead them after experiencing nearly eight years of a failed theoretician in the White House.

~

America's quadrennial re-invention

This election year, 2016, finds my European friends particularly confused. They don't understand America (especially American politics) and why we take so long to choose our Presidential candidates and why we don't hold a speedy election and get on with the business of governing. The thing they are most confused about, though, is why we are constantly re-inventing ourselves, politically, every four years. I lived overseas for 24 years. Twenty of those years were spent in one unbroken period as a U.S. diplomat. I was continually under the gun to explain who we were as a nation and why we did the things we did as a people. You want a tough job? That was a tough job, and if you don't believe me, just ask any contemporary political historian or sociologist.

Fortunately, I managed to de-code many of our official actions by relating them to our Constitution and our Bill of Rights which helped explain the decisions taken by our Supreme Court, for example. That seemed to satisfy them, at least temporarily, but it wasn't enough. I got questions about American interventionism, American expansionism, American capitalism, racism, gun violence, illiteracy, religion, homophobia, crime, drugs, our perpetual scandals like Nixon's Watergate and Clinton's sexual escapades. The list went on and on.

This year, I'm getting questions about why we don't just grow up and decide if we want to be a left-leaning liberal social democracy like many European countries or some hybrid capitalist-centric right of center thing? What they're really asking is, "After nearly 240 years shouldn't you know who you are, what you want and how you're going to go about getting it?" If you think about it seriously, you'll have to admit that it's a reasonable question.

Haven't we figured the whole thing out yet? Don't we know ourselves and our history well enough to be able to decide which path we want to follow: for business, for governance and for our society at large? Do we want to respect the rights of the individual above all else, adhering to the letter of the Constitution, or are we willing to trade some of them away in order to secure the rights of the collective?

If you look at the disharmony among American voters and their dissatisfaction with our country - that cuts across ideological and political party lines - you'll have to conclude that we can't find a balance. There may be many reasons, but some smarter people than I believe that America suffers from a social construction called *ideological schizophrenia*, but it might be that the truth lies closer to something called, *Multiple Personality Disorder* which is an abnormal condition in which the personality becomes so fragmented that some of the various parts cannot even communicate with each other.

If we take two simple things like *governance* and *leadership,* there is no way we can compare their current definition and practical application to those of yesterday when our Founding Fathers were cobbling together our Constitution. Their dreams of a strong republic were based on an unwavering belief that the de-centralization of power would eventually bring about a society worthy of the industry that gave it life. What they hadn't counted on, however, was that successive generations would forget their sacrifices at the hands of an occupying power.

They couldn't envision that future Americans would fall off the ideological wagon and ultimately succumb to their own self-interests. In short, they underestimated just how spoiled we could become and how blasé we could be about what Alexis De Tocqueville called, "The Great American Experiment." To my European friends, I must say that it appears we've turned our back on our elders and forgotten that each generation has an irrefutable and undeniable responsibility to the previous one. That is the sacred pact that a free people make with one another in order to secure the future for their heirs. We had better remember that and decide who we want to be soon, lest circumstances decide our identity for us.

~

A night at the comic opera

I forced myself to watch the Republican debate last night on CNN, and I must honestly say that the experience brought me not even a smidgeon closer to picking a favorite candidate. It did, however, make me want to book a trip to *Never-never land West* (Las Vegas) if only to sit in what must be the gaudiest bordello-like theatre anywhere on the planet. I'm speaking of the debate venue, the Venetian Hotel. With all the pre-debate publicity, you would have thought that the event was going to be an indoor bullfight between Spain's most famous matador and its most ferocious bull, but as it turned out it was nothing more than a cheap version of a no-plot Marx brothers film without the laughs.

The cast of characters/candidates were almost caricatures of themselves, courtesy of a mountain of media hype and previous debate performances. The only new things were the questions posed by CNN's grand old man, Wolf Blitzer, and his journalist partners: Hugh Hewett and Dana Bash.

Personally, I was hoping that CNN would have sub-contracted the job out to either Don Rickles or Lewis Black, but all seemed to handle their task reasonably well. I was struck by a couple things, though. First was the absolute woodenness of nearly all the candidates. It was as if 'Poison Ivy' (the eco-terrorist from Batman escapades) had sprayed them all with a dose of *Pompous Powder* and then handed them over to Mr. Spock from Star Trek for a mind meld and an auto-suggestion to *act Presidential*. It appeared to me that each candidate had also pre-selected one of his peers for targeting and had rehearsed an Ann Richards one-liner to deliver at just the right moment (Ann Richards was the Texas Governor who opined at the 1988 Democratic National Convention, "Poor George (Bush). He can't help it. He was born with a silver foot in his mouth."

The questions were definitely stacked to elicit visceral responses from all candidates on how they felt about Donald Trump's positions and his bombastic comments which left me a bit suspicious that a Trump campaign mole might have been on CNN's payroll. What <u>was</u> glaringly different with this debate was the way the candidates pivoted to something totally different almost immediately after being asked a pointed question. It made me think of Charles Durning's portrayal of the Texas Governor in 'The biggest little whorehouse in Texas' as he danced the Texas *side step* around every direct question, leaving the reporters dumbfounded.

But this was Las Vegas, after all -- gaming capital of the world, birthplace of sleight of hand, card-palming and misdirection -- so I guess that we all got what we came for, a king size combination of a kindergarten free-for-all and a game of sandlot baseball where everybody asked Wolf Blitzer to "pick me, pick me, so that I can speak!"

One and a half-hours of one-upmanship, interruptions, Donald Trump's childish grimaces and gross generalities later and I was fast asleep, so I missed the last 30 minutes of the debate and the closing statements. I'm betting that even if I <u>had</u> stayed awake it wouldn't have made a dime's worth of difference. THIS debate moved the Republicans one step closer to permanent exhibition status at Madame Tussaud's wax museum.

~

Are Presidential debates passé?

Americans have been watching their Presidential candidates debate each other for over a couple centuries and while some debates have provided a fair amount of illumination, more of them have, at least lately, been generating more heat than light.

I watched all of them, including the Vice-Presidential debates, for the last three Presidential cycles and feel supremely qualified as a layman to give you my honest assessment of their usefulness. Are you ready? Drum roll, please....near zero usefulness, unless of course you are a masochist. Before I go into the details, let's look at America. We're DIVIDED along very clear ideological lines. The Right wants to stimulate the pockets of wealthy capitalists and let the wealth trickle down. In contrast, the Left wants to take the wealthy capitalists' money and forcibly spread it around like manure on an Iowa cornfield in the hopes it will bring in a bumper crop.

The great American gap is even wider at the education, ethnicity and gender levels. We've become an incredibly ignorant populace, pitifully unaware and unconcerned about our own history (and the reasons for it). Our higher education system and its professors are heavily politically biased, and we're busy turning out new versions of old hippies from the 60s but with highly advanced social media skills that would be the envy of every old radical. Many of our graduates have little or no knowledge of America's grand experiment, and absent that knowledge, they don't have a prayer of understanding how to preserve it or improve it. Our ethnic and racial divide is greater now than at any time during the last two-three decades, despite having elected our first half-Black President eight years ago.

We are no closer to understanding what it's like to be a young Black man in inner-city America than a young Black man has at identifying with a financially-strapped White middle class suburban dweller. We don't travel in each other's circles and we don't speak each other's languages. Most Whites don't have Black friends and most Blacks don't have White friends and neither of them have many if any Hispanic friends. We stick to our own 'tribes' and our own private space and don't venture forth into the confusing *foreign* territory of those different from ourselves.

On gender and religious freedom issues we're really confused. To abort or not or to abort, to allow abortion in the third trimester when a fetus can survive outside the womb or to even allow fathers of these vulnerable human beings any influence in the decision-making? To embrace or condone homosexual marriage or to accord the Federal government the right to force religious organizations or the owners of private companies to pay for contraception for their employees? Have we reached the point where it's acceptable and even advisable for women to subordinate their personhood in favor of their gender and be used as pawns or objectified and made the victims in a phony war on women promoted by the Left for the sole purpose of getting a woman elected President?

That, ladies and gentlemen, is the divide that is playing itself out in our Presidential debates along with the other fabricated wars between the rich and the poor, race against race and the educated against the uneducated. Americans have finally been de-personalized and reduced to pure demographic sub-groups by the campaigns. We are no longer a nation made stronger by our diversity, but one divided by it. And that's why the debate formats are no longer relevant because the issues are too complex and too important to be debated in ways that only promote the sensationalizing of our differences and forcing these questions to be answered in two-minute segments.

Instead of moderated debates, which have proven to be prime time platforms for partisan moderators asking salacious tabloid questions, we need to move towards a conversational format where the topics are announced by a non-questioner facilitator. We need to let the candidates talk with one another, uninterrupted and uncensored, with a strict timed cutoff for each topic. Unless these changes are made to the way we assess our candidates, we will not get the truth about them or understand their views. There is an old saying that, "the camera doesn't lie." Now it's time to put it to the test... without the interference of biased moderators who happily place their thumbs on the scale.

~

As much fun as giving blood

The first of three 2016 Presidential debates is now history, and as a spectator, I have to say that it was about as much fun as giving blood. No one won tonight. Instead, everyone lost, as both candidates proved once again that neither one of them is supremely qualified to sit behind the Resolute Desk and be Commander-in-Chief of the world's top superpower. The 90-minute debate revealed no secrets, uncovered no new weaknesses, nor did it give any voter any reason to believe that by electing either one of them that America will be any closer to solving its most pressing problems. Instead, it only reinforced the notions that Hillary

Clinton or Donald Trump supporters already had about their candidates. It has been said that there is only a small sliver of undecided voters left to sway because most voters have already made their choice. This leaves the debate as providing only entertainment value to voters. On that score, it came up short as well. It was more welterweight than heavyweight fight with no knock-out punches finding their target. The redoubtable manager from 'Rocky' would have said, "That's OK, champ, we was jes toyin' with her." If both candidates lost, then the question becomes, "Who lost the least?"

The answer to that depends on what you were hoping to see from the encounter. As a traditional debate, Clinton probably scored more points, but the average person might have viewed it, differently. Street fighters would have definitely given Trump the nod. Here's how I scored the debate: Hillary Clinton succeeded at showing us that she studied for her 'exam' and that she's really good at memorizing and repeating talking points, but this we already knew as she is a product of the rote school of government. Her stature and stage presence was heavily scripted, controlled and stable throughout the debate.

Her tone was supercilious as if she were flying a few thousand feet above her rival and looking down on him. Her body language gave away nothing and she made no eye contact with Mr. Trump. She was focused and disciplined in her responses though she pivoted away from them when necessary to land a few pre-arranged blows on Mr. Trump's finances, on his attitudes towards women and his 'racist' tendencies. She was not friendly nor was she forgiving. She was, quite simply, herself. Mr. Trump, on the other hand, was unscripted and sounded like the final exam (the debate) was just a pop quiz and responded to Mrs. Clinton's taunts in predictable Trumpian fashion with rambling disconnected sentences.

In short, he took Mrs. Clinton's bait and she played out the line until it was time to set the hook which she did (and often), releasing him only to hook him again. Trump was repetitious and meandering, calm but probably seething beneath the surface. While his eye contact with Mrs. Clinton was frequent, it was cold like the eyes of an inanimate alabaster statue in a museum. His command of the issues was uninspiring, choosing, instead, to stay on the periphery. The few times he ventured forth into the no-man's land of details, he quickly brought himself back to the safety of generalizations.

Their performances were predictable: hers, the consummate politician and his, the seasoned straight-talking businessman. While they showed us nothing new, they did make us realize that this year's election has become the ultimate crap shoot for America. We have only ourselves to blame for elevating two such questionable people to the pinnacle of Presidential candidates. There will be a day of reckoning, and it is November 8th when we must choose between the two. God help us all.

~

Authenticity in politics

Much is being made this year about authenticity in politics. If there ever were a bigger, more glaringly obvious oxymoron, I haven't found it yet. Politics by its very nature is about seduction, salesmanship with a bit of subterfuge thrown in for good measure. I know that the idealists among you will be wanting to banish me from the island for that remark, but hear me out. I've known and worked for a fair number of politicians and top salespeople in my time, and none that I can recall ever once came up to me and asked, "Do you think I'm being authentic enough?" Now just because they didn't say it doesn't necessarily mean they didn't <u>want</u> to say it or thought it.

I get that, but the fact is that politics is first and foremost about getting elected, and even the most well-meaning people will say what other people want to hear once in awhile. That doesn't make them full-blown phonies; it just makes them human (and, of course, politicians).

Take this year's crop of two dozen some odd candidates. At the start, there were 17 Republicans, 5 Democrats and a couple of Libertarian/independents. Do you really think that any one of them was truly authentic, that they never put on the politician's mask or ever told a lie? Of course not. You're smart and savvy. You can see through the populist fog they create. You know that the truth has many faces and that it is subject to some interpretation. There are facts and then there are the candidates' facts that offer more spin than a high-speed blender. That's been, to quote a current candidate, "the art of the deal" since man first discovered the art of lying.

Let's take that the two front-running candidates: Donald Trump and Hillary Clinton. Some would call them both two-faced. Others would say they're chameleon populists. A third group might just accuse them of being bald-faced liars. And you know what? They're all a little bit right.
Trump has played the high stakes corporate board game for so long that he's actually <u>become</u> his strategy. He's the pragmatist's pragmatist in business and is now segueing into the political arena. Hillary Clinton? Well,

117

we're all familiar with her history of 'creative storytelling' about her *namesake*, Sir Edmund Hillary, the sniper fire landing in Bosnia, the video for Benghazi, her email server, etc., etc.

Despite both candidates' downright fabrications, misspeaks, and selective populist pandering to special interest voters' groups, I would submit that both are authentic in the sense that they know that they're not fooling anyone and that they are not pretending to be anything other than what they are, each and every time they take the stage or rush to make a promise they know they can't keep. The real question is, "What does that make us?" Are we nothing but willing participants in a game of Liar's Poker, trying to guess how many times we're being conned by the other players or does it go deeper than that?

Maybe our society has just gotten so used to being lied to that we have accepted it as the price of admission for living in a modern world. There is another explanation, and it is that we've ceded our vote on whether or not to punish the offenders for their phoniness TO the offenders, and they're in no rush to locate the Sodium Pentothal. It could also be that we have given them tacit permission to act that way because we, too, have embraced the crooked path and see it now as an authentic choice. To quote a famous political strategist friend of mine, "It's easier to meet a virgin teetotaler in Las Vegas than to find an authentic politician." I don't know what that says about virgins, teetotalers or Las Vegas, but it's pretty clear to me that it's not flattering to politicians.

~

Beware of the big dog

I admit that I occasionally saunter down memory lane in my mind, but I sure don't want to re-live the Clinton years of 1993-2000. First, there's the audio of their campaign song - "Don't stop thinking about tomorrow" - that I can't get out of my mind. Next, is Bill Clinton's own achy-breaky voice that is meant to disarm you in an old-timey Southerny sort of way. The visuals are equally as bad with his jagged index finger poking the air like an old Nike Ajax missile leveled straight at you. What I fear most is his return to the White House and the toll it would take on that wonderful residence. After all, it took years to get the house back to its normal state (and return the furniture the Clintons took with them 'by accident'). And now we're going to elect his wife and give him free reign of the place to do what he does best? Folks, it's not *1600 Peccadillo Avenue* we'd be turning over to Arkansas' favorite son; it's the people's house...my house, your house, our house.

Those not worried about a repeat of his sexual shenanigans should consider this: the White House would give him the perfect base of operations to ply his trade of extracting contributions from world leaders for his Clinton Foundation and arranging million dollar speaking engagements for himself. Talk about fox in the hen's house!

His track record with women speaks for itself, and I for one don't want him anywhere near young impressionable women or older wiser women either, especially in the White House. While people my age may have a lower tolerance for that sort of thing, millions of voters were in diapers while Mr. Clinton was trolling for new 'adventures' back then, and these young people don't remember the shame we felt at his bold denials about "...not having sex with that woman, Ms. Lewinsky." Impeachment and the suspension of his law license for lying under oath was too good for him according to some of my female friends. Had they had their way, a *surgical strike* would have been their choice of action.

What amazes me (somewhat) is Mr. Clinton's polling numbers. In a recent Bloomberg poll in November, he still comes away with a 60% favorable rating (34% unfavorable). While the company doesn't say what the age demographic was I'm going to stick my neck out here and guess that it was heavily weighted towards millennials and millennial Democrats. The Republicans I know wouldn't let the man deliver pizzas to their kids' babysitter let alone welcome him back to the White House, so that begs the question: "Will Bill Clinton be an asset or a liability for Hillary Clinton in the campaign?"

A recent exchange between Mrs. Clinton and Donald Trump over some remarks of his that she says are sexist may portend how the Trump people are going to handle a 'Bubba redux' on the campaign trail. It's called, the *glass house defense.* By turning the accusation back on Mrs. Clinton, vis-à-vis her husband's sexual predilections, the Trumpians will re-open the door to Mr. Clinton's skeleton-filled closet that has been boarded up for years and marked, "Closed for Rehabilitation." I'm hoping that Mrs. Clinton will be asked some very straightforward questions about her prosecution of the 'war on women' and the hypocrisy she owns for condoning her husband's behavior and mounting a hit squad (back then) to stifle the 'bimbo eruptions' caused by her wandering Bill.

I also want her to answer questions about a possible conflict of interest with the Clinton Foundation while she was Secretary of State as well as her penchant for prevarication. Maybe then we can get down to the business of flushing out the truth about her positions on a range of issues.

If that's not possible, then I hereby give my proxy to Donald Trump to take off the gloves and mix it up...with both of them. If nothing else it will be fun to watch.

~

Black and White Facts Matter

Democrats are gearing up their message machine to convince America's African-Americans that they have their backs, that only the Democratic Party can give them a path to prosperity and that a vote for Hillary Clinton will ensure it. There's only one problem with that, and it is that the Democratic Party has consistently failed Blacks in America, right down the line. Students of history know that it took nearly an act of God to convince Democrat legislators to vote for Civil Rights legislation in the 60s.

Since then, Democrats have failed to capitalize on the promise of that legislation. They have not worked well enough or often enough with Republican Presidents or with Republican Congresses to put into place meaningful Government programs that would create sustainable well-paying jobs for Blacks.

Instead, they have consistently fought for entitlement programs that would lock them in place in an unbreakable cycle of government dependency rather than give them a helping hand up to the middle class. To add insult to injury, the Obama Administration has done precious little in nearly eight long years to address the growing divide among the races in America. Some even say that the President has squandered a once in a lifetime opportunity and has actually made things worse. History will decide.

Question: What do Blacks really want? Answer: The same things that all of the rest of us want: safe communities and adequate housing, a good education for their children, gainful employment, a path to upward mobility, an equal voice in decision-making and respect. Given our common aspirations, why, then, is there such a disconnect between the average Black voter and the Republican Party and their allegiance to the Democrats?

That answer is also simple. It's because the Republican Party has not presented a sufficiently convincing case for the things it believes in AND it has not engaged the Black community where it lives.

A few speeches to the NAACP and occasional visits to Black churches won't win the day with Black voters. Only a concerted effort to visit the inner cities and engage its leaders and ordinary citizens in an on-going dialogue about their issues and challenges will help to spread the Republican message of inclusiveness. Black Americans must be made to understand that the Republican message is <u>America's message and their message</u>.

It is one that's rooted in the individual - based on an unwavering belief in personal independence, personal freedom, personal empowerment, personal accountability and equal opportunity through equal access to education and jobs under an economic system that rewards initiative.

If we are to make any progress, we must move beyond mere messaging to a facts-based discussion on the persistent problems that face Black America. The facts are within everyone's reach and speak volumes, but not to everyone. This is especially true for Blacks themselves who often feel demeaned by them or feel that they are only cited to place the blame solely on their shoulders. There is absolutely no question that an intensified dialogue is needed and that it must shift into high gear and soon, otherwise we are bound to see increased desperation among Blacks, many of whom have already lost all faith in their government and its leaders.

It is, therefore, no surprise that we are witnessing the rise of Black activism and demonstrations from organizations like 'Black Lives Matter' much of which is due to a widespread perception that 'White-dominated' institutions like law enforcement and the courts are to blame for the Black community's plight. Closing the racial divide on a social level will take considerably more time than improving the economic one, which is why we cannot wait for the next Administration to do something. We need a racial reality check by both Presidential campaigns before a single Black vote is cast. Only then will the Black community have a chance to see which candidate and more importantly, which Party, is willing and able to help it tackle their problems. Voting by tradition is not the answer.

~

Blackboard jungle warfare?

While watching the Sunday morning political shows and listening to the pollsters go on and on about demographic groups, I detected that <u>education</u> was a key factor (at least this week) in the media's choice of a theme to use to support *their* candidate, Mrs. Clinton. Whether this is just their latest attempt to promote the narrative that stupid people vote for Trump while smart people for Clinton, I don't know, but I suspect it has more than a little to do with helping the Clinton campaign firm up its 'educated voter' demographic.

The polls seem to indicate that the better educated voters (both men and women) prefer Mrs. Clinton to Mr. Trump while the lesser-educated voters (especially men), side with Mr. Trump.

Here are a few facts. According to U.S. Census data, there are about 209 million Americans over the age of 25 and nearly 67 million of them have a college degree. That means that 70% of them (142 million) don't have a college degree. Both Donald Trump and Hillary Clinton would like to move all of them over to their respective columns, but it seems right now that Mrs. Clinton cares more about wooing the better educated to her camp.

Voter gender and education according to the Pew Research Center

MEN - Men are divided in their party loyalty (roughly 44% are Democrats and 43% are Republicans) except when it comes to married men. Here, Republicans lead with 51% to the Democrats' 38%. Republicans have an edge when it comes to White males with 49% versus 40% for Democrats. Among Black men (and women), the Democrats hold an overall 80% to 11% advantage over Republicans.

WOMEN - Married women are equally divided as to their party loyalty at 44%. Unmarried women are clearly in the Democrats' camp by 57% to the Republicans' 29%.

EDUCATION - Democrats hold an overall advantage when it comes to college-educated voters by 49% to the Republicans' 42%. The figure for those having post-graduate degrees and leaning Democrat is higher for both men and women at 57% to the Republicans' 35%. (The figure is even higher for women holding those degrees; it's 64% to the Republicans' 29%.)

Facts from the Presidential Election of 2012

- In the Presidential election of 2012, 133 million people voted. That represented an increase of 1.8 million people from the number that voted in 2008.

- In 2012, the voting percentages by age group were: 45% for 18-29 year-olds, 59.5% for 30-44 year-olds, 67.9% for 45-64 year-olds and 72% for 65 and older.

- In 2012, there was a net decrease of 1.8 million youth voters' votes. The number of votes from 30-44 years-old also decreased by 1.7 million.

- In 2012, 20.5 million votes were cast by voters between the ages of 18-29; voters 30-44 years-old cast 30.8 million votes; voters 45-64 years-old cast 52 million votes and those over 65 years-old cast 29.6 million votes.
- In 2012, women voters cast 4% more votes than men. Women voters, 18-29 years-old, have outpaced men in their voting percentage since 1996, hitting their peak at 8% in 2008. The reverse is true for older (65+) female voters who, since 1996, have continued to lag behind male voters. In 2012, their rate was 3.7% more votes.

Is there a war on education?

It appears from all the campaign rhetoric that the Democrats are engaging in what can only be called a demographic war, aiming to pit educated against lesser-educated Americans by tapping into the *education prejudice* of the elite ruling class. To me, this is an extension and deepening of the political elitist/establishment versus outsider war that has characterized both campaigns for the past few months. Some may even call it a *managed civil war* using education as a weapon of mass division.

It's easy to muster support for better and more education opportunities for all Americans. Unfortunately, those calls to action are usually made by the educated elite and can arouse more than a little suspicion among the demographic they're designed to help. Often, the call for more opportunity can be viewed as condescending and even patronizing. Both the Clinton and Trump campaigns have voter bases that encompass many different demographics. One of them is the educated voter. A significant portion of Clinton's base is the educated elite, who all have 'accredited knowledge' as a common link.

As graduates of the halls of ivy, they know better <u>because they've been taught that - told that they know better</u> - and they have the diplomas to prove it. In some cases, they have huge student loan debt that will take years to pay off. That's why Mrs. Clinton is making her 'free college tuition' pitch so loudly. She knows it will be hard to counter it because everybody wants a well-educated populace and because it hits home with two important demographic groups: youth voters and their parents.

Trump, on the other hand, is appealing to the bedrock, American voter that has come up from the ranks from the 'school of hard knocks,' is street smart and in many cases is self-made. These voters have watched how the left-leaning ideology of elite ruling class Democrat government officials and bureaucrats has kept them from the inner circle of influence. They are hoping that Trump will reward their loyalty by returning the U.S. to a true meritocracy and wrest power from an entrenched, academic, top-down governance model.

This is definitely not the time to pit yet another demographic group against another. We've already had enough divide-and-conquer politics this year. A sheepskin on a wall is not proof of wisdom and should not be the litmus test for entering the arena of power or influence...neither should it be ignored altogether. Well-educated or not, we all should heed the master carpenter's advice when it comes to choosing our candidates, "measure twice, cut once."

~

Bush vs. Gore once more?

Sixty-two days. That's all that's left before we know if we've elected a seasoned political operative or a professional outlier as President. If you listen to the mainstream media and especially the patron saint of America's Left, Amy Goodman, of National Public Radio's *Democracy Now*, you would believe that Donald Trump is a combination of Genghis Khan, Vlad the Impaler and Dr. Strangelove and that Hillary Clinton is channeling Joan of Arc, Harriet Tubman and Mother Theresa. Both characterizations are wrong, of course, but that doesn't stop the anti-Trump forces from proffering doomsday scenarios if Trump is elected.

"America will totally disintegrate. We'll have race riots and economic ruin and become a police state. He'll create international chaos. The stock market will collapse and our country's image abroad will suffer a deadly blow. No one will ever take us seriously again." And on and on it goes. The anti-Clinton forces, too, (especially the Super PACs), are in 'take-no-prisoners mode' and are pulling out all the stops to convince us that she's sick, weak, untrustworthy and downright malevolent.

This is more than just politics. This is all out political thermonuclear war, and we are all at ground zero. We've entered a bottomless black hole where no light or truth can live. Some will say that our only way out of that hole is to reject both major party candidates and elect a true *Third Way* candidate like Gary Johnson or write in Bernie Sanders' name on the ballot. I don't mind telling you that the prospect of having either one of those characters sitting in the Oval Office scares the stuffing out of me in a way that Trump and Clinton don't. I would agree, however, that America could benefit from having a new major political party that represented those of us that espouse a more center right conservative approach bordering on the Libertarian, as the way forward.

Considering that most of America has probably already decided who they're going to vote for, the die is probably cast on the popular vote, unless, of course, an 'October surprise' finds its way into the race. The question is, would anything sway the committed Hillary or Trump voter from voting for their candidate at this point? I don't think so. America is dug in. It will stand by its man/woman no matter what, and if that is true, we will, most certainly, see another Bush vs. Gore cage match in our immediate future.

Why? Because popular votes don't elect our President. Electoral votes do, and this is the hypocrisy of our system that denies us a true 'one man one vote' election. There have been three times in our history where one candidate won the popular vote and the other the electoral votes. One of those was the 2000 election. While there's good reason to believe at this point that Mrs. Clinton has the electoral vote advantage due to the high numbers of Democrats living in high electoral vote states, something could happen in the waning days of the campaign to change all that and create a jump ball for the swing states which could tip the balance.

If Mr. Trump really wants to win this election he'll have to capture all the states that Mitt Romney won in 2012 plus carry Ohio, Florida, Nevada, maybe Colorado, one ten-electoral vote Midwestern state and/or Virginia. That is an uphill path for Mr. Trump, but the race is already tightening and if it keeps up we could very well see a repeat of Bush vs. Gore play out two months from now. I don't know about you, but I don't have the energy for another cliff-hanger vote count, nor do I want our Supreme Court involved, especially the current one. That's why I hope for a huge voter turnout and a massive win on November 8th.

~

Conventional wisdom in an unconventional election

As a political analyst, I must confess that this Presidential election is baffling on so many levels, not only in terms of the candidates themselves - who certainly didn't come out of central casting - but also for the influence of unusual circumstances (like an FBI criminal investigation). I'm not the only one who's constantly second-guessing his models. Many of my colleagues are collectively scratching and shaking their heads in amazement at the events that are shaping the two campaigns. At this point, it's probably best if I threw out a hypothesis so you know where I'm coming from. Here it is:

Most of the pollsters will be wrong in their predictions. That goes for the punters in Las Vegas as well as the major media outlets and the prognosticators at the Republican National Committee and the Democratic National Committee. That obvious lack of certainty will impact the election because it will 'force' more voters to head for the polling places out of a heightened sense of worry that their candidate will lose if they don't.

Having gone out on that very long limb, let me list the top 20 issues (in no special order) that will motivate those voters:

1. Our leaders have betrayed us by not solving the country's problems
2. America is losing its traditional values and its moral compass
3. We have lost control of our borders
4. Home-grown terrorism is on the rise and government can't stop it
5. The Middle Class has been decimated by government's mismanagement of the economy
6. America will never completely recover its lost jobs from foreign countries or grow enough new ones
7. Our educational system is a mess
8. America's minorities are 'hyphenating' their allegiance to the USA
9. Race relations are worse now than eight years ago
10. Our tax system is in bad shape and is preventing the growth of small business
11. Gender and generational conflicts are being used by politicians to divide us
12. Life in our inner cities is worsening
13. Violent crime is claiming more innocent victims
14. Our new heathcare system is failing to deliver on the Administration's promises
15. America's energy policy does not reflect its true resources
16. We have no coherent, cost-effective, environmental protection policy
17. We are over-regulated on all levels
18. Our Supreme Court is too politicized and not focused on Constitutional arguments
19. We have lost faith and confidence in our institutions
20. We feel disrespected around the world

I'm sure we could add another 20 or more items to that list, but those are the big issues of concern to most Americans this election cycle. As of this writing, we have a little over four months to go before we vote for either Hillary Clinton or Donald Trump. Never before have two Presidential candidates been so different in their approach to issues, campaigning, public statements and their speaking styles than Clinton and Trump. Both, however, have much in common. Each represents an 'establishment' (Hillary Clinton – professional politicians and the Washington elite and Donald Trump – big business).

Both have high untrustworthiness ratings among their own constituents and among opposition voters. Both are nearly 70 years old and are grandparents. Both are 'East Coasters' living in New York State (though Mrs. Clinton comes to New York via Illinois, Arkansas and WASHDC) and both grew up in privileged homes. What is unconventional is the paths each took to bring them to this point.

Donald Trump parlayed a million dollar loan from his father to amass a huge personal fortune through shrewd real estate deals and kept his wealth by taking liberal advantage of our country's bankruptcy laws. Clinton married early after college and rode her husband's coat tails to the Governor's Office and finally to the Presidency. Then she parlayed name recognition and a change of address to win a Senate seat and later, in 2008, used her Washington insider status and failed Presidential campaign to secure a cabinet position while her husband was busy raking in money for the family's foundation. Those are the facts.

During the next few months, we will experience a true clash of titans, an epic struggle for the 12-15% of America's voters that will make the all-important popular vote difference.

The problem is that popular votes alone don't win Presidential elections; electoral votes do. The conventional wisdom would have us believe that the Democrats hold the electoral vote advantage with their bi-coastal and Midwest Blue State coalition (with Pennsylvania and a few swing states thrown in for good measure). They may be right...but there is also the distinct possibility that they are overly optimistic, especially in a year where a 'Third Way' candidate like Donald Trump can bring a sizable number of angry, dissatisfied voters out of the woodwork to challenge the conventional wisdom and the odds-makers. Watch carefully how the events of the next few months play out.

Remember, Ronald Reagan was behind in the polls just a few weeks before the election when in the final debate with Jimmy Carter he turned to President Carter and said, "There you go again," and we all remember how that turned out.

~

Crossing the Rubi(o)con

The worst thing that people used to say about American politics was that it was a blood sport. And while that description may still be true, it doesn't tell us everything about how the game is being played in 2016 and how much blood will be spilt. In fact, there's probably no one single phrase that can adequately capture the interplay between the Republican candidates as they slash and burn their way towards winning the most serious job in our land.

After last week's debate in Texas and the subsequent antics of two candidates in particular, we can now say that we have finally crossed the Rubi(o)con, that once inviolable line between bad taste and worse taste. I'm speaking of the puerile name-calling and the acting-out of grown men on a national stage in front of millions of prospective voters.

Some of the exchanges between Donald Trump and Marco Rubio dealt with body parts/accessories like big ears, small hands, bouffant hair, spray tans and bodily functions like profuse sweating and uncontrollable bladders. After awhile, I thought I had accidentally switched channels and was listening to Dr. Sanjay Gupta wax medical about anatomical anomalies. The other possibility was that I had been transported back to my grade school play yard when 'Knuckle-Job Jimmy' was threatening to steal my milk money while taunting me with pointed accusations about my boy/manhood.

Unfortunately, it was real, a battle of the insult titans, who succeeded in clipping the barbed wire of the 'No Trespassing' sign and entered a political minefield from which no one returns unscathed. At a time when every precious second counts, these two top Republican candidates chose to waste a golden opportunity to communicate with us. Instead, they chose performance art. I don't know where these childish barbs rank on the scale of political tactics, but I do know where they rank on the 'discomfort meter.' They are off the chart for most of us. And while I understand the need to raise one's profile and/or electability in voters' minds right before Super Tuesday primaries where 595 delegates are at stake, I still can't wrap my mind around a candidate like Marco Rubio who

128

spent the last few months trying to assure us that he was the 'adult in the room' only to see him go from kindly Dr. Jekyll to evil Mr. Hyde in the time it takes to say, "Your mother wears combat boots."

I expected Donald Trump to ratchet up his ad hominem attacks, because that's his modus operandi -- crush or be crushed and let the devil take the hindmost. But to see kindly Marco Rubio as a serial besmircher? It does not compute. Someone must have given him a popularity poll that showed him trailing Trump badly and on a trajectory to lose his home state of Florida. I can't think of any other reason for such an abrupt tactical switch.

Our 180 degree turn away from serious discourse signals the end of an era. We have now become Uncle Remus' impatient *Br'er Rabbit* who demanded civility from the *Tar-Baby*, and when he didn't get it, punched him, got stuck in the gooey stuff and was eventually thrown into the briar patch by *Br'er Fox* who left him for dead. I hope that our 'Br'er Rabbit' of civil political discourse learns his lesson and manages to leave the thorny thicket of personal attack politics and lives to fight (more wisely) another day.

~

Democrat love letter eulogy

Day three of the Dems' convention was a showcase for two politicians on their way out the door: Barack Obama and Joe Biden. In his speech, President Barack Obama showed all of us once again that he never met a stage he didn't like. His speech was a Mulligan stew of ingredients, including a healthy dose of self-approbation for his own tenure as President in which he used all the familiar buzz words of his previous campaigns like *audacity* and *hope and change* and *yes, we can*. These were catnip for Democrats to remind them of who's still in charge and what they owe the egotist-in-chief who this evening was more concerned about maximizing his face time with the American people than with elevating Mrs. Clinton to a seat next to him on Mount Olympus.

We witnessed yet another vintage Obama performance tonight as our Orator Laureate delivered a great speech that was designed to burnish his own record and secure his place in history. Fortunately for him, all his self-congratulatory prose was loaded onto his indispensible electronic friend, that rhetoric prosthetic, the teleprompter. We have come to know our President not only as a great speechmaker, but also as a performer and entertainer who never turned down an opportunity to stand in the spotlight and be adored.

Tonight was no different. Looking like the world's problems were squarely on his shoulders (unlike his other frequent TV performances on Jimmy Kimmel, etc.) and exuding a practiced seriousness with his trademark upward-turned jaw and steely gaze, he proceeded to talk about an America that only exists in the minds of his sycophants and speechwriters. Predictably, Donald Trump was portrayed as dangerous and seriously out-of-touch with the 'real' America of Barack Obama and Hillary Clinton, but then that's what we expected of the President... yet another fanciful flight from reality. Otherwise, how could he make the claim that there's nothing wrong with America that a little togetherness can't fix?

And how could he have the temerity to equate Mrs. Clinton's attendance record with a list of *accomplishments* that qualify her for his job? Precisely. <u>She is every bit as unqualified to be President now as she was in 2008. Perhaps more.</u>

The TV cameras whirred and the teleprompter did its duty, faithfully rolling out all the crowd-pleasing words on each of the three plastic screens before Mr. Obama who has come to depend on it like a man with an incurable addiction. Indeed, the teleprompter may have earned itself a coveted place in the annals of political history as it has turned ordinary men into oratorical giants and saved the bacon of others who couldn't put together a coherent sentence with duct tape. So day three was the big build-up for the acceptance speech of the first woman nominee for President. President Obama, Vice-President Biden and Vice-Presidential candidate Tim Kaine all collaborated to set her table, carefully arranging the flowers and making sure the Presidential silverware was polished and ready for her speech on Thursday.

While the final hand has been dealt in this, the final game of the Dems' poker tournament, there is still one Joker outstanding and it's the yet undisclosed emails purported to be held by Wikileaks' founder Julian Assange. Will they be released before Mrs. Clinton's big moment or will Assange play Texas Hold'em and save them for another date? Either way, the Dems deserve their moment with their candidate. Let them have it. There will be plenty of time for dirty politics next week and on until November 8th.

~

Dewey vs Truman, Goldwater vs Johnson or Bush vs Gore?

If history really does repeat itself, which part of history will repeat itself in 2016? Will we see a clash à la Thomas Dewey versus Harry Truman (1948), a redux of Barry Goldwater against Lyndon Johnson (1964) or a Bush vs Gore (2000)? I'm betting we'll see all three in some shape or form but with the same two 2016 candidates. Here are my predictions...

Donald Trump (DT) will survive the Republican Convention nomination process to become the Republican Party's candidate for President. Hillary Clinton (HC) will easily sweep the Democratic Party's votes to become their standard-bearer. Judging by the primary campaigns, the general election campaigns will look something like this: Trump will accuse HC of being a liar and will focus primarily on her 'blame it on the video' and Benghazi failure to protect the lives of four Americans.

He will also reach back in time for other highlights of now famous HC lies. He will paint her as a total political animal that will say anything and do anything to further her own career, case in point her choice to set up her own private email server so as to protect her own personal communication. Assuming she brings up his 'misogynistic' comments, he will counter with her record in the State Department of not calling out countries with bad human rights records for their abuse of women AND point to her foundation's acceptance of millions of dollars in contributions from those same countries. Pushed, he may even point to her actions in defending her philandering husband by setting up a 'Bimbo Attack Squad' which character-assassinated the VOB - victims of Bill.

DT will call into question HC's judgment, citing the above incidents, and will call attention to her lack of actual management experience. Should she retort that she was 'CEO' of the State Department, he will respond by saying, "How did that work out for you? You never fired one person in connection with the Benghazi debacle?" He will also pick up the Carly Fiorina line about her being the most traveled Secretary of State by stating that, "Travel isn't an accomplishment."

Finally, to counteract her alliance with and loyalty to the Obama Administration, he will play the populist/hypocrite card. He will accuse her of pandering to special interest groups like Blacks and Hispanics to pump up her vote by falsifying the record of the Obama Administration, of which she was an integral part. He will point to America's anemic economy, the median income drop, the $19 trillion national debt, the dramatic chronic unemployment rate among African-Americans and their feeling of helplessness and hopelessness which has led to a breakdown of respect for authority and the rise of racial animus.

Hillary Clinton will launch a multi-front, multiple-demographic campaign against DT that will include: a relentless attack on him for being a woman-hater, a minority-hater, an immigrant-hater and, in general, being a bully. She will use his own words against him, taken from rallies and debates and media interviews. On the economy and his contention that he is a successful businessman, she will bring up his four corporate bankruptcies and question if his success should be measured in the number of failures he's had. On the military and America's security, she will stress her close contact with the joint chiefs and with the SECDEF and her many visits to 'war-torn' areas and ask DT when he last visited the troops or had a meeting in the Situation Room. HC will try to rattle his composure by simply hitting him where it hurts...between the lips.

She will use her superior rhetorical speaking ability to help him dig a hole for himself where he can put all of his generalities (the only thing anybody in America has heard from him on any subject)! Finally, for the coup de grâce, HC will take a page from the Lyndon Johnson playbook and portray DT (as Johnson portrayed Goldwater in the famous "Daisy Girl" ad) as an unstable person whose finger must never be allowed near the 'red button.' The original ad against Goldwater only aired once on Sept. 7, 1964 and featured President Johnson's voice saying, "These are the stakes, to make a world in which all of God's children can live, or to go into the dark. We must either love each other, or we must die."

Bloodied and browbeaten, both candidates will await the outcome of the election on Tuesday, November 8th. It could very well end in a Dewey/Trumanesque manner where the conventional wisdom of the pollsters and the pundits will not prevail. Indeed, the 2016 polls could be wrong as they were on September 24, 1948 just six weeks before the election when Gallup had Dewey up by 8.5 points. The problem then, as it could be this November, was that the mood of the country was changing daily, almost hourly. After the Truman win, Gallup and Roper did an analysis of the votes and found that one of out seven voters made up their minds in the last two weeks of the election. If that is the case this year, stay glued to the TV, because it won't be over until it's over. Remember Bush vs Gore?

~

Dinner table warfare

I attended a pretty fancy dinner the other evening with some pretty high-powered government, academic and business people. I was prepared to be diplomatic and low-key and focus on non-confrontational, non-political topics. Things went fairly well for the first half of the evening, but as my fellow diners relaxed after consuming their entrees, the topic of conversation suddenly switched to local and national politics.

Never one to shy away from an exciting and stimulating conversation, I decided to dive into the shallow end of the 'pool' and make a few, what I thought were innocent comments, about American politics. Given the state of our polarized and partisan political climate, people were cautious in venturing their honest opinions. However, after a few minutes, calm gave way to a gathering storm which was preceded by a few *trigger words*. You know the kind I mean, like *Russia, special prosecutor, sanctuary cities, illegal immigration,* etc.

Suddenly, you could see the battle lines being drawn, and our small table (one of three) was sharply divided and showed it. I can't say I was shocked, but I was a bit surprised that the gloves had come off so quickly. While watching the parrying and thrusting take place I couldn't help but think that at this very moment hundreds of thousands of dinners like this one were taking place - in barbecue joints, food courts and in five-star restaurants across the country.

I imagined the temperature heating up as America's most challenging problems were being hotly debated by passionate citizens as they wolfed down their burgers and beef Wellington, risking the need for the Heimlich Method. "This can't be happening at my table," I thought. But happening it was. All that was missing was a unanimous Congressional declaration of dinner table war. Normally, a voice of reason would emerge and break the tension with a joke or an attempt to change the subject to a less incendiary one. This never happened. One topic did gain traction, however.

It started with a statement by a university professor who mentioned that her daughter was attending a very expensive college and she had shelled out $64K/year to keep her there. She said, "In Europe all higher education is free and that's the way it should be here in the USA." I couldn't hold my tongue. I said, "Why should I have to share the cost of your personal financial decision to send your daughter to a prestigious university?

What if I were a childless, middle-aged, single man (and taxpayer) and didn't want to pay for somebody else's children's education? We're not Europe."

Predictably, the "You didn't build that" argument was thrown on the table and my fellow diner said, "We all stand on the shoulders of everyone else and we are all one big community. What helps one helps the other." I gulped and collected myself. I told her that there was an element of truth in her statement - that we all benefited from the good deeds of others and the investments of their families. I then countered with a question, "If that is the case, and I am helping pay her tuition, shouldn't I be entitled to some of her future earnings?" After hearing that, she suddenly went silent and the topic did, too.

I managed to overhear a bit of the talk at the other tables. It was rising and falling, but thankfully, the dinner was coming to a close and the discussion was moving to what writers call a denouement (a wrapping up). On my way home, I played out the scenes in my mind and thought about how our divisive politics has now intruded into almost every aspect of our personal lives. Things like simple dinners have now become emotionally-charged events and even the most innocent conversations have become mine-strewn battlefields just waiting for an unsuspecting foot (or word) to set them off. I'm afraid that fate has dealt us a bad hand and there isn't much we can all do to stop its escalation, so I have made a personal decision...I'm going to stop eating and maybe you should, too.

~

Embarrassment of riches versus party of paucity

The Republican Party's presidential wannabes need to stop wasting their buckshot on skirmishes with each other and focus on the real issue that could get them nominated. I'm speaking of the 'embarrassment of riches' Republican field of nine outstanding candidates compared with the paucity of only three candidates for the Democrats. Nothing points up the differences in the depth, breadth and character of the two political parties more this year than who each has actually brought to the party.

The number of candidates that have thrown their hats in the pre-primary ring is actually a direct reflection of the willingness of the parties to accept divergent views and diversity of personalities. The Republican National Committee (RNC) has shown it is unafraid to let its hair down and leave its thumb off the scale so that any and all comers could stand up and show themselves as yet another public face of the Republican Party. Such a no-fear attitude is testimony to the party's self-confidence, despite its loss in the Presidential contest of 2012 where the pre-primary field was also large.

Some critics would say that the Rs have trouble distinguishing between doing what's necessary to win and their fidelity to principals. Still others would posit that they are too ready to fall on the sword of their own convictions and would defend a public display of their internal differences even if it means losing races. Both could be partially right, but what does that mean for the Republicans' chances of taking the brass ring of the presidency this time round in 2016?

To answer that, let's look at that embarrassment of riches to see how an imaginary cabinet might stack up comprised of the Rs' candidates: Secretary of State, Carly Fiorina; Secretary of the Treasury, John Kasich; Secretary of Homeland Security, Marco Rubio; Secretary of Defense, Ted Cruz; Secretary of Commerce, Jeb Bush; Secretary of Education Secretary of Health and Human Services, Dr. Ben Carson; Secretary of Health and Human Services, Rand Paul; Attorney General, Chris Christie, Chief of Staff and the list goes on.

All could assume their new roles, get quickly up to speed and be assured the support of the electorate. For the Democrats, the imaginary cabinet is even more difficult because of the paucity of current candidates (Hillary Clinton, Bernie Sanders and Martin O'Malley). The Democrat field stands in stark contrast to the Republicans' because many potential Dem candidates have been put off by the ideological rigidity of the Democratic National Committee (DNC) and its unbending view that a candidate must not only be chosen on the basis of strict adherence to Democratic Party principles but also must fit the mold of the right ethnicity or gender...or be the 'next in line.'

So far, Republicans have not seized the day and maximized their opportunities on or off the debate stage. None have called out the thin field of Democrat candidates on their views or the DNC's reasons for offering Americans such *weak tea*. While concentrating their fire on Americans' fear and anger they have totally ignored the supremely clear path for criticizing the Democrats: their pitifully small field; their eagerness to pre-ordain Hillary Clinton (and thereby stifle open debate); and for being a party that prefers a no dissent, lock-step, Primary march to lock up its nominee. This suppression of openness and subordination of the desire to seek a public consensus on who should represent the party should be worrisome to the Democrats, but apparently, it isn't for whatever reason.

This leaves a gaping hole in their credibility and one that Republican candidates need to exploit if they are to move past their internecine disputes and gain traction as a whole. The candidate that rises above his own talking points and redirects his aim away from his own competition and towards the Dems' Achilles heel will ultimately gain in the polls.

~

Fifth column attack by the fourth estate?

Jan Erik-Olsson robbed a bank in Stockholm, Sweden, back in the 70s and held a few people hostage. The hostages thought they were going to die and formed a kind of 'traumatic bond' with their captors and even defended them after they were released AND refused to testify against them in court! That gave us what is now called, 'Stockholm Syndrome' (it was first called 'Norrmalmstorgssyndromet' after the address of the bank).

In the U.S., we got a closer look at this attachment when Patty Hearst, the Hearst newspaper heiress, was kidnapped by the Symbionese Liberation Army and later forced (or persuaded) to rob the Hibernia Bank in San Francisco on April 15, 1974. A year later, she was captured and shocked everyone with her story about being brainwashed by her captors.

She went to trial, and the prosecution said that she was, "a rebel in search of a cause" while her attorney, F. Lee Bailey, maintained she was coerced to commit the crime after extensive mental browbeating. Hers was a story perfect for the media which lapped it up and served it piping hot to TV and print audiences for nearly a year. On March 20, 1976, Hearst was convicted of bank robbery (a Federal crime) and use of a firearm in the commission of a felony and got a 35-year sentence. So much for the brainwashing defense.

The story doesn't end there, though. Thanks to our old pal, President Jimmy Carter, Hearst's sentence was commuted to the 22 months she had served, and she was released in 1979. Later, on January 20, 2001, in his last day in office, another Democrat President, William Jefferson Clinton, gave Patty Hearst a full pardon.

There have been other instances of brainwashing that point to its influence on our lives. Take the tragic Jonestown, Guyana, mass suicide where over 900 men, women and children willingly drank poison-laced Kool Aid on the order of their cult leader, Jim Jones. Brainwashing is real and I think that we're seeing the latest attempt at it on a nationwide scale, today, by an alliance of the media and certain members of the general population. Their aim? Setting the hook in the minds of other impressionable and angry people already predisposed to hating the President.

That's a pretty bold statement, I realize, but recent studies of major media stories seem to underscore the media bias of the anti-Trumper *journalists* with unceasingly negative narratives that have now reached well over 75% of all stories filed since candidate Donald Trump's nomination back in 2016 up to the fourth month of his Presidency. If this is true, and there is a coordinated effort on the part of the mainstream media to take down Mr. Trump, it can only be regarded as a fifth column attempt by the fourth estate to wrest power from a lawfully-elected President.

In that sense, their acts are no different from the backroom collusion and price-fixing of the nineteenth century 'robber barons' which, eventually, led to the 1890 passage of the Sherman Act. One of the other unfortunate by-products of monopolies is complacency. Companies aren't interested in creating better products because, as monopolists, why should they? They already have their market share! This is, in my opinion, the problem with a media monopoly...no incentive to improve their products. It's simpler and cheaper for them to re-package existing stories that are built on gossip, innuendo or anonymous sources' information into a Willy Wonka Chocolate Factory, assembly-line product. No one, except the President himself, dares to call them out or label them for what they truly are, fake news purveyors. While that irritates them, it doesn't deter them.

There must also be an element of AI (artificial intelligence) at work among the denizens of the press, because they are rapidly reaching new depths of journalistic perversion and *media-ocrity*. Outlets like the Washington Post, the New York Times and CNN are serving up their own unique blend of 'dump-Trump' claptrap with every new issue or program they produce.

Their strategy is simple: keep up the pressure to gain new readers and viewers, hoping that will translate into higher advertising rates and a captive audience that eagerly awaits the next serving of journalistic red meat. In their attempts to radically influence us, brainwashers frequently underestimate two things that act as a shield against idea manipulation. One is the strength of our basic core beliefs and the other is our will power. Just as there are some people that cannot be hypnotized, there are millions of Americans who cannot and will not be brainwashed into believing that they see a kindly grandmother offering a slice of apple pie when she's really a wolf wearing a starched apron holding an axe.

137

First line in the water

Anyone who saw and heard Senator Ted Cruz from Texas announce his run for the presidency today in front of a crowd of 10,000 college students at Liberty University in Lynchburg, VA, saw a man of conviction and confidence. Speaking for 40 minutes without a teleprompter or notes on a stage in the round, the Senator challenged his audience to 'imagine' (a theme he would use throughout his speech) a Cruz presidency that re-ignited and protected the flame of America's Constitution.

Senator Cruz laid out only a few concrete actions he would take. Instead, he concentrated on the big picture. Enthusiastic applause erupted after his comments on re-invigorating the job market, repealing Obamacare, protecting the lives of the unborn, standing up for the first and second amendments and re-balancing America's foreign policy. Largely seen by many as the champion of the Tea Party Movement and the hard right of the Republican Party, Cruz used today's occasion to re-define himself by softening the edges of his usual steely countenance with a personal and patriotic appeal for support of his candidacy for the nation's highest office. He spoke quietly yet passionately about his family's faith and the role that it has played in his family's life and history.

Speaking to a youthful and largely conservative-leaning audience of twenty-something college students with strong religious convictions, Cruz pulled no punches in his appeal to recapture our Constitution and was met with generous applause as he took the audience through important dates in American history starting with George Washington in 1775 and ending in 1933 with Franklin Roosevelt's 'nothing to fear but fear itself' speech.

He seemed to connect strongly with the prevailing undercurrent of 'courageous conservatism' in the hall as he did a four points compass pivot, turning slowly towards a different section of his audience at specific points in his speech never once faltering or losing the speaker-audience connection. Public speaking is Cruz' tour de force as is his ability to maintain the personal connection and keep the audience' focus on him as he moves seamlessly from one idea to another without breaking stride. This is in sharp contrast with President Obama who often needs re-focusing pauses between moves from teleprompter right to teleprompter left, thereby reducing the personal connection to his live audience.

Ted Cruz is a natural public speaker while Barack Obama's style is that of the TV anchorman. The difference between the two men was starkly evident today. The immediate challenge ahead for Senator Cruz is convincing enough potential donors that he can unify the Republican Party around his 'courageous conservative' battle cry without alienating the Republicans' more moderate base or the Tea Party wing <u>and</u> be able to sway enough independents and Libertarians (to say nothing of Democrat-leaning minorities) later on to make the all-important electoral vote win happen for the Republicans. While there are still well over 500 days to the election, in political terms the timing was perfect for Senator Ted Cruz' announcement. The games have officially begun.

~

Giving hope the old heave ho

The Democrats had better be careful this Christmas season. If they think they're going to rebuild and reinforce their ranks by calling out 'hope' and President-elect Donald Trump for offering it, they need to know that they're headed down a blind alley where a bunch of American patriots are waiting for them. I read, recently, that Indiana Steelworkers' Local 1999 boss, Chuck Jones, slammed Mr. Trump for inflating the numbers of jobs that would be saved at the Carrier Plant in Indianapolis and for giving "false hope" to workers that they would keep their jobs. While I expected a full-court press on the President-elect by every Democrat that could draw breath, I didn't think I'd see them attack their own sacred cow (hope) just before Christmas!

Let's put things in perspective by turning back the clock to the glory days of Barack Obama's first campaign for President. There were two words mentioned at every single whistle stop, campaign rally or were present on bumper stickers and posters around America. The words were 'hope' and 'change.' First came hope, then came change. It was clear that Mr. Obama's followers felt that hope was MIA after eight years of a George Bush Presidency, so the natural thing for them to do was take it out of mothballs and then apply it like a fake tattoo to Mr. Obama (who gladly took up the mantle of being the next messenger of 'the word'). He was happy to run a campaign based on emotion.

At the time, nobody challenged either his right to reach out to new voters with a hopeful message or the basis on which he hoped they would hoping right along with him. Obama had no accomplishments to point to, no successes under his belt, no real experience in either governance or management. In short, he *hoped* you'd overlook all of that and concentrate on tomorrow and put HIS past in the back of the bottommost drawer of that old chest in the attic of your memory.

It worked. There was such a compelling need for hope that it broke free of the constraints of cynicism that had held it in place. Americans came 'home' to their faith in the future. Nearly eight long years later, hope was now a hit and run victim, limping away from the scene of the accident that was the Obama Administration...until Donald Trump breathed new life into it at America's political roadside. Trump essentially ran two campaigns: one for the downtrodden and disaffected and one for the angry activists. Both campaigns were based on a deep and abiding hope for and belief in America's future - and not the future promised by the Obamaites.

His was an old time future that was based on America's past fidelity to conservative values. For his good Samaritan work in resurrecting hope, he earned criticism from the Left, proving two things: that no good deed goes unpunished and that Liberals now feel that they own 'hope' lock stock and barrel. It's theirs, and woe betide any man who would take it and 'pervert' it to his own ends. No, hope may only be used to further the Liberal agenda, Liberal thought, and Liberal dreams. The Democrats apparently feel that they hold its patent and all rights are reserved...for them. So what's a new President to do? Offer Americans dryer than dust platitudes or old worn out impossible promises?

Should Mr. Trump only give us the facts and not exercise the bountiful energy he possesses or try to inspire us with the spirit of the possible? That's actually what hope is. It isn't the facts, though it does sometimes rely on them. Rather, it's belief in the possible, based on a set of truths about ourselves and an honest assessment of our strengths and weaknesses. If the Democrats or labor leaders continue criticizing hope, they will make it impossible for our nation to heal, to achieve or to work together. And while hope may not be a plan, without it, there's no need for a plan.

~

halloweensurprise@FBI.gov

I can hear the computer keyboards clacking away as reporters start preparing their post-election stories. There are still two possible scenarios, but the mainstream media are working on a Hillary wins story with the headline, "Hillary blowout, first woman Pres." While these folks aren't even considering the possibility of a Trump victory, they still have a back-up story ready with the headline, "Billionaire steals election; mourning in America." Fox and the 'Right-leaning' media are a bit more cautious, but they, too, have two stories ready. The first, "HRC scores touchdown; FBI wants instant replay." The second is, "New American brand, Trump 4U."

A stressful year, yes, but exciting. Election 2016 has been like one of those $19.99 obscure product commercials at 2:00 am in the morning..."But wait. There's more!" Indeed. More shoes have been dropped in this cliff-hanger election than by Imelda Marcos' maid at the Malacanang Palace in the Philippines. Just when we were ready to count Hillary out from illness, she bounces back, and then so does Donald Trump after his pool hall remarks from a decade ago. Enter the *spoiler*, FBI Director Jim Comey, who, according to sources, may be dressing up this Halloween as Judge Roy Bean, the famous 'hanging judge' from Val Verde County, Texas after he sent the following letter to his employees on Friday, the same day he sent *another letter* over to the Congress declaring he was 're-opening' the HRC email investigation:

"To all:
This morning I sent a letter to Congress in connection with the Secretary Clinton email investigation. Yesterday, the investigative team briefed me on their recommendation with respect to seeking access to emails that have recently been found in an unrelated case. Because those emails appear to be pertinent to our investigation, I agreed that we should take appropriate steps to obtain and review them. Of course, we don't ordinarily tell Congress about ongoing investigations, but here I feel an obligation to do so given that I testified repeatedly in recent months that our investigation was completed. I also think it would be misleading to the American people were we not to supplement the record. At the same time, however, given that we don't know the significance of this newly discovered collection of emails, I don't want to create a misleading impression. In trying to strike that balance, in a brief letter and in the middle of an election season, there is significant risk of being misunderstood, but I wanted you to hear directly from me about it.
Jim Comey"

Predictably, the meanstream media reporters couldn't believe their eyes when they saw Comey's letter. "How dare he throw the election into question for Ms. Hillary? He already absolved her. What Republican got him to change his mind and how could he ever think of going trick or treating after dropping this bombshell?" This was especially disturbing to the likes of CNN and the Washington Post and other *Hillary True* cheerleaders that were already planning their Inauguration Ball coverage and looking forward to their front row seats at the first woman President's press conferences <u>and</u> sipping champagne with the Hollywood glitterati for the next four years.

For the reporters on the Right and the Trump campaign, it was like getting a last-minute reprieve from the Governor - who disguised as Carlos Danger (aka Anthony Weiner) - told the hangman that he would have stand down for awhile to give the Feds a chance to look at the 10,000 emails that 'Carlos' and his wife, Huma Abedin (HRC's confidant and Vice-Chair of her campaign), have stored on their shared laptop. Meanwhile, the real barometer of the election, costume shops in Washington, DC, are still reporting equally strong sales for both Trump and Clinton masks. One costume, however, is outpacing all the rest. It is that of a computer server with the words, "Tempus fugit" and "Nov. 8th" stenciled on it. What a country!

~

Headlines and headliners

Our lives are made up of headlines that express, in a few words, what we are feeling and experiencing as a society and as individuals, but headlines don't always reflect the truth. Often they reveal more about the headline writer than the event in question. Take today's front page headline in the Albuquerque Journal that precedes the short piece on Donald Trump's visit to Mexico where he met with President Nieto: "Trump vows to oust millions in U.S. illegally."

What was the headline writer's intent in picking out this one aspect of Trump's visit and his five-point immigration plan? Was he trying to provoke the reader with an interpretation of Trumps' comments? Trump never mentioned he was going to 'oust' all 11 million illegal immigrants. What he said was that he would take the worst of the worst first (lawbreakers) and send them back. Then, he suggested that he would make the rest go back to their home countries and register themselves before an eventual return to the U.S. That's not *ousting*. When we think of 'ousting' we think of someone being forcibly and physically ejected from a nightclub by a bouncer. Bad choice of words.

Then there's the obvious alternative reading of the same headline to mean that Donald Trump would oust them illegally (in an illegal manner). Sorry, but that's clumsy. With all that Trump and Nieto talked about yesterday, wouldn't it have been better not to fan the flames of Hispanic anger by writing a different headline like, "Trump's Mexican rapprochement" or

"Trump vows better relations with Mexico" or even, "Trump meets Nieto for immigration peace talks." Those headlines say something positive.

That brings me to the power of the editor and the power and imagery of words. When I picture an editor in my mind I think of Sinbad the Sailor, standing astride a huge body of water (like the Colossus of Rhodes) with a huge scimitar in one hand, blade glistening in the sun. He's looking at my copy and thinking, "How can I hack this to smithereens?" I know it's probably unfair, but editors do really wield considerable power. Their red pens can turn a story with oomph into a puff piece with just a few key word changes. Editors are concerned with two principal parts of speech: adjectives and verbs. Adjectives describe a person or situation and verbs indicate action; both can turn a saint into a sinner or the reverse. This is also true in the Presidential campaigns.

Candidates' speechwriters' give life to otherwise dry rhetoric with controversial and sometimes piquant adjectives. With Trump it's *crooked* Hillary, and with Clinton it's *dangerous* Trump. Each campaign is trying to paint a word picture for you, knowing that certain words trigger specific images and emotional responses and can imbed themselves into your subconscious like a wood tick. Our language is one big barnyard full of words that can be used to demean, denounce, denigrate, dehumanize and destroy. They can also uplift us...but not this year. Dale Carnegie is nowhere to be seen ("Be hearty in your approbation and lavish in your praise.").

I swear the speechwriters and the editors have been burning the midnight oil in a quest to unearth the nastiest and most innuendo-filled words that can be hurled at their opponents. It's just a matter of time before they escalate the attacks by using *second coming* type headlines (this refers to the huge type size reserved for cataclysmic events or the second coming of Christ). My worry is that Christ will come back during one of our Presidential Elections and HE won't be able to get any media 'ink.' What's worse is that some agenda-driven editor will slough off the event with a headline like, "Son of God returns home - no room at the inn...again."

~

How do great societies die?

If you believe the doomsayers, especially during Presidential election years, our society is rapidly headed for the dust heap of history. Our best days are behind us and the only thing we can look forward to is our certain demise as a democracy and a free speech loving country. To prove their thesis they point to our diminished standing in the world, the high rate of gun-related crimes, worsening race relations, pervasive joblessness and a blatant disregard for law and order.

There are other factors that would seem to bolster their claim like the recent incidents of wanton terrorism in the homeland and the growing schism between America's ethnic groups (some of which are only too happy to protest anyone in favor of enforcing our borders/laws). They decry the media's lopsided reporting and their pursuit of sensationalism, always looking for the next gory story instead of concentrating on the moral turpitude exhibited by our leaders. Then there are the renegade TV commentators and guest 'experts' who are always ready to character-assassinate anyone who disagrees with their positions on virtually any subject.

The loss of trust in our public institutions is probably their biggest worry and best exhibited by both parties in a Congress that ranks lower on the trust scale than used car salesmen (apologies to used car salesmen). Our current Presidential candidates are a close second, not trusted by large numbers of their own parties! Ask older generations of Americans what they miss most in our society and they'll probably cite civility, forthrightness, honor, loyalty and accountability. Ask the younger generations and they'll probably tell you *a job* and real prospects for the future. History shows us that most societies don't explode. They implode.

It happens when the pillars of their institutions that support them break down or are hollowed out by indifference, indecisive leaders or lack of public involvement. The speed at which the societal dominoes fall can be breathtaking, or it can be imperceptibly slow.

Society watchers don't always agree on how to interpret the signs, just as pollsters don't always analyze their findings, accurately, leaving special interest groups to pursue their own agendas without benefit of the facts. The truth is that societies like ours <u>are always changing</u>, shedding old beliefs and embracing new ones, and while those changes sometimes represent progress, they can also signal a turn for the worst.

That's why it's vital that we not shy away from having spirited national discussions, debates and then elections. Soon, both political parties will hold their conventions. Each will present carefully stage-managed events designed to shore up support from their base and will fire shots across the bow of the opposition if not directly amidships. There's nothing wrong with ordinary partisanship. We expect political parties to advocate for

144

their own positions. Partisanship becomes dangerous, however, when it kidnaps our attention and directs it away from our real problems.

No society can effectively tackle its own problems if it is mired in partisan bickering or if it rejects the orderly processes that enable lasting change. One of those is the rule of law and lawmaking. The recent horrific murders of police in Dallas tell us that we're entering a new and dangerous phase of our society's evolution. Will we circle the wagons and choose the *strength in numbers* approach or break ranks and take the *every man for himself* path? We'll find out soon as we are about to meet at an ideological crossroads. The choice we make in November will surely guarantee which direction our country will take. Will it be one of greater openness and inclusiveness or one that views every opportunity to grow as a problem in search of a solution?

~

How to move the millennials

In the absence of a Republican or Democrat African-American change agent candidate, the scramble is on for both parties to woo millennials to the ballot box. This will not be an easy sell for either party, but it is absolutely necessary for Republicans as they try to find the additional three million votes they will need to win the presidential election.

There is divided opinion on whether to mount a significant push for those votes, however, as some political strategists simply don't want to 'go there' and would prefer concentrating on shoring up 'the base' and picking up votes from the ranks of the undecided or independent voters rather than entering the maze of complex and thorny millennial issues. Not going there, however, would be a mistake on two levels.

The first is that Republicans' need to develop a successful short-term vote acquisition strategy and the second is a long term need to grow their base among a group that will one day hold power in America and remember who did or did not court their support.

The election of 2016 will not be a conventional election because we are not living in conventional times. The current front-runner candidates reflect that. There are parallels with the past we should be looking at that can give us some insight into how youth voters will vote this time around. One example is the Kennedy-Nixon election of 1960 when America was turning away from militarization in favor of greater introspection, despite the Cold War.

JFK embodied the youthfulness of that race. Ironically, he was of the same generation as Richard Nixon (Kennedy was born in 1917, Nixon in 1913). His world views were formed by war and were anything but isolationist. Later, we saw Robert Kennedy and Eugene McCarthy corner the youth vote by appealing to the anti-war sentiment of the time. The economy was not a prime driver of the youth vote then; ethics and America's foreign policy were.

The economy did become a prime driver among young people later in the 1980 Ronald Reagan election. The youth vote then was a curious mix of those who wanted us out of all war, those who wanted jobs and those who were deeply committed to changing the way America was run, post-Jimmy Carter. The ideological youth voter split was growing. The hard core of the Left had stiffened and split itself into two groups: committed one-world leaning Democrats and die-hard, anti-war, anti-politics activists. Republican youth became hardened fiscal Conservatives. Messaging to all these groups was incredibly difficult due to the groups' divergent ideologies. A pointed message to one group would have effectively alienated the others.

Both parties essentially gave up courting them until the Clinton/Bush election and then re-doubled their efforts in the elections of 2008 and 2012. The Democrats had successfully attracted a new generation of idealists and were able to move them farther left. Unfortunately for them, millennial optimism faded along with their hopes of finding employment during the Obama years.

What makes the millennials different from their hippie grandparents, their one-worlder and conservative parents? The answer lies in their attitudes toward: the economy (they're floundering as second tier or non-participants), the environment (they're more knowledgeable and committed today), foreign affairs and war (they're fed up and confused), technology (they're heavily invested in it), social mores (they're more open-minded and are early adopters of non-traditional alternatives to the status quo), etc. The easiest way to reach this very diverse voting group is to do three things: first, embrace them rather than fear them; second, be open and non-judgmental with them and third, understand their issues.

Being a youthful candidate in appearance and demeanor also helps. Candidates wishing to succeed with this group must understand that millennials can be persuaded to their point of view...they just need a sincere invitation to - and be a part of - the discussion.

~

Is America ready for a super-sized CEO?

In 2012, voters rejected a top CEO for America's top job. Mitt Romney had it all: stellar resume, proven leadership qualities, great track record, yet he came up short with voters in favor of what many would say was an inexperienced orator bent on reversing decades of America's progress. The Republicans were shocked that so many voters preferred the soaring rhetoric of a man who'd never managed anything larger than the staff of the Harvard Law Review to their golden boy from corporate America. Now, nearly four years later, the Republicans have two candidates who've made names for themselves in the business world: Carly Fiorina, former CEO of Hewlett Packard and real estate billionaire, Donald Trump.

For many on the Left, the mere thought that the corporate fox could be invited into the hen house of the Executive Branch sends shivers down their spines. Many cannot envision a worse scenario, especially at a time when both houses are dominated by *evil corporatists* masquerading as Congressmen and Senators who, if left to their own devices, would allow fracking everywhere, sell off America's precious National Parks, de-fund Planned Parenthood, roll back the gains made on national healthcare and allow America to drift into racial chaos.

The contrast between the two parties could not be greater; the Democrats are worshipping at the altar of socialist ideology in the guise of Vermont Senator Bernie Sanders, and former Secretary of State Hillary Clinton is busy trying to decide how far left of her current positions she should move to keep Sanders in check while keeping a watchful eye in her rear-view mirror on Massachusetts' Senator, Elizabeth Warren. Not to be outdone, the Republications are also exhibiting real paranoia about being viewed as the party of the *super-rich one percenters* as they are led by the opposition media through the scenes of elections past to earlier times when the electorate perceived them to be a bunch of elitist ne'er-do-wells. If this perception is allowed to take root (again) the Rs' chances of not only winning this election but winning <u>any</u> major election in the foreseeable future will be infinitesimal at best.

The one person that can swing public perception the Republicans' way is, ironically, the one that can also swing it the Democrats' way...Donald Trump. If Republicans are smart, they will persuade him to make his campaign a referendum on American capitalism and encourage him not to dwell on his personal wealth but instead speak about the good America's corporations do, using his life story as a 'teachable moment' for younger voters. THAT success story is powerful enough to counter any claims by the Left that American business is the enemy.

The choice is clear. Republicans must use the system of free enterprise and enlarging the economy to win votes. By keeping their powder dry and not pointing out the major flaws in the Obama economy, Republicans will make a critical mistake. They will give the Left both the time and opportunity to spin and revise history and use fear to persuade voters that big business is bad but bigger government is synonymous with benevolent government. Donald Trump needs to move the debate instead of being the subject of it.

~

Is the GOP on life support?

I've been a GOP watcher since my teens when Richard Nixon was campaigning against John F. Kennedy, and while I'm supportive of Republican (read: Conservative) values I haven't always been on board with the Party's candidates. That's nothing unusual for me as I've always been a critical thinker rather than an *all-in* supporter of the man on the ticket.

I didn't support Goldwater, was completely for Reagan, lukewarm on Bob Dole, totally behind Bush '41', squarely in Bush '43's' corner, on simmer for John McCain and totally committed to Mitt Romney who I thought had the absolute perfect resumé to lead America. This year, we Republicans had the largest field of candidates ever, but ended up with the least likely nominee (if you look at our last 50 years). Donald Trump has pushed old-style traditional Republicans into an untenable position by his unorthodox campaign style, his over the top remarks, his personal life and his tendency to bite the hand of the party that feeds him.

He has been at war with the Party's old guard, the RNC, the House Speaker, the media, with women and literally anybody that would challenge or disagree with him. He has waged guerilla warfare as well as conventional war against his detractors, and instead of building coalitions, he has repeatedly avoided them, seemingly unaware of their importance to his campaign. In that aspect, alone, he has broken the mold of traditional campaigning and chosen to dare anyone to attack his position.

He has, for all intents and purposes, cloaked himself as Col. William Travis at the Alamo and thumbed his nose at the overwhelmingly large Santa

Ana army and mooned them from the parapets. We all know how the battle of the Alamo ended, but we are still not sure how the Trump insurgency will end, though many of us Republicans have an inkling. Without the cavalry of millions of stealth supporters and closet 'Trumpians' coming to his rescue, he will fail. Their support is the 'Hail Mary' pass of all times, the longest of long shots but if successful, will put him in the pantheon of political high-stakes gamblers.

If unsuccessful, it will forever mark him as the 'man that killed Jesse James.' The only difference will be instead of being Robert Ford, HE will be Jesse James, having engineered his own demise. For some strange reason, many Republicans are completely okay with this kind of glorious death - as if it is okay to have waged a losing campaign as long as you went out with guns a blazing!

This is where I part company with my Republican compatriots. I see no glory in losing well on your own terms, especially when there is so much at stake. A couple years ago, I co-authored a book on the Republicans and on their chances for winning future Presidential elections ("How Republicans can win in a Changing America"). In it, my co-author Lance Tarrance and I took the Republicans' temperature and analyzed the steps they needed to take to win back the White House.

Admittedly, this was pre-Trump, but we did predict that the only way forward was with a candidate that represented what we called, "The Third Way." We felt that to win, the Rs needed a new type of populist candidate that could bring new voters to their ranks. The difference with our strategy and the one that's playing out today is that we based our projections on an addition of voters not a subtraction of important groups like moderate Democrats, millennials, Hispanics and women. We had not factored in Mr. Trump's alienation of the Party's leadership, which appears to be the case.

I have repeatedly said, in recent months, that we should look at this election not as a contest between two candidates, but rather one between two competing ideologies - and that the stakes are just too high to focus on the flaws of two individuals. The mainstream media has made that ideological contest impossible because of their singular devotion to Mrs. Clinton and their willingness to throw fair coverage of Mr. Trump out the window. It seems now, that according to recent polling, the Democrats are gaining valuable ground in not only swing states, but also in states where the Republicans had a slim chance of winning. They are gaining ground among some important demographic groups: White

149

suburban women, millennials and with ethnic voters. Is there anything that can save the Trump campaign at this point? Only a massive voter turnout from Mr. Trump's own core supporters coupled with a low turnout among former Bernie Sanders' supporters, with women and with disgruntled Hillary Clinton supporters can turn the tide. I'm afraid, that absent that, Mr. Trump will end up as a footnote - albeit a big one - in the 2016 Presidential Election year.

~

It's dodgeball time in the GOP

By all accounts, the Republicans seem to be choosing up sides for a serious game of dodgeball. This week, prominent, old guard, party elites like Mitt Romney, former President G.W. Bush and even House Speaker Paul Ryan all expressed their dissatisfaction, each in their own way, with the presumptive Republican nominee. Romney and Bush decided to boycott the Republican convention altogether while Ryan stated that he wasn't ready to endorse Trump...yet.

In politispeak that means he's playing a waiting game until Trump comes to him for a Pow Wow and is ready to seriously discuss not only his style, but also issues like trade, immigration, the budget, healthcare and national security. If there is no meeting of the minds and these issues are handled poorly it could cause a deep fissure within the Party and alienate Trump from its conservative base.

It is, after all, Ryan's job is to keep the House squarely in Republican hands, and he's understandably concerned about the 'down ballot' seats that are in play this year. That's not really anything new, though it is rather unusual for a powerful man like the speaker to poke the bear so publicly. Trump expressed measured surprise, but it's hard for me to believe that his scouts on Capitol Hill didn't give him a head's up that something like this was in the offing.

If those scouts <u>didn't</u> know it, then it's high time to install the red telephone between the Speaker's office and the penthouse in Trump Tower to explore ways to solve a nagging conundrum: many moderate Republicans don't want to relegate civility and traditional party views to the broom closet, but by not giving the field to Trump, they risk starting a cold war with the man who's going to head their Party in June. Clearly there is major horse-trading going on, but if the right horses don't get traded it could lead to a serious division between the two party factions in

Cleveland, and THIS could severely weaken the Party and prevent it from unifying in the few months leading up to election day.

This, however, is the way things are done in GOP land. Instead of airing its dirty laundry in the shade, away from the media spotlight like the Democrats do, the Rs open the windows and let the stink of their disagreements find a breeze that happily transports it to the waiting media. Some will say that *both* parties need this kind of transparency, that to keep such conflicts private is to deny the rank and file the truth. While they may have a point, such things also have a way of careening out of control, and losing control in public is Kryptonite to power politics. My guess is, that for the next six weeks (until the end of the primaries), we'll see a nuanced game of media dodgeball played out before the American public between Donald Trump and the Republican Party's elders.

It's anybody's guess how much this will hurt the Party (or help the candidate). One thing is certain, however, Republicans better keep an eye on their hourglasses because time has a way of slipping away. They could very well lose the momentum they gained after Trump's victory over his last two remaining rivals. This is a temporary advantage over the Democrats and it won't last long. Candidate Trump needs to make the most of it with carefully chosen appearances, well-crafted speeches and side-by-side photo ops with powerful Republican Party faithful not to mention marshalling his surrogates for a full-on encounter with minority groups, women and independents.

Many pitched battles lay ahead in the weeks and months to come, and many Republicans are silently praying that their only enemy is the Democrats.

~

It's official…we can now stop holding our breath

The world can now exhale. Hillary Clinton has announced her candidacy for the Democratic Party's nomination for President. And what a surprise it was. Mrs. Clinton kept us all on pins and needles in the same way that an eight-month pregnant woman suddenly declares she's going to have a baby. *Mrs. C* is perfectly willing to play the part of Richie Cunningham's mom and giggle a little when adoring admirers call her that. 'Happy Days' is here again! Actually, I think Mrs. C's rise to the top is testimony to *America, the possible* where a poor rich girl from the Midwest can go to a great school, become a lawyer, marry an ambitious man, ride his coattails to power then grab some of it for herself. It's not a new story but it's a true story and serves to remind us that anything can, and usually does, happen in this wonderful country of ours.

As the father of daughters, I'm also glad that women have now reached the top of the political pyramid. I truly am. Unfortunately for them, in order to stay there they must first plumb the depths of the subterranean chambers of that pyramid to learn the secrets of success: how to deceive, use subterfuge, speak in forked tongues, be duplicitous and do the dance of the political pharaohs. (Notice for woman readers I didn't use a female comparison like Salome. I should get some points here.)

For those of my Republican readers who think they will be able to simply resurrect the waning days of the Bill Clinton Administration and tar Mrs. C with that brush, I say to them, *fugetaboutit.* Her hubby would probably say, "That dog won't hunt," and if anyone knows hunting it's ole Bill.

If Ronald Reagan was the Teflon President, then Bill Clinton was the Kevlar President. Not only could he deflect almost anything but he also had the uncanny ability to sense the right moment to ask for forgiveness...and usually got it! His wife, on the other hand, is not the keeper of the political barometer. While she uses many of the same tactics to win (act first; ask for forgiveness later) she can't quite pull it off because she doesn't possess her husband's charm. She is the bad cop to Mr. C's good cop, and if there is any image that's hard to shake, it's that of bad cop. Columbo she's not.

It's a pity, too, because America needs a tough leader right now, one that towers above the fray but that can mingle with America's middle. In fact, it's to that latter group where Mrs. C is headed for support: to college campuses (women), to the shop floor (unions) and to America's needy neighborhoods (mostly minority voters). She will be reminding them of the greatness of Democratic Party ideals. Her crusade will be to recapture the rapture of middle class opportunity, and she will make the case that class warfare was invented by upper-class Republicans and it was they who fired the first shot in the war on women.

Here's my prediction: if Mrs. C is able to survive the walk through the Republican gauntlet of Benghazi and email hearings and be able to talk around her thin government resumé in much the same way as the junior Senator from Illinois (Mr. Obama) did in 2008, then she will have proven herself worthy of the Oval Office in the minds of many undecided voters.

While America's middle class family of today has no resemblance to the Cunningham's, the Cosby's or the Cleavers. Mrs. C knows that the closest thing America <u>had</u> to 'Happy Days' was her husband's term in office, and she's betting that she can rekindle the spark that propelled him to that office in 1993.

It's an ambitious goal, especially after being part of an administration that used a form of creative destruction to remind us that the past was just a pipe dream. I'm reminded of a great quote on ambition; "Great ambition is the passion of a great character. Those endowed with it may perform very good or very bad acts. It all depends on the principles that direct them." So said Napoleon Bonaparte. Make of that what you will.

~

Last lap of the masquerade parade

I always enjoy watching the last lap of just about anything. This year it's the Presidential race. It's not that I have a perverse hope that the candidates will crash and burn like stock cars. It's more about watching how their strategies and tactics change. Before Labor Day, the candidates are not usually wedded to fixed strategies. They try a little of this and a little of that, stick their toes in the cultural waters and dabble with clever one-liners about their opponents. They are also somewhat selective of who interviews them and when (Mrs. Clinton's hesitancy about holding press conferences shows more than average caution as she has now gone well over 200 days without holding one).

The rationale for this marathon-type pace is, that at this point, candidates are usually pretty confident of the support of their base prior to Labor Day (after which most pundits say is when voters start concentrating on the election) and they want to fine-tune their images and their rhetoric to address the undecided and swing voters. This tactic isn't new, but it is more obvious today as the candidates approach the home stretch.

While Hillary Clinton has always been out front with her *it's our time* approach to women (aptly reflected by the popular bumper sticker, "A woman's place in the White House"), what's noticeable now is the increase in intensity of that message as Labor Day draws near. Mrs. Clinton's stepped up attack on Donald Trump's fitness to even be accorded human being status let alone take his candidacy for President seriously is a narrowing of tactics to maybe three to four messages and/or themes that will dominate the last 60 days of her campaign. Mrs. Clinton's

153

first message is: "A vote for me is a smart vote" (as opposed to voting for Donald Trump which is just plain stupid).

Message two is the *glass ceiling message*: "It's time for a woman" (subtext: look at gender - not me personally - and remember that men have fouled things up for far too long). Message three is the *them and us* theme: "Stand with me and I'll fight the evil rich 1% Republicans for you and preserve the legacy of *si se puede* Obama." Finally, message four is the *inclusionary theme* to every undecided or minority voter: "Join us. Be a part of the winning team; let's all move America forward, together."

The Clinton campaign is clever. They have kept up the pressure on Donald Trump, personally, and have used his own words against him at every turn with sarcasm, name-calling and every other tactic to cut him off at the knees. Before Hillary Clinton, there was another successful Democrat politician that took the road less traveled for women by poking the bear with a sharp stick. It was Ann Richards, former Governor of Texas, who, at the 1988 Democratic National Convention, said of George H.W. Bush, "Poor George. He can't help it. He was born with a silver foot in his mouth," proving conclusively that Democrat women could also act scorpion-like and strike with deadly words.

Trump's messaging on a number of issues is rapidly *evolving* now that a new campaign team has taken the reins, and it appears that his generals are worried. They are reaching deep into their bag of tricks for messages that will soften his previous comments on immigration, for example, in order to capture a larger share of the Hispanic vote. (His speech in Wisconsin on Black America's problems was another example of a new outreach to the African-American community.)

The campaign is hoping for a "There you go again" moment like Reagan had with Jimmy Carter during the debate of October 28, 1980. If Trump's people can persuade the electorate that their man remotely resembles Reagan <u>and</u> can cast reasonable doubt in the minds of fence-sitting independents that Hillary Clinton is a Nixonesque figure given to conspiracy and lying, they may have a chance of winning more of the popular vote.

But, as we all know, that won't be enough. Trump needs to move some important electoral votes his way. States like Florida, Ohio and Pennsylvania are critical. Michigan, Colorado and Nevada would help, too. And while Virginia with its 13 electoral votes is a long shot, it's still worth a shot. The question then becomes, "In the 70+ days remaining, must Trump don his chameleon mask and selectively pander to all the smaller demographic groups?" Will he adopt the Clinton model of using phony accents to make his points with Black America or turn his *Make America Great Again* cap backwards and launch into a political rap number to capture millennials? I shudder to think what will happen in the next two months as these two campaigns change course and move from the asphalt of the Daytona Speedway to the dirt of the demolition derby.

~

No-fault immigrants

Can we all agree that the children of illegal immigrants are no more at fault for being here than is the driver of a car hit by someone without a valid license while legally entering an intersection? Last Friday, the President raised the stakes in the immigration debate by announcing an enforcement 'slow-walk' of deportation for approx. 800,000 illegal immigrants who came here involuntarily as teenagers or younger. This will increase support for the President from some ethnic communities, but the one he wants the most is the Hispanic community. What his administration forgets is that most Hispanics are law-abiding citizens and look down on those who break our laws. I firmly believe that most Hispanic voters are like any other voter. They vote their conscience and not their ethnicity.

It's anyone's guess whether the President has the right under the "Immigration and Nationality Act" to set the pace for identifying and deporting illegal aliens like *no-fault immigrants,* but if his authority is challenged it will undoubtedly result in a brouhaha costing millions of taxpayer dollars, time and political capital. Our immigration policy must be discussed, but not in a piecemeal fashion, and neither party really wants the whole issue debated months before an important election because both parties could lose important votes.

There is an aspect of Mr. Obama's policy that could end up hurting all of us...the infusion of 800,000 new workers into an already dismal and growing unemployment situation. This will certainly anger the millions of unemployed workers, and that could translate into opposition to candidate Obama come November. The plight of the no-fault immigrant is clear. They are not to blame for the sins of their fathers (or mothers). While deporting them would be justified in the eyes of the law, it would hardly be consistent with the culture of a compassionate country. There is a way forward that could please both the absolutists and the relativists in this debate.

155

A special status should be created for them: *no-fault immigrants.* Those without felony convictions, who are under 18 and who can demonstrate that they came here involuntarily should be permitted to stay. They would need to register with Homeland Security and the State Department within a specific time period and then apply for a temporary residency card. Then they must get a real social security number and a work permit from a special office in either HS or the Department of Labor.

They would not be allowed to collect food stamps or welfare benefits but would be allowed to collect unemployment benefits like anybody else. Finally, they would be fingerprinted and issued a special forgery-proof ID card, submit to annual interviews by HS for a five-year period and have their income tax records reviewed by the IRS. Before the end of five years or on their 18th birthday they would have two choices: be deported to the country of their birth or apply for U.S. citizenship. Should they choose to apply for U.S. citizenship, they would follow the same procedure that all would-be citizens follow: return to their home country, submit an application at the American Embassy and wait their turn (back in the U.S.) to be processed <u>behind</u> all those who came before them.

The United States should be not be in the business of breaking up families, but neither should we turn a blind eye to our existing immigration laws. If we don't find a solution now, we will soon have to deal with the next generation of no-fault immigrants.

~

No veneer politics

It's Super Tuesday 2016, and several of my friends have been complaining loudly to me about the tone of the Republican candidates' rhetoric. They say that they are sick and tired of hearing the candidates' vitriolic personal attacks on ethnic groups, on our trading partners and on each other. They have also bemoaned the lack of civility and decorum in the debates and on the campaign trail.

I've listened patiently to all of them and have noted their frustration with our entire election system which starts with candidate selection through the primary process and on to the general election. The complaints haven't stopped there. They've railed against the Supreme court ruling on the 'Citizens United' case which allowed corporations and other organizations to enjoy the same status as individual campaign contributors. I've listened to them criticize the inordinately long time our election process takes with all its many candidate debates, town halls and whistle stops.

I've heard them harangue the actions of the Political Action Committees (PACS) and the sleazy campaign attacks, courtesy of the opposition research teams. I've tried my best to discuss each and every complaint they've raised, but nothing I say seems to appease them. That's why I took a short break to collect my thoughts and try to find the real reasons for our political dysfunction. Here are a few of them...

1. We have the wrong governance model. At this point, with this much basic ideological disagreement, we could benefit from a parliamentary system where the voting public elects members to a two-chamber parliament. The majority (winning) parties form a government and agree on a leader (Prime Minister) to head the current government. The cabinet posts are decided by the winners, according to the size of their majority in the election. If the government cannot pass a budget, for example, a vote of no-confidence could be taken and the government would fall which would lead to a new election. The Prime Minister would call the date for the new election and candidates would have a restricted amount of time to campaign.

2. We spend too much money on our campaigns. Candidates should be required to accept a combination, public-private campaign financing scheme where 1/3 of the money comes from a federally-established fund, 1/3 may come from the private sector and up to 1/3 may come from the candidate him- or herself. A cap of $500 million would be placed on campaign spending for a national office and $200 million for a Congressional seat.

3. We need term limits. Our elected officials spend too many years on the job. We need to limit Senators to two terms (12 years) and Congressional Representatives to six terms (also 12 years). As an aside, I would like to see fewer lawyers in our legislature so that more 'ordinary citizens,' could serve, but I would be satisfied to see term limits as a good start at reforming the system. Our Founding Fathers never intended that our elected representatives have lifetime service; that was reserved for Supreme Court justices.

4. We need term limits on Supreme court justices. A person's brain cells, energy and judgment deteriorate over time, and there is absolutely no reason to keep justices on the bench into their 80s. Justices should serve

no longer than 25 years, no matter their age, and no justice vacancies should be filled during a Presidential election year.

5. We need a balanced budget. If we are to get our financial house in order, keep our currency stabilized and head off these yearly government shut-down threats and continuing resolutions, we're going to need to give our legislators some cover by passing a balanced budget amendment to the Constitution.

While some of the foregoing suggestions might help change the tenor of our politics and return us to a more civilized form of political intercourse, I'm not sure they will solve the widely-differing philosophical and ideological disagreements of our two political parties which have kept us at loggerheads and actually caused the total meltdown of civility. In short, we're tired; we're frustrated and we're angry... at record levels in our country. This incivility is the by-product of all that fatigue, frustration and anger, and it's not going to stop any time soon.

In fact, it's going to get worse as we proceed towards the election of a new President. Even after that it's not going to stop. So to my disappointed friends, I say, "Welcome to the brave new world of American politics. You better get used to a daily fare of confrontation and coarse conversation as America is on a forced march back to its revolutionary war 'Spirit of '76' roots. It's just too bad that civility has to be the first casualty on that new battlefield."

~

Reclaiming our political currency

The world is a dangerous and chaotic place and it is filled with power-crazed dictators, terrorists and way too many nuclear devices. Americans need to stand firm, respect each other and our Constitution and the rule of law. We need to safeguard our national interests at home and abroad and fight for our freedom whenever it's threatened. That's one view, shared by many who've lived in this world for a half-century or more. There's another school of thought, though, and it is usually held by idealists, those to the left of the political ideological spectrum and our young.

The world will continue on a steady path towards peace and prosperity if only we keep the dialogue going, but progress is being slowed and negatively impacted by the forces of capitalism and those on the right that are unwilling to recognize the need for rapid integration into a world community where borders are unnecessary and where everyone shares equally in the wealth of others. That's the way I see the divide, and while you may see it differently, I believe that we can agree on one thing...that most of us disagree with one another these days. Personally, I see no way out of the ultra-partisanship that plagues our country.

We might as well resign ourselves to the new, old tactics of the sixties: protests, occupation of public buildings and sit-ins. And THAT'S just the Democrats in the House of Representatives! Outside, on college campuses, things are even worse. Students are demanding 'safe spaces' that are free of uncomfortable or objectionable speech as if the First Amendment doesn't exist. Republicans are being accused of being racists simply because they want our immigration laws enforced or if they disagree with a President that routinely abuses his Executive Branch authority.

We are down to two choices for President: one an entitled, power-driven, habitual prevaricator and the other a shoot-from-the-hip, bombastic, real estate magnate that has managed to amass a fortune despite four business bankruptcies. We are faced with a political *Sophie's choice*. No matter which candidate we choose, it will be a loss for at least half of us. This is not the first time Americans have had to choose between the lesser of two evils, but it is, at least in my memory, the first time we've had to choose between two such vastly different Presidential candidates. Though much is made of the 'establishment' versus the 'non-establishment' monikers applied to the candidates, both in fact represent their own particular establishments.

Mrs. Clinton represents the career politician, elite, ruling class and Mr. Trump is squarely the 'poster boy' for American business. So if you're looking for an anti-establishment candidate, you had better check out the Libertarians' menu...or you could always write-in socialist Senator Bernie Sanders on your ballot.

Ironically, our former colonial masters, the British, may be showing us the way towards recapturing our sovereignty from an overbearing government. On June 23rd, Britons reversed their self-imposed fealty to the ruling class of the European Union by a vote of 52% to 48%. Our English cousins decided to rip up their membership card in an organization where they were founding members. For 43 long years, Englishmen and Englishwomen watched their sovereignty steadily erode.

159

Like the frog in the slowly boiling pot, they were unaware of the danger that lay ahead of them. Fortunately for Britain, the issue of immigration woke them up and they were able to jump from the boiling pot and demanded a referendum on remaining in the EU (BREXIT). To their government's credit they got it, and 72% of the public voted with 52% choosing to call it a day.

America is also that frog. We've watched our freedoms be slowly taken from us by unprincipled politicians. We have ignored our own self-interests (at our own peril) and continued to elect leaders that give us more of the same, time after time. Perhaps it was just political fatigue that led us to relinquish OUR sovereignty to those with greater determination and perseverance. The truth is, Americans are tired, angry and frustrated. We have, I believe, finally reached the breaking point, and like the British, understand what's at stake and will turn out for this Presidential Election in record numbers.

In 2012, Barack Obama won re-election with 52% of the popular vote. In 2016, Britons took their country back by the same margin. There is a lesson here. It may be that a slim margin is better than no margin at all or it could be that you can fool some of the people all of the time but not all of the people all of the time.

~

Republicans, Democrats, conventions and democracy

Well, it's official. Donald Trump is now the Republicans' choice to enter the squared circle of American politics and face down Madam Secretary, Hillary Clinton. True to form, the Republicans' first night was a donnybrook between the Rules Committee, party leadership and the no-Trumpers who shouted, stood on chairs, raised their fists in anger and proved, once again, that the elephant of the GOP has a long memory and can make a blood-curdling trumpeting noise when threatened - even in its own circus tent.

It proved, too, that the Republicans are ready to take on their own in an open forum with the whole world watching. Call me crazy, but I truly believe that THAT openness speaks volumes about a party often accused of being too restrictive. Granted, there was behind-the-scenes maneuvering going on to get the nine states' delegates that wanted rules changes and a roll call vote to fall away to only five, but that is called politicking. Both parties have foot soldiers that go behind the lines to work their magic, and both parties rarely emerge from a convention without a few bruises and minor lacerations. The Republicans are different from the Democrats, however, in that they do their blood-letting in the open.

Will Donald Trump now automatically be loved by every Republican in the convention hall and outside on the streets of America? No, but many fence-sitting Republicans (and opponents of his) will fall into line during the next 3½ months. That is also the nature of American politics. If anyone believes that the Democrats are in lock-step with one another in their support of Mrs. Clinton, they are sorely mistaken.

One look at the face of Bernie Sanders will tell you that's not the case. Millions of 'Feel the Bern'ers' will need time to shift their support to Mrs. Clinton, but it will probably happen, though perhaps not to the degree and speed that the Democrat hierarchy (and Mrs. Clinton) might wish. It will take some persuasion, but given the Democrats' history it will come to pass.

Expect the next few days of the Republican Convention to gather steam as it goes through its "Make America (fill in the blank)_____" themes, all designed to attack both the sitting President and the Democrat hopeful. Some call conventions a slaughterhouse environment where the opposition candidate is brought in on the hoof and then systematically cut to pieces by a carefully stage-managed butchering by party loyalists and celebrities. Both parties do it, but not with equal fervor and relish. The Republicans will try their best to link Mrs. Clinton with her former boss and swear up and down that she had no mind of her own (and followed him blindly down the wrong path) AND *personally* made wrong decisions on a whole host of topics.

8They will call her a pathological liar for Benghazi and for 'Servergate' and portray her as an enemy of the Constitution and of traditional American values. They will point to her many scandals, her poor judgment and her lust for power as the coup de grace.

The Democrats will intensify their campaign of *reasonable* Hillary, *calm cool and collected* Hillary and of a Hillary *for all people and all seasons*. She will be placed on a pedestal on the moral high ground above the *evil, dangerous, racist, megalomaniac,* Trump. From her perch, she will shower her supporters with the right Democrat poll-tested buzz words, delivered in carefully-coached measured tones UNTIL it is time to ratchet up the rhetoric (watch the poll numbers for the switch).

161

Then, she and her campaign will plunge the knife in for the kill. This approach will be timed perfectly and be accompanied by an avalanche of TV ads and surrogate speeches given by darlings of the Left. Mrs. Clinton will portray herself as the only one that can heal America's wounds, bring us together, stop the racial strife and keep us safe because she LISTENS while Donald Trump only TALKS. Our conventions must look to the outside world like shark feeding frenzies to foreigners tuning in to Sky News, BBC or Deutsche Welle (or even CNN International).

Can we blame them for not understanding how we got to these convention moments, through a Byzantine primary system complete with Super Delegates that can change their minds about who they will nominate (the Democrats) or those that are locked in to vote the way their states voted (the Republicans)? No. We can't blame them, nor can we explain to them how such a democracy can allow Electoral College votes to nullify a popular vote victory. Stay tuned for more this week and next when it's the Dems' turn. There's never a dull moment in American politics.

~

Reversing the outsourcing wave

According to the U.S. Dept. of Labor, in January of 2009, America's labor force was 154 million with 7.8% unemployed or 12 million people. In January 2016, the labor force was 158 million with 4.9% unemployed or 8 million people. What those numbers don't tell you is how many millions of Americans have been shut out of the labor force by outsourcing, corporate down-sizing, age discrimination, insufficient skills or conversion of full-time jobs to part-time ones. Millions of Americans have simply given up looking for work.

During President Obama's time in office, which admittedly included one of our country's most terrible recessions (something he didn't cause), the number of jobs created have not kept pace with those persons entering the workforce (something he is partially responsible for). Those are the simple facts whether you're a Republican or Democrat, liberal or conservative, independent or socialist.

America, once the envy of the manufacturing world has quietly become an old dowager with nothing more than her celebrated past to comfort her as she makes her way through the modern world of emerging markets and low wage jobs. That said, the USA is still populated by millions of small businesses that tough it out every time a new existential threat pops up like profit-crushing high minimum wage legislation and the 80,000 plus pages of new regulations this year that serve to create the conditions for outsourcing and capital flight.

Economists all know this (as do the rest of us), but we've been taught that we should leave the solutions to all those 'bright minds that are working on this.' Unfortunately, many of those bright minds are protecting shareholders first and foremost, and if there are opportunities that lay beyond America's borders, that's where the boardrooms go.

Immediately after WWII, profit was considered normal and not something to be ashamed of. Today, corporate America is in a quandary. It wants to beat its own drum and trumpet its own successes because it's good for share prices, but it also knows that it must be careful about mentioning how much of that success is due to outsourced jobs, foreign manufacturing contracts or overseas investments. This corporate schizophrenia is part and parcel of daily life in the communications departments of most big companies.

The opportunities for outsourcing America's jobs are also embedded deep in many of our trade agreements like NAFTA and the TPP, giving corporate America more reasons to move work offshore to places like Mexico and the Far East. Investments follow the markets and market demand provides jobs. It's simple, really. One would think that our market of over 300 million people would tip the job scales in our favor with a massive wave of employment, but it hasn't.

Why? One reason is that many of our largest companies have been unabashedly greedy and felt no allegiance to the American worker. Add to that the fact that our government leaders haven't understood the basic DNA of American business, nor have they made it a priority to engage top business minds to round out their education, and you have two out in the ninth inning. The results were predictable, and we are now paying the price for that willful ignorance... unbridled outsourcing.

Job growth, outsourcing and offshore investments will soon become issues in our Presidential election. Democrat Presidential candidate Senator Bernie Sanders already castigates big business at every opportunity and Republican candidate, Donald Trump, complains loudly and often about China and Mexico stealing our jobs. Corporate America had better get ready for an onslaught, because this issue raises the hackles of any American whether employed or not.

Staunch 'free trader' types that believe that it's perfectly acceptable - even desirable - to have a manufacturing presence offshore (rather than a U.S.-based one) that serves the U.S. market will say there's nothing to fear, "The market will correct itself." Sorry, but the market won't correct the real issue of ideological differences or the question of how much is too much or too little when it comes to our workforce and off-shoring. That's a role for our citizens, our government and the private sector to work on together. We need to elect a President that understands business <u>and</u> human nature and is smart enough to know how to use each one with a plan that strengthens our domestic labor force while keeping us competitive in world markets.

If we don't, we might as well dispense with 'country of origin' stamped on our products. "<u>Not</u> made in America" will be enough.

~

Rocky throws in the towel

The stage was set, the spectators were in their seats, and in walked the champ. White-haired and looking unfazed by months of battle for his party's nomination, Senator Bernie Sanders, the Rocky Balboa of the far left, took the stage for his last fight before retreating from the public eye. All that was missing was the triumphal music theme and craggy 'Mick' the manager to make the scene perfect for Philadelphians. Instead of a seven-foot tall Russian opponent, Sanders had to shadow box with the absentee Republican candidate, Donald Trump.

When the bell rang, instead of coming out swinging, Sanders had to 'endure' a full four-minute ovation as if he had already won the fight. Meanwhile, in a remote location, Donald Trump was busy 'tweeting,' telegraphing his blows to the Twitter universe, millions more voters than occupied the Wells Fargo Arena seats.

After throwing a barrage of punches at Trump he missed his real target, the <u>Democratic National Committee</u> and its rabid Hillary Clinton supporters that populated that organization and that methodically worked to defeat him from behind the scenes. Not a single punch landed on his closest opponent, Hillary Clinton, who benefited from the DNC's below the belt blows. Instead, Sanders chose to fight the good old fight he fought throughout the Primaries, targeting the 1%, the evil rich and stood tall for the underprivileged, downtrodden Americans who've been left out of the American Dream.

Sanders got even – a little – by challenging his supporters to show up for the big vote tomorrow, on the future of the Super Delegates. That was the only punch that resonated. The fight was one-sided as was expected and without a referee. It also showcased future contenders like former Mayor Cory Booker and now Senator from New Jersey and former Consumer Protection Agency head and now Senator from the far far left State of Massachusetts, Elizabeth Warren. Both clearly punched above their weight and launched haymakers and swung wildly at capitalism and the demon Republican nominee.

The Democrat crowd got their money's worth and their pound of flesh despite the fact that only one boxer occupied the ring. All left the arena satiated, however, ready for the next bout scheduled for Tuesday. While 'Rocky' may have taken a dive without mentioning the rigged system that assured his defeat, he left the ring standing tall and unbloodied and vowing to continue to take the 'Revolution' to the next level. The winner? Bernie Sanders, the aging Socialist pugilist from Vermont, a true champion that showed the odds-makers they were wrong to count him out before the bell.

~

Scoring the South Carolina Republican Debate

It's been ages since I've tuned into CBS for anything let alone a clash of titans of the Republican variety, but tune in I did last night to witness the R's six-pack of candidates, absent the provocative Governor of New Jersey, Chris Christie, businesswoman Carly Fiorina and all the others who've dropped out over the last week or so. The debate was faster paced without them, but candidates still only got a minute each to answer the questions, hardly enough time for details on anything, but plenty of time to dive into the mud of personal attacks.

Be that as it may, CBS is to be congratulated for its moderatorship and organization. The audience, on the other hand, should have gotten a few lashes of the cat-o-nine-tails for their rudeness. I could see, even from a distance, that the audience' outbursts irritated the moderators as well. I must admit, that I don't know how you can inject civility into an audience that has a propensity for shouting, except perhaps to give them all a pint of Old Crow laced with a valium an hour before entering the auditorium.

It was obvious that all the candidates were well-prepared for this last debate which precedes the South Carolina voting by only three days. Their advisors had done a good job in grinding off their rough edges with a few possible exceptions, and they were ready to return fire with fewer pre-tested sound bites (there were no "There you go again" moments of the Reagan variety, for example). While everyone will probably score the debate differently, here's my take.

Debate moderators - A; Their questions - B+, The audience - C on civility, A for enthusiasm. The candidates (in alphabetical order): Governor Jeb Bush - B+ for poise and succinctness and B for exhibiting restraint and courage for his defense against the Trump onslaught (Trump attacked his brother's handling of America's security and the Iraq War), Dr. Ben Carson - A for soft spokenness and sincerity and B+ for his overall answers; Senator Ted Cruz - A- for debate skills but C for losing his composure while animatedly discussing his disagreement on his stance on immigration with Senator Marco Rubio; Governor John Kasich - C for annoying repetition of his accomplishments in Ohio and D for not recognizing that the audience didn't want a 'peacemaker' on the stage, and F for attempting to portray himself as one. Senator Marco Rubio was, in my opinion, the clear winner last night.

I give him an A for his engaging presence, an A+ for his arguments, an A for connecting with the audience and a B- for letting himself be sucked into a duel with Senator Ted Cruz (which ended in a draw).

Finally, there's Donald Trump. I agonized over this one, but I give him an A for being Donald Trump, a D for a failed attack on Jeb Bush through his surrogate brother, an F for not accurately reading the mood of the live audience (they were friendly to Jeb Bush that evening), and for his overall performance I give him a C+. If Trump is to win over the undecided voters which number around 14%, he's going to have to improve his demeanor on stage, be less caustic and try to find a facial expression that is more to the friendly side of the scale.

All in all, this debate was more of the same, but it did have an air of immediacy to it as everyone is sensing that the race is narrowing to perhaps three people: Trump, Cruz and Rubio. If I'm right, Bush, Carson and Kasich will probably stay in the race until Super Tuesday but remain in low double-digit or high single-digit territory.

And the final score? Rubio, the winner on points - a TKO (Technical Knock Out), Trump and Cruz, tied for second. Bush a distant third, followed by Kasich and Carson tied for last place. It's now up to the good people of South Carolina, the first real southern state of many, to choose their man.

~

Skirts against the shirts

It finally happened, and we have both candidates to thank for it. I'm speaking of the final throes of a campaign in what has now become the front lines of a new uncivil American Civil War that is pitting men against women. Just when we thought we had made significant progress in closing the gender gap, the Clinton campaign launches an all-out attack designed to separate the sexes and focus on the 'evil male oppressors' by linking all Conservatives to what they claim is the *misogynist billionaire and Republican candidate, Donald Trump.*

Building on the gender skirmishes of the previous election with the 'contraception battle' spearheaded by the young activist Georgetown University student Sandra Fluke who wanted her birth control pills paid for by the Feds, to what the Left has deemed an unwarranted and unfair attack on Planned Parenthood by undercover videos on ' fetus harvesting' and the reprehensible comments made about the Little Sisters of the Poor for wanting an exemption from the Obamacare mandates for providing contraception to their lay workers, the crescendo of 'gunfire' has led to full-on demonization of the arch 'woman-hater' - Donald Trump - for his admittedly stupid and macho remarks of a decade ago.

The gates of civility have been breached and the gloves have come off as the Clintonistas have trained their fire on recruiting the female vote by telling them that this election is an existential struggle <u>between them and us,</u> their male brethren. This is a blatant and transparent ruse to move the female voting needle Mrs. Clinton's way, and it has been exacerbated by her actions which are even more repugnant: her objectification of women and their use as pawns in her political chess game to win the Presidency. It is also proof that the old Roman strategy of divide and conquer is now firmly ensconced in American identity politics. It is also ironic that the Clinton campaign, which has as its battle cry, "Stronger Together," would take this lowest of low road tactics. It begs the obvious question, "What part of Stronger Together does this have to do with uniting Americans?"

By destroying that which makes us truly strong...our bedrock gender relations, Mrs. Clinton has shown her true colors and they are not the red, white and blue of *one people out of many.* She and her army of surrogates are doing irreparable harm to the last bastion of our true strength - the defense and protection of all people - <u>men and women,</u> to live and work in harmony. She and her campaign should be ashamed of themselves for pounding a stake into the hearts of all of us who have fought to ensure equality by de-gendering our nation rather than giving preferential treatment to one group over the other. The idea is simple: see ourselves as people first, not demographic sub-groups in some campaign strategist's master vote-getting plan. In these final two weeks of the most divisive political election in our recent history we must resist the urge to further devolve into single-issue or special interest partisans. Instead, we must focus on the real enemies of our democracy: bigotry, intolerance and apathy. We should remember Benjamin Franklin's quote: "We must indeed all hang together, or most assuredly, we will surely hang separately." Do your part and vote for the unity of all people and reject the false flag of a phony war on women - or any group for that matter. Uncertainty and fear should have no role in deciding the outcome of our future.

~

So goes Iowa?

Well, it's official. We're off and running in the great Presidential Election of 2016. The farmers, merchants and ordinary people of Iowa have spoken. Iowans have been pretty proud of being the political compass of the United States and harvesting winners for the Republican and Democratic Parties. Actually, though, during the last nine presidential terms (or 36 years since 1980), Iowans chose the right nominee six times, but of those six, four were sitting Presidents, nominees who were seeking a second term and got it (Ronald Reagan, Bill Clinton, George W. Bush and Barack Obama).

Two of them didn't get their second terms (George H.W. Bush and Jimmy Carter). Looking at the Iowa Caucus winners for the Democrats' nominee, three became President: Jimmy Carter, Bill Clinton and Barack Obama. The others: Walter Mondale (1984), Dick Gephardt (1988), Tom Harkin (1992), Al Gore (2000) and John Kerry (2004) never made it the White House. On the Republican side, the only first-time caucus winner that became President was George W. Bush. The others left at the sidelines were: George H.W. Bush (Reagan lost to him in Iowa by 2% in 1980 but beat him out for the Party's nominee that year), Bob Dole (1988), Mike Huckabee (2008) and Rick Santorum (2012). The latter beat Mitt Romney by only 34 votes.

That leaves the final score for Iowa at: Republican nominees that got to be President (excluding second term Presidential runs) at a whopping 1; for the Democrats, the score is 3. As they say, those are the facts, but that doesn't take anything away from the friendly folks in Iowa who braved the elements and a Byzantine system of organization to negotiate their way to the finish line. In case you're wondering just how complicated the whole system is, imagine you're a member of an Iowan square dance club.

You've been practicing your steps with your partner after work and on weekends for years. It's Monday night and you're dressed to the nines in your finest hoe-down duds. You've motored over to a local Iowa barn that is usually trimmed with colored lights and a raised wooden stage for dancing. This night is different. You enter a darkened barn with a dirt dance floor covered with sand. You take your place with Mary Ellen, your partner, and the band, which is forty feet away kicks off with an obscure Russian folk melody played in a crazy non-square dance tempo. The square dance caller is speaking Arabic and he has a lisp.

That's the equivalent of an Iowa Caucus. There are 1,681 precincts in Iowa where registered party members meet to elect delegates to county conventions, and there are 99 conventions, one for each county. The county conventions then select delegates for the Presidential nominating conventions, and it goes on from there. In 2012, Iowa changed its system of 'winner take all' to a proportional one where each candidate takes away the proportional number of votes that he/she won in percentage terms.

Caucus-goers meet in schools, firehouses, libraries, private homes and a host of other venues for only one hour to talk-up their candidates to one another and then begin to negotiate votes from those who eventually see the error of their ways (some anyway) and change their votes to other candidates. These usually small 'gatherings of neighbors' is a folksy and personal method of cajoling and arm-twisting and this year led to a win by Texas Senator Ted Cruz with 28% of the Republican vote, businessman Donald Trump with 24% and Florida Senator Marco Rubio with 23%.

The numbers for the two Democratic Party candidates were razor-thin. Former Secretary of State Hillary Clinton prevailed with 49.9% to Vermont Senator Bernie Sanders' 49.6%. I hope the whole thing was worth braving the cold Iowa Winter for these brave Mid-westerners and for those mythical square-dancers that are probably close to doing themselves in right about now.

~

Super Delegates: Arranged marriage or managed infidelity?

Winning the Republican and Democratic nominations for President has reminded us that our system of choosing nominees is hardly transparent or simple to understand. I'm not speaking of the one-man one-vote system that we use in our general election, but rather of the highly-partisan 'Super Delegate' (SDs or pledged delegates) system that serves to stack the delegate deck and has now given candidate Hillary Clinton over 500 delegates (470 of which are SDs versus 70 for her rival, Senator Bernie Sanders), despite Sanders' win in the New Hampshire Primary and his razor thin loss to Clinton in Iowa.

For the Democrats, 2,383 delegates are needed to win their party's nomination out of a total of 4,763, and most of these will be apportioned according to who wins the individual caucuses and primaries that are either proportional or 'winner-take-all.' If that were the only game that was being played, it would be a fair way to choose a nominee, but it isn't. The additional layer of Democrat SD votes (712) that are in play also serves to tip the scales in favor of the candidate that has extracted the most promises of pre-primary support from the SDs.

The Democrats' Super Delegates are comprised of distinguished party leaders, elected officials, all sitting members of the Democratic House and Senate and all Democratic governors. In the Presidential election of 2008, for example, SDs accounted for about 823 votes or 20% of the entire delegate vote. Democratic Party SDs will attend their party's convention, and while in theory they are free to support any candidate they wish, most have already pledged their allegiance and their votes well in advance to certain candidates (in this case the vast majority to Hillary Clinton which accounts for her substantial lead in SDs).

There is a light at the end of the nomination 'tunnel' for the Democrats. Should their SDs wish to change their minds and their votes and support a different candidate at the convention, they are free to do so. Most are well aware, however, that their Democratic Party bosses have long memories and will probably refrain from switching their votes. Not to be outdone, the Republicans have their own SDs (roughly 168 or about three from each state which are comprised of the top three Republican officials in their states), but 95% of them are required to support the winners of the individual states' caucuses or primaries and are not allowed to bargain their votes away; 5% may do as they wish.

To win the Republican Party's nomination, a candidate must get 1,237 delegate votes out of the total of 2,472. As of this writing, Donald Trump has 67 delegates. Ted Cruz follows with 11 and third place holder, Marco Rubio has 10 (John Kasich has 5 and Dr. Ben Carson has 3.)

This two-tiered system of pledged and unpledged delegates is flawed if not borderline undemocratic. If we really want to level the playing field in how we choose our Presidential nominees we ought to consider focusing on the issue of Super Delegates, and while we're at it, we might want to take on the 800 lb. gorilla in the room, our 'Electoral College' with its 538 electors that *really* elect the President and where there is no constitutional provision or Federal Law that requires them to vote according to the results of the popular vote in their state! Voting should never be a marriage of convenience between our conscience and fear of losing face. Neither should it be so removed from transparency and simplicity that the average person feels no loss in abstaining from voting.

~

The Democrats add another scandal

The controversial website Wikileaks decided to help the Democrats by adding a little more excitement to the upcoming Democratic National Convention. Seems they dumped twenty thousand emails, originating from all levels of the Democratic National Committee, on their website. The emails reveal that several DNC officials were openly supporting Hillary Clinton's campaign (what a surprise) and may have colluded with her campaign staffers to find ways to sabotage her opponent, Senator Bernie Sanders' chances of getting the Party's nomination. After a long rules committee meeting yesterday, Congresswoman and DNC Chairwoman, Debbie Wasserman Schultz, decided to throw in the towel and resigned her position, effective Friday. Long time Democratic operative, Donna Brazile, is replacing her.

You have to hand it to the Democrats; they got their scandal out there before their convention even opened its doors as opposed to the Republicans that got blind-sided last week by Senator Ted Cruz with his non-endorsement speech. There is another tranche of emails expected from Wikileaks, soon, and Democrats are holding their breath, hoping that the release takes place in the wee hours of the morning as opposed to prime time. There is already considerable tension among Bernie Sanders' supporters who feel that the Primaries were rigged and that the DNC was 'in bed with' the Clinton campaign. One wonders if Hillary Clinton will invoke her now famous quote from another interview, "At this point, what difference does it all make?" Probably not. In fact, many expect the scandal to be buried deep in the bowels of Philadelphia's Wells Fargo Convention Center until unearthed and replaced by a larger one. Republicans are not going sit on their hands while the Democrats turn on the fog-making machine to divert attention away from their intramural election rigging. They're already doing interviews with the media as we speak.

The Russians are coming! The Russians are coming! "Pssst, tovarish, please pass the decoder ring. We have to get this hack of the DNC's computers finished before Comrade Putin comes back from his phone call with Julian Assange. You know how long it took us to sweep up after we hacked Madam Secretary's server in Chappaqua. I don't want a repeat of that with the DNC hack, so let's get a move on!" That is a fictional conversation, but, according to the Democrats, it could have happened – that the Russians could be behind the intrusion into the DNC's computer system AND be responsible for a possible attack on Mr. and Mrs. Clinton's basement bathroom server. While there is no evidence at this point that Russia is involved, there is a real worry among Democrats that there is another digital shoe to drop – that a few thousand more Hillary Clinton emails could suddenly turn up on the day she is to address her convention.

The one perplexing thing, at least for Republicans, in the DNC scandal – and in all Democrat scandals like Benghazi and 'Servergate' for that matter – is that nobody ever gets fired! In this case, Congresswoman Wasserman Schultz who headed up the Democratic Party's now thoroughly disgraced DNC, resigned. Not fired mind you, resigned. Shortly thereafter, she was promptly named the Honorary Chairman for the Hillary Clinton 50-state election campaign. That's chutzpah, Hillary Clinton style. Who said that the Democrats don't take care of their own? We might find some disagreement on that score by talking to a few Bernie Sanders supporters that thought the Democratic Party was playing it straight down the middle with them. The convention should be interesting at the very least, thanks to Wikileaks...and maybe the Russians. Spasiba.

~

The 'finalis disputatione'

The last of three Presidential debates will be held tonight. For those of you too shell-shocked by the campaign to understand that sentence...this is the last debate. No more. Finito. It will be held in the pleasure center of America's corpus, that quintessential city of entertainment and gambling, Las Vegas! Yes, folks, deep in the city that never remembers anything, that doesn't know you're here if your wife calls, or that only exists to fulfill your every fantasy and desire for wealth and happiness, our two remaining candidates for the Presidency will duke it out before an audience of upwards of 70 million bloodthirsty American TV viewers.

Instead of allowing Caesar's Palace to host it, where lions would have been the perfect arbiters of good taste, the event will be held at the Thomas & Mack Center at the University of Las Vegas not far from the glitz and gaudiness of the Vegas strip. My fantasy scenario for the evening would have gone something like this, however...The lights dim twice and rise again at the T&M Center hall. (I kept the venue as it was too late to change it, even in my mind.).

The stage, which has a sawdust floor and is surrounded by a twelve-foot steel cage with only one entrance/exit (a door made of shards of glass), is illuminated by two searchlights that spread their beams over the cage as the two candidates are introduced by none other than lion tamers and illusionists Siegfried (Fischbacher) and Roy (Horn). Both are clad in their LV stage costumes and both are riding white tigers down a ramp located high in the rafters of the hall to the absolute delight of the audience that is all dressed in classic Roman togas.

Roy (the dark-haired and more ostentatious of the two) clears his throat and bellows..."And now I give you her mightiness, the irresistible, HILLARY!" Madame Secretary walks in dressed in a willowy long toga with a gold breastplate over it. She has a huge sword dangling from a scabbard that is attached to a waist cord made of braided gold ("Something I just whipped up at the last minute from some leftover donations to the Clinton Foundation," she said.) Her hair is done up high and in the shape of a helmet and is protected by what looks like two golden serpents with intertwined tails. ("My stylist put it together from jewelry on loan to me by some campaign donors," she stated.)

No sooner had she reached her podium (hand-carved to resemble a chariot from the movie Ben Hur) than the voice of Siegfried boomed over the microphone (Sigfried's the blond one with the heavy German accent that sounds like a cross between Henry Kissinger and Arnold Schwarzenegger). "Ladies and gentlemen, put your hands together for Donaaaald Truuuump!"

Trump enters the stage also dressed in a toga but with the laurel branch of the Caesars crowning his orange/blond locks. He is giving the 'thumbs-up' sign to the audience as he enters the steel cage and stands behind his own podium which is also made into the shape of a chariot but with specially-formed scythed blades that extend a full-three feet from the sides. "These," said Trump, "are so crooked Hillary doesn't get near my real estate." The giant door is closed with a thud and the moderator, Chris Wallace, who is dressed as an executioner in all black leather with silver studs on his arms is carried onto the stage by six recent Syrian immigrants dressed as Nubian slaves.

(Their spokesslave commented that this was the only job they could get that didn't require extreme vetting.) The debate begins with questions about immigration, foreign affairs and Obamacare, but is quickly sidetracked to Mrs. Clinton's emails and Benghazi by Trump who is now rattling his chariot as if he is careening around the arena in pursuit of her. She pivots and heads down the 'woman assault path,' alleging that Trump has bedded most of Las Vegas' women, to which he replies, "That's not true, simply not true, not in the high-season, anyway." The audience erupts in waves of raucous laughter, and sensing he has them on his side, Trump flashes a broad smile and takes a bow.

His moment in the sun is short-lived, however, as moderator Wallace fires off a missile, "Is it true, Mr. Trump, that you and Vladimir Putin were lovers in the 1970s?" "Absolutely not," says Trump. "You're confusing me with Yoko Ono and my opponent Hillary Clinton. Vlad and I have never met and we have never ever exchanged any love letters as was reported by that sleazy rag, the Washington Post, or as I call it, the "Washington Post-It Note for the illiterati." After a few more heated exchanges between the candidates and the moderator and amid heckling by the now extremely excited audience, the debate is nearing its climax.

As a surprise to everyone, Bill Clinton has now walked onto the stage and is standing outside the cage. He has begun to address the audience. Looking every bit an emperor, WJC throws his toga trail over his shoulder and begins to speak. "Friends, Las Vegans, countrymen. Lend me your ears. I have not come to praise Hillary nor to condemn Trump. I come to offer myself to you instead of these two totally unworthy candidates. You know in your heart that you want me back, so let's make it official. All in favor of having another four-year Big Dog administration, raise your hands."

Hands start going up by the hundreds until nearly the whole hall is a sea of arms pointed toward the heavens. Getting the approval he sought, Bubba gives the nod to Wallace who promptly pushes a button and releases the debate floor beneath the candidates which sends them both to the basement where their screams and the sounds of white tigers' growling waft through the floorboards until silence once again returns. The third debate is over, but the games are just about to begin as William Jefferson Clinton has just announced his candidacy and the clock will start anew as he begins his campaign, but not before spending a few days *taking in the sights* from his penthouse suite high atop Caesar's Palace. The last camera shot we see is Clinton smiling at us as he puts out the "Do Not Disturb" sign alongside his emperor's laurel crown on his doorknob and then disappears from view.

~

The (nearly) great Democrat debate

Lincoln and Douglas it wasn't, but the Democratic Party debate of last week was, perhaps, a template for what we can expect debates to look like from now on. Ironically, the Democrat field included a bunch of old White guys (OWGs), something the Democrats have been accusing the Republican Party of being for many years. The only diversity representative was Hillary Clinton who managed to out-man the men, by answering questions with a presidential pondus that all on the stage could envy. Those expecting a donnybrook among the five were surely disappointed as CNN demurred from posing the really tough questions that would have set them against each another (something they did with impunity in the previous Republican debate). That's not to say it wasn't entertaining. Senator Bernie Sanders performed true to form haranguing capitalism, the 1 vs. 99%, income inequality and generally acted the part of the graying modern-day activist, something Saul Alinsky would have been proud of.

His decibel level and passion were high and he didn't shy away from throwing Wall Street and all the other greedy rich under the socialism bus. He was also short on details, something he shared with the other candidates. Governors Chafee (Rhode Island) and O'Malley (Maryland) talked, understandably, of their accomplishments, but lacked the fire in the belly that one would have expected from underdogs in the race. Chafee's demeanor was ramrod stiff and his performance was lackluster. O'Malley took the high road of speaking in dulcet tones of vision and inclusionary politics (let's all get along).

I couldn't help but think that his frequent looks to his right, to Hillary Clinton, was a deliberate attempt at some potential VP posturing. The most disappointing of all was Senator Jim Webb whose resumé as former Secretary of the Navy and accomplished author was eclipsed by a wooden and uninspiring delivery. He was clearly a fish out of water in what was a sea of forced calm. He had his chance to shine by talking of the real foreign policy dangers we face, but ran afoul of the clock that ticked away his opportunities. Mrs. Clinton stole the show and even got a welcome 'reprieve' from her Benghazi and email troubles by a statement from Sanders, "I think the Secretary is right. And that is, I think the American people are sick and tired of hearing about your damn emails." The crowd erupted and Mrs. Clinton reached out and shook Sander's hand with a big, "Thank you."

CNN moderator, Anderson Cooper, did his level best to keep everybody on time and on point and asked some good questions, but nothing terribly penetrating or personal except for one that went to Hillary Clinton's credibility and her frequently changing positions on major issues. As a graduate of the Bill Clinton School of Deflection she handled herself like a pro. She dodged and weaved like a tight end running wide of the tacklers. Those who prefer a polished pol had reason to rejoice, as for the rest of us that prefer specific answers to specific questions we were left wanting. Unfortunately, we Americans have become accustomed to that stereotype, but that's not to say we like it.

That is evident by the poll numbers that show Mrs. Clinton as untrustworthy or worse. The good news (for some) is that we will have ample opportunity to see her and her Republican rivals in action for another year. There is still one more choice left to be made and that is whether we prefer an 'outsider or insider' candidate. Will we support a radical change that will put a neurosurgeon, a real estate magnate or a former computer company CEO at the top of our wish list or will we fall back on the tried and true career politician from the Democrat or Republican field to lead us into the future? Stay tuned for more as we navigate the road already heavily traveled through the months ahead. I can hardly wait.

~

The (new) American (voter) revolution

There was no single *shot heard round the world* to mark the start of the newest American voter revolution. We didn't need it; we all knew it was coming. After the last two hand-offs of the Presidency from Democrat to Republican to Democrat it was bound to happen. If our skepticism and distrust of our leaders wasn't earned solely by the decisions of all three Presidents, the stalemates in our divided Houses of Representatives, several highly controversial Supreme Court rulings, numerous Executive

Orders issued by the current President then all the various political scandals of both parties insured it. The result of which is a uniform 'throw the bums out' mentality by the voters.

This fight is now playing out for all of the world to see in a flight to the extremes of ideology from the campaigns of avowed socialist Senator Bernie Sanders on the left to that of populist businessman Donald Trump on the right. The polarity is astounding. While their positions on most issues may have nothing in common with each other, both agree that the devil is not in the details but rather in the halls of power in Washington, DC, aka the 'Government,' or if you prefer, the 'swamp.'

THAT is a pitch that resonates and one that will help them ride the crest of the anti-politician wave through the first few primaries UNTIL they get tarred with their own brush and <u>become</u> the politicians, themselves. It's inevitable. No one can continue to speak in generalities forever. Sooner or later Bernie Sanders will have to explain how his 'Robin Hood' philosophy of stealing from the rich and giving to the poor will work in practice, and Donald Trump will have to go into detail about how he will "Make America great again" and pay for all his promises WITHOUT a little help from Robin Hood.

Even after writing two books on the American voter and the American political system, I still have great difficulty in predicting where this is all going simply because there are so many wildcards in this particular card game. Not since the Vietnam War have I seen such a split in the American electorate and such widespread and intense distrust of politicians. While the Tea Party may have been the visible manifestation of that discontent on the right, it was piggybacking on years of growing dissatisfaction with government overreach and mismanagement. The same goes for 'Occupy Wall Street.'

American voters are chomping at the bit (again) for change. They want their country back, their lives back, their jobs back, their self-respect back and yes their <u>faith</u> in their fellow man and their elected officials back. They want safe drug-free schools, neighborhoods without sexual predators, crime under control, the border secured, an opportunity and a pathway to a well-paying job. American voters don't want partisanship to the point of inertia, a world where we play no role nor one that sees us as an unwanted aggressor. They also don't want tyranny in any form, whether from government leaders, their rules and regulations or from oligarchs in the business world. They're fed up with race hustlers and with phony racism.

Mostly, they're tired of having to stand at the barricades or march to the ballot box every four years to preserve what's left of *their* ideology.

They're gasping for air and don't want their country to go down for the third time, so they're getting ready for one final battle that will not only decide the country's political direction but also Americans' livelihoods for the foreseeable future. The wrong outcome of the 2016 Presidential election will almost certainly guarantee that millions of American voters will drop out of the process and embrace an 'every man for himself' strategy instead of a 'one for all and all for one' course.

~

The new pachyderm shift

On Tuesday, the Hoosiers of Indiana cast their lot with Donald Trump and helped him push the last brick into place for the *house that Trump built*. His rivals soon took to the stage and announced the suspension of their campaigns. This left a clear field for the most non-traditional Republican candidate since Barry Goldwater to confidently sprint towards the nomination in Cleveland.

Whether they knew it or not, Indianans effectively fired the first shot in the general election campaign (though the Democrats have yet to crown Hillary Clinton). So, instead of waiting until after the June 7th primaries, the Trump campaign will be in general election mode until the actual convention voting takes place in July.

There are a fair number of Republicans, among them House Speaker, Congressman Paul Ryan, sitting on the sidelines now. All are wondering if they can support a candidate who's managed to break every commandment of traditional campaigning. They're wondering if they have the courage to go public with their support for him lest they be accused by the opposition of being a bigot, a racist, a woman-hater or a bully-lover. These timid souls may in fact become a 'ghost army,' waiting at the periphery to bolster the main line of defense when the Democrats start lobbing the heavy artillery at the Party. They could also be regarded as the new Republican 'silent majority' - largely unwilling to show their faces (or their hands) at the political poker table until the last possible second.

All will demand strong, reasoned leadership from a commander-in-chief that doesn't turn the other cheek after the first punch is thrown. While many are fearful that an alpha male's hands shouldn't be anywhere near the levers of power, another group is counting on it. Unfortunately, both

178

populate the same party. That's why both groups must come together NOW and form a coalition of the willing that includes moderates, independents AND the new deal (*Art of the Deal*) Trump supporters.

There's no room on the bus for fence-sitters or grudge-holders if the Party is to remain a politically-viable force for spreading a conservative message. To spread that message, the Party must enlist a sizable vanguard of capital 'R' Republicans to backstop Trump when he speaks about the virtues of capitalism, conservative values, safeguarding our homeland and making the economy work for everybody.

This is not a wish list; it is a must do list if the Party is to shake off the negative publicity that continues to dog Mr. Trump's own campaign comments. Candidate Trump has forced the Republican Party into a kind of 'Sophie's choice' situation, where it must choose the least painful of two options...to change dramatically or to fade into obscurity. The burden of that choice must be borne by all Republicans; no one is exempt from it. There is no middle ground. Either Republicans work together to get their candidate to soften his rough edges and adopt some positions that won't alienate potential voters in November OR they must resign themselves to another humiliating loss at the ballot box.

In the musical "Jesus Christ Superstar" Mary Magdalene sang, "I don't know how to love him." This song reflects the sentiment of many Republican voters (especially women voters) who see Trump the man as a walking contradiction - a bewildering combination of two incompatible people inhabiting the same body. One says he loves them; the other questions their value. And they're not the only ones. Add all minorities and moderates to that list and you have a sizable voter deficit. Some epic bridge-building must take place during the next few months. THAT is an existential task. If something isn't done, the Party will experience a silent, steady bleed as its moderates head for the lifeboats and the open sea, abandoning the devil they like the least.

~

The people's choice

The first Republican debates for the Party's Presidential nominee were a resounding success with many of the Party faithful, but they also prompted a number of negative responses. Here are just a few of them: "I think that if Mr. Trump is going to participate in what amounts to a beauty pageant then he ought to be wearing a swimsuit, himself." This was followed by another viewer that said, "They all looked like used car salesmen, so the RNC ought to hold the next debate on a car lot." Another viewer opined, "At least none of the candidates had tattoos or wore earrings." A senior Republican analyst was overheard saying, "If this is a meat market, I'm becoming a vegetarian."

The opposition, predictably, had something to say, though it's possible I misheard the statement from the head of the DNC that went, "You call these candidates"? I call them glorified Fuller Brush men. I doubt if they could even spell campaign let alone mount one. They're all amateurs with sky high hopes of grabbing the brass ring away from OUR candidate-in-waiting, Hillary Clinton, who, as everyone knows, was pre-destined to become Commander-in-Chief and take up the torch from her husband."

Matter of fact, now that I write that from memory, I'm pretty sure that I misheard her. What I actually think she said was, "The Republicans are all morons and misogynists. None of them have ever held a real job, unlike Secretary Clinton who has done everything AND single-handedly fought for the rights of our 99% and all the underprivileged masses around the world. No other woman in all of American history can touch the hem of her garment when it comes to experience and commitment to the downtrodden."

I shared that quote with Hubertus, one of my Republican friends. He wasn't as sanguine as the DNC chief. Matter of fact, he went all Trump on me and started reciting all the scandals that Mrs. Clinton has been involved in. There was *Troopergate* (really her hubby's scandal), *Whitewatergate*, *Travelgate*, the *Bimbo Hit-Squadgate*, *Benghazigate*, *Email/Servergate*. Hubertus was on a roll, but I had to stop him before his head exploded.

"My friend," I said. "Let's keep this thing fair and balanced. Isn't it true that there were also scandals among the Rs? What about *Bridgegate* (Governor Christie)? And *Motorboatgate* (Senator Rubio)? How are the Republicans going to handle the press AND narrow down the field of candidates so the American voter can choose among them"? Are you just going to wait for the primaries?"

At this point Hubertus pulled himself up to his full height, threw out his chest, leaned in towards me and said, "We've got that figured out. We're going to radically transform the debate process and demand that the Dems do the same. Here's our plan...we will hold the next debate under water and give the candidates scuba gear with built-in microphones and a regulator that automatically cuts off their air supply if they go over time with their answers. That will probably eliminate a couple. We'll hold the third debate at 'Six Flags Over Texas,' and instead of a debate stage, all candidates will be strapped in to the "Pulverizer" (Six Flags' own monster roller coaster ride). This will lighten their responses (and maybe their lunch), automatically, and will help winnow the field by two or three by the end of the day.

"Wow, that will certainly shake things up," I said. "What about the final debates between the Republican and Democrat nominees?" Hubertus smiled. "I don't want to let the cat out of the bag just yet, but I can say that we have borrowed some ideas from the ancient Romans, and we will be auditioning some animals very soon."

~

The shot heard round the world...again

It's almost over. Just two days to go before the Election of 2016 and three days before the start of the new American Revolution. That's because, if Hillary Clinton and her party win, we the charter members of the basket of deplorables of America (conservative Republicans), will be fighting her and her Progressive friends and supporters on November 9th to preserve what is left of the greatest political experiment on Earth.

Make no mistake. Mrs. Clinton is not a moderate or a closeted middle-of-the-road Democrat. She is a dyed in the wool Liberal and represents the newest and most serious threat to millions of God-fearing, law-abiding, family-oriented, traditional Americans who have been living lives of quiet desperation these last eight years watching their freedoms be systematically stripped from them by an ultra-Left leaning administration.

While our current form of Progressivism may differ from the hegemony and colonialism that was practiced by the British Empire that governed us until our first American Revolution in the late 1700s, it is, nonetheless, every bit as dangerous to our core values and our rights as expressed in our Constitution and Bill of Rights. For those unsure of just what Progressivism or its more modern cousin, Secular Progressivism is, it's a belief system that is non-religious-based (and sometimes vehemently anti-religious). It supports an immediate and fundamental change from America's traditional values and conservative thought and instead advocates for a rapid and thorough movement towards liberalism that would give preference to the rights of the collective over those of the individual.

181

It is an ideology that has steadily infected our politics and permeated our entire culture in a myriad of ways from bathrooms to battleships. Just the name 'Progressivism' is a gross misrepresentation of a belief system that has more to do with socialism than with promoting the individual liberties won for us in our first American Revolution. I would contend that there is absolutely nothing redeemable in subordinating the rights of the individual, for it is the individual that creates the collective, not the other way around.

Secular Progressives have joined the liberal crusade with the caveat that any movement towards liberal group-think must avoid association with religion or the practice thereof. They will often point to a specious argument to bolster their case. It is: "Isn't it better to sacrifice the liberties of a few when the liberties (or welfare) of the many are at stake?" It's also a frankly un-American choice when seen against the backdrop and intent of our Constitution, and it reminds me of a quote from Ben Franklin, "Those who would give up essential liberty to purchase a little temporary safety deserve neither liberty nor safety."

The birth and first few decades of Progressivism from 1890-1920 were largely focused on improving the lot of America's middle class at a time when our rapid industrialization was leaving many workers behind and was treating them as expendable cogs in corporate America's *wheel*.

The rise of labor unionism helped to improve the living standard of many workers, but Progressivism then became a political movement that turned its focus on the whole of U.S. society. To be sure it was difficult then (and now) to argue with the Progressives' belief that many of society's problems like poverty, greed, racism and violence can be reduced or even eliminated with a good education and a safe environment, but that was an unreasonably simplistic cause and effect argument because it ignored, and continues to ignore, the advanced state of American politics and life, in general.

It was mostly the high-handed manner in which Progressives pressed their case (a forced, top-down approach) that created and strengthened the enormous opposition to this new form of social engineering. That was until the bad times of the Depression hit, and America again flirted with it. The after-effects of the Russian Revolution of 1917 were striking and it was clear for all to see that the seizure of individuals' rights did the opposite of what was expected.

The emphasis placed on the collective and de-emphasis on the individual led to a breakdown of openness, elimination of willful, spirited cooperation and destroyed independent thought and creativity. The collectivist approach led to a fear and loathing of authority and a retreat from all that empowered it.

Human nature takes over when human beings' rights are abridged by centrally-managed, top-down and top-heavy bureaucracies. A lack of respect for authority ensues (because absolute authority usually ignores the wishes of the governed). The work ethic suffers and public greed increases as everyone scrambles to make sure he/she gets his 'fair share' of subsidies, all provided by an ever-dwindling base of producers and taxpayers.

As is so often the case with well-meaning people, their motives may be good, but their methods of effecting change can be disastrous. This is true when Progressivism runs wild with its own power to legislate - either from the Legislative Branch, from the bench of the Supreme Court or from the Oval Office. Any ideology, which favors the rights of the collective and subsumes those of the individual - and when given unlimited power to seed itself and grow unfettered or unchallenged in the boardroom, schoolroom or in government - presents a real and present danger to our democracy. And no matter how attractive the messenger, the message of a totalitarian ideology that would limit the individual's power over his/her own lives is reprehensible.

While Theodore Roosevelt may have been a colorful figure and proponent of the idea of Progressivism in his day, his fifth cousin, Franklin Roosevelt, made it happen with several controversial programs, the first of which was the 'CCC' (the Civilian Conservation Corps) which was essentially a paramilitary organization. The columnist Jonah Goldberg, describes it this way, "Enlistees met at army recruiting stations; wore World War I uniforms; were transported around the country by troop trains; answered to army sergeants; were required to stand at attention, march in formation, employ military lingo...; read a CCC newspaper modeled on Stars and Stripes; went to bed in army tents listening to taps; and woke to reveille."

Again, while no one can dispute the need for something bold to put men to work during a crisis, many can dispute the way it was done...entirely by government. Later, Roosevelt would institute the National Recovery Administration (or NRA) and extend the reach of government even further. It should be noted that this was also being done in other parts of the world at the same time, but by very different governments like the National Socialists in Germany. Interestingly enough, the leaders of both the U.S. and Germany used the power of demagoguery to accomplish their goals and consolidate their power as has our current President. Though one government then may have been benign while the other was malignant, they both used some of the same tools of persuasion.

On Tuesday, America will vote for its President, but more importantly, it will decide which ideology it will support. Will it be that of the Progressive demagogue who would forcefully re-distribute America's wealth, dilute or eliminate the rights of the individual and increase the power of the few and influential in Washington, DC or will it be the other demagogue populist who has played on the anger and disappointment of the average man and who promises to return power back to people by sweeping his broom in the corners where all the spiders of Progressive group-think reside? I have already voted - not only my conscience - but also my fidelity to the values and ideals that made this country great and will, with God's help and blessing, make it great again.

~

The single-market Stockholm Syndrome

Stockholm Syndrome is a condition that is defined as <u>identifying with your captors.</u> *Think Patty Hearst and the Symbionese Liberation Army.* It can also apply to companies that have been convinced into believing that putting all their (export) eggs into one (single export market) basket is a great strategy. Let's use our closest market, Mexico, as an example.

Say you're a big manufacturer and the customer that buys your components instructs you to send them to Mexico where they are assembled into his products across the border in a maquiladora. On the surface it's good business for you to help your client lower production costs by sending your parts to be assembled by Mexican workers who earn considerably less than those of a U.S.-based company. Let's also say that the bulk of those finished products are re-exported back to the U.S.

In this case, the lower production costs mean lower retail prices for American consumers. The downside with this scenario is that American workers lose out. Sure, they get *other* jobs (like shippers, consolidators and warehousers) to take the place of assembly and quality control jobs, but they are generally lower-paying jobs than the ones we lost, AND they are very susceptible to market downturns. Manufacturing jobs are also susceptible to market downturns, but the difference is that American

184

companies that manufacture close to home not using foreign contract manufacturers or assemblers can more easily shift production or reduce it quickly (and without penalty). Those using offshore manufacturing are essentially locked in by foreign contracts that may be difficult to break. To those profiting from the maquiladora strategy, congratulations. I just don't believe that that strategy optimizes flexibility or grows U.S. jobs.

Some have said it's even downright unpatriotic. That icon of the 'Apprentice,' Donald Trump, recently made a statement (February at CPAC) that, "Mexico is not our friend. I'm not just talking about the border. Mexico is ripping off the United States big league and we have to do something." That's an extreme viewpoint in my opinion. What I suspect he meant was that NAFTA and the maquiladoras present opportunities that cost-driven U.S. companies cannot ignore, AND that we have helped them beyond the point of simple neighborliness. NAFTA does much good, but it is also the business equivalent of affirmative action, tilting the scales of fair trade by, among other things, disadvantaging American contract manufacturers and assemblers.

Our recent quantum leap in exports to Mexico, according to a report from the U.S. Dept. of Commerce has, to use the words of a well-known border/maquiladora proponent, made 'south' - the southern part of New Mexico - a (manufacturing) "powerhouse." It's especially true if *south* means south of the border - in Mexico. Exports to Mexico (for maquiladora assembly and re-export) have grown the stats substantially and focused New Mexico's gaze on places like Santa Teresa as a consolidation hub.

Fortunately, many New Mexican communities' direct exports still originate from all over our state and help retain valuable jobs <u>in their own communities</u> like: southeastern New Mexico (for dairy products and foodstuffs), Albuquerque (for aviation and non-electrical machinery equipment) and Artesia (for refined fuels), etc.

If we really want to win the export 'war' we're going to need to remember that <u>depending on a single market to the exclusion of all others is a strategy of extreme vulnerability.</u> While we should be grateful for the Mexican export market, we need to look beyond it to the rest of the world's markets, and we need to produce even *higher* value exports <u>here</u> and increase our overall finished goods export volume to those foreign markets. We can all be seduced by our own ambition from time to time and start believing our own PR, especially when we're too heavily invested in one market, but Single-market Stockholm Syndrome can be hazardous to our exporting health.

The bottom line is that more markets equal more opportunities. More companies selling in more markets equal even more opportunities. It's as simple as that. In any case, we need to re-negotiate NAFTA as a first step towards re-balancing the scales.

~

The Smolder in Boulder

The mood was electric or at least static electric as the Republican candidates stood poised to take on the hit squad of CNBC moderators and questions that were better suited to battlefield interrogators than to professionals from a national network. The 'Smolder in Boulder' made the first Democrat debate look like a wake for an IRS agent.

Boulder, Colorado doesn't exactly spring to mind when one thinks of the perfect venue for a Republican debate as the city is so heavily Democrat-leaning, nor would one immediately think of CNBC as the epitome of a fair and balanced network to conduct it, but the wheel stopped there after Fox and CNN had their turns. The evening started out with a lot of 'jump balls' as candidates scrambled to get microphone time on the heels of questions to their competitors. CNBC moderators threw out plenty of red meat to them, egging on the candidates to criticize their peers.

Predictably, Donald Trump went on the offensive and criticized John Kasich for being on the board of Lehman Brothers, implying that he was not the populist he claimed to be but one of the Wall Street establishment. Trump continued his parade of generalities throughout the debate leaving us with more questions than detailed answers. There was no shortage of barbs thrown at each other, but later in hour two the candidates turned the tables on CNBC calling them out for rude and stupid questions such as one on Fantasy Football which prompted a rebuke from Chris Christie saying that with all the serious issues at stake that CNBC would choose such a ridiculous question and waste viewers' time was unbelievable.

At a point, it seemed that the candidates circled the wagons and were unified in their disdain of the questioners. There were, to be fair, a number of questions about the serious challenges facing voters on the economy, the budget, a few on immigration but none on foreign policy or race relations, for example. Healthcare, entitlement programs like Social Security and Medicare were debated roundly with most candidates reverting to their own talking points while some like Marco Rubio spent his time on specifics. Rubio also took a personal question on his own

186

finances and pivoted to the problems facing America at large, making a great case for his candidacy. Ben Carson remained gentlemanly throughout but stumbled briefly when asked to explain how he would turn around the American economy. He recovered his balance and collected his thoughts, but it was obvious that economics was not his strong suit.

John Kasich was Mr. Ohio and never missed an opportunity to speak of his accomplishments in turning around that state's economy and used his time to speak of his vision for applying the same solutions, nationally. Huckabee and Paul acquitted themselves well when they were called on (which was not often) and answered every question with poise and conviction. Moderator Becky Quick was CNBC's Trojan horse and used her soft spoken style and understated demeanor to deliver several body blows like questions to Donald Trump on comments he made about Marco Rubio being too close to Mark Zuckerberg (allowing too many H1/B1 visa applicants into the U.S.). Trump denied saying it but was proved wrong by Ms. Quick's follow-up quoting the comments as coming from Trump's own website!

Jeb Bush held his own in the debate but was severely understated in his answers. While he made no mistakes, he left no lasting impression as being presidential, either. Unlike other candidates that relied on trumpeting their accomplishments while being in office he, regrettably, lacked enthusiasm. His low key approach proved, to many, that he resembled Trump's assertion of him being a "low energy" candidate.

Carly Fiorina, on the other hand, delivered a solid performance in giving fluid and well-thought out answers, especially when she was queried on her time as CEO at HP and talked about her stint there in the context of America's struggle to climb out of the 15-year bond and stock market hole. Ted Cruz was at the top of his game and gave carefully edited, and seemingly unscripted, answers to every question. He appeared calm and collected and scored big with the audience that responded very enthusiastically to him.

As previously stated, the second hour was definitely the demise of CNBC as nearly all the candidates threw them under the 'media bus' with criticism of their sophomoric questions. The audience was in complete agreement and responded with boos at one point. The winner of the debate? It was the Republican candidates as a whole as no one candidate stood head and shoulders above the others. The other winner was the issues which, unlike in the Democratic debate, were not AWOL.

~

The three faces of the Republican Party

Face 1. The Establishment Elite
Face 2. The Populist Republicans
Face 3. The Moderate Republicans

There has never been an election year in modern memory that has surprised us more, shaken us up more and thrown the Republican Party off its axis more than this year. My co-author (Lance Tarrance, a nationally recognized pollster) and I saw this coming back in 2013, long before we wrote our newest book, "Breaking Republican" (2015) which predicted the rise of an *outsider* or as we call it, a 'Third Way' candidate.

Face 1 - The Establishment Elite

That prediction aside, we also called for a quick and thorough self-intervention by the Republican Party in our first book, "How Republicans can win in a changing America." Unfortunately, the Party did not heed our call, but instead decided to let things play out on their own after the humiliating loss of a truly fine candidate, Mitt Romney, to Barack Obama in 2012. In doing so, they proved the old adage that, 'the undertaker can take his time because his customer isn't going anywhere.'

While it may not be fair to place the entire blame on the party elite for their reluctance to do any meaningful soul-searching, it is fair to hold them accountable for their ignorance of the realities that were staring them squarely in the face. These were: an America in tatters, headed by an inept Administration that allowed gender, race, generational and economic conflicts to fester; that ventured into dangerous international policy waters; and that showed its true colors by abusing its power...and our Constitution.

The worst sin of all, however, was the elite's refusal to acknowledge the changing/changed American electorate and an incorrect assessment of the extent of their anger and resentment for all who held positions of authority within the Government and the Party. Republicans have also had grievances with their leaders and elected officials, but those grievances have usually been addressed well before the Party asked its faithful to fall in line while being given their marching orders before major elections. This time they weren't, and the Party would soon pay a high price for its intransigence.

188

The greatest threat of all to the Party was the refusal of its leaders to change and adapt to the new reality of the rise of the low-information and high-emotion voters - voters that had been discounted as unimportant long ago. In short, after throwing open the shutters that protected them from the elements of dissent and disagreement, Party elders found a lynch mob of angry people who were ready to take down America's 'ruling class' of professional politicians and sacrifice everything to rescue the country and a way of life they loved.

These were not radicals; they were people from all wings of the Republican Party. They were not just Tea Partyers or single-issue proponents or fringe elements. They were the working middle class and the silent millions who went about their daily business, secure in the knowledge that the Party they served and supported would honor their obligation to keep pace with the times and evolve, especially after being trounced in the last two Presidential elections. How wrong they were. The Party wasn't listening, nor did it have its finger on the pulse of the massive growing unrest that would soon explode in the Primary Season of 2016.

Face 2 - The Populist Republicans

A new political and generational paradigm had arrived...unbridled populism. It was threatening to the establishment because it was neither prepared for it nor understood it. This new Republican brand of populism was not born with the announcement of Donald Trump to run for President in the summer of 2015 nor was it conceived with the formation of the Tea Party, though each had its own separate and profound impact on it. It had been slowly fermenting in every corner of the U.S., in every small town and every big city and in the minds of millions of dissatisfied, disgruntled Americans for the last 7½ years of the Obama Administration.

And while it may be difficult to pinpoint exactly when the new Republican populism reached its critical mass, it's probably fair to say that a few influential individuals were key in helping propel it along. One was Senator Rand Paul and another was Senator Ted Cruz, but the second stage booster rocket that carried it beyond the Republican establishment's political gravitational pull was a larger-than-life billionaire businessman, Donald Trump. Here was a candidate that could articulate, though often in an inarticulate way, all the pent-up emotions and grievances that many Republican and independent voters had been yearning to actualize for years, but had been kept in check by the Republican Party establishment.

189

The establishment's motives for preserving the status quo weren't evil or Machiavellian. They were, however, woefully misguided in their decision to continue promoting candidates that adhered to accepted 'traditional' methods of political engagement. Had they been listening carefully they would have realized that their base was already way past the boiling point and was now demanding <u>new</u> rules of engagement that were grounded in the reality of the new political paradigm of populism.

Face 3 - The moderate Republicans

There is a tendency, particularly among the media, to paint all Republicans as a uniform bunch of anti-government, law and order, pro-big business types. And while many Republicans do identify with that description, there are also many that place themselves somewhere in the middle of the Republican political spectrum, especially when it comes to certain social and leadership issues. These are the Party's moderates, and their disagreements are often about degree and process. They are the softer voices among the throng of more vocal members. They participate, but usually quietly. They hesitate to rise from their seats and clap loudly or chant "USA, USA, USA" and they are often confused about the animated nature and assertiveness of their Party brethren.

They are equally bewildered by the political tactics used by their elected representatives. Despite their confusion, they remain loyal and steadfast in their support of the Party's overarching goals and vision. This year is testing their wisdom, their resolve and their patience as they see the Party's front-runner populist candidate barrel through the Primary contests, winning nearly everything in sight accompanied by an unusually shrill and often confrontational tone. They are keeping their powder and their criticism dry, waiting to see if populist rhetoric and bombast will give way to hopeful words and a positive Republican message of which they can be proud.

The moderates of the Party are many and far from naive. They realize that the stakes in 2016 are perhaps the highest they've been in thirty-five years and are willing to 'let it all ride' as the political roulette wheels spins for another couple months before a nominee is chosen. In July they will be faced with a choice. Will they accept the will of the majority or a plurality of populists or will they seek shelter in neutrality or worse, self-imposed political hibernation, until it is <u>their</u> time again? Should they choose the latter, the real question is, "Will the Party still be there for them when and if they return?"

The ultimate pile-on

Today's media coverage of the Presidential election reminds me of a Rugby match where the players all fall on the one poor sod in possession of the ball in the hopes of crushing him with their collective weight and effectively sidelining him. Seems that we've now reached the point where all of the cable news media outlets (except Fox), all the big three mainstream media TV networks, most of the major newspapers, all Democrats, and even some prominent Republicans have decided that they hate Donald Trump...a little more than they hate Hillary Clinton. CNN and the Washington Post have been on a months-long vendetta to do Trump in, and I cannot even begin to count the emails I get from the Post and others on a daily basis in which they portray DT as a modern-day Hitler, Mussolini, Chairman Mao, Paul Pot, Idi Amin, Sadam Hussein or other nefarious historical despotic figure.

Time out. We need to think this thing through. Yes, it's true that Donald Trump says things that are over the top and sometimes head into the next valley, but who of us hasn't made statements we've later regretted or that were misinterpreted or misconstrued by others? I'm not apologizing for - nor defending - his many ill-advised comments, but I am saying that to compare him to evil dictators for those statements is the antithesis of defending disagreeable speech and open discourse.

If I were a news journalist, I'd probably be tempted to write about the 'crazy Donald,' too, but I wouldn't assume to know what's in his heart. I'd cover his actions and deeds and compare them to his rhetoric, just like we should with every person, be they politician or ordinary citizen. I'd have to give Mr. T. the benefit of the doubt and the presumption of innocence until proven otherwise.

It's true that he has called for a 'time out' or moratorium on allowing citizens of countries with a history of supporting terror against America into America (until we can figure out who they are), but what he's really saying is that we need to be vigilant and look at the facts about terrorism and who is committing it. An honest and thorough vetting of these people is not racist or bigoted. The truth is we need a better vetting system and we need it before we experience any problems, not after they've gained entry into our country.

191

And regarding America's illegal immigration problem...do we need a wall? You bet we do and one with state-of-the-art surveillance. Without a border, Mr. Trump says, "We have no country." The man's right. The border needs to be secure, and we need to immediately turn the illegal border-crossers around and point them back south from whence they came.

On his remarks about Hillary Clinton's trustworthiness? Have at it, Mr. Trump. It's not as if Mrs. Clinton is playing by the Marquess of Queensberry's rules. She's using everything and every media partisan at her disposal to skewer you. What's happened within the last couple weeks, since the end of the Republican Convention, is that DT is pushing back on his *handlers'* suggestions as to how he should be engaging the public. While he might give in to them and do the occasional endorsement (Paul Ryan, John McCain and Kelly Ayotte just recently), the rest of the time he is being himself and doing and saying exactly what he wants.

Unfortunately, those times are the ones that get him into trouble, but he's being guided by personal experience and the golden rule of success: 'if it ain't broke don't fix it.' He knows that he will lose support if he is perceived as a typical politician, and he also knows that there is a price to be paid for disingenuousness - loss of trust - and that is something Hillary Clinton will soon find out...or will she?

Mr. Trump's biggest mistake thus far is assuming that everything that works well in business will also translate as a winning strategy in politics and that every popular brand (his included) should be able to withstand criticism from its detractors. Maybe that was true in the 'old days' when media bias was not so pronounced and widespread, but 2016 is different, especially now that the media has found a man they love to hate! The opposition has also been joined by assorted bigwigs in the Republican Party that are afraid of losing constituent votes if seen as Trump supporters.

The Clinton media meat-grinder is well-oiled and has surrogates/agents everywhere like Paul Begala, Lanny Davis, John Podesta, Van Jones, Don Lemon, Amy Goodwin, Charlie Rose, all of Hollywood celebrityville, Jeff Bezos, former Bill Clinton advisors, Mothers of Black Lives Matter members, AND even some unwitting Republicans who've wandered into the Democrats' carefully spun web of faux *inclusiveness*. I feel a wave building, and it's not surfable. It's deadly and verbal. The signs are the invocation of Nazi Germany, the Holocaust and racial animus. If we must revert to the Nazi past and dredge up the demons of the Third Reich we better take a hard look at the former Minister of Propaganda, Joseph Goebbels, the creator of the 'Big Lie'. Goebbels was a dedicated man, dedicated to propagating untruths. His formula was simple. Don't go for the small lie. If you're going to lie, lie big, then make sure you have a campaign that insinuates and shouts it from the rooftops, often.

Make the lie believable by hitching it to something people *want to believe* or something they are actually seeing happening in real life. Then connect it to a villain and make the villain the subject of incessant attacks. Let the lie be the wave that carries your boats to the shore of people's conscious thoughts.

In Goebbels own words, "If you tell a lie big enough and keep repeating it, people will eventually come to believe it. The lie can be maintained only for such time as the State can shield the people from the political, economic and/or military consequences of the lie. It thus becomes vitally important for the State to use all of its powers to repress dissent, for the truth is the mortal enemy of the lie, and thus by extension, the truth is the greatest enemy of the State."

Once any lie is circulated widely enough and enough negativity is built up, more and more people will lend their words and support to it. That's what's happening today with the 'never Trumpers.' I would guess that the Clinton campaign is both ecstatic about the ground-swell of Trump criticism and worried about it. After all, that which can be done to one's enemies can also be done to one's self. The bottom line is that this is an existential election. The Presidential candidates are actually not as important as their ideologies. One will make America 'great again' and the other will make it 'more of the same again.' The voter needs to remember that going to bed with a clear conscience has a price...as does living one's life without one.

~

The U.S.-Mexico relationship: A study in vulnerability

It's time for a *come to Jesus* meeting of the minds on our attitudes to our neighbor to the south. We need to face the unpleasant fact that our relationship is increasingly starting to feel like a marital estrangement of two people that initially loved one another, but over time have found little in common. Those are big words, and I know that to even give voice to them will rattle people that are heavily invested in building bridges of amity and commerce between our two great countries, but they must be said if we're truly interested in closing the fear, animosity and skepticism gap. Let's look at the facts...

On trade, Mexico is our third largest trading partner (nearly $600 billion in two-way trade). Mexico is our second largest export market. It's also our third largest agricultural export market taking nearly $20 billion of our foodstuffs, annually. Mexico is also the third largest exporter of goods to the U.S. Unfortunately, the U.S. runs a huge annual trade deficit with Mexico (over $60 billion). In simple terms, Mexico sells more to us than we do to them. U.S. companies have invested over $100 billion in Mexico while Mexico has invested under $20 billion in the U.S.! (source: U.S. Trade Representative's Office). Based on the statistics, some in the new U.S. Administration would characterize the relationship as pretty one-sided, especially after having experienced nearly 24 years of NAFTA. Statistics don't tell the whole story, however.

The truth is, that while Mexico has managed to lure many blue chip American manufacturers south of the border, those same companies have profited, mightily, from NAFTA and have taken advantage of Mexico's lower labor costs to produce goods that are then shipped back to U.S. consumers at prices that are lower than if they had been manufactured in our country. That's the good news, but it's also the bad news.

Our manufacturing sector has suffered greatly under NAFTA and has lost well over 600,000 jobs since its inception back in 1993. It would seem nearly impossible to unring that bell and return the majority of those jobs to the U.S., but the Trump Administration is intent on trying by re-negotiating the agreement and by encouraging U.S. manufacturers to stay in the U.S. This should worry both Mexican AND U.S. companies that have come to rely on the maquiladoras as a cheap production source. It should also worry a few major U.S. border cities like El Paso and to a lesser degree those in southern New Mexico if new 'border taxes/surcharges' are applied on Mexican-made goods headed for U.S. markets.

At some point, the pressure could become too great and U.S. companies could pull back from the Mexican market (because not enough U.S. exports to that country are actually consumed in Mexico but are simply re-exported to the U.S.). Their fall-back position could be a re-assessment of their manufacturing and investment strategies. They could very well abandon their operations there, reduce or even cancel their manufacturing contracts in Mexico. It's simple math; new export surcharges would add more to the cost of their goods bound for the U.S.

and negate the advantages of cheap Mexican labor. In short, America's trade and investment future with Mexico is uncertain.

There is another major industry that Mexico and the U.S. share: tourism. According to travel reports, Mexico is the U.S.' top foreign destination with over 28 million Americans visiting that country every year. In total, Mexico derives over $14 billion/year from international tourists, much of it from Americans. It's estimated that Mexican visitors to the U.S. are in the 15-17 million visitors/year range. Tourism promotion in Mexico is done at the national level (SECTUR, the Ministry of Tourism) while U.S. tourism promotion is done at the state and city level.

The bottom line is: <u>both nations need each other's tourism</u>. The Institute for International Education estimates that of the over one million foreign students in the U.S. only about 18,000 are from Mexico (this does not include illegal immigrant students). Even at that low number, Mexico still ranks 10th in terms of all international students here. By contrast, U.S. students in Mexico only number about 3,000. It is estimated that one million people cross the Mexico-U.S. border, legally, every day and that over 4,000 commercial vehicles will do the same and carry with them about $1.4 billion worth of goods.

About 34 million Hispanics of Mexican origin live in the U.S. Of that number, about 11.4 million of them were born in Mexico while the rest were born in the USA or self-identify as Hispanics of Mexican origin. They account for 2/3 of the entire U.S. Hispanic population. Their median age is 25 (source: U.S. Census Bureau). It is estimated that one million American citizens live in Mexico. The U.S. and its border states still have an illegal immigration problem with Mexico even though illegal border crossings are down. Illegal immigration has plagued the U.S. for far too long and must be addressed with a major adjustment to our immigration policy. We desperately need a plan to secure our border, deport dangerous criminals and regularize the status of undocumented persons that have lived here, peaceably, for many years.

Congress must decide which path to take towards legalizing residency and/or providing a pathway to citizenship for America's illegal aliens. We owe it to ourselves and to those millions hiding in plain sight to find a solution that will fix the problem. We also owe it to our relationship with Mexico to close our border to future illegal immigration and stop the flow of drugs being smuggled into our country. In short, one-sided solutions will not solve two-sided problems, and the sooner we understand that, the quicker we will be able to create a new relationship based on a realistic and mutual understanding of just how much we need each other.

~

The very best fences

Folk wisdom has it that "good fences make good neighbors," and while that may be true, it isn't the only criterion for keeping peace with one's neighbors. Take Mexico, for instance. We've been their neighbor and have experienced border problems ever since the 'Mexican Cessation' (the name for the region of modern day southwestern USA that was ceded to us by Mexico under the 1848 Treaty of Guadalupe Hidalgo). This area was no suburban backyard; it encompassed 529,000 square miles and was the third largest acquisition of territory in American history. It came about after U.S. troops invaded Mexico City in 1848. Mexico had only been independent from Spain for 27 years at that point and didn't capitulate from the war nor cede the land, easily. In a very real sense, the country was lucky that the vocal minority in the U.S. that wanted to annex all of Mexico didn't get its way!

The treaty was signed, and the U.S. Treasury cut a check for a cool $15 million for an area that amounted to approximately 15% of the entire USA. Considering the land seizures (including all of Texas), Mexico lost 55% of its pre-1836 territory under the Treaty of Hidalgo. While the treaty effectively ended the Mexican-American War, it didn't end disputes over land. One of those was the actual surveyed area around El Paso and the Mesilla Valley which presented problems for both the U.S. and Mexican governments.

It was eventually solved with the *Gadsden Purchase* on April 25, 1854 under which the U.S. paid Mexico $10 million. However, the Mexican people felt betrayed by this land sale that was agreed to by their leader, Antonio López de Santa Anna, and they made their feelings known, loudly and often. Many scholars say that this is the point in history that seems to mark the birth of the undercurrent of ill will toward the United States that exists today among activists who feel that the U.S. 'stole' Mexican land.

Our relationship with Mexico has undergone and survived many ups and downs over the last one and a half centuries. Our two peoples have gone to each other's schools, intermarried, invested and worked across each other's borders. At times, our relations have been very strained, and the rifts have been plainly evident. Internal economic and social struggles have plagued Mexico for many years, and a porous border with the U.S. has not helped calm the fears nor assuage the anger of ordinary

196

Americans that feel abused and assaulted by illegal immigration and a steady stream of narcotics pouring into our country.

On the other side of the coin are the 'open borders' and 'reconquista' (reconquest) advocates that still poke at the age-old sores of that Mexican resentment over the 'theft' of Mexican territory. Speeches given by the President during the U.S. Presidential campaign and actions taken by his Administration have done nothing to tamp down that resentment. The good news is that we now have an opportunity to honestly air our grievances with one another. Maybe we can remind ourselves of the importance of our relationship and that will encourage us to renew our pledge to work together to find mutually-beneficial solutions for the future. Now that that opening exists, it is up to both parties to admit, that while good fences may make good neighbors, the *best* fences are those that are well-maintained and properly reinforced, that protect both neighbors and are not so high as to prevent us from talking over them.

~

The voluntary partitioning of America

We've been experiencing a political migratory movement in the United States for some time now. Liberals are taking over America's cities while conservatives are leaving for the suburban and exurban areas. The migration is also leaving some states *true blue* and others *blood red*. Take California for example. While about 25% of the population there self-identifies as conservative or Republican, that leaves 75% that don't, and their voting patterns clearly tell us where they stand: a Democrat Governor, Democrat House and Democrat Senate. They also stand with two feet planted in an economic sinkhole, but that's another story.

Who are these liberals that are moving to (or remaining in) both coasts and urban America? They're a demographic hodgepodge, but they do have a few things in common: a world view that eschews conflict, an environmental belief system that accepts 'global warming' (and a hatred for fossil fuels), a pro-legalized drugs mentality, a view of religion as the "opiate of the masses," a pro-abortion stance, a preference for government-as-nanny role over a free market driven economy, an anti-gun bias, a desire to 'protect' Americans with safe spaces and political correctness, an open-border belief along with an illegal immigrant-forgiveness attitude and a common hatred of conservatives and Republicans. And the conservatives? Who are they and why are they leaving urban America? They are God and country first people.

They uphold traditional American values and believe in personal freedom and personal accountability, the free marketplace (of ideas, opinions and commerce), are pro-Constitution and very pro First and Second Amendment, protectors of the unborn, are against the legalization of drugs, oppose illegal immigration, support the equal and consistent application of our country's laws, are against violent protests, want swift and impartial justice for criminals but also demand victims' rights. They want a smaller more responsive government that respects the individual's privacy and feel that America is only safe when it has a strong defense.

Conservatives support religious freedom and believe that atheism and secularism must never replace America's foundational beliefs in a "creator." While I'm willing to concede that these are generalizations and that there are probably some people that don't fit the entire mold of either one, I still contend that if you can see yourself in more than half of each of them then you are either a Liberal or a Conservative.

The word, 'migration' describes a temporary condition, where a group of animals or birds, for example, leaves one locale for another only to return to their original home after a period of time. This is not the case with America's political migrants. Theirs is a one-way migration and is based on a conscious desire to move to a physical place where the preponderance of residents belong to their own *tribe* or share their own ideology. That hypothesis is based on current voter registration and voting patterns, political parties' local and state office-holding, state laws and states' re-districting. We will have to wait another three plus years to examine the data that will come out of our 2020 census, but as far as the newly naturalized citizens go we should get an indication of how they feel in the 2018 mid-term elections.

We are already ideologically split as a nation, and maybe even more divided now than at any other time in our history except for the Civil War. We have packed up our ideologies and political partisanship and have moved - and are moving - to physical political 'safe havens' or refuges from uncomfortable or opposing thought. These safe havens are pockets in communities within states and can also be entire states.

Those states that are *blue* or *red* have governments that reflect the values and beliefs of their citizens. We saw how they voted in November of 2016 and we heard their voices support or denounce Donald Trump...and are becoming louder with each passing day. We can expect more of the same as time goes by because we have become more politically estranged from one another. It's anybody's guess where all this migration will lead us. Will

198

liberals' laws that seek to 'equalize' wealth help them realize their idealistic view of America or will they send them on a journey certain to fiscal calamity (like California)? Conversely, could we see the building of a ideological fortress around conservative communities? While no one expects laws to be enacted that mandate wholesale political partitioning, I do believe we will see a continuation of voluntary one-way migration to towns, cities and states that will self-identify, politically and ideologically, in much the same way ordinary voters do.

This trend could dramatically change America's communities and the way they market themselves. I can see the ad campaigns now. "Come to California, the *anything goes* state. If you can dream it you can have it...for awhile." Then there's Colorado. "We're high on you (especially if you're a Democrat)!" How about Chicago, Illinois? "Where liberal thought becomes liberal action, especially in our streets!" For the conservatives there's Texas, "We've got space to pace..and a free Glock to every newcomer!" Louisiana, Alabama and Mississippi would join forces in a regional campaign. "Come to the only coast that lets you breathe free." The possibilities are endless.

~

Those seemingly endless wars on women

Somebody has to pull back the curtain on this whole subject of the wars on women. We don't have a war on women. There are actually several of them. One war is a religious-based war perpetrated by those men that hide behind Sharia Law and other medieval theologies as they endeavor to keep women subjugated and under their thumbs. The indefensible acts of violence committed in the name of religious beliefs against young girls and adult women around the world are truly reprehensible and shouldn't be tolerated or supported anywhere, least of all here in the USA. That said, this war is real and does exist, right now.

The second war is perhaps the longest-running of them all. It is a *silent war* that hides behind centuries' worth of men's beliefs that women are both objects (of desire as possible mates or for purely amorous purposes) and subjects (of their protection and reverence as wives and mothers). This complex relationship with women has led to a lot of male confusion throughout the ages, but has seen an upward ratcheting with greater intensity in the 20th and 21st centuries. While we men may desire women for their beauty, talent and attractiveness, we also seek their company to complete some missing part of ourselves. Outside of our intimate personal relationships in the home, we can be intimidated by women when they compete with us in the workplace, for example. I maintain that the reasons for that intimidation have less to do with sexism than with our conflicting feelings about them (we cannot both desire such women and accord them our protection, simultaneously, so we try to ignore their gender and compete with them using all the tools in our toolbox).

This 'anything goes' attitude can appear discriminatory against women by today's standards, but if women want a seat on the board or the CEO's job they must play by the same rules of engagement that men do. Obviously, there must be laws that protect women (and men) in the workplace against sexual discrimination and that level the playing field, but laws have another purpose to fulfill. They must provide the structured environment that make it easier for us to make the necessary personal changes in our attitudes that will, over time, make the laws obsolete. As with any major aspect of our society, we have tended to concentrate our focus on what's wrong – or yet unaccomplished – with women's issues. While this may be natural, it's important that we also celebrate the advances of the women's movement.

Our younger women are the obvious beneficiaries of the gains made since women's suffrage, all the EEO regulations and even the Roe vs. Wade decision. All of this progress has come at great cost to thousands of women (and unborn women) over time, but it should also be stated, for the record, that men have been involved in improving the lives of women and have not been disinterested bystanders. There has been a downside to women's gains, though. It was an attitudinal backlash against men – and not just against those men that opposed women's further emancipation – but against all men, by some women.

While it was at its peak in decades past, it has taken a generation or two to subside, but it is hopefully on the wane. Unfortunately, there are still men that would like to see and interact with women in 'traditional,' male-dominated ways, but they are, I believe, the minority. These 'leftover men' are feeling a loss of power or influence, and it is natural for them to cling to the past until they can see this transition as a positive development. We must try to make them understand that their lives and careers will benefit from including a different set of values, attitudes and practices than their own in the workplace and in society in general. That is the final battle in this second war on women.

There is a third, more insidious, destructive and phony war on women, and it is being perpetrated by those on the Left. It involves an aspect of women's lives that is now mixed together with politics as well as being a

200

values issue. Described as *women's reproductive rights* and centering on a 'woman's right to choose' it encompasses all forms of abortion on demand, and is really a human rights issue that includes the horrific third trimester abortion when fetuses that could survive if they were born early were not given a chance. For those valuing life, third trimester abortion is reproductive hegemony and should be considered a 'hate crime' because it discriminates against a defenseless group (the unborn).

Another aspect of this new phony war on women is the current female Democratic Party's candidate's desire to break what she and many other women see as the final glass ceiling of the American Presidency. I believe this is a fabricated war because most men do not oppose having a female President. As such, it should not be characterized as a: them or us, either or, man or woman contest. For a couple centuries preceding ours, men have been voting for other male candidates with little or no consideration of keeping women from elected positions (largely because laws prevented women from appearing on the ballot). Granted, those were unequal times, but to tar all men with the same discriminatory or sexist brush now is flat out wrong.

Voters today have both male and female candidate choices and they select them for the most part on their qualifications. Look at local, state and federal races. We now have a significant number of women in positions of power and authority in the Supreme Court, in Presidential administrations as Cabinet Secretaries, in the House and Senate and in governorships. The vast majority of them have won their seats fairly and squarely without playing the gender card. Now is not the time to turn back the clock and pit men against women in an unnecessary and imaginary conflict, especially after the peaceful transition and gains we have made. No American is served by a gender-based civil war.

~

Throwaway diatribe

What in heaven's name made Romney do it? The diatribe on Donald Trump, I mean. Was it too quiet around the old Romney homestead, or was the former Presidential candidate asked by the RNC to step up to the plate and deliver a bean ball pitch at the new 'outsider' candidate before the ninth inning? If you believe the latter, good luck in unraveling that ball of twine and playing Woodward and Bernstein in search of 'Deep Throat.' That trail is colder than a Hillary Clinton handshake. The RNC and the Republican 'establishment' will not be admitting to pushing Romney out there like a decoy during duck season anytime soon. The mere fact that a stand-up guy like Mitt Romney would break Reagan's 11th commandment ("Thou shalt not speak ill of a fellow Republican") and insert himself so forcefully into the middle of the Primary sweepstakes is confusing at best. Many questions come to mind like: "Did the RNC promise their support for a Hail Mary Romney candidacy?"

"Did Romney agree to the poison pill because he knew he wouldn't run again and had nothing to lose?" Or, "Was this all about Romney's legacy before the Party turned out the lights on him?" There are those in the Republican establishment that believe that if Trump wins the nomination it will be the end of the Republican Party as we know it. I freely admit to holding the same opinion. The difference is, I do not believe that it would be a bad thing to excise the tumor of staid, establishment thinking that has governed the Party's actions leading many to view it as an aging, lumbering pachyderm in search of the Elephants' graveyard.

Republicans have lost the last two Presidential elections because they have not been quick enough, strong enough or smart enough to realize that the mood of the electorate and America's demographics were changing. Because of the establishment's decision not to change their thinking, they have viewed the gathering storm of growing voter dissatisfaction as something transitory, not realizing that these prevailing winds were actually the harbinger of a tornado that would swoop down and devastate their plans for a revival of the 'good old days'.

News flash. The good old days are gone with those winds. The Republican establishment had better realize that the barometer is predicting unstable weather for the coming months. Now is not the time to ignore reality. Nature tells us that the only trees to survive such devastating storms are the flexible ones. Intransigence and ignorance of the forecast is no excuse, but is a sure recipe for disaster...at the polls.

There is no doubt in my mind that many Republicans believe that the RNC leadership has simply been re-arranging the deck chairs on the Titanic for the last eight years by not listening to the impassioned pleas of their own members to put up candidates that are prepared to take the ideological fight to the Left. By refusing to do so, they have made a colossal mistake, just as Gov. John Kasich did a few weeks ago at a public debate when he offered himself as peacemaker to the live audience only to realize that peace was the last thing on their minds. Surely Mr. Romney must have known that his remarks about the Republican front-runner would sound like sour grapes after his three-million vote loss to President Obama.

He should also have known that he would incur the wrath of Donald Trump, a man who does not take personal attacks lying down. In short, Mitt Romney not only poked the wrong bear, but he poked the wrong bear in the wrong place...in front of its supporters. This was not just a tactical mistake, it was a stupid one, because if there's one thing we've observed during the last few Primaries it's the remarkable devotion and resilience of Trump's supporters. They will not be persuaded to ditch him just because a failed candidate says they should. Mitt Romney's 'street cred' may not be gone, but it will be up for review after the echoes of this throwaway diatribe fade.

~

Time to outlaw people?

I've tried to stay away from this topic but can't any longer. First, let me say thanks to everyone who's written anything serious on the subject of gun violence. There's no question that we need to keep the conversation going about our Second Amendment (as we do about other Amendments as well) otherwise we will not revisit them when it's necessary.

That said, may we please have a moment of silence for the hundreds of thousands of people killed each year in wars, suicides, domestic abuse, gang conflicts, drive-by shootings and gun accidents? It seems to me that there are only two points of view when it comes to gun control: those who want it (even to the degree of banning all firearms) and those who don't want any more laws. AND there are two points of view about gun violence. If you recognize them as partisan and applicable to a specific political party, you are wrong. Some Democrats and Republicans cross party lines on this issue.

Viewpoint 1. -- By banning or severely restricting all weapons, America will be safer by removing the killing tools (firearms), AND this will lead to a massive reduction in murders because it will eliminate or reduce the human impulse towards violence.

Viewpoint #2. -- By banning or severely restricting all weapons, America will become more dangerous as only the criminals, the mentally deranged and domestic terrorists will have the tools to kill AND it will not reduce or remove the natural human impulse towards violence.

There. Where do you come down on the question of banning or severely restricting firearms? If you say 'yes' to number one you are probably ignoring human nature and are more idealistic (read: hopeful) then

203

pragmatic. That is your right, of course, but just be aware of the consequences a ban would have on the <u>illegal</u> sale of weapons. The sale would rise, and none of these purchasers would go through a background check. More firearms - not fewer - would enter the underground market and that would likely increase the incidence of crime and murder and make more law-abiding gun-owners, victims.

If you choose number two you are not an idealist, but a realist. You believe that human nature is, well, natural, and that people will always be killing people by any and all means possible: rocks, tree branches, baseball bats, knives, bombs, cars and guns, of course. You also believe that everyone has the right to protect himself/herself in a free society and that the Second Amendment doesn't only apply to a regulated militia. In addition, you also believe that restricting the right of people to protect themselves <u>is also a crime</u> and should be punishable. Hear that Chicago, New York and D.C.?

While the media and the Administration and, yes, the Democrat Party's Presidential candidate may be spearheading view number one and the Republicans' candidate view number two, it really isn't as simple as that. Reasonable people of both parties point to the First Amendment and say that there must be limitations on free speech (the 'You can't yell "fire" in a crowed movie theatre' argument).

Therefore, there must also be room for some limitations on the right to keep and bear arms. That's why we have Federal Firearms licenses for sub-machine guns, for example, and why you're not allowed to keep a working rocket launcher in your front yard or use an RPG (rocket propelled grenade) when you're angry with your neighbor. Those are weapons of war, and as such, should, in my opinion, be regulated.

The purchase of semi-automatic weapons (today's typical handgun) and revolvers should continue to be regulated in that the purchaser must pass a State Police background check in order to buy the gun and subject himself to a waiting period if he resides in another state. Gun show purchases of semi-automatic weapons (on the premises of the gun show) should also be subject to the buyer's passing a background check. Personal sales made outside of gun shows should not. In the case of persons having <u>documentable</u> bona fide mental health problems, there should be an official statement made by more than one medical professional that has examined the patient and will attest to the patient's unstable mental condition.

204

As for illegal firearms and those used in the commission of a crime, they should be destroyed and the perpetrators tried for committing crimes with a firearm and incarcerated. Illegal aliens committing crimes with firearms must serve the same sentences but then be deported back to their home countries. Should they re-enter our country, illegally, they should be slapped with a mandatory sentence equal to their original sentence.

It's time we acknowledged that people possessing a firearm for the sole purpose of self-defense are better able to defend themselves when police can take upwards of 15 minutes to respond to a 911 call. Murder rates are high in cities with tough gun laws. Why is that? Is it because criminals don't like to step up and volunteer for background checks or is it because there are just too many guns on the streets, or is it because certain neighborhoods in Chicago, Detroit, New Orleans are too dangerous for even the police to go?

Try telling an inner-city youth living in a dangerous gang-infested neighborhood that his family doesn't need a firearm for protection, or tell elderly persons walking home from their banks on Social Security payday that they don't need a deterrent to mugging. Take away the guns from law-abiding innocent people and you've just expanded the victim class. There will be people, largely anti-Second Amendment opponents, who will use the mass slayings in Orlando to their political advantage.

They will use the 'angels of our better nature' approach of viewpoint one (we can rehabilitate our society away from violence by outlawing weapons) to move our emotions towards the passage of new, restrictive laws. As painful and disruptive as it might be, it's important that we continue the dialogue on gun control, because to deny it would only embolden the anti-gun groups to go underground and work behind the scenes, out of public view.

We must also realize that there is a huge gray area, or better said, a neutral zone for further conversation, but before we go there, we must settle the question of which viewpoint is right, number one or number two. Unless we do that, we will not be able to make any meaningful progress on regulating firearms away from those who shouldn't have them. And who are those people? They are: convicted felons, the bona fide mentally ill, terrorists, some illegal aliens, drug abusers, abusive spouses and children. What other measures should be taken to reduce incidents like the attack in Orlando? Answer: armed bodyguards at venues of high risk, less restrictive concealed carry laws that allow for concealed carry at more places like shopping malls, theatres and other large public gathering spaces <u>and</u> nationwide, all 50-state (and the District of Columbia) reciprocity for concealed carry license-holders.

America must come together on this issue, otherwise those presently on the *reasonable* side of the argument will be forced by conscience <u>or their government</u> to join the *unreasonable* group that is advocating for wholesale bans of certain weapons and severe limitations on the rights of innocent people to protect themselves. We must at least agree on whether gun violence, or any violence at all, is the result of human nature or human nurture or some combination of both. Then, and only then, can we move to plug the holes in our gun laws.

~

Trump cops a feel of the swing states

I would love to be the State of New Hampshire – not live in New Hampshire, mind you, but **BE** New Hampshire or more properly the media in New Hampshire. I heard a news report today that said that the Democrats were spending upwards of a $120 million on ads to support their candidate for Senate there.

Really? A hundred and twenty million dollars to win a Senate seat? That's practically unheard of in a State known mostly for its license plate, "Live free or die" and maybe granite and trees. I visited NH many years ago but I'm hard-pressed to remember anything significant about it. I'm also willing to admit that that might say more about me than New Hampshire, but that doesn't change the fact that my memory of the state is totally blank. I'm going to bet you, however, that Donald Trump remembers New Hampshire just like Florida (another battleground state) where he spent the entire day yesterday at five different rallies.

Hillary Clinton understands how important wins in critical 'swing states' or 'battleground states' are to her electoral vote total as well. That's why <u>she</u> was in New Hampshire today, to counter the 'Trump Effect" with a message that sounded like a war cry, delivered by her sister-in-arms, the faux Indian herself, Senator Elizabeth Warren, from neighboring Massachusetts. Senator Warren tried to spoil Trump's gains in NH by turning his 'Hillary's a nasty woman' remark made in last week's debate against him by underscoring that "nasty women also vote." Clever. Campaigning is about timing and messaging, and the best time to use opponents' words against them is when they're fresh in everyone's minds. That's what the HRC campaign is doing now – especially in the swing and

206

battleground states. Pollsters, too, are having a field day, in places Ohio, Pennsylvania, Utah, Colorado, Nevada and even in the Midwest where some believe that states like Michigan and even Wisconsin are in play.

Under normal circumstances in a normal Presidential Election year, pollsters would be experiencing the late stages of "Pollster Euphoria," a mixture of anxiety and excitement as they roll out their final polls in these closing two weeks. This year, however, all bets are off owing to two candidates whose unfavorables make regular polling extraordinarily difficult if not impossible. Pollsters' reputations are also on the line. One interesting poll came from Investors' Business Daily (IBD) that has accurately predicted the last three Presidential Elections. Their poll showed Donald Trump ahead of Hillary Clinton by a few points. The 'Real Clear Politics' average of polls tells a different story, however. It shows Clinton in the lead by four points.

National polling has gotten some competition this year due to the importance and fluidity of the swing and battleground states which has spurred more regional or individual state polling. But there is also another confounding variable or *wild card* in polling this year and that is the emergence of a new, possible 'stealth voter' that may be hiding his true candidate preference for Donald Trump out of fear of ridicule from friends, family or co-workers. I have a feeling that the Trump campaign is actually counting on this new voter perhaps because they have seemingly conceded the votes of many Blacks, Hispanics and women to the Clintonistas. Republicans had better pray that there are, indeed, several million of those 'stealth Trump voters' out there, AND they had better hope that they are concentrated in high electoral vote states, otherwise the bulk of the electoral map will remain in Democrat hands and insure yet another Presidential defeat for the Republicans.

~

Trump ship deserting sinking rats

For those of you who haven't been following the American Presidential election and all the revelations that have come to light, permit me to top up your cocktail of the bizarre...

Last week, new previously *misplaced* Hillary Clinton emails were revealed, along with transcripts or snippets of speeches she made to foreign governments or Wall Street benefactors. In them, she advocates for a hemispherical open borders situation when it comes to trade and, presumably, immigration. We don't know which is actually true because

Mrs. C. won't release her own transcripts of these speeches - the same ones that netted her millions of dollars in speaking fees from the people she now publicly bashes for preying on poor folk like you and me.

In one of the Wikileaks' documents, HRC is quoted as saying that it's necessary for a politician to have two opinions on issues: a public one and a private one. If that is the case, it sounds like she is playing both sides of the street, hedging her bets and not telling the truth to one of the groups. Back where I come from, we call that 'sneaky,' and while others may have a more piquant name for it, it all comes down to the same thing...somebody's being lied to. These new discoveries just add a little more speculation to Mrs. Clinton's lack of veracity.

While Hillary is busy trying to deflect any media attention from the new emails, Republican candidate Donald Trump is trying to find a Kevlar umbrella big enough to shield him from a growing storm of media inquiry about a ten-year old tape that reveals his seamier side when it comes to the fair sex. In this tape, he wallows in words that describe his ability to 'storm the gates of beautiful women's citadels' (my poetic substitute phrase for some pretty explicit low-rent locker room language). This tape was a real October surprise and one that sent journalists' hearts a fluttering, prompting them to ask any prominent Republican they could find what he/she thought of Mr. Trump's comments.

Predictably, and presumably to save their own skins/seats, many Republican bigwigs denounced the comments and rescinded their support for DJT. This caused the Trump ship of presumptive state to part ways with the self-serving Republican *rats* that had gathered on the gunwales of the Trump Titanic and had jumped to calmer, safer waters. Trump must have heard their screams as they hit the water and was reminded of his pilgrimage to the altar of the Speaker of the House to get his blessing. Now it must seem that he is in danger of losing it and will experience a slow steady bleed of even more influential Republicans ready to dust off their *holier than thou* tee shirts, rush to the microphones and separate themselves from their only hope of winning the White House.

It's said that Democrats brainwash their young, but that Republicans eat theirs', and the latest *Trump Tape* is a textbook example of political cannibalism at its best (worst). While it may be too early to wave the checkered flag on Mr. Trump's performance during the second Presidential Debate of last night, I'm willing to bet he did well enough to continue trying to make Trump great again. We should all stay tuned as there is plenty of time left for another October or even November surprise for both Mr. Trump and Mrs. Clinton. In fact, my more conspiratorial sources tell me that Vladimir Putin has approached the Trump people and has offered himself as a replacement for 'The Donald' if he decides to pull out. Apparently, Putin tried the same thing with the Clinton camp, but they wanted to charge him a multi-million dollar re-stocking fee, and in a fit of anger he turned them down and told them that he would "bury them" in emails. What a campaign year this has turned out to be!

~

What America's youth want from a candidate

Much has been said about the political divide between the established (older) voter and the millennial (or younger) voter in America. Researchers, pollsters, think tanks and pundits have all weighed in or are looking for the magic formula to analyze this important group of 18-35 year olds. The reason is simple. They want to be able to predict with some certainty how they will vote and for whom. In conducting their research, companies are using social media and cell phones and have trained their people in the vernacular of America's young.

I fantasize about how a call center conversation would go with a millennial. Ring, ring (to cell phone). Answer: Yo, it's Bobby. Talk to me. Caller: Hey, it's 'Wewanttoknow Polling.' Got five for some data transfer? Bobby: It's a maybe, but I'm pretty busy checking out the new iwatch at Best Buy. Can you make it three? Caller: You got it. Couple of questions...first what's with Hillary? Are you cool with her?

Bobby: Yeah, if you're into yesterday. How old is she, 80? Caller: Actually she's only 68. What about the other Democrat candidates? Do you know any of them? Bobby: Sure, Bernie something. He's like ancient but makes it seem fun. Caller: What do you mean? Bobby: He's like, you know, a young guy trapped in an old dude's body. He sometimes reminds me of my poli-sci professor. He's a big radical, too.

Caller: OK. Do you know any of the Republican candidates? Bobby: Are you for real, man? I don't hang with the Rs. They're like super toxic dudes, always ragging on the poor fence-jumpers. Man, they're like the Hillary, sooo yesterday. Except maybe for the Rand Man. He's cool. He's like one of us, a free thinker. Don't know any of the others except for 'Big 'D,' the Trumper. I wish I knew what stuff he's on and where he got it. I want some of it!

Caller: What about the campaign issues. What do you know? Bobby: That's a no-brainer, man. I'm into 'freebies.' I owe $50K in college loans, man. I got no job, am living in the old folks' basement and am really bummed out. I'm not about to do the Walmart parking lot thing or move in with my buds, so the candidate that gives me the most is gonna get my vote. Caller: OK, I hear ya. But what about the other issues like the Iran nuclear deal?

Bobby: I'm cool with the deal, I guess. The Iranian dudes are just trying to make ends meet. I mean it's criminal to keep them from buying stuff like iphones over some stupid Plutonium. Everybody knows they're going to cheat, anyway. Caller: You mean you think it's okay that they get the bomb? Bobby: Yeah. Look at us and the Russians. We got a bunch of them and we ain't set 'em off yet. I figure they'll forget about it once they've done their shopping and are chillin' out with a cold one. Caller: Alright, what about other things that matter to you, like social issues? Bobby: No time to deal with those now, man. It's my turn to be waited on and this Best Buy babe is HOT! Later. (Hangs up.)

I would have asked the caller if this was a typical call. I'm sure he would have replied, "No, of course not. This guy knew what a Republican was."

~

What makes a voter?

Ask just about anyone what makes a great voter and you'll probably get a variation of the same answer...one who seeks the truth about the candidates, follows the important issues of the day and who is well-informed about them. Ask the campaign managers and they'll probably give you a simple more direct answer like: one that votes for their candidate. To them, THAT'S a great voter.

Dig a bit deeper into the inner workings of the campaign analysts' and strategists' minds and you'll hear: a voter they can attract with the right message, a voter that can be poached from the opposition, a voter that will not change his mind no matter what their candidate says or does and lastly, a voter that contributes to the campaign. Each type of voter is important to a campaign, but some are more important than others and make up a bigger part of the candidate's base. The highest ranking might go to the voter that contributes money to the candidate's campaign.

Why? Because no voter that donates his hard-earned money is going to admit he bet on the wrong horse and change his vote. Next might be the candidate's most ardent supporters whose loyalty will not be compromised regardless of their disagreement with the candidate over a single issue they deem important. (These are the 'totality voters' who see the candidate's whole views and not just positions on single issues as being the decisive factor in their support of him.) Slightly down the value chain are voters that are moved by the candidate's message or position on a single issue (single-issue voters).

They are a bit more prone to jump ship if they perceive that the candidate has changed his position on *their* issue. Finally, we come to the 'poached' voter that has been convinced to desert his first-choice candidate. This group is the least loyal, the thought being, "If they were wooed away once, they can be wooed away again." The next level of voters are their subsets and are split up into specific demographics like age, gender, education, race, ethnicity, urban/rural residence, marital status, financial situation, voting frequency, etc. The whole voter 'tree' is hung with these identifiers and subsets which are like Christmas ornaments of various shapes and sizes. The only thing connecting them is the tinsel (their motivation to vanquish the opposition).

The campaign pollsters are the ones that have the all-important task of identifying which voters are which and then figuring out how many of them are actually telling the truth. There are a number of groups that may play a pivotal role in getting either of the presumptive nominees from the Democrat or Republican side, elected.

To nobody's surprise, the important voting groups this year are women (particularly single women), minorities (particularly Blacks and Hispanics), disaffected (angry) voters, and Independents (42% of the self-identified electorate). The polls will be flying fast and furiously in the coming months and will be used to bolster each campaign's success in attracting these voters AND for amassing much-needed campaign funds.

The Republicans will be trying to shore up their base of older, White, high school-educated, male voters, married women over 40, evangelicals and conservative-leaning Independents, while the Democrats will be concentrating on winning over their base of college-age voters, union members, younger single women, Blacks, Hispanics, left of (Democrats') center middle-aged Progressives and independent voters. Both groups will be courting first-time voters and will be engaged in aggressive new voter recruitment drives.

211

There are two major things driving this election for the Democrats: 1. their dedication to continuing the Obama Administration's path towards social, racial and economic equality and 2. the election of the first woman President. The Republicans see this as an existential election, largely a contest between good and evil that encompass: the goodness of *free range* capitalism leading to economic opportunity, personal freedom and government accountability versus the 'evil' of government excess, overreach and abuse of power.

The major issues for the electorate are (according to many exit polls taken during the primaries): the economy (jobs and wages), bloated runaway government (excessive national debt, executive power grabs and legislative gridlock) and security (personal and foreign). Second-tier issues include: immigration, education, healthcare, our military budget/readiness, and social issues. With a little over five months to go before election day, voters of all stripes still have ample opportunity to assess the candidates' strengths and weaknesses and throw their support behind them before voting on November 8th. The choices we make for President, Senate and Congress this year will determine America's course for decades to come.

~

When civility isn't on the menu

Both Hillary Clinton and Donald Trump will be flanking His Eminence Cardinal Timothy Dolan, the Archbishop of New York this evening at the posh Waldorf Astoria Hotel in New York City. And the reason? It is the annual Alfred E. Smith white tie dinner held to raise money for Catholic charities and to which the Presidential candidates are invited - under the banner of civility. Civility, you say?

What's that and how could it ever share the same sentence with words like *Republican* and *Democrat* or *Clinton* and *Trump*? Good question, but while this dinner may be hopelessly out of step with our political times, it's the only game in town since the annual "Dinner of Nastiness" organized by the mainstream media had to be canceled. The reason? The journalists couldn't decide on the level of nastiness they wanted to exude and because their keynote speaker, the uncrowned queen of nastiness, Congresswoman Debbie Wasserman Schulz, was disinvited as some considered her to be too much of a 'softie.' That last part was actually not true, but could have been considering the vitriolic nature of the political campaigns and the destructive tactics of the DNC. So, Mrs. Clinton and Mr. Trump will be on the dais with the venerable Cardinal.

It's anybody's guess who will bring up the subject of the recent Clinton campaign emails that demean and denigrate the Catholic Church. I just wish I could be a fly on the tablecloth to hear the exchange about politics in religion and religion in politics among these three individuals. Timothy Dolan is known to be a fair-minded and resolute man and one that does not shirk from his office when he feels that his church is under fire, so let's hope the microphones are sensitive enough to pick up the Cardinal's words. It bewilders me that the Democrats are bulletproof on issues that reveal their hypocrisy like the missing emails and the sabotage of their second candidate and their pay-for-prey thugs that disrupted Trump rallies, not to mention their attacks on religion.

It's as if we Americans have reached both our saturation and boiling points, simultaneously, and that we've decided to simply turn off the gas and empty the tank of any/all civility and/or belief in the system or its leadership. The *dinner of civility* will probably end on a contrived high note that speaks about enemies sitting down together in a verdant glade, smoking the peace pipe of amity. As for me, I'll be looking for the tell-tale signs of cracking veneers.

I'm reminded of another Alfred E. and that's Alfred E. Neuman, the mascot and cover boy of Mad Magazine. Impish, troll-like and definitely not PC, THIS guy would have planted whoopee cushions on the guests' chairs and rigged up several stink bombs to go off during the speeches. HIS dinner would not have been pretty, but it would have been memorable which is more than I can say for tonight's high-roller feedbag, although...with a fellow like Trump at the table, anything's possible.

Watch for the crinkling upturned edges of Trump's mouth and look to see if he is fidgeting in his chair. Try to analyze his body language and then look over at Hillary's bodyguards. If they're moving towards her, one of two things is happening: either she is feeling a bit queasy after the heartburn she got from Chris Wallace' questions last night about the Clinton Foundation, or she's having a panic attack at the thought that Donald Trump could actually win the election by corralling the Catholic vote! Civility can be tough to chew, especially when served cold by a cleric who doesn't share your views on his flock. My advice, Mrs. Clinton, is to pick at your food, thank His Eminence profusely and leave before they serve the bananas Foster.

~

When playing it safe isn't

Punditland is full of folks swearing that Donald Trump's campaign is on the skids. The *meanstream* media has always had it in for Donald Trump because he never fit their idea of what an American President should be. First, he wasn't a Democrat (which most in the media are). Second, he wasn't polished enough like their heroes Barack Obama and Bill Clinton who were masters of political rhetoric. Third, he wasn't a career politician and fourth, he was a no-nonsense, straight-talker that was prone to go off script.

In short, he didn't fit the profile of a modern, feel-your-pain, politically-correct, leader of the Free World that would kowtow to America's adversaries. No, Trump was an outcast, an outlier, not one of the *right-thinking* people. On top of that he was a successful businessman and actually built things of value rather than appending his name to some obscure legislation or flying around the world on the taxpayers' dime, negotiating bad deals for America. He wasn't part of the Washington establishment, though he did rub elbows with them when they needed him for re-election donations. He was the proverbial wealthy estranged uncle who came to Thanksgiving dinner armed with a turkey and a bottle of brandy and a treasure trove of slightly off-color stories that wowed the children but embarrassed the adults.

Donald Trump was a prisoner of his own desire for success and driven by his own ambition. He never clocked in because he had never clocked out! He was always on the job, mixing business and pleasure in a way that the press despise (unless they're included in it). Trump is at his best when surrounded by adoring fans, but the media somehow labels that as narcissism, ignoring the legions of lock-step Obama supporters that hung on his every word as if he were clad in sandals, robed up and walking in Jesus' footsteps.

Hillary Clinton is not a man of the people. She's often referred to as a *wonk*, a *policy nerd* or at the very least, officious. She's not a natural campaigner judging by the practiced smiles and rehearsed nods she dispenses on cue. That's not to say that Mrs. Clinton doesn't like people; she just likes them on her own terms and for her own purposes. She's practiced in the art of political flesh-pressing, having learned at the knee of her husband. Mrs. C. is disciplined, methodical and persistent, lawyerly traits that apply to over half of Washington, DC. One thing she's unfortunately not, is imaginative or creative, and that sets her apart from her Republican opponent, Donald Trump.

214

Mrs. Clinton's campaign is now urging everyone to "play it safe" and to "go with the one you know." The other night, during the second Presidential debate, she referred to watching a movie about Abraham Lincoln when she was asked why she would have two different points of view at the ready - one for the public and one for herself. At that point, I was convinced she would channel our 16th President and quote his remarks from an 1864 speech when he said, "An old Dutch farmer, who remarked to a companion once that it was not best to swap horses when crossing streams," but she didn't. That would have been a natural segue out of the thicket of unbelievability she created for herself, but instead she pivoted, preferring to stay on safe ground.

Donald Trump doesn't always play it safe, nor does he always play by everybody else's rules. He is a punter. He calculates the odds, looks at the probable outcomes, assesses his competition and plots out his moves. Occasionally, when the likelihood of success is within striking distance, he invests his money, places his bets and stays in the game until the wheel stops spinning. In short, he uses creativity, instinct and information <u>before committing his resources</u>. That's good management and something you can't learn in school or in the narrow, incestuous world of politics. Those who would portray Trump as a loose cannon, an unstable character or would call him dangerous or unfit to serve as America's President are ignoring five basic problems facing America that demand new thinking, unorthodox measures and new solutions.

They are: 1. the critical need for good management to dig us out of our $19 trillion hole of national debt, 2. the re-positioning of America's place in the global marketplace, 3. the threat of domestic and international terrorism, 4. the revitalization of our labor force and the creation of millions of new jobs, and 5. the growing racial tension that could soon engulf us.

Politically speaking, now is not the time for America to worry about staying on the same safe horse, for that horse is exhausted. Instead, we need to find a better place to cross the stream.

~

Chapter IV
Hillary Clinton and Donald Trump

Who is the real Hillary Clinton and what does it even matter at this point?

My apologies to HRC for borrowing her sentence from the Benghazi hearings, but It was irresistible. Truth be told, Hillary Clinton has been a net positive for many groups of people like the media and Republicans this season. Up until Senator Bernie Sanders' campaign gained traction, hers was the watering hole for many Left-leaning political and special interest groups to slake their thirst and be rejuvenated. Among them were: hard core feminists, the alternative lifestyle community, pro-abortion advocates, Hollywood celebrities and many in the ranks of America's well-heeled donor class - both in and outside of Wall Street.

To Mrs. Clinton's credit, from her early days as Arkansas' First Lady to her short time as Senator from New York and finally Secretary of State, she has generated more firestorms of passion than any other female politician in modern times. No one can argue that she has boldly made her mark in the pages of America's political history books. BUT it has come at a high price for her party. While capturing three million more popular votes than candidate Trump, she successfully alienated a huge swath of the American electorate (62 million people to be precise) and opened up a sinkhole of despair and disarray for her fellow Democrats.

Mrs. Clinton has always straddled the chasm of Americans' love and hate but somehow she has always managed to escape unscathed. This time, however, she couldn't close the sale in the 2016 contest for America's top job. The reasons were many, but the one most often cited is that she was simply a bad candidate and that her style was wooden and insincere. She was heavily scripted and at times appeared smug, overly confident, condescending and sharp. There was precious little humor or authenticity in her rhetoric, but there were occasional glimpses of truth like when she said that the coal industry (and coal jobs) would go away if she had any say in the matter.

The denouement was, of course, her "basket of deplorables" comment about all Trump supporters. THAT effectively cost her the independent vote and maybe the election. Millions of words have been written about Mrs. Clinton and many more will follow. This election, more than any other, revealed her true nature and unwillingness to shoulder the blame for losing.

Many believe it is this 'blame avoidance' that will disqualify her for any future office. On the plus side, she has helped the Dems close the 'Clinton chapter.' Her defeat served as a political high colonic for them and may have liberated them from the past. They can now move forward and embrace new ideas and new candidates that could help them move away from the fringe elements in their party, back to the center. Nothing is certain in politics, however, especially when the Clintons are involved. Democrats could, of course, decide that moving towards the center is an ideological dead-end street for them and will choose the Bernie Sanders/Elizabeth Warren path, instead.

If that happens, it's possible that the next generation of Clintons (Chelsea) will step up to *save* the Democrats from themselves. If the past is any indication of the future for the Clintons, I believe their family will remain engaged in Democratic politics. They are, after all, the quintessential political Zombies.

Millions of words have also been written about Donald Trump, and in the coming months and years many more will find their way into print, on blogs, in the nightly news and in Op Eds in America's newspapers. Unfortunately, many of them will be lies and 'fake news,' made to look real by the anti-Trump industry, the *Resist* movement and Organizing for America.

While it's true that most Americans love a winner, many on the Progressive Left despise conservative Republican winners and are doing everything they can to either unseat our 45th President or throw insurmountable roadblocks in his way. Their goal is to stop the recalibrating of our economy, the remaking of our social construct and the rehabilitating of our foreign policy, all while touting compromise (on their terms, of course).

I have some psychologist friends who believe that Donald Trump is suffering from 'Narcissistic Personality Disorder' and that he needs help. When I asked them if this is something that many successful people and leaders have, they hemmed and hawed and danced around their answer. On Trump, they countered with, "Well, we can't be absolutely sure about him because we haven't examined him or treated him." Precisely. This is one of the ways many on the Left take down somebody they don't like or disagree with. They diminish them or question their bona fides...or their mental health.

It is one of their most favored tactics and will continue, unabated, until the accusers are called out for being the smug, self-righteous people they are AND are held accountable for their words and actions.

For many on the far Left, Donald Trump should only have the right to exist in reality TV or in a skyscraper in midtown Manhattan. He should never, ever, be allowed to speak for the vox populi. He definitely should <u>never</u> have been allowed to be President, but President he is. The following articles are an attempt to understand both he and Hillary Clinton.

America, Inc.?

"The chief business of the American people is business." That quote came from an unlikely source, President Calvin Coolidge. He went on to talk about business in a speech where he compared it to religion. To him, business was like religion and he committed all his passion to both. "The man who builds a factory," he wrote, "builds a temple... The man who works there worships there." In 1925, old Cal gave a speech about the press in which he said, "There does not seem to be cause for alarm in the dual relationship of the press to the public, whereby it is on one side a purveyor of information and opinion and on the other side a purely business enterprise.

Rather, it is probable that a press which maintains an intimate touch with the business currents of the nation, is likely to be more reliable than it would be if it were a stranger to these influences. After all, the chief business of the American people is business. They are profoundly concerned with producing, buying, selling, investing, and prospering in the world. I am strongly of the opinion that the great majority of people will always find these are moving impulses of our life."

Down through the ages, Presidents have had their ups and downs with industry moguls and unions, often battling them in public. One remembers John Kennedy's fights with the steel industry and Ronald Regan with the Air Traffic Controllers (Reagan fired them all). The push-pull relationship will always be there as government spars with the private sector and vice versa. It is their nature to be combative and to constantly seek the upper hand. We allow it and nurture it because we are a country that believes that success comes from constructive confrontation.

The free flow of commerce guarantees opportunity, but it also guarantees that there will be occasional conflicts and abuses. There is a fine line that separates self-interest from national interest. We are lucky when the lines merge, but when they don't we grow farther apart, become receptive to greed and repair to our respective camps where we hoard our wealth, keeping it out of America's bloodstream where it only benefits the few at the top.

I believe that this is the crux of our current national skepticism about big business, and it has spawned the growth of an 'us versus them' mentality. Not enough capital has trickled down into the ecosystem of small business or into the hands of willing and innovative entrepreneurs. The result has been the emergence of the 99% vs. the 1% opposition forces.

Opportunity is now seen as the province of the moneyed few, and our young people are increasingly seeing themselves as victims of an American pipe dream. We have gone from an energy crisis in the seventies to an orgy of quick profits in the post-recession eighties (which birthed a 'get rich quick' mentality) to a flattening of expectations in the nineties to a depression of confidence in the first decade of the new millennium. To quote a famous preacher, "America's chickens have come home to roost." Eight long years of tepid growth with excruciatingly high unemployment has shaken our will and sent us on a downward spiral of self-doubt and left us questioning our core values and our ability to get back up on the horse that threw us.

Enter a billionaire President who was regarded by many as the last best hope for rebuilding our crumbling economic defenses and who would help us find the courage to start over. Many who voted for him were people of little means or were just the working poor. It may seem strange to those who don't know America or Americans that these were the people that would put a rich man into office, but they did. And why? Because the average American is an optimist and a believer *in what works* and is not afraid to put aside envy when it's in their own self-interest.

While America's business is business, that doesn't necessarily mean that America can be run like one, at least not like a sole proprietorship. Our current President seems bound and determined to take a crack at running the country as if it were a blue chip enterprise, but what kind is it? A casino where the house has the advantage or a factory of ideas? Can we be moved in a direction that will raise all boats on a sea of opportunity or will we revert to our old ways? Donald Trump is the consummate leverager. It's his specialty, and like many others growing up in a time and a place where real estate developers got rich using other people's money, he now is faced with an enormous challenge that goes well beyond the borders of his own portfolio. He must now use *America's money* to make America great again.

The question is, "Is there enough confidence, grit and money left to make lemonade out of America's lemons?" Will the American people give him the latitude and freedom he needs to put its savings on a winning number or will he face a backlash if he doesn't act swiftly enough to please them? At some point, even his own personal charisma could lose its cachet. His mandate to govern could be eroded by a few key legislative losses leaving him without critical support. We saw him snatch victory from the jaws of defeat in his personal life, but those were different times with a whole lot less to lose.

America is not like a corporation nor a reality TV show. It is a shark that must be constantly moving and fed a steady diet or it will be resort to attacking its own. Calvin Coolidge wasn't charismatic like Donald Trump, but he had a keen insight into the American psyche. He understood what makes us tick and he had abiding faith in us. It is in all Americans' interest that Donald Trump channels the wisdom of his predecessors and comes to one critical realization...that we are all shareholders in America, Inc., and without us, even the best CEO is useless.

~

Analyzing the Progressives

The Democrats have found a candidate - Hillary Clinton - that will take them 'back to the future,' to the good old days when her husband occupied the Oval Office. The only trouble with her candidacy is that the good old days will not return upon her election, at least not the way some Democrats hope. Hillary was supposed to be a moderate Democrat like her husband, but she is exhibiting uber Left tendencies if you believe her campaign rhetoric and is now calling herself a 'Progressive.' For those of you who are not aware of what Progressives want, let me give you a few examples...

Progressives are for bigger more centralized government with more power siphoned off from the states and funneled upwards to strengthen Washington policy makers. Progressives want an 'equalization' of income (translation: higher taxes on the rich and nearly rich and more entitlements for everybody else). Progressives want more EPA regulations and a rapid move towards alternative energy no matter the cost to our economy. They want super stringent regulations on all firearms, special taxes on ammunition, the elimination of concealed carry permits and more gun-free zones. Progressives want amnesty for all illegal aliens and do not want to spend money to secure the border with Mexico. They also want a clear unencumbered pathway to U.S. citizenship (not only residency) for illegal aliens.

Progressives want to strengthen the President's hand (when he's a Democrat) by supporting more Executive Orders. They want a massive reduction in military spending and implementation of a doctrine of 'soft power' (translation: words) to replace peace through strength or any option of military action. They are in favor of expanding a woman's 'right to choose' (abortions) any time even in the third trimester, increased sex education in the schools and favor a more 'active' role by school administrators in students' lives.

221

They support 'relaxed' (translation: downward adjusted) education standards that take the child's *feelings* into consideration instead of their grades. Progressives are for making the establishment of charter schools difficult so as to keep students in public schools, and they support a 'federalization' of education. On the university level, they want student loan forgiveness and free college tuition to all.

Progressives are for spending money we don't have (incurring even more national debt) to put people back to work on infrastructure projects which they want to reserve for unionized labor. They are for using the power of the federal purse to force states into submission and accept a broad range of Progressive ideas such as a single-payer healthcare system and mandatory maximums on healthcare services for senior citizens using a 'cost benefit' calculus (the Ezekiel Emanuel model that caps a person's 'useful life' based on economic considerations).

They are for regulating business, not only through taxation but through new rules in the workplace (federally-mandated minimum wages they call 'living wages' and for federally-mandated maternity leave, etc.). Progressives are for social engineering that makes everyone 'equal' regardless of where they already stand on the earning or learning curve. Progressives are against 'right to work' laws and participation regardless of the workers' preferences. They are for higher 'user fees' for federal roads, national parks, for federal lands and for anything the federal government owns or manages.

Progressives are in favor of 'wellness surcharges' on snack foods and other foods or beverages containing *too much* sugar or that are high in calories. They are for imposing these same regulations in all schools and in private businesses like restaurants. They are for increasing gas taxes to get people to either buy more fuel-efficient cars or to stop driving altogether. They are for 'forgiveness' for those incarcerated on drug charges and for releasing hundreds of thousands of 'non-violent' offenders into our communities.

They are for legalized marijuana, nationwide, and for spending less on law enforcement that would be used to apprehend drug users. Progressives are for making America religion-neutral, removing all references to God from our money and from any public building and for denying individuals the right to express their religious beliefs in their own private businesses. Finally, Progressives are also for stifling dissent and disagreement on subjects they have deemed, *settled*.

"Asked and already answered" may well be the Progressives' motto when it comes to shutting down debate on issues like global warming, for example. You probably won't hear these statements made in such a categorical way by candidate Clinton, but listen carefully for the *newspeak* and the nuances in her campaign speeches and rhetoric. You may need a Progressive decoder ring to fully interpret them, but make no mistake, they are there, even if between the lines.

~

Benghazi must continue to speak to us

Along with millions of other Americans, I have been following the Benghazi hearings. From that very tragic day on Sept. 11, 2012 when our Consulate and later its annex were stormed, I watched in sadness as armed terrorists crashed through the barriers of these facilities and began shooting and looting, ultimately killing four of our citizens.

Since I was a part of that diplomatic world for 20 years it brought back a flood of memories of many dedicated people and the procedures they used to safeguard against, or at least ameliorate, such attacks. There are some things that the average American is not aware of, however. One of those is the Marine Security Guard Program and the tougher than nails Marine Security Guard Detachment (MSGD) personnel that are assigned to our embassies around the world.

The size of the embassy and the threat level of the host country usually determine the size of these contingents of seasoned young professional Marines, most of whom are in their early 20s. They typically serve one hardship tour and one *normal* tour of embassy duty before their time in the program is up. In total numbers, the program comprises nearly one full battalion of the Marine Corps.

These brave young men stand guard over our facilities and are fully prepared to give up their lives if necessary to protect the thousands of Foreign Service Personnel who are assigned to our embassies. (*A little known fact, however, is that their primary responsibility is to safeguard the classified material in an embassy along with securing the facility as well as protecting its personnel.*) They're constantly training, keeping themselves in top notch condition (I know, I trained with a few of them and was fortunate to befriend many more). The MSGD is headed up by a Master Sergeant or Gunnery Sergeant who reports to the Regional Security Officer (RSO) in the embassy who in turn reports to the Ambassador.

The RSO is part of the State Department's Bureau of Diplomatic Security (DS), the security and law enforcement arm of the State Department. On a local level, the RSO liaises with host-country security forces, helps to set up training programs for them and for the many private security guards who protect our facilities overseas. They also participate in assessing threat levels at post and then communicate that information back up the chain of command.

The MSGD and the RSO are well-trained well-disciplined professionals. They know that any hole in our security plans will be exploited by our enemies and that can cost lives. Benghazi is a case in point. There are many unanswered questions about our security there that address the level of training and loyalty of our local guards at the consulate.

There are other even more painful ones not widely discussed in the press such as: "Why did our Ambassador even go to Benghazi at a time when it was widely known to be an extremely dangerous place? Why were repeated requests for more and better security refused by the State Department?" And finally, "Why was no military unit sent to Benghazi to at least intimidate the attackers with a show of force to get them to stand down before lives were lost?"

To me, the answers to these questions are more important than ones concerning the inane and deceitful *talking points* offered up by the White House and State Department or which numbskull thought it entirely appropriate to cite a totally unrelated video as the cause for the attack. Preposterous. One of the principal reasons offered for not giving the military 'go' order was the time it would have taken to get to Benghazi (as if we would have known in advance how long the attacks would last!). We must let the Benghazi hearings continue until we get the facts. We owe it to the victims' families and to all who willingly put themselves in harm's way to protect us.

~

CC: The FBI

The recent brouhaha over the FBI Director's re-opening of the Hillary Clinton email investigation has prompted a couple thoughts from my very overloaded brain. Whatever your feeling about the *Mulligan* that FBI Director Comey took last Friday, we have a serious timeline problem with looking at what appears to be 650,000 emails now residing on the laptop belonging to Anthony Weiner and his estranged wife, Huma Abedin.

Even with a meta-data search to identify those emails with Hillary Clinton's name on them I would guess that it will take the FBI way more than eight days to read them and make a determination on whether classified material passed to Ms. Abedin's computer from Hillary Clinton's private server.

I am assuming that the FBI will be looking for the following: a) whether classified material was sent from Mrs. Clinton to Ms. Abedin from Mrs. Clinton's private server; b) whether this information was also shared with others with no security clearances (like Mr. Weiner for example); c) whether classified material was stored on an unsecure device (their joint laptop); and d) why didn't Ms. Abedin disclose to the FBI that that device was one that could contain official work-related emails.

There are more twists in this whole matter than there are curls on Debbie Wasserman Schultz's head and they're more difficult to follow than any average voter should be asked to do which is why I believe we've entered the *glazed eyes* stage of the election. This is the stage where voters have already made up their minds about Mrs. Clinton, and these voters can be broken down into a few groups.

Group #1 wants a woman President and they don't care how crooked and duplicitous she is. Group #2 wants Hillary Clinton because they like Bill Clinton and want to return to the 'glory days' of his administration. Group #3 wants a Democrat to continue changing America in a 'third Obama term'. Group #4 wants nothing to do with Donald Trump and would vote for a hologram before they'd vote for him. Group #5 wants Hillary Clinton because they actually believe that Machiavellian tactics and subterfuge are the only ones that can work in today's America and that Mrs. Clinton has proved that she is a master of them. To be fair, there's also a sixth group that feels she is the best qualified to run the country, but that group, too, doesn't see the email/classified information situation as a deal breaker.

The hypocrisy and double-speak coming out of the mouths of HRC's surrogates today is astonishing. I swear hundreds of them are on conference calls every morning listening to Robbie Mook, Clinton's campaign manager, telling them what they all need to say that day. Today it is, "stress the word, 'unprecedented' when you're speaking to the media about what Comey did." Not waiting for the conference call was the Senator from Nevada, Harry Reid, who sent his own letter to the FBI yesterday saying that Director Comey "might have broken the law" by announcing his decision to re-open the investigation.

(The law he's referring to is the Hatch Act.) I hasten to point out that this is the same Senator that has no qualms about spreading rumors on the floor of the Senate (in 2012 he accused then Republican Presidential candidate, Mitt Romney, of not paying Federal income taxes by saying, "So the word is out that he (Romney) has not paid taxes for ten years").

Let's say that the FBI keeps its investigation open and Hillary Clinton is elected President. What will happen then? Several possibilities exist: 1. President Obama could pardon her for any wrongdoing before he leaves office; 2. she could take the oath of office and thumb her nose at the FBI and appoint a new, hard line Attorney General. (The problem there is that she would also need a Democratic Senate to approve the appointment of the new AG so that she could put indirect pressure on Comey); 3. she could also do what the Clintons do best and simply delay the process and run out the clock of Americans' patience; 4. the other more outrageous choice is to simply pardon herself for actions taken when she was a private citizen and "spare the nation all that wasted time and energy that a further investigation would cost."

Either way, Time Magazine will surely have to name "Emails" as their person of the year in 2016 as we have truly entered the political equivalent of the 'Twilight Zone' where time, space, and relativity are all perpetually rolling around and exchanging places in a constantly spinning tombola drum. There is another possibility that no one is considering, however, and it is that most of the 650,000 emails have nothing whatsoever to do with government or politics or classified information. They could all be about Chelsea's baby shower, chocolate chip cookie recipes and Mrs. Clinton's yoga. And the rest? They could easily be innocent conversations between Mrs. C. and Ms. Huma on what in the world to do about 'Carlos Danger.' Any bets, anyone?

~

Christmas in Clintonville

Seventy years after the debut of Frank Capra's film, "It's a wonderful life," Hillary Clinton took on the persona of amiable George Bailey of the Bedford Falls Building and Loan. Instead of appearing in rural New York, though, Hillary rolled into the Democratic stronghold (53%) of Warren, Michigan to speak to a crowd of businesspeople about her economic plan for America. Mrs. Clinton wasn't going to let Donald Trump one-up her on proposals for putting Americans back to work or for kick-starting our lackluster economy. Instead of speaking to captains of industry, her audience was a mixed bag of union members and Democratic Party

226

stalwarts at Futuramic Tool and Engineering Company. Like George Bailey, she wasn't going to let old man Potter (played by the evil skinflint Trump) steal the show or the town from the decent hard-working men and women. No sir, this was a time of reckoning. Armed with an endless stream of promises and an inexhaustible Santa's bag of freebies, Mrs. Clinton was out to entice voters of every stripe - except those who believe in the power of Capitalism and the magic of the free market - that it was she, and not the pretender Trump, that would make America great again by "standing together," again.

Promises flowed like cheap plastic necklaces at Mardi Gras. Tossing out *free college for everyone*, *tax breaks for child care*, *more subsidies for Obamacare* and *billions for infrastructure* to create new high-paying jobs, all that was missing was a Hooverian reference to a *chicken in every pot*. Warren is close to America's poster-child city of all-time bad management, Detroit, and like Detroit its fortunes depended on some form of auto-related industry.

Unfortunately for them, the automakers saw the handwriting on the wall years ago and began moving operations out of the state, citing high taxes and abysmal municipal management as the reasons. Many were Mexico-bound and found our southern neighbors very willing to cough up every single benefit from Bill Clinton's NAFTA agreement to lure them away from the high-operating cost environment of Estados Unidos de América.

Undeterred by the reality of the past and believing in fairytale Robin Hood economics, where stealing from the rich and giving to the poor wins the day, HC and company played to the 'togetherness' theme - where the rich must belly up to the bar and give according to their ability to those (poor) according to their needs. To her credit, she didn't break stride, speaking with that deep conviction that only those who've successfully brainwashed themselves have. So she George Bailey'ed through her speech without even a single 'aw shucks' for punctuation. And while the speech may have not moved her political needle very much, the point was to look calm, collected and in control in the hopes that her lapdog media partners would take the cue and contrast her measured tones with Donald Trump's double forte monosyllabic harangues.

In a balance sheet duel, Hillary's George Bailey was no match for old man Trump's Potter who could buy and sell him a hundred times over, but Hillary had a secret weapon. She knew that envy is a very powerful tool, and that while people may respect wealth and success they don't always admire or like wealthy <u>people</u>.

227

She's betting on that internal human struggle to win back some White working class voters, but she is taking no chances, which is why she and her campaign will be throwing haymakers at Trump every day for the next 90 days until he finally gives her the keys to the 'Building and Loan' on November 9th...unless he can foreclose on Hillary's empty promises before then.

~

Delete before writing the answer?

When I worked overseas in our embassies we were expressly forbidden to use our personal email accounts for official U.S. government business. It was that simple. End of sentence. When we needed to communicate back to headquarters in Washington or to folks on the outside we used our official email account.

Another alternative open to us (for government communication) was our classified cable system. Cables could contain any one of a number of designations ranging from Unclassified to the highest Top Secret classifications. We could also choose to send a letter that would be hand-carried in the official pouch back to headquarters by a special government-authorized courier. These options are still in use today.

Those folks who preferred to communicate by telephone did so, but time zone differences often made it difficult. Many of them used phone calls to be more open and direct AND avoid leaving a paper trail. So when the New York Times broke the story about our former Secretary of State's use of private email accounts (over a dozen for herself and others) to do government business through a private server in her home I was pretty amazed. My amazement increased when I heard that Mrs. Clinton didn't bother to turn over her official emails until the NY times story 'outed' her – a full two years after her departure from the State Department!

'Servergate' has been embraced by all the Hillary haters as proof that the secretive Mrs. Clinton has not changed her spots since the days of protecting her husband in the Arkansas Governor's Mansion and the White House. Many Democrats who believe in transparency have also criticized her for poor judgment if not downright flaunting regulations that she, herself, made subordinates observe at the State Department. Mrs. Clinton's decision to circumvent the system is not defensible on any level. Her excuse, *the need for convenience*, doesn't wash. She could have used two cell phones: one official, one private (a common practice among government employees).

If she didn't want to carry the second one herself she could have entrusted it to her aide (another common practice). If she wanted to use a telephone instead of sending an email from a smartphone she had frequent access to a secure phone and could communicate an official message to anyone she chose. Only the call (the number and duration) would have been identified and not the content, unless of course she was being monitored by the NSA.

If you don't buy the 'convenience' argument, then what other motive would she have had to end run the system? The only logical conclusion for anyone other than a dyed in the wool Hillary supporter is that she wanted to keep the public, the prying eyes of the media and the EOH (enemies of Hillary) out of the loop on how she conducted her business. Mrs. Clinton assured us that her 'team' (whatever that means) went through her entire cache of Clinton server-archived emails in a few weeks and determined that only 30,000 (50,000 pages) had 'official' content.

The rest were all private and were summarily destroyed. Excuse me? Who gave Mrs. Clinton the right to operate with only a private email address in the first place or to do her own search of her own private server and make those determinations? Those are the questions I'd like answered. By the way, the State Department now says that it would take them many months to search the emails she gave them to determine if any are releasable to the public, and the exercise would cost the taxpayers, millions.

You're telling me that the State Department can't find a dozen trustworthy people who could be sworn to secrecy, put in a secure room and do that job in a week? C'mon. Focusing on the emails given to the State Department is an example of Clinton legerdemain – look here, don't look there (at the contents of the private server in Chappaqua, NY). That's the 'X' that marks the spot. I say the Congress should subpoena the contents of the server by making a clone of it, retrieve the 'deleted' emails and then take THAT data to the secure room with the examiners. Email sure has come a long way since 1971 when Ray Tomlinson (a U.S. programmer working with the ARPANET) sent his first test emails to himself from one computer on his right to another on his left. Nowadays, we can make the ones we don't like <u>disappear at will</u> AND pretend that they never existed at all!

~

Feeling like Fagin

I'm racking my brain trying to remember how I felt about Donald Trump before I knew he wanted to be our President. My earliest memory goes back to the 1980s when he was busy grabbing New York headlines for some real estate deal or divorce. I can't remember which. I'd probably put him in the same category as the fictional Gordon Gekko character or the all-too-real Michael Milken and Ivan Boesky, men whose egos clearly outstripped their humanity.

It was probably not fair of me to do so, as I never met any of them, but I did stay at a Holiday Inn once and I did see the movie musical 'Oliver.' If you've ever read Charles Dickens you know he's obsessed with two basic themes: honesty and wealth (or the lack thereof). Dickens would have had a field day with America and our politics had he lived now instead of the 19th century when he wrote Oliver Twist.

For the sake of argument, let's say he's still around. I think he would have taken on the persona of one of his own more unseemly characters, Fagin, the not-so-loverly ringleader of a group of down on their luck young pickpockets. Back then, Fagin was a fixture of the London underworld, an essential evil, thrown together by fate with other unsavory fellows in an environment reminiscent of Wall Street.

Wherever you went in London you were bound to run into Fagin, and in the 1968 movie version of the book, you hear him sing a song that is unforgettable. Some of the lyrics are: *"I'm reviewing the situation. Can a fellow be a villain all his life? I think I'd better think it out again."* Yes, Dickens would be Fagin, today. In fact, Fagin could be Donald Trump's campaign manager. In his interview for the job by candidate Trump, I see them both sitting at a huge table across from each other in a massive conference room in an opulent office overlooking midtown Manhattan. Trump is dressed impeccably, but Fagin's suit is off the rack and is poorly fitting. Trump notices everything about him from his unkempt hair to the wart on his chin which he can't stop staring at. The questioning goes like this.

<u>Trump</u>: Mr. Fagin, I can't help but noticing. Your suit is really terrible. Where did you get it? And why would you wear such a thing to an important interview? <u>Fagin</u>: I'm glad you asked that. I looked long and hard for something that would catch your attention. I thought about Armani or something ridiculously expensive, but then I said, no. He sees those all the time. Best go to the warehouse store for a factory second.

230

Worked, didn't it? You noticed. Trump: OK, I admit it. You got my attention. Let's talk about your last job. It says here that you were a 'Liberator of unnecessary items.' What's that? Fagin: Well, Guv, I was a kind of speculator, if you get me drift. I'd see a nattily dressed gent with an attitude and figured he needed to be relieved of some of the burdens of his life. You know, take pity on him and lift him out of his anxiety and guilt about being rich.

Trump: You mean you stole from him? Fagin: I'd prefer to say that I entered into a silent partnership, where I leveraged the assets at hand for an up-front benefit. Trump: Are you also a lawyer? Fagin: Heavens no, sir. I'm an honest thief! Trump: How are you with the media? Fagin: Know them well I do, and every beat reporter knows old Fagin, too. Why I've probably picked every one of their pockets at least once. That goes for their bosses, as well. You see, I'm irresistible. Seems everybody wants to pick my brain, and while they do I lift their wallets. It's human nature. People actually want to be stolen from, they do.

Trump: Last question. Do you think you can make me President? Fagin: Possibly. How dishonest are you? Trump: Plenty, but I never steal from my friends. Fagin: How many friends have you? Trump: None. Fagin: Pleased to meet you, Mr. President.

~

Flat is just...flat

I was raised in the Midwest, in the farm country of southern Wisconsin, with plain speaking people. These were not harsh or insensitive people mind you, they were just folks who knew a lot of nouns and verbs but often came up short on adjectives. Some would call them plain spoken. Others would say they were just plain. I simply called them, 'my people.' There was something easily recognizable about them, too. Their flat Midwestern delivery frequently sounded like the low hum of electricity passing in overhead power lines or occasionally like the metal on metal of worn out brake linings.

The upside to Midwesterners' speech was that their pronunciation was rumored to be almost devoid of any regional accents that characterized other Americans' speech. But, there is no getting around saying it, it was also irritatingly flat, not even a half-note's variation, up or down. I can always tell when I'm in the company of another Midwesterner, especially from my home state of Wisconsin. It's like the metronome in my head suddenly stops in mid-course and all the other ambient sounds around me are suddenly still - like birds that have stopped chirping just before a storm. I am often transported back to my rural roots whenever I'm with such a landsman, but I must confess that there's one of them that makes me want to rush to Midwest headquarters and turn in my membership card to the heartland. It's Democratic Presidential candidate, Hillary Clinton. Mrs. Clinton, (who hails from the Chicago suburbs) is an expert at adopting special regional accents like that of *down home* Arkansas where she resided for over a decade with hubby Bill. I'm also reminded of her accent pivot in her Selma, Alabama speech where she attempted to win over a largely African-American crowd by Blackifying herself with an affected old-timey Black dialect: "I come too far from where I started from."

But no matter where Mrs. Clinton's lived, like New York and Washington, DC, for example, she always seems to revert back to her Chicagoland tone, style and cadence when she gets excited. It's happening right now as she intensifies her travel throughout the U.S. in these remaining two weeks of what has become a campaign of nastiness on steroids.

On a personal level, my problem is that I don't see how my ears and my patience are going to survive if she gets elected President. I am deadly certain that the combination of her flat and often harsh speaking style, coupled with her intense facial steeliness, will be nearly impossible for me to digest - so much so that I may even be forced to stop watching and listening to any Presidential speeches or press conferences for the next four years. And while most people could probably do that, it would be disastrous for me, someone that needs to write about such things with some regularity.

That's why I've been thinking about a few solutions. What if Mrs. Clinton's staff found a doppelganger to replace her for all public appearances and then contracted with a voice double to dub over all her vocalizations? They could use somebody like Emma Thompson or Meryl Streep. Actually, there a number of women that could step up and do the job, and I'm pretty much okay with most of them, just as long as they don't choose Elizabeth Warren. That would be like adding fingernails on the blackboard to worn out brake linings.

~

Geriatric Presidents and amateur diagnosticians

This week I saw all major news networks and cable channels scramble to give their on-staff doctors some face time and do 'drive-by analyses' of the health of our two Presidential nominees. We all heard about the various types of pneumonia, the danger of dehydration, the scourge of high cholesterol and of freaky psychological conditions like Narcissistic Personality Disorder along with painful descriptions of drugs like Coumadin and Statins and their role in preserving life. We laymen had to don our stethoscopes and lab coats and pop in videos of Marcus Welby, MD, Dr. Kildare or Ben Casey and then dust off our Merck manuals in order to make some sense out of what has now become 'Dancing with the MDs.'

I have a mortal fear of hospitals and dread going to the doctor so you can imagine my anxiety after tuning in to hear about our near septuagenarian candidates' medical conditions from TV-based GPs and the kind of probing and prodding that surround giving them a clean bill of health. If I were running for President I'd be tempted to fake the doctor's statement and say something like...

I have examined the patient and I consider him to be in reasonably good health for an old coot. Yes, he needs to lose a little weight and probably exercise more, but then so do 200 million Americans. I worry that he doesn't drink especially considering he's a politician. As far as his mental faculties go, he is a tad crazier than the rest of us if for no other reason than he wants to be President and expects to work 12-15 hour days for a ridiculously tiny paycheck, have the un-Godly responsibility for the security of a nation that ignores the dangers of the world around them and expects to be criticized for everything he does. I have advised the patient now candidate over the years and he has never disappointed me. He has consistently ignored my suggestions which leads me to believe that he has a lot of common sense.

While I realize that he will be the oldest President ever taking office, I have every confidence that he will last at least three years in the job without suffering a total breakdown. I would expect that the first thing to go will be his patience at about month three. Later, at month six, his sense of humor will desert him, followed by a pronounced desire to take frequent vacations and play copious rounds of golf at about the beginning of year two. (This will help with the weight loss.)

He will then start exhibiting a desire to take midnight strolls with his Secret Service detail in search of the perfect cheeseburger and begin his mornings with a round of 'five-card stud' with his Joint Chief of Staff and male Justices of the Supreme Court. During the third year of his Presidency, his wife will notice a number of behavioral changes that will indicate the onset of Presidential buyer's remorse syndrome. He will frequently utter statements

233

like: "Why me? What do those Democrats want from me, blood?" "Do I really have to give another idiotic State of the Union Address and lie about the condition of the country?" Shouldn't we get a pet raccoon like Calvin Coolidge had?" "What about cancelling Christmas at the White House this year?"

Lucky for all of you, I am not running for President this year (even though I am an old codger) and in "reasonably good health," so the above letter need not be written nor will I have to go in for a physical, once again proving that there are considerably more benefits to being a voter than a candidate.

~

Getting to know Donald Trump's America

Most of us knew Donald Trump was exaggerating when he said that he would build a wall and that Mexico would pay for it. We also knew that repealing and replacing Obamacare would take more than a few months to accomplish. We're not stupid; we were just tired of hearing the same worn-out, pathetic and boring lines from other Republican as well as Democrat candidates. We wanted something different. We wanted fighting words, words we would have used ourselves.

That's why it doesn't really make any difference if Mexico pays for the wall or we turn in a few million Green Stamps or raise billions with neighborhood bake sales to pay for it. We weren't EXPECTING it to happen. Get it? We wanted a champion, a street fighter from New York, someone over the top instead of another plastic politician cut out of the same DC mold we've seen for decades.

OK, now that we have him, what do we do with him? Should we embrace his unique leadership style or do we try to change him? Should we encourage him to be more Republican or let him find his own balance amid the Hounds of the Baskervilles in Congress? Tame him or turn him loose? House-break him of his twitter account or sit back and enjoy it, knowing that while he is our leader he is also his own man, and to lobotomize him of his personality would be giving in to mediocrity? There are those that would gentrify him, make him more acceptable, a clone of Barack Obama. Somehow, I can't see that as an acceptable solution. He's not going to go on the talk show circuit because he realizes (as his predecessor didn't) that his office is above trading one-liners with either of the two Jimmies. Been there, done that.

He knows he has work to do and is intent on doing it, and if you think the trips to Mar-a-Lago are just Trump junkets, you don't know the man. He's a self-proclaimed workaholic - wherever he spends the weekend. He's driven to succeed, not to get by. Atmospherics are just that for him, atmospherics. There's no deeper or hidden meaning in the trappings of the office for him. While he likes the pomp and circumstance of the office, he's results oriented.

Does he have a thin skin? Sometimes, but not when it truly counts. In those situations, he's the man of steel. Ask his staff, his wife, his generals and the Republican voter. Does he easily brook criticism? No. Does he look for dissenting opinions? Yes. Does he always take the advice he's given? Probably not, but then, who does? Does he have a vision for America and a plan to realize that vision? Yes, and it's simple…rebuild American pride and confidence, domestically; regain the respect of the world's nations and return us to a position of international pre-eminence by relying on time-tested proven American values.

We lost our edge and our balance over the last eight years. We got soft and complacent. We gave up on capitalism and democracy and avoided confronting our fears and getting in touch with our true beliefs. We let things slip and allowed the tail of Progressivism to wag the dog of common sense (and two centuries of success). We became convinced that we were a doddering old fool of a country, hopelessly out of step with the rest of the world instead of the place where dreams are born and things happen. Donald Trump is not going to single-handedly turn everything around for us. That's our job under his leadership. It's about time we put away the hurt feelings and the protest signs and got on board the ship of state. Pack a lunch and a change of clothes; it's going to be a long and bumpy voyage. Or…stay on the dock and whine about not getting a stateroom with your own private balcony. We'll miss you at the Captain's Table, but we'll be happy to give your dinner to someone who deserves it.

~

Hillary Clinton, this is your life…almost

America made history today on the second day of the Democratic Party's convention with the nomination of the first woman as a major party's Presidential candidate. It was done by a state-by-state roll call vote until Vermont proposed it be done by acclamation. Later in the evening, convention proceedings morphed into political theatre with the addition of former President, Bill Clinton. The stage was set, and all that was missing was Ralph Edwards calling the nominee out from behind the

235

curtain with a big "Hillary Rodham Clinton, THIS is your life." That job was left to Mrs. Clinton's husband who proceeded to tell us a bedtime story in his familiar homespun Arkansas way, giving us a 'once upon a time' litany of his wife's accomplishments from their first meeting up to the present... almost.

Bill Clinton used a clever trick to appeal to a wide number of delegates as he mentioned her life's travels from one city to another, eliciting applause and cheers with a Rand McNally-like travelogue, proving once again that the Clintons know what moves a crowd to its feet.

Mr. Clinton chose to deliver a resumé that was designed to be seen through a folksy family-ground lens. What he left out (understandably) was all the painful and embarrassing chapters that we who watched their lives unfold KNOW about their real relationship, one that was contentious, often destructive and sometimes on life support. Potus 42 neglected to mention her bad judgment as Secretary of State and her many avoidable controversies that continue to tear our country apart. Glaringly absent were her current scandals that speak volumes of the 'other' Hillary, the one we all know to be self-absorbed, controlling, truth-averse and laser-focused on power.

Many of us remember her demeaning women with comments on not wanting to bake cookies or by cozying up to foreign countries that abuse women. The other major theme of President Clinton's speech was an attempt to portray his wife, who is unquestionably the poster child for the political establishment elite, as a 'change-maker.' This was no accident, as focus group testing has shown her to be viewed as highly untrustworthy and the consummate insider rather than a fearless politician ready to venture outside the bubble of expediency. Winning is not incidental to Mrs. Bill Clinton... it is everything.

Day two was masterfully orchestrated to win the woman vote, the family vote, the minority vote, even the disabled vote with a softer message of inclusiveness that screams, "Hillary is a mom. Hillary loves children, and Hillary is on your side." It was pure Madison Avenue all the way, right down to the DNC's *fight song* sung by a chorus of young, 'cool' singers reminiscent of "We are the World." In short, day two was designed for the heart not for the head.

Day three will see an appearance of President Barack Obama who will be there to burnish his legacy by assuring the delegates that by helping Hillary Clinton become President, America will become whole by seamlessly moving into an Obama third term. Democrats are quick to point to Obama's 56% approval rating as proof that he can help Hillary Clinton win the Presidency, especially if she embraces his policies more vigorously in the coming months. What Democrats fail to consider, however, is that many Americans may have just recently warmed to Mr. Obama precisely because he will be leaving office soon!

One final thought, and this is for all of us, whether we're Republicans or Democrats. We Americans are too easily and too often seduced by rousing speeches, lofty rhetoric and fancy stage dressing and are far too susceptible to emotional tugs on our heartstrings. The political parties, their candidates, campaign strategists and convention managers know this and do their level best to avoid the 'boring bits' of policy. Instead, they serve up conventions that appeal to our pleasure centers. This is their job, and so far neither the Republicans nor the Democrats have disappointed us. If only they would.

~

Hillary's blue dress back from the cleaners

FBI Director, James Comey, testified before Congress today and answered questions about his agency's long investigation into former Secretary of State and Presidential candidate Hillary Clinton's use of a personal server to conduct official U.S. Government business. Democrats portrayed the hearing as a *witch hunt* (which may be a slam at all law-abiding witches and a very un-PC sexist remark) while Republicans claimed it was an attempt to seek answers on why the FBI did not recommend the case be turned over for criminal prosecution. Comey reasoned that "no reasonable prosecutor" would take the case. That is, of course, in a normal court. What was left unsaid was that there is a larger court that has already ruled on Mrs. Clinton's role in what must now be characterized as a huge public fraud.

The court I'm referring to is the court of public opinion where reasonable people who've listened to Mrs. Clinton's numerous statements about how she never did this and never did that have concluded that she was either: a) incredibly calculating in firewalling the truth by managing her own emails in a server in the basement of her Chappaqua, New York home which was also used by her husband and the Clinton Foundation, b) incredibly stupid, negligent or naive in doing so, or c) she just didn't care.

Reason a) shows her arrogance and willful disregard for protecting the nation's business. Reason b) demonstrates exceptionally poor judgment

237

or seriously questions her intelligence. Reason c) reveals a hubris and Machiavellian streak that should clearly disqualify her from becoming America's next President. Any one of those reasons would have prompted an honest candidate to withdraw from the Presidential race...if we were living in the Watergate years, but this is the *new America* where power or the desire for power corrupts, absolutely. It is also a time when the American electorate is so scandal-weary that it is willing to sweep such 'indiscretions' under the rug of history just to be done with it all.

This, of course, is what the Democrats, who have been infected with a terminal case of Clinton infatuation, are counting on. They hope our memories are so short that we have forgotten about all the trouble that the Clintons have caused over the past two decades. Another possible motivation is the desire to see our first female President and that this desire is so strong that voters will forgive her actions and let bygones be bygones.

In my time as a U.S. diplomat serving at eight embassies and one consulate, I was well-versed and routinely instructed in how to recognize and handle classified material. The regulations were simple and transparent. You never took classified material out of the embassy. You never copied it and took it out of the embassy. You never sent it by email or by fax out of the embassy. You never altered it by removing headers which clearly identified it as classified material and sent it out of the embassy, and you never left any of it on your desk when you went home.

You locked it up in your classified material safe. If you did leave it out, and the Marine Security Guard Detachment found it while doing their rounds, you would either get a security violation or a warning. If you got three such violations you risked losing your security clearance and would, probably be sent back to D.C. in disgrace.

In my 20 years of service, I left one 'Limited Official Use' (LOU, the lowest classification) document on my desk, and the next morning the Regional Security Officer called me into his office whereupon he gave me the document back with a warning that this should not happen again. It never did. I learned my lesson. In Hillary Clinton's case she trafficked in sending, receiving and archiving official U.S. Government documents (both classified and unclassified) in her basement and made herself a target of ordinary hackers and foreign governments, alike. But Hillary's real 'blue dress' - the smoking gun of all of this scandal - is her seeming inability to tell when a SUBJECT was classified.

Even a first-year, rookie Foreign Service Officer can sense when subject matter is likely to be of a classified or sensitive nature. Surely the leader of the State Department, and especially Mrs. Clinton with all her government experience, should have been able to recognize that reports of conversations with foreign leaders and their opinions about U.S. policy were not something to blithely send around the email universe to some one thousand recipients. While Mrs. Clinton's blue dress may have just come back from the FBI cleaners yesterday, the indelible stain of bad judgment is still there for all to see...if they choose to.

~

How to poke the new bear

Here I sit tapping on the keys and thinking that it seems that Donald Trump has always been a part of our lives. For some that's a terrible thought to ponder, I realize, but it feels like he's always been there in our frontal lobes where our cognitive skills reside along with our emotional expression, memory, problem-solving, language and judgment capabilities. Somebody once called the frontal lobe the 'control panel' of our personality. I've been listening intently to the political talk shows and following comments made by prominent Democratic Party Senators like Charles Schumer from New York.

The latest comment of his was to slam Trump for his 'twittering.' On this topic, Mr. Schumer is not alone. In fact, the volume of stored-up negativity towards the President-elect and his *bodaciousness* is spilling over the dam in the form of young people's protests, declined invitations by so-called 'Hollywood A-listers' to perform at the Inaugural galas, etc. Judging by the vitriol and the opposition to Mr. Trump, we had all better run to our closets and put on our chain mail armor, for the attack arrows are about to be headed Republicans' way. For those of you whose chain mail is slightly out of fashion, amazon.com is selling (seriously) a special suit for only $77.95.

It's not like we didn't know this was coming. We knew the moment all the Obama sacred cows like Obamacare, immigration, Supreme Court nominees, EPA regulations, political correctness, etc. were herded into Trump's sights and pronouncements by the Democrats' Swiss Guard that they were moving into attack formation. It's quite natural that the Democrats' eight long years' worth of work to systematically create a new status quo would be defended to the last man, woman or epithet.

And to be sure, the battle lines are being drawn, quickly, to align their defenses and mobilize their offense to take the fight directly to their common enemy. We can expect many of the same old tactics will be used to obstruct any effort to dismantle that which Mr. Obama has created. The Democrats will attempt to de-legitimize Mr. Trump's status as President and demean him, personally, as someone 'unfit to serve.' Everything he, his cabinet or the Republican-dominated legislature does, will be defined as either anti-American, racist or contrary to the 'true' American way.

His supporters will be likened to the brain-washed followers of Jim Jones' 'Peoples Temple' of the 1970s or worse. They will be branded as demagogues, dullards or White Supremacists, bent on taking America back to the days of segregation and rampant bigotry. There will be no honeymoon for the Trump Administration as half the country will see itself as 'date raped' by an unfair system that elected a President without a majority of the popular vote.

In just a few weeks, America will have entered the first phase of a domestic cyber war where the mainstream media and especially the social media will be the principal weapon of (Trump) mass destruction. Leftist bloggers will inundate the Internet with malicious personal attacks on the new President along with plenty of disinformation and 'fake news.' New opposition groups will be formed and new money will be raised from angry donors of the small-to-large variety that feel betrayed by the system. This is a far cry from bi-partisanship, a term which may well be relegated to the back pages of an archaic English lexicon.

Given the mounting opposition, it begs the question, "Should Trump even try to bring such a hopelessly divided country even one step closer or should he ignore the protestations and simply forge ahead with his agenda to "Make America great again?" If he chooses the latter approach, will he not be making the 'Obama mistake' to go it alone and thereby exacerbate the division? More importantly, can he accomplish his goals of re-making America without the support of the other half of America?

We have four years to find out, but the bigger question is, "Do we have the collective stomach to endure four more years of entrenched push-back?" I doubt it unless he makes some early and significant gains on several fronts like Obamacare, unemployment, immigration and the Supreme Court. These are the big issues, but the smaller ones could easily impede his progress on the larger ones, and that's where the Democrats are hoping to trip him up. They will constantly question his authority and his motivations, hoping to weaken him and delay his actions. It's not a new tactic, but it seems to be the preferred method of the Left...destroying the village in order to save it.

~

Lies, downright lies and outright lies

"Liar, liar, pants on fire, hanging from a telephone wire," now that's a blast from our childhood. Today, it's become a common refrain used by combatants on the political right starting with the President and on the left starting with the fourth estate - the press. (Note: The term fourth estate used to refer to forces outside the established power structure using medieval three-estate systems. Historically, in Northern and Eastern Europe the term referred to rural commoners. Today, it's the media.)

President Trump can justifiably lay claim to ramping up the search for liars and their lies by repeatedly calling out the media for reporting a flurry of 'fake news' and now 'very fake news' stories about subjects ranging from Russia's involvement in the 2016 Presidential election to the dismissal of General Michael Flynn from his post as Director of the Defense Intelligence Agency. Indeed, the President has become a kind of reverse lightning rod, shooting high voltage accusations at the media for not doing their jobs at vetting sources or for specializing in 'second-hand' or 'cut and paste' journalism. (This is the style where reporters take stories written by others and then modify them slightly or run them unchanged without any substantiation or attempt at investigating their veracity.)

To be honest, the press has brought their low approval ratings on themselves by taking sides in the political debate. They loved JFK and were lukewarm about LBJ until he escalated the Vietnam War. Then they hated him. They also hated Nixon and were amused by Ford. They were supportive of Carter...for awhile. They didn't like Reagan because he went over their heads, directly to the American people, and slaughtered a few of their most sacred cows. They weren't particularly fond of Bush '41' because he was too reserved and didn't give them enough spice for their columns. They loved Clinton because he was hip and because he loved their spotlight until they covered his impeachment hearings. The press despised Bush '43' and characterized him as a cowboy or bumbling bumpkin. Then came Barack Obama and the media fell in love...again. It was JFK redux. In Obama's case, lies that came from the Administration or directly from the President's own mouth were dismissed as 'mis-speaking' or things 'taken out of context.' Now, with '45' the press is enraged and on a crusade to bring him down.

241

The new reporter's handbook has basically re-defined lying. It is now considered *anything that a Republican or conservative says that doesn't please the media.* Gone is the time-honored tradition of checking and re-checking sources and tracking down facts. Media organizations that had previously cautioned their reporters to 'get it right' are now saying 'get it any way and anywhere you can, and if you get it right that's a bonus.'

Occupants of the White House must also shoulder their share of the blame for obfuscation and doing that little sidestep that actor Charles Durning danced in his portrayal as the Governor of Texas in the movie, "Best Little Whorehouse in Texas." These were some of the lyrics he sang as he sashayed through the Texas State Capitol Building: "Fellow Texans, I am proudly standing here to humbly see. I assure you, and I mean it - Now, who says I don't speak out as plain as day? And, fellow Texans, I'm for progress and the flag - long may it fly. I'm a poor boy, come to greatness. So, it follows that I cannot tell a lie. Ooh, I love to dance a little sidestep, now they see me now they don't - I've come and gone and, ooh I love to sweep around the wide step, cut a little swathe and lead the people on."

Lying has become gentrified, rehabilitated. Everybody does it, so can it really be that bad after all? Enter the downright lie - sometimes confused with an exaggerated outrageous statement said for shock value. It often comes with tongue firmly planted in cheek. It is packaged into a statement that no one except the press would take seriously like Trump's own comments on his supporters' love of him: "I could almost shoot somebody and not lose voters." While technically not a lie because it is unproven, reporters don't care. If it was an unproven or hypothetical statement said to make a point it's as good as a lie to them. In order to please the media, Trump would actually have had to shoot someone.

The outright lie can also depend on the liar's motives or be something said that is so patently over the top that nobody would ever confuse it with the truth - the kind of falsehood that makes people laugh out loud at its absurdity. The mainstream media is especially good at being indignant because they have no sense of humor. I fear that the level of media self-righteousness is keeping them from doing their job AND for ferreting out the truth. Without any real reward for doing so, we are doomed to keep getting the kind of news (much of it spun beyond recognition) that has characterized the eight years of the Obama Administration. Don't look for any improvement any time soon.

~

Mirror, mirror

Okay, we've reached critical mass on this whole 'Trump is a crazy man' crusade. It's now time we ask all the psychologists - armchair and certified - to take a long hard look in the mirror (after removing their gargantuan egos and checking their self-righteousness at the door) and tell us why they have departed from the practice of using the so-called 'Goldwater rule' of not diagnosing people without even speaking with them.

For those too young to remember Senator Barry Goldwater from Arizona, he was also a presidential candidate who many believed was, to use a non-professional term, *just plain nuts*. The Senator was perhaps the most conservative political candidate Americans had ever seen run for the nation's highest office. He quite honestly scared the stuffing out of liberals and even some Republicans for his stance on a number of issues and for his controversial statements. Psychologists at the time were almost wetting themselves with fear and were chomping at the bit to diagnose poor Barry G.

In February of 2017, a psychologist by the name of Dr. John Gartner, broke that rule by starting a petition to remove President Trump from office because of what he called, "serious mental health issues." Last month, the same Dr. Gartner gave a speech to a group of 'highly respected' psychologists and psychiatrists at Yale University in which he reiterated his warning about Trump's mental condition. Feeling absolutely no reservation to keep their diagnoses to themselves about what they perceive to be the President's mental fitness, they linked arms to uniformly declare, <u>without ever talking with Mr. Trump</u>, that he too, like Senator Goldwater, is crazy as a loon.

To date, Gartner has about 48,000 signatures from fearful mental health professionals who feel that the Trump Reich is right around the corner. To read his speech it sounds like we better call 911 and immediately dispatch the men in white coats to put Mr. Trump in a strait jacket before our Republic is turned into a fascist state. To them, we have a crisis, but the crisis to me smacks more of mass paranoia on their part. Could it be that their fear is based on profound regret that a pathological liar (which would have been more medically preferable to them) lost the presidential election and they are simply acting out? I would posit that the reason for their snap diagnoses could be that these highly accredited docs have a problem distinguishing between the reality of politics and campaign hype and everyday reality. Their knee-jerk quackery in remotely analyzing a complex and controversial man without actually getting him on their couches is an indictment of their unprofessionalism as a group (something I don't believe they foresaw when they gathered at Yale). By coming out of the analyst's closet, they showed their true colors and makes me believe that perhaps they should take one of their own tests to determine if they have some deep-seated neuroses or worse yet, psychoses.

After they've done that, I would suggest that they all be required to sit down with a few ordinary conservative Americans for a few hours and discuss their feelings about their mothers, their toilet-training and a few other sensitive issues they're so fond of asking us. I think that at the end of those sessions we'd discover that they are no different than many other angry liberals that are upset at Hillary Clinton's loss. By abusing their Hippocratic Oath and discarding the prevailing practice of the 'Goldwater rule' they are not worthy to pass judgment on anyone let alone the President of the United States.

While I do not advocate taking away their licenses, I do think we should reevaluate the esteem to which we hold them. We might want to consider enacting some regulations, maybe capping their fees to say, $32 an hour (my co-pay charge for visiting my GP) and making them give us a disclaimer about their mental health and have them take a Rorschach ink blot test before we reveal even one of our most innermost secrets to them. Finally, we should make them give us an unconditional warranty that their sage counsel will improve our lives. After all, if my mechanic can give me a two-year or 24,000 mile guaranty of their work, my shrink ought to be able to do the same.

~

Neurosis roulette

I have two very good friends; we'll call them Aaron and Emily. Both are eminently qualified, internationally experienced clinical psychologists. Both have treated patients with some pretty serious problems ranging from substance abuse to suicidal tendencies. With all of that experience, I thought that evaluating our Presidential candidates would be a walk in the park, but I was wrong. It seems that Hillary Clinton and Donald Trump are not the stereotypical figures that many of us would make them out to be, but they are the 'gift that keeps on giving' for the medical profession.

Starting with Donald Trump, they both agreed from what they have observed, that he has exhibited all the signs of a person with a textbook disabling personality disorder called, "Narcissistic Personality Disorder (NPD)." This is taken right out of the 'Diagnostic Criteria from the

244

Diagnostic and Statistical Manual IV' which lists the criteria for all the psychological problems/disturbances that psychologists and psychiatrists use to diagnose clients. *At this point I have to add that Aaron and Emily aren't in the habit of rendering conclusive diagnoses without first examining their patients, but they wanted to be responsive to my request and told me that these are just their opinions based on what they've seen of the candidates thus far, from afar.*

It seems that NPD is traceable back to a person's early childhood and how they learned (or didn't learn) empathy or how they understood and related to other people's needs. Here are nine of the recognizable traits that a person suffering from this disorder might exhibit:

1. a grandiose sense of self-importance
2. a preoccupation with fantasies of unlimited success, power, brilliance, beauty or ideal love
3. a belief that he/she is 'special' and unique and can only be understood by or should associate with other special or high-status people or institutions
4. a need for excessive admiration
5. a sense of entitlement i.e. unreasonable expectations of especially favorable treatment or automatic compliance with his/her expectations
6. interpersonally exploitive i.e. takes advantage of others to achieve his/her own ends
7. lacks empathy and is unwilling to recognize or identify with the feelings or needs or others
8. envious of others or believes that others are envious of him/her
9. exhibits arrogant or haughty behaviors or attitudes

After mulling these over for awhile, I thought about how they might be explained by *chemistry*, but Emily said, "No. It's not that or their brain connections as you might see with Manic Depressives or Schizophrenic disorders; it is the very structure of their personalities that have been stunted in some way that stops them from being able to look beyond themselves and feel empathy for others."

She continued with, "It starts early on in their lives and speaks to a problem that the child cannot accept - that people do not like them or that they could be wrong." Emily said that many children come to grips with the source of these feelings, in stages, as they learn coping strategies during the maturation process while helped along by nurturing parents.

People with NPD <u>don't learn these things</u>, and in fact spend most of their time in trying to maintain the feeling of being safe. They also regard any criticism of themselves as threatening and will need to be struck down as quickly as possible by destroying anyone who offered that criticism. In short, no personally-directed negativity will be allowed to stand unchallenged. People with NPD see the world as revolving around them, and there's seldom room in their world for anyone else. Emily said that policy will always play a subordinate role to personality and that losing is never an option because self-preservation is their overarching need.

The interesting thing to me is that none of this is conscious behavior, which is why the first step must be to convince the person of that fact before any meaningful change can take place. She said that there have been some successes along the way, and some people have turned themselves around with therapy and by learning to read the signs before they act. "So, there's hope for Trump, then," I said. "Maybe," offered Emily. "Couldn't Trump just be a first-class narcissist and not have this NPD," I asked. "It's possible, but highly unlikely because he has exhibited more than a few of the telltale signs of the classic NPD sufferer," she stated.

"What about Mrs. Clinton," I said, "Isn't she a narcissist, too, AND a pathological liar?" Emily gathered her thoughts and chuckled to herself and replied, "No, she's just a stupid liar and can't seem to stop. She digs a hole for herself with her lies and then just digs it deeper by lying some more." From an amateur observer's point of view, I guess it's fair to say that we have two Presidential candidates that ought to excuse themselves from the race and come back in 2020 after getting some professional help. Just before hanging up the phone I asked my final question. "Aren't all people that seek powerful positions narcissistic and controlling?" Emily took a moment and said, "That goes with the territory of ambitious people who seek power and influence. While everyone needs a healthy sense of self-worth and confidence, I believe that we should only elect those people that have found a good balance between their own egos and empathy for others."

To this I responded, "With that in mind, we should be careful for what we wish for because we might just get it!" "You said it, not me," concluded Emily, "though I think that Oscar Wilde said it first." I stood corrected, a whole lot better informed and just a bit confused, but at a much higher level.

~

No more glass ceilings or glass slippers

There's good reason to praise Hillary Clinton for breaking the glass ceiling and receiving her Party's nomination for President. As the father of two daughters I get it, but I got it long before Mrs. Clinton became the nominee. I watched women rise to positions of power in corporate America (General Motors, Hewlett Packard, Yahoo, etc.) for decades. I also saw them win elected office as Congressional Representatives, Senators and Governors. Women have been Cabinet Secretaries in several Presidents' cabinets and attained high rank in our military not to mention occupying three seats in the Supreme Court.

This would lead many to say, "You've come a long way, baby," to quote a famous advertising campaign in the 70s. In my view, we don't need to prove anything more to ourselves about our attitudes on equal opportunity and equal access to a level playing field for women. I think we've pretty much eliminated most of the legal and other barriers that once kept women outside the circle. Now that I've said that, let me get right to the heart of this article. I support having a woman President...just not THIS woman for President.

Not only does Hillary Clinton not have the right experience and skills to lead our country through these dark economic and perilous national security times, but she's power-crazy, controlling, deceitful, untrustworthy and to quote those that know her well, too vindictive to be entrusted with the nation's top job. Does she love children? Sure. Was she a good mother? Probably. Does she like the average person/voter? A little, depending on what they can do for her. Is she fond of money? Absolutely, as her fees from Wall Street speech-making attest. Was she an effective Secretary of State? Depends on your definition of 'effective.' Is she honest? Definitely not as 'Servergate' and Benghazi show.

Mrs. Clinton's trustworthy numbers are nothing to write home about, and no number of barn-burner speeches given by powerful Democrat men and women are going to move that needle in the right direction with discerning voters. Watching the Democratic convention this week I was struck by the disproportionate number of minorities and women mounting the Dems' stage. This was no accident, for Mrs. Clinton desperately needs over 90% of African Americans, over 50% of Hispanics and at least the same number of young women PLUS her 'normal' Democratic voter base to show up at the polls in order for her to take home the brass ring of the Presidency. That's why the convention looked more like a gathering of the NAACP, NOW, La Raza and Black Lives Matter.

This outright pandering to minorities is identity politics at its worst, especially because it's happened before with the last two elections of Barack Obama and we all know what the Black and Latino communities got in return. Nada. Nothing. Zero. Based on that experience, if I were a minority voter I wouldn't vote for any Democrat for President let alone Hillary Clinton.

If I were a young woman I wouldn't vote for her, either, as she's done nothing to convince me that she has my interests at heart other than to guarantee my right to an abortion on demand. There has to be more to being a woman than that, right? Aren't women Americans, too, and shouldn't they consider themselves Americans first and women second or third or fourth after religious persuasion, ideology and other determiners? I tried to teach my daughters by example. When I owned my own businesses, I hired the best qualified people, often women, to key positions. I supported women while in the Foreign Service by consistently recommending them for promotions, and I tried my best never to judge a book, any book, by its cover (hard or soft).

I don't like Hillary Clinton for many reasons, but the biggest is that I don't view her as a particularly sympathetic person. I watched her mess up the healthcare portfolio that her husband gave her back in 1992. I saw her during 'Travelgate' and 'Whitewater'' and how she handled her husband's many infidelities. I saw her delay, deny and stonewall on 'Servergate.' I cringed at her lies on Benghazi and nearly cried when she told the parents of the fallen four that their sons died because of a video. I don't trust her nor do I trust her husband who wove a fairy tale love story for Democrats the other night about their relationship and his undying devotion to the best "change-maker" he had ever seen. More Clinton claptrap. I'm not buying it, because I'm not a fool <u>and</u> because I trust my instincts.

This is not the 'Matrix' and she's not Neo. She's not the <u>one</u>. The Oracle knows it. Morpheus knows it. You know it and I know it. Now it's time to get real, shake off the cobwebs, put away the *togetherness* signs and come to our senses. Think back to the Hillary Clinton that bad-mouthed her husband's paramours as 'trailer trash;' that made life miserable for Monica Lewinsky; that lied about ducking sniper fire in Bosnia and on and on and on. Having said all this I don't expect you take out your checkbook and write a big one to Donald Trump. I don't want you to switch sides and immediately support the Republicans. I just want you to think about who Hillary Clinton <u>really is</u> and what an America with her as President would be like. Don't be fooled again.

248

Passing the mantle of deplorability

I've been busy trying to think of a few good things to say about a possible Hillary Clinton Presidential win. And while it's been hard for this committed Conservative, I think I have come up with one. By winning the Presidency, Mrs. Clinton would finally be able to pass the baton of deplorability (to use her own special word) to Massachusetts Senator Elizabeth Warren as the most deplorable or frightening woman in American politics.

With a Presidential win, Hillary Clinton would move to the top of the food chain, to the bubble of White House protection, where criticism would no longer be allowed to cross the line of Secret Service acceptability and where strong derogatory comments would be viewed as potential threats. A Clinton win would require Republicans to find another vessel for their ire. That vessel has to be *comrade* Elizabeth Warren, the poster child of 'benevolent socialism' and enemy of the landed class. Yes, it is Elizabeth Warren, who has moved up to "most deplorable" status and who always brings a gun to a knife fight and who would rather cut her opponents off at the knees rather than lower herself to a compromising position.

EW also makes herself an easy target with her caustic, categorical statements about anyone of the Republican persuasion that dares call her orthodoxy about the pernicious nature of capitalism and the need to re-distribute Americans' wealth, into question. Warren's persona is that of a committed revolutionary. All that's missing is the dull gray uniform and the red star usually reserved for a worker's cap. Her rhetoric makes one think that the Czar is alive and well in the USA and that his strings are being pulled by the evil capitalist moguls who are bent on controlling all the levers of power and oppressing the masses...and that she is the only one that can save us.

There's a lot of that saviorism going around on both sides of the aisle these days, but Senator Warren's borders on the other worldly. This is not an exaggeration or a figment of imagination of some brainwashed right-wing ideologue. It is based on Mrs. Warren's track record in government, her speeches and her actions. All I can say is that we Conservatives can breathe a sigh of relief that she chose to sit out this Presidential race and let her sister-in-arms (Mrs. Clinton) take the pole position...for now.

Mrs. Warren will bide her time and <u>will be a candidate in 2020</u> after Mrs. Clinton has dug such a large hole of debt for us and fouled up our economy so badly that the voters will be scrambling to support a candidate that promises a plan to *Robin Hood* the rich and get America back on sure financial footing again. Enter St. Elizabeth, protector of the downtrodden, the economically disadvantaged, America's old and new minorities, women and financially upside down college students. The list goes on and on and represents a growing base of new Democratic Party voters that will welcome the relief of new entitlement programs and of a single-payer government-run healthcare system - all to 'protect the little guy' from the big bad wolf of Wall Street and America's corrupt CEOs.

The only trouble with that scenario is that Mrs. Warren will have alienated all her big donors <u>before her campaign even begins</u> and will have to go to the well of the average person whose pocketbook will already have been picked by higher prices at the pump, the supermarket and by friendly Uncle Sam's tax boys. I'm afraid, that by 2020, deplorability will be the least of our problems.

~

Playing the 'Lemming card'

I can't believe that some of us are still talking about voters as if they were one-dimensional beings and that the Democratic Party is still playing what can only be called, the *Lemming card*, when they talk to women. <u>What's even more perplexing is that many women don't seem to care that they're being treated as objects by the same party that claims it's the Republicans that are objectifying them!</u> Pandering (or if you prefer *pimping*) to special interest groups like women to satisfy their need for recognition is now part of the Dems' political playbook and they have taken it to a new level this year by portraying Republicans and their Presidential candidate as anti-woman. Their rhetoric goes something like this...

"Donald Trump is a misogynist and will do everything to disempower women and disenfranchise them from making any progress in their forward march towards total equality in the workplace, in the home and in the world. If in charge, Republicans will repeal Roe vs. Wade, close down Planned Parenthood Clinics, prevent women from achieving workplace wage parity, stifle their opportunities, limit their equality under the law by approving anti-woman, right-leaning Justices to the Supreme Court and generally keep their boot on the neck of all women."

The actual narrative may be a little different, but that's the gist of it. Democrats hope that all women will stand as one with their candidate, Hillary Clinton, a woman who talks the talk but walks a very different walk when it comes to paying her own staff, accepting donations to the Clinton Foundation from countries that abuse women, and as mentioned in the last Presidential debate, was an enabler and perpetrator of attacks against women who were sexually victimized by her husband.

Her actions and words have been directed at destroying the reputations of her 'husband's women' like when Mrs. Clinton said that Bill Clinton accuser, Gennifer Flowers (who had a 12-year relationship with Mr. Clinton) was just "some failed cabaret singer who doesn't even have much of a resume to fall back on" or her attack on young White House intern Monica Lewinsky which she labeled as "a narcissistic loony toon" or her comments to George Stephanopoulos on accuser Connie Hamzy, "We have to destroy her story."

No one expects a wife to graciously forgive her husband's sexual escapades nor to feel overly compassionate towards his paramours (or victims), but I would wager there are very few wives that would place the blame squarely on the other women and then go after them so systematically and with such vengeance as Mrs. Clinton did.

In a 2015 interview with 'The Federalist,' Hillary Clinton clearly showed that she could speak from both sides of her mouth about women when she said (about sexual assault survivors), "That any woman who reports an assault should be heard and believed, and there should be a process that is in place — not made up every time that something like this happens — to examine what she is saying, to begin to hear from people to make some kind of decision that is viewed as fair to everybody, because it does need to be fair to everybody. But many women like her feel that they are basically being asked to remain silent. That nobody wants to hear from them, that nobody wants to believe them, and nobody wants to have the comprehensive services that they need."

When her personal history is viewed in light of remarks made in recently discovered emails on her having "two points of view: one private and one public," the only conclusion that can be drawn is that Mrs. Clinton is a serial hypocrite when it comes to having women's best interests at heart. It's hard not to conclude that she views women as pawns in a political power game to ride her gender to the White House.

The real question is: "Are American women voters so easily persuaded to ignore the reality of Mrs. Clinton's actions, subordinate their skepticism, and actually vote for her just to get a woman elected President?" If so, we have truly become a nation of Lemmings who will ignore the perils of the sea below and happily follow each other over the political cliff. Call me crazy, but I have more faith in American women and their ability to see the real face behind the two-faces of Hillary Clinton. We'll see if I'm right on November 8th.

~

Probation and the nation

Ninety days used to be the standard probationary period for a new employee. Management was fairly comfortable that it could accurately assess a new hire's strengths and weaknesses during that time. Not anymore. It seems like America (and the rest of the world) feels that two weeks is long enough to judge its new President, so the word has gone out that Donald J. Trump, 70-year old, successful multi-billionaire who has run several companies and employed upwards of 20,000 people should be held to a higher standard than the average worker and only be allowed a couple weeks on the job before he's fired.

Back in 2008, a young, one-term Senator with no financial, managerial or international experience was elected to the nation's highest office on the emotional message of "I'm not George Bush" and "hope and change." For the next eight years, Barack Obama proved his lack of experience in a number of *bone-headed* decisions that drove our fragile vehicle of commerce over the cliff (of course it was all George W. Bush's fault).

He then proceeded to dally and dither, whither and thither on the international scene, spending his time drawing lines in the sand and posturing for the cameras. His was the 'decision by default' Presidency that proved the adage that if you left a pile of papers on your desk long enough, they would eventually go away.

The current occupant of the White House has a different style. It's called what you see is what you get. Example...if you heard him make a campaign promise in 2016, you will probably see him fulfill it in 2017, 2018, 2019 or 2020. If there's one thing that Donald Trump knows, it is that he doesn't have much time before the forces of political nature catch up to him and restrict his forward movement. Until then, he will blind us with his speed and decisiveness. He told us that "we would get tired of winning," but what he <u>didn't</u> tell us was that he would break the Presidential sound barrier with a flurry of executive orders his first two weeks in office!

The reasons are clear to those that know Mr. Trump. He's a true workaholic that is driven to succeed. Detractors will say that it's because of his narcissistic personality. To that I say, "So what?" I'd rather have a CEO that knows who he is and what he wants than someone who is on a 'journey of personal discovery' while in the White House. Donald Trump eschews hope and change for hope and change' sake. Hope without a plan is for saps. It's actions that count. And if you aren't up for the challenge, "You're fired."

The President has surrounded himself with the same type of men and women. They're not theoreticians, not academics, but people with street smarts and, yes, money. None of them are apologizing for their wealth, nor should they. When our system works well it is like an ever-expanding apple pie. By removing one slice you actually leave room for another <u>larger</u> slice to take its place. The Left doesn't understand that, and that is why they will always oppose people like Donald Trump. Mr. Trump knows this and that's why he's moving fast, leaving the media in doubt as to which 'outlandish' thing to cover. What his opponents haven't figured out is that <u>this is a strategy not an ideology</u>. His enemies will call this 'unfair.' "He should go slower and give us time to catch our breath (so that we can formulate our own plan on how to bring him down)."

No, the President knows better. By not giving them time to regroup, he makes them play his game and forces them to oppose everything he does instead of being selective - a little like using a howitzer to kill a sparrow.
Sooner or later, he believes, they will end up shooting themselves in their own feet and anger the American public. Time will tell if he's right. I just hope I can keep up with this tireless President apprentice.

~

Protesting the protestors

Oh, California, wherefore art thou California, the California of old, the California of civility and openness? Leave it to the Golden State's University of California (Berkeley Campus) to resuscitate the "Free Speech Movement" of 1964-65, but this time <u>without the free speech</u>. It seems that that campus' undergrads, imported rabble-rousers and quite a few professors were offended by the very idea that an opposing voice was attempting to penetrate their PC and safe-space protected little bubble the other evening. So, as typical à gauche anarchists generally do, they created havoc and destroyed public property to protest the scheduled speech of one Milo Yiannopoulos, a Greek-born British journalist who happens to write for a right of center website, Breitbart News. Of note is the fact that Mr. Yiannopoulos' speech was sold out and, with very short notice, he was able to help the organizers raise the necessary funds for extra security to protect himself and his audience.

A similar situation was largely averted in Albuquerque, New Mexico nearly two weeks ago as the Acting President of the University of New Mexico quite correctly waived the extra security costs for Mr. Yiannopoulos' speech at the Student Union Building. It would appear that New Mexican snowflakes have a slower melting point than UC Berkeley's, and while there were protests in Albuquerque, they were not as destructive and dangerous as those of our Californian cousins'.

It seems that we all have now entered, 'the year of living dangerously' where ski masks, Molotov cocktails and baseball bats have replaced the slide rules, skateboards and backpacks of our university students. Goodness knows many students have a right to be angry. Some have five-figure student loans and no jobs for them when they leave the safe space womb of the halls of ivy.

Many will graduate with degrees in obscure and commercially undesirable subjects that only qualify them for another bite of the University 'apple' (a Master's program). With that to look forward to, I can understand their frustration, but taking to the barricades to bite the hand that feeds them is not a very productive use of their free time.

I suppose they're also angry that they have four years of conservative political policies to endure, spearheaded by a President that they despise, whose party ran the table and now is rolling back all the social 'gains' that were made during the *cool guy's* presidency. If they're honest with themselves, maybe they'll admit that they don't have a lot of personal experience to fall back on when it comes to criticizing successful people for their success. It's always much easier to say "they didn't build that," that their wealth was unfairly earned, and that successful people should be embarrassed because they have money. Shame on them. They should be giving it all away to the truly needy...like college students.

We had all better batten down the hatches as we're in for a rocky ride as hundreds of hundreds of thousands of disgruntled Democrats, ex-Bernie Sanders supporters, *Black Lives Matter* and *Occupy Wall Street* members, along with angry hard-core feminists, join forces with student activists to

254

vocally - and with occasional violence - push back hard at the new Administration's conservative policies. Our first Amendment will be used as both a shield and punching bag by both sides in the coming years as we figure out how to tackle protests against non-PC speech and the protestors that would attempt to stifle its free exercise. There's no question that university administrators will play a decisive role in allowing or disallowing future speakers their time at the podium. Significant challenges await campus police and local police forces as they attempt to keep order.

Some key questions must be asked before future demonstrations get out of hand. The most important one is, "How much latitude will university leaders allow their student bodies before they call in the uniformed forces to quell protests that have the potential to escalate to the point of violence or destruction of property?" They had better have a plan, because I can guarantee you that the protestors do.

~

Queen for a day

The stage was set. The table was cleared. The name card was freshly printed and the seats were packed with an anxious audience. And then the curtain rose as the gavel sounded and the latest investigation on the events in Benghazi, Libya of Sept. 11, 2012 were off and running. The guest of honor was coiffed, smartly clothed and ready to be the roasted on the spit, all prepared for her by the Congressional Select Committee on Benghazi. The *host* was Congressman Trey Goudy, former prosecutor and now chairman of a committee that is so divided that it could be dubbed the Hatfields and the McCoys.

It was not the Spanish Inquisition or the Nuremberg Trials, but it was not "Queen for a day" either. Jack Bailey was nowhere to be found, and there was no diamond tiara on a velvet pillow waiting for the winner. It was hardball and the batter up was none other than former Secretary of State and Presidential candidate, Hillary Rodham Clinton. Mrs. Clinton was not without visible means of support, however. Her lawyer, David Kendall (from Bill Clinton impeachment fame) was in the camera line as was Congresswoman Sheila Jackson Lee from Houston (who never met a TV camera she didn't like). The Ranking Member, Congressman Elijah Cummings (D-MD) was loaded for bear as was Congressman Adam Smith (D-Washington) and the rest of the Democrat members who were all determined to save Mrs. Clinton from a bad performance. Little did they know that Mrs. Clinton didn't need them. Her manner was calm throughout the proceedings.

There were no, "What difference at this point does it matter" outbursts by Secretary Clinton, only an attempt to run out the clock by answering questions in what might be called the Joe Biden School of Debating (why use 100 words when a thousand will do). It worked. She looked and sounded Presidential except for occasional body language which betrayed her impatience with what the Democrats called a "prosecutorial" line of questioning.

I don't think that Republicans actually thought they would find a 'smoking gun,' but I'm sure they hoped to prove three things: 1. that Mrs. Clinton failed to manage a terrible crisis by delegating authority to underlings; 2. that she failed to protect an American installation and four Americans who died because she was more interested in shifting the blame to an anti-Muslim video to ensure President Obama's (and her own) legacy and; 3. that she was trying re-write history knowing that she would run for President.

There was also a fourth, perhaps less important, but nonetheless germane...her possible conflict of interest by continuing an email relationship with Clinton family friend, Sidney Blumenthal, who was trying to get a contract in the Middle East. The questioning was fast and furious (from the Republican side) while Democrat committee members gave Mrs. Clinton space and time to collect her thoughts by asking questions about securing <u>future</u> State Department facilities. The exception was Rep. Adam Smith who harangued the Chairman and the Republican side for wasting $4.7 million of taxpayer money on unnecessary hearings saying, "We haven't learned one new thing from all of this."

The real victims of the hearing were (again) four dead Americans who couldn't be present to offer their testimony because they suffered excruciating deaths from smoke inhalation in a poorly-secured building that was under siege by heavily-armed insurgents that didn't attack them because of a video. These brave men deserved better and so did their parents and loved ones, some of which were in attendance at the hearing.

I cannot imagine what they were thinking listening to the former Secretary invoke 'State Department speak' as she passed the buck for the lack of security to her 'security experts.' The ghost of former President Harry Truman must have been weeping at her pathetic attempts to shirk her responsibility for the massacre in Benghazi.

No matter what one thinks of Mrs. Clinton's tenure at the State Department and her handling of the Benghazi tragedy, we must give her high marks for being an excellent lawyer. She knows how to make short shrift of troubling and controversial questions, turn the tables on her interrogators and pass her own blame on to others.

If this ability is one that qualifies a person to become President of the United States, then Mrs. Clinton has earned a shot at the Oval Office. If not, then she should disband her campaign, apologize to all of us and go quietly into the history books and let future generations give her a thumbs up or thumbs down.

~

Repurposing the status quo

I've learned many things in life, but one of the most important is that if everybody is telling you to do something it's probably best to step back and question why. Recently, the British publication, "The Economist," came out against Donald Trump and predicted that if he were elected President, it would set off a nuclear-type trade war.

Normally, I don't pay attention to The Economist which I view as the maven of the economic ruling elite, but after economist Ben Stein called them "Left-wing punks" this morning on Fox Business News it got me thinking about how the forces that constitute the status quo and make up the 'prevailing wisdom' in any given situation are getting really nervous about the possibility of a President Donald Trump setting up shop in the Oval Office. That got me thinking about how we are all too willing to let the 'experts' define what prevailing wisdom is and then tell us that it would be suicide to disagree with them.

As of this writing, much is being said about the Republican elites who are donning their flak jackets and retreating to their War Rooms in order to carve out a plan to stop a candidate that has captured the attention and support of millions and who is constantly rattling his saber at the establishment. The whisper campaign of 'brokered convention' is intensifying and has been handed off to the rank and file of the Party via the media, and of course, the opposition has welcomed it with open arms.

It appears that Mr. Trump has become a threat to the *prevailing wisdomites* that include lobbyists, big money donors and entrenched politicians. His rejection of corporate money has sent up a signal flare that his arm might not be very twistable and that his agenda to 'Make America great again' might be vastly different from theirs. His kind of independence is the thing that makes power brokers cringe as it is anathema to their doctrine of keeping the candidate dependent on the establishment.

This is not to say that Mr. Trump couldn't be a Trojan Horse, happy to be wheeled inside the gates of WASHDC after which he would proceed to do whatever's necessary to win like the pragmatist he says he is. I have never read "The art of the deal," but I had it explained to me by one of my friends who said that if Genghis Khan and Sun Tzu had both lived at the same time they might have collaborated on the 'Donald's' book. For admirers of Trump, that's good news, as they feel that today's America needs a battle-hardened leader that can withstand the Left's onslaught and repel attacks from his own people, simultaneously.

The real question is, will a Trump nomination and eventual elevation to President be the equivalent of the American victory at the Battle of the Bulge or the Greek defeat at Thermopylae? In order for the powerful status quo to be re-purposed, it will take more than a single victory at the ballot box. It will require the creation of a super coalition of America's *general interest groups* to fix our economy, repeal and replace Obamacare, repair our infrastructure, make us competitive in the world marketplace, create jobs and tackle the many social challenges facing our society.

One should never underestimate the power of those who feel under attack, and that goes for America's power elite and special interests. Should a Trump Presidency become a reality, his attempt to take on the status quo would not be an easy fight. He should know that it's not enough to have *amor patriae* (love of one's country) especially when confronted by the full force of America's Left. That goes double for those from within his own party AND from the American ruling class for whom he represents an existential threat. Trump should watch his back but remember that "fortes fortuna adiuvat" - fortune favors the bold.

~

Screwtinizing Donald Trump

There comes a point when most of us say, 'enough is enough,' but we are living in extraordinary times when journalists never bother to leave their desks to write a news story; when anonymous sources have replaced bona fide, on-the-record ones; and when editors freely abrogate their responsibility to properly vet reporters' hatchet jobs on the media's enemies. The man who has become their target is the American President who has only been in office for five months.

We all know who the media ninjas are: CNN, The Washington Post and the New York Times, among others. These once respected news outlets have now become houses of ill repute, happily churning out highly questionable 'real news' stories about Russia, collusion, impropriety, pay for play and treasonable acts committed by presidential campaign officials, a political party and our new President. What used to be called, 'yellow journalism' has now become de rigueur and the modus operandi for a literary lynch mob dedicated to destroying an administration and a single individual. I'm sad to say that they are acting like a bunch of uncontrollably angry fanatics.

These are tough words, but the incessant attacks on the veracity of Donald Trump and even his family have already proven that fair and balanced reporting has been relegated to the dust heap of journalism and no longer plays any part in truth sleuthing. It is, instead, only fuel for ratings and fodder for the legion of anti-Trumpers who gleefully revel in every sound bite, vitriolic and demeaning word and phrases uttered on a daily basis by legions of talking heads and 'experts' trotted out by news producers or editors. Networks like CNN have nearly given up covering other major events unless there is some connection to the 'Russia' story.

What was formerly one of America's leading purveyors of international reportage has now sunk to the level of panderer - all in the name of ratings. One can look back to CNN's coverage of the Gulf War in the early 90s as a high-water mark in that network's history. It was excellent, timely and balanced with reporters like New Zealander Peter Arnett who risked his safety to broadcast from the Baghdad Hotel as rockets landed in nearby neighborhoods.

What happened? Partisanship happened. Competition happened, and with it a major swing Left of the political middle happened. CNN couldn't resist the lure of the advertising dollar and gradually became a mouthpiece of the Progressive movement. Later, it would take up the anti-Second Amendment cause with Englishman Piers Morgan as its Don Quixote on a series of programs that railed against gun ownership, using America's mass shootings to hammer home the point that guns must be removed from Americans' hands. Morgan's show was cancelled in 2014 after three years of haranguing gun rights organizations and angering millions of gun owners.

259

CNN needed another cause, and the easiest and most ratings friendly target was businessman/candidate Donald Trump whose controversial style and comments were perfect for non-stop criticism by anchors like Don Lemon and Anderson Cooper. Both jumped on the anti-conservative bandwagon during the Presidential campaign of 2016. Their marching orders were clear to all who watched the channel: bring down the Republican Party, insure a victory for Hillary Clinton and destroy Donald Trump.

Their strategy was to surround themselves on their nightly broadcasts with former Bill Clinton supporters and Democratic Party operatives and link arms, speak with one voice and launch an all-out guerilla media war of innuendo, underpinned by a false narrative that Donald Trump was either deranged, demented or demonstrably dangerous and unfit to be President.

One of their tactics proved that nothing was beneath them as debate questions were given to the Hillary Clinton campaign team by Donna Brazile, a CNN employee. After Trump's election, CNN intensified its efforts to discredit him and have kept up the pressure ever since by filing a number of stories with anonymous sources and even some false ones about the Trump Russia 'collusion.' CNN has kept its fake news spinning in the air like so many circus plates until just this week when a directive from the CEO's office seemed to put the brakes on the geyser of unsubstantiated reporting. CEO Jeff Zucker directed his newsroom not to air any more Russia stories unless approved by the executive. If the past is prologue, however, this will not have much effect on any future unprofessional journalism at the network as the seeds of their discontent with the President and his Party are sown deep and will continue to germinate beneath the surface.

~

Should we forgive Hillary?

Every President has it within his power to pardon wrongdoers or grant clemency to criminals. That includes full pardons, commutation of sentences or rescindment of fines. That's a fact. It's in the Constitution (Article II, Section 2, Clause 1). It doesn't, however, allow Presidents to grant clemency to those prosecuted under states' laws. There is even an Office of the Pardon Attorney set up to handle potential pardonable cases. This office works with the Attorney General and the President's office in arranging the final pardons. The most famous pardon in the last half-century is Gerald Ford's pardon of former President Richard Nixon for his part in the Watergate crimes, and while that may have been *the* big pardon headline of our time there have been many pardons throughout history that were more than a little controversial.

Let's start with Abraham Lincoln. Lincoln actually pardoned over 300 people in his time in office. Among them were 264 Dakota Indians that attacked White settlers during the Sioux Uprising in 1862. President James Madison pardoned two pirates (Jean and Pierre Lafitte) for their assistance in the war of 1812. Andrew Johnson was the Kingfish of Presidential pardoners, giving pardons to 7,000 people during his presidency. Presidents Garfield and Harrison were the only two Presidents that gave no pardons. (Harrison died shortly after taking office and Garfield was assassinated.) One pardonee, George Wilson, who was convicted of robbing a U.S. mail train, refused his pardon from President Andrew Jackson and opted to stay in jail!

War has a way of causing our tempers to boil over, but time gives us pause to find compassion. At least two Presidents have pardoned former enemies (mostly Confederate officers right after the Civil War), but one man, Frederick Krafft, a socialist, was convicted under the 1917 Espionage Act and sent to jail for attempting to cause insubordination and disloyalty among members of the armed forces. It seemed that Krafft was preaching on a street corner against the U.S.' entry into World War I and some soldiers in the crowd took umbrage at his remarks and filed charges against him.

He was convicted, sentenced to five years in prison and fined $1000. President Woodrow Wilson gave him a full pardon after he had served a little over a year. More recent pardons have also caused a few storms of discontent. Richard Nixon commuted the sentence of famous labor leader Jimmy Hoffa (for fraud and bribery) and pardoned Lt. William Calley (convicted of murder in the My Lai massacre). Even 'Tokyo Rose' (Iva Toguri D'Aquino) who for years attempted to get GIs to desert their posts and surrender to the Imperial Japanese Army through her broadcasts on the radio during WWII was pardoned by President Gerald Ford!

On his last day in office, President Bill Clinton pardoned his own brother, Roger, for drug crimes; Marcus (Mark) Rich for tax evasion and illegal trading with Iran; Susan McDougal for her part in the Whitewater deal and 16 members of the violent Puerto Rican terrorist group (FALN) that set off 120 bombs in the U.S., most of them in New York City.

So far, President Barack Obama has pardoned a little over 1,000 people during his eight years in office. Many of them have been for cocaine possession and conspiracy to distribute the product. One wonders if that has anything to do with his own previous use of cocaine. Should President Obama spare the country more Federal inquiries of Hillary Clinton by telling future Departments of Justice to go pound sand and leave the poor woman alone?

Should he short-circuit any more attempts to find the truth about her role in the deaths of four U.S. citizens in Benghazi and leave us all guessing for the rest of our lives? Should he include any 'pay for play' with the Clinton Family Foundation and the State Department in the pardon and make it an all-inclusive one that basically exonerates her for any wrongdoing in her entire life in Government? Those are probably academic questions, but they could be debated during Mr. Obama's last weeks of his Presidency. I'm anxiously awaiting the morning of January 20th to see if '44' thumbs his nose at '45' by pardoning HRC as a parting shot to a man who doubted his birthplace and his right to be President.

~

The caveman in all of us

For the last four years I've hosted a monthly man's political discussion group, and as you can imagine, the temperature has gotten pretty hot from time to time as the members of our group come from the right of Charleton Heston to the left of Susan Sarandon. We have a few moderates, too, but we call them Independents. Oh, and we have a Libertarian who acts as our moral compass and always helps us find true North when things get too extreme. We meet over the lunch table (no sharp objects only plastic cutlery) and often have a single malt whiskey waiting in the wings, just for political emergencies. We usually have a specific discussion topic, and this month's was Hillary Clinton.

I'd gone to great lengths to read about Mrs. Clinton and even created a board game based on her life. I also bought a door prize – a really tremendous Hillary nut-cracker - which I raffled off. Fittingly, the uber liberal member of our group (let's call him Will), won it! A year or so ago we added an out-of-state member from Texas via Skype to our group. Dr. Michael is an old friend of mine with whom I've spent dozens of hours talking politics. He's a man with an insatiable curiosity, quick mind and terrific sense of humor. He took to the group and the group to him, immediately.

Today, we started by going through Hillary's early pre-Bill Clinton life, moved to her marriage and time at the Rose Law Firm, her eight years in the White House as First Lady, as Senator and finally as author of "Hard Choices." I admit that for years I had never been a Hillary fan, especially after watching Emma Thompson's portrayal of her in Primary Colors. Then there was her internal SWAT team that handled the 'bimbo eruptions' associated with her husband's paramours. I wasn't thrilled with the exaggerations she's peddled about being named after Sir Edmund Hillary or landing in Bosnia under sniper fire, either. However, I tried to put all that behind me and focus on her recent past, her time as Secretary of State.

This was a more challenging task because Mrs. Clinton really didn't have any high points during the five plus years of her tenure as principal Obama administration frequent flyer. Actually, the thousands of miles spent in visiting 112 countries didn't produce much in the way of results, but I'm sure proponents of Mrs. Clinton will say that she 'helped restore America's credibility on the world stage.' I'm willing to let history be the judge of that. There was one defining moment in her time as SECSTATE (if you don't count the moronic *reset button* episode), and it was the whole sordid Benghazi business. This was a time I'm sure she'd like to forget, especially the eyeball-to-eyeball confrontation with Benghazi victims' families at Edwards AFB. You remember, she said that they (the administration) would get the men who made that video.

I can't help wonder what it took to get her to say that to the fathers, mothers and wives of the four dead Americans, full-well knowing it wasn't a video that caused the attack on the Benghazi Consulate and CIA safe house. Surprisingly, my friend Will and I agreed on Hillary and on what kind of strength it takes to go the distance in a rough and tumble political campaign AND what that says about a person's character.

What we didn't agree on was the next subject of our lunch...*relativism as it relates to political decision-making and policy-making.* I'm the absolutist. Will is the relativist. I tried to bore a test hole into Will's mind to see if I could find the locus of his thought processes, but the bit kept slipping as we went round and round in a circular argument about the Constitution, consistent application of the law, Executive Branch overreach, etc. Finally, I could feel my patience subside and my demeanor slowly change into that of a caveman. I was, ironically, proving one of Will's points...that we are all pretty primitive no matter how sophisticated the subject matter of our conversation.

~

The ever-changing never-changing Donald Trump

Political strategists are amazed at the chameleon-like ability of Republican front-runner Donald Trump to adapt to the rapidly-changing political winds of the 2016 Presidential race. There is an equal number of political pundits that are equally amazed at the *unchanging* nature of Donald Trump as he barrels his way through the first caucuses and primaries. So which one is the real Donald Trump?

According to the man himself, he says he is able to adapt and change and be what he needs to be to be successful. In other words, he is no different from any other career politician except that he's better than most at doing it AND he has a track record of success to fall back on. In simple terms, he's a man who knows himself well and who has walked the walk of a successful life, keenly focused on his goals, full-well knowing that he must adapt to survive and thrive (four corporate bankruptcies and subsequent ascent from their ashes are testimony to that).

At times he has exhibited shades of Yogi Berra, Harry Truman, Lee Iacocca and Oral Roberts, but he has also shown himself to be a convincing patriot. A perfect example of the need to improvise and adapt quickly was Trump's recent close encounter of the religious kind with the Holy Father, Pope Francis, who saw fit to question Trump's right to call himself a Christian.

Trump could have responded in any number of ways, but chose a softer more measured approach which helped him keep the Catholic vote and gave the Pontiff time to walk back his remarks. That shows maturity and good judgment and should serve to allay some fears about Trump's tendency to return deadly fire, quickly. Trump's a realist and has made his fortune by betting on human nature; by using his instincts; and by cleverly allocating his resources in order to leverage his position.

To say that he is a deal-maker is not to disparage the man. It is high praise, unless of course, you are among those who are against any form of compromise and see 'deal-making' as selling out. Trump will need to attract a variety of demographic groups to lock up the nomination. At present, a large number of them are in the Cruz camp and show no signs of deserting their man just yet. The question then becomes, "Is there enough anger out there to fuel two candidates?" Trump is betting that he can keep Americans' anger and frustration simmering as he moves from win to win until shortly before Super Tuesday when he should, in my opinion, add another message to his campaign quiver...that of *action-based hope.*

This would not be the empty rhetorical hope of then-candidate Obama, but rather an experience-based hope that is rooted in Trump's successes (something that neither Obama nor Hillary Clinton could offer). If it were up to me, I would like to see Trump launch a version of JFK's "Ask not what your country could do" message of American engagement alongside his, "Make America Great Again" theme.

Neither Ted Cruz nor Marco Rubio can play the Trump 'experience matters' card as neither one has ever run anything larger than a Senate office, so they must focus on something that is uniquely theirs...a deep and abiding understanding of how Washington works (so that they can fix it) along with an appeal to younger voters, minority voters and idealists that 'this is their time and their chance' to reset politics for the future (the implication being that Donald Trump is rooted in the past).

All three will probably adopt a few new themes and messages that will be tested in the coming primaries, but they are likely to be more highly-targeted demographically-specific ones, designed to bring the numbers of Hispanics, Blacks and young voters (especially women) up over the Republicans' abysmal 2012 campaign levels. So it's on to Super Tuesday with essentially a three-man bobsled race towards the finish line. The first order of business must be for each man to stay on board, especially in the tight turns.

~

The Republican Alamo?

For those of you who aren't Midwesterners or Republicans, what I'm about to say might not make any sense to you, but hear me out, please. Rural Midwesterners like me were raised on Republican values even though our parents may have been Democrats.

My generation grew up with a value system that was based more on the Ten Commandments than the first ten planks of the Republican or Democrat party platform. We were religious, read the Bible and believed it. We gave back to God the things that He expected of us: faith, honesty, loyalty, devotion, hard work, respect, patience, forgiveness and compassion, and we passed these things on to our families, neighbors and country, too. It didn't much matter which political party we supported as

265

long as that party shared those values. I would like to believe that the same is true today. Make no mistake, we 'hayseeds' will support whichever leader has actually lived according to those Judeo-Christian ideals.

And while some may characterize this Presidential election as a contest between two diametrically-opposed ideologies, I believe it is more than that. It is an existential threat election that will either strengthen our American values or render them completely useless. Should the Left prevail, it will continue on the now eight-year long path of systematically dividing Blacks against Whites, the rich against the poor, man against woman and young against old. It will stack the Supreme Court with justices whose political and philosophical allegiances will prompt more *Ginsburgian* remarks as they feel emboldened by a lack of public condemnation thanks to an Administration that has linked arms with a do-nothing or say-nothing media.

Promoting self-censorship and a growing reluctance to criticize the power structure would be the way for the new Clinton Administration to govern us, a continuance of the Obama effort to reverse the polarity of the majority and the minority in America. It would also allow for a growing build-up of tension in minority communities, now being promulgated by race hustlers whose only desire is to see an ever-widening gulf between the 'oppressor' and the 'oppressed.' The purpose? To see that the underprivileged are granted more social programs designed to keep them squarely where they are instead of moving them up the economic ladder through meaningful employment.

Much is asked of many who can little afford to give it, but this would not stop a Clinton Administration from asking all of us to give 'til it hurts through a <u>wealth equalization and income re-distribution program</u> (dubbed a 'socially-conscious' tax reform scheme) that would enable the Federal Government to socially engineer the country towards achieving 'economic justice for all.'

In the years leading up to the 2016 election, Hillary Clinton took millions of dollars in speaking fees from Wall-Street companies, ostensibly to help her *grow America's wealth pie.* Unfortunately for Wall Street, Mrs. Clinton has been finding new ways to target <u>them</u> as the bogeymen of America's economic decline while she re-sizes the slices they will get. While this may be the way politics is played in Washington, DC, it doesn't play well in Middle America. Chicanery and back-stabbing aren't our pathway to the Promised Land.

We know that if you don't water your crops with more than promises, they will die. We don't respect flimflam artists or fast-talking tractor salesmen, and we certainly know what fertilizer smells like. That is why many of us are voting Republican this year, because we also know what success looks and sounds like AND we're just flat tired of the tail wagging the dog. Do we think that Donald Trump, an East Coast city slicker with a strawberry blond bouffant hairdo who often trips over his own tongue, is our idea of the perfect candidate?

Hell, no. But we do know the brand of snake oil his competitor is selling, that talk is cheap and the sand has almost run through democracy's hourglass. We know, too, that this may be our last shot to plow America's field of dreams and we sure as heck can't get there with someone who lies to mothers, widows and orphans...and all the rest of us.

~

The worst man for the job?

President Trump is a billionaire, and many of his cabinet picks are wealthy individuals who have made fortunes either in the stock market or in their chosen fields. For those on the far Left, like Senator Bernie Sanders, that fact must immediately disqualify them to serve their country.

Sanders prefers *men of the people*, ordinary men from the middle class, for the top departmental jobs. Apparently, being well-to-do and successful and willing to leave your wealth imprisoned in a blind trust isn't enough for him or Elizabeth Warren and all the other Left wing zealots in the Democratic Party. Bernie appears to believe that having money somehow makes you insensitive to the plight of those without it. That may very well be true for some, but surely not for all Americans of means. If wealth is the kiss of death for a cabinet member or politician, then half the Congress and Senate should divest themselves of their holdings and resign their positions. Former Senator and Secretary of State, John Kerry (who is married to Theresa Heinz Kerry, the heiress of the Heinz fortune) is one. So was our 41st Vice-President, Nelson Rockefeller, and the Kennedys. The list goes on and on.

Being rich in America used to be pretty swell. People looked up to you, wanted to be like you and learn your secrets of success. These days, you're a pariah, a greedy capitalist dog, something lower than a pedophile scoutmaster. Your motives for serving your country are suspect. "After all, why would a rich person want to give up making lots of money to become Labor Secretary or Secretary of Education? It just doesn't make sense!"

American employers used to look for the best qualified people to take senior positions. A person's bank account didn't figure in to their decision. Having wide-ranging life experience was also a plus. If you had failed and managed to get back on your feet, so much the better. Americans used to love a winner.

Winning definitely isn't what it used to be. Every child playing sports is classified as a winner, just for playing the game. Ask any parent whose son took home an end-of-year 'trophy' for suiting up for Pop Warner football if they think their boy is a winner. "Of, course," will be the response, so why then is Sanders and company making such a big deal about accomplished cabinet nominees?

The answer is simple. It's not egalitarian. It's not *fair* that someone who is successful should be allowed even more success. After all, aren't there other less-successful people out there that should be considered for these important jobs? Shouldn't the President have recruited his candidates from the ranks of the unemployed, for example? THAT would have made sense to people like Sanders who has never run a business or made a payroll. Come to think of it, he shares that lack of experience with our 44th President who named a number of wealthy people to top positions (like Jeffrey Immelt, CEO of General Electric, who became Head of his Economic Recovery Advisory Board).

Then there was Hillary Clinton whose net worth at the time of her appointment as Secretary of State was estimated to be $31 million. What about Mr. Obama's Chief of Staff, Rahm Emanuel, who sat on a nest egg of over $11 million in 2010? I suppose the foregoing were acceptable exceptions to the 'Sanders Rule' which is: "It's alright to be rich as long as you hide it and you are not a Republican." Truth is, the pages of American political history are replete with the stories of wealthy people from both parties. If Senator Sanders and his anti-capitalist colleagues really believe that we should be *fishing the other end of the lake* for less successful people to head up our agencies and departments, then maybe he should be using different bait to catch the attention of the majority of Americans that feel that the best man (or woman) for the job is still the one that's most qualified for it.

~

Three cheers for Bill Clinton

I think it's about time we all thanked Bill Clinton for everything he's done for our country. Maybe Elizabeth Barrett Browning could help us with her Sonnet #43, "How do I love thee? Now there was a romantic woman as her later years would reveal. But back to our 42nd President.

We owe Bill Clinton so much that it's really hard to begin. "Let me count the ways." We owe him for returning our values to us and for our re-discovery of right and wrong after the truth came out about his abhorrent behavior in the White House with "that woman, Ms. Lewinsky" (and the legion of paramours throughout his time in the Arkansas Governor's Mansion). Yes, we must thank him for being a serial adulterer and for causing the country so much pain and costing us so much money in his impeachment hearings. Why?

Because his rapacious quest for the 'gentler sex' taught us that Presidents' feet are also made of clay and that we must stop all this hero worship of men in power. *It's interesting to note that two of Mr. Clinton's idols, JFK and FDR, also 'wandered' from time to time.* Weakness comes in all forms, and while that kind of temptation is not exclusive to Presidents or to Mr. Clinton, it is something Presidents would do well to avoid. Television broadcasts of Commanders-in-Chief pointing their crooked fingers at the camera and lying about their peccadilloes do not look good in re-runs on YouTube, especially if their wives are running for the same office.

But, should sons (or wives) really bear the responsibility for the sins of their fathers (or husbands)? The Bible is pretty equivocal on the subject (see Deuteronomy 5:9 and 24:16, Exodus 20:5 and 34:6-7 and then Ezekiel 18:20). I suppose that if the Bible is divided on the issue then we, too, should cut Mrs. Clinton some slack for her husband's transgressions.

There is a favorite idiom of mine that is unambiguous about guilt and reputation. It is, "A man is known by the company he keeps." While that is more 'today' than the Bible, it is also about the past and is one of the best ways we can determine whether a person's actions match their words or philosophy. On that score, we need to thank Bill that his trists were only with women and not tête-à-têtes with avowed domestic terrorists like some Presidents we know. We must also thank *Bubba*, as he is affectionately called by his down-home admirers, for marrying Hillary Rodham back in 1975 and velcro'ing her to his coattails. Theirs has been a whirlwind journey through numerous high-profile political scandals and

269

intrigue, starting during his Governorship and moving through Travelgate, Whitewater, an alleged 'Bimbo eruptions hit squad,' Benghazi and now the famous unsecure private email server. That said, it's not been all bad for the Clintons. After leaving the White House "nearly broke" they took the moonlight carriage ride through the wealth-laden streets of the 501(c)(3) tax-exempt organization neighborhood, amassing a fortune with their Clinton Foundation.

Bill Clinton was, and still is, a very popular and iconic figure among Democrats. Unfortunately, he also is a figure that evokes disdain and disgust among non-Democrats. Recently, Mrs. Clinton announced that she had a new job for him when she is elected...fixing the American economy. Nothing like entrusting a man who never owned a company, never created a single job or ended up "nearly broke" after leaving an eight-year long, six-figure job to right size America's ailing economy. Bill Clinton may be many things to many people, but I will always be thankful to him for one major undertaking...the 2000 authorization to use the Global Positioning System (GPS) for civilians. With that action, '42' actually saved lives and marriages. No longer would wives berate their husbands for taking wrong turns and ending up in Butcher Holler. Bill, you have my vote, but not for your wife.

~

Trump presidency creates new industries

It's time to give President Trump a little credit for his clever use of creative goading that has led to the massive stimulation of the American economy in just one short month! Take the protestors, for example. The 'Million Women's March' on Washington may have been the first group to have kick-started the new opposition economic miracle. If we assume that there were only a quarter million women that descended on Washington on January 21st, they had to have gotten there by car, bus, train or plane.

If each of them spent just $200 on round-trip transportation and stayed at a Holiday Inn in the nation's capital or just outside the District in neighboring Virginia or Maryland they probably paid $100/night, times two nights, at least. Even protestors get hungry so they had to eat at least twice a day, and at DC prices they could easily have racked up $30/day per person. Then there were those cute pink stocking caps with ears. Figure $10 apiece. Their printed signs probably cost a pretty penny, too. All in all, that march probably brought in a couple hundred million dollars or more to transportation companies, hotels, restaurants, printers, etc. Not bad. After the inauguration, the protest class (especially the more violent ones) really shifted into high gear, taking to college campuses and creating mayhem. Here we have other items they purchased locally (no imports from Mexico or China) like alcohol for their Molotov cocktails, lots of Balaclavas to hide their faces, standard issue hooded sweatshirts and, of course, their army surplus gas masks and combat boots (great for kicking in plate glass windows).

Add this to transportation charges from Uber drivers, the costs for replacing broken windows and the repair or replacement of other public property that was destroyed and the 'heroes of the revolution' should get the equivalent of the Medal of Freedom for their contributions to their local economies. Yes, dissension is good business for America's businesses. It's great for the non-profit, special interest organizations and politicians, too. Take Senator Elizabeth Warren, for example.

After she tried to read a 40-year old letter from Dr. Martin Luther King, Jr.'s wife, Coretta King, denouncing Senator Jeff Sessions on the floor of the Senate (and was promptly shut down by a Senate rule that prohibits the impuning of a fellow Senator), it was reported that donations to her political coffers soared! I'm sure that angry Liberals are also giving more money to Congresswoman Nancy Pelosi, Senator Charles Schumer and Senator Bernie Sanders, too.

Then there are the lobbyists and the lawyers - the hired guns of DC. They will switch allegiance at the first whiff of money and sue anybody for anything. We can always count on them to charge, mightily, for their services. Case in point, former Attorney General, Eric Holder, has been hired to 'help out' California to the tune of $25K/month. What a bargain!

The media are also big winners. Filing negative stories about the President gets the Trump haters' blood boiling and that increases ratings which also raises the advertising prices networks and papers can charge for airtime or column inches. Who loves you, baby? Trump does. With every over-the-top statement he makes, the presses turn faster and our flat screens and smart phones flicker brighter. Every network political 'contributor' with a political axe to grind or a cheap shot in their back pocket is invited to be a panelist with others of their ilk to trash talk the President and take home a few thousand shekels for venting their spleen on national TV.

Every time Mr. Trump's family is skewered (like his daughter, Ivanka, whose line of clothing was not renewed by the politically correct West Coast clothier, Nordstrom's), Trump supporters step up and buy more of her clothing at other stores to show their solidarity. Finally, recent stock

271

market gains show that American investors have more confidence in our economy now and are buying more shares. That adds value to our country's bottom line. All this proves my point that protesting pays off big time for America. It's the industry that keeps on giving, and Mr. Trump knows this which could be why he delights in getting under the skin of his detractors. I say, up with the First Amendment! It's better than a tax cut or a border surcharge or even the repeal of Obamacare. It's so typically American.

~

Tyranny is tyranny

I've seen comparisons made of President-elect Trump to Hitler and comparisons of Trump's followers to the "Sturmabteilung" or 'SA' (the 'Storm Detachment' that helped Hitler spread his message of national socialism in the late 20s and early 30s). It's hard for me to believe that my countrymen, let alone some of my intelligent friends who have never lived through such abject tyranny could compare a populist businessman turned politician with a power-mad dictator like Adolf Hitler - a man who started a world war and was responsible for the murder of millions of innocent people (3% of the then world's population).

It just goes to show you that the Left, its media lapdogs and academics have done an exemplary job of convincing us that there is only one right path to travel, politically, and it is theirs (now who's sounding dictatorial?). Their years of spoon-feeding us their PC pablum that we were oppressors of nearly every living soul as well as unkind and unfair to one another has worked its insidious magic and turned liberal Americans into world-class reactionaries that would gladly shut down free speech or at least limit it to their own definitions.

They happily condone the need for 'safe spaces' on college campuses where conservative thought and the mere mention of Donald Trump's name throws the little snowflake students into convulsions. Lately, this intolerance of our past has led one college to pull down the American flag from its campus because it was "causing the students too much consternation and anxiety." While it may be tempting to draw parallels between ourselves and 1930s Germany when national socialism rose to the level of a state religion, the argument cannot hold water when held up to the sunlight of certain facts. Germany was paying huge war reparations. Its economy was in shambles and its national pride was suffering. It was perfectly poised for a 'savior' that would come and shake up the power structure and tell the people they were the chosen ones and create new enemies that needed to be vanquished. Adolf Hitler was their man, but he was not really chosen by the people, at least not in the election of 1932. He lost by nearly 6 million votes but later won, when on January 30, 1933, he was appointed Chancellor by then President Paul von Hindenburg who was 84 years old and in frail health. A month later, following the Reichstag (Parliament building) fire which Hitler's henchmen set, von Hindenburg suspended civil liberties and paved the way for dictatorship...and Hitler.

Donald Trump had demonstrated no real interest in running for President until June of 2015. The only 'fires' he set were the fires of excitement under voters who wanted a dramatic change from the policies of a politically-correct new Left *tyrant* who used Executive Orders to carry out his will instead of that of the people. Hitler had wanted political power ever since his departure from the military after WWI. Donald Trump ran an open and transparent political campaign in contrast to Hitler who persuaded a number of knuckle-dragging thugs to be his *Gauleiters* (regional Nazi Party leaders) - acolytes in villages and towns that would be loyal to him and push for his candidacy. Their reward? Local power.

Trump funded his own campaign and promised to empower the American people, not regional party hacks. Trump ran a multi-billion dollar business before throwing his hat in the ring. Hitler was nearly penniless. Trump ran the gauntlet of a primary system and beat out 16 other candidates on the debate stage. Hitler used subterfuge to come to power.

Hitler knew nothing about running a business let alone the economy of a large country. Trump had made a fortune running businesses. Hitler ran on a platform of hatred for the 'others' (largely the Jews). Trump pledged a closer relationship with Israel. Hitler sought to govern through doubt. Trump chose to campaign on the certainty of America's potential. Hitler was the supreme orator. Trump was a stump speaker, often repeating himself and frequently sounded like a child sloshing around in a mud puddle after a new-fallen rain. It's probably here, with Trump's bombastic remarks, that his detractors are looking to make their case for tyrannical predilections.

Granted, they have a rich field of Trump statements to choose from that could, on their surface, make one think that Donald Trump is a wolf in sheep's clothing. And while I might agree with them that the President-Elect might have fooled some people into thinking he was an ultra hard-liner on immigration, geopolitics, etc. by his, admittedly, off-the-cuff statements, he didn't, to paraphrase Abraham Lincoln's quote, "fool all of the people all of the time." The actions he will take, post-inauguration, will prove his opponents wrong when he makes good on his promises to safeguard America's borders to say nothing of balancing our geopolitical interests through the application of common sense diplomacy.

Until it can be proven that Donald Trump murdered anyone, burned down a government building, masterminded his Presidential win by buying off voters or rigging the ballot boxes, I am going to assume that the 62 million plus people (and 306 electoral votes) that put him into the winner's circle, were smart and not prejudiced, bigoted, homophobic, misogynistic, war-mongers or White Supremacists. I'm convinced that they just wanted their America back where it belongs, resting comfortably under a Constitution that <u>protects</u> not attacks freedom of speech and that doesn't permit a forcible homogenization of citizens into a politically-correct contrived image of what the Left thinks an American <u>should</u> look like.

~

Watch the shiny object

Americans have got to stop acting like mesmerized children at a magic show. This goes for all lawmakers, the media and the general public. It will not be an easy task because we have become addicted to being mesmerized, to having our gaze deftly shifted to the magician's right hand while his left is busy readying a rabbit for a quick pull out of his top hat.

This is the current state of presidential politics emanating from the big magic show stage on 1600 Pennsylvania Avenue. It's strange that so many people, especially those in the media, were so slow to recognize Twitter messages, political pep rally speeches peppered with monosyllabic prose and comments steeped with innuendo as part of the act of a president who wants us to suspend our reality and adopt his own personal brand of it. What were we expecting when we elected him? That he would suddenly 'convert' from his New York real estate ways to senior statesman who spoke in dulcet tones and smiled benevolent smiles while kissing the rings of Democrat Congressmen and Senators?

Did we really think that this tiger would - or even could - change his stripes and choose the bedside manner of friendly old family doctor over that of a Manhattan real estate magnate? I am sure that there were many that thought his act was just that - an act - and that after a few months he would surprise us all with a Jimmy Stewart impression of Mr. Smith goes to Washington.

Sorry, Virginia, there is no Santa Claus, tooth fairy or Superman, and there is no chameleon inside the Donald Trump suit. He is what he is, and he has been telling us that for years while spinning an exciting web of intrigue and mystery around his persona (which, I believe, he sees as something distinctly apart from himself). The more discerning among us have observed him say one thing and do another, say two things and then reverse himself, and then say three more for years. We've read his 'Tweets' with head-shaking disbelief and then heard him try to redeem himself by forgiving the very person he's attacked (Attorney General Jeff Sessions is the latest victim) by saying, "he's a good guy, really, but...."

There's always a *but*, an open door out of the corner he's painted himself into, an escape route. Somebody has always given Donald Trump a second chance because we're Americans and we always want to give the other guy a break, AND because we want to be associated with a winner, with someone powerful, charismatic, appealing. We want to forgive him for his lapses of judgment because he is human, fallible, like us, and we want to be forgiven for our transgressions, too.

I knew who we elected back in November of 2016. I saw the shiny object, too, but being an older voter experienced in the ways of the world, I knew that the country was in for more than just four years of ideological disagreement. We were going to war, and Donald Trump was not going to lead the country like an Eisenhower, but like a Patton, itching to engage the enemy on their turf using his unique blend of unorthodox tactics. He was not the Redcoats, standing in a perfect firing line waiting for the revolutionaries to show up. HE was among the Yankee militiamen laying in wait, up in the trees and behind the shrubs.

Donald Trump is a figure that inspires and leads, but he also has the capacity to disappoint. His path is built on leveraging...everything: ideas, money, goodwill, expectations. He raises people's spirits and then hopes that they will stand with him when the chips are down and the piper must be paid. Contrary to his own declaration about not being a politician, he has always been a politician, coalescing support, making alliances, eliminating the obstacles in his way while keeping his eye on the prize du jour. He is NOT a fool, a bumpkin, a knave or a lightweight. He's clever, wily and thinks several steps ahead. He uses the tools at his disposal to achieve all that is possible. Then, when he succeeds at his task, he reinvests in better tools to achieve even more. Sometimes the investment is his own and sometimes it comes from others.

Any eighth grader can tell you that a 100lb woman can move a 400lb boulder with the right amount of leverage. President Donald J. Trump is busy doing what has worked for him throughout his life, and he is busy making the media whitewash his fence while the rest of us help him carry his water, hoping with every step that we've made the right choice.

~

When enough is just too much

The word of the week is...impeachment. And who do we most associate it with? Your favorite Congresswoman, Maxine Waters of Los Angeles, California of course - a woman who never met a TV camera she didn't like. She and others like her care little for civility, the benefit of the doubt or anything that resembles fairness when she cavalierly throws around *impeachment* as if she were asking to 'please pass the sugar.' I get that the Left wants President Trump to pack his bags and fire up Marine One to take him back to New York, but folks, that's just not going to happen. If you think Richard Nixon held on to the Presidency as if it were a winning lottery ticket you don't know Donald Trump.

Here's a reality check. All of you wanting Trump's head on a stick had better do some self-medicating and immediately assume the Lotus position. The man is made of steel. He will hang on to the Presidency like a capsized sailor to a life raft in a sea of sharks. He will use every breath in his body to resist any attempt to throw him out of office, so all of you who are devoting so much of your time and energy to this pursuit should regroup and think about using *your* energy for something a little more productive. Volunteer for some charitable work, or better yet sign up as a missionary to Syria or North Korea.

I'll keep your dinner warm while you're gone. I get about a dozen anti-Trump stories sent to my smart phone, daily, from the Washington Post (WP), and if you were to ask me which of the media outlets that hates and despises Mr. Trump the most, first place would have to go to the WP. Following closely on its heels would be CNN and MSNBC in a tie for second after which would come the New York Times. (The online 'media' like the Huffington Post and Politico are in a class by themselves.)

I have been a subscriber to the WP's digital stories for a few years now, but I am seriously considering canceling my subscription as <u>enough is just too much</u>. The level of vitriol is so great that I'm convinced that the WP must have found its political writers among the ranks of some militant ex-wives or ex-husbands club or at an S&M bar in San Francisco. The level of

276

anger and attack from these sources deserves mention in an article in the New England Journal of Medicine under the title, "America's new hating class: Can they be treated?"

Back to impeachment. Okay, let's say that Donald Trump is impeached. His Vice-President, Michael Pence would become President. If you think that soft-spoken President Pence will be receptive to a Democrat agenda and break down in tears with the first negative story run in the WP I have a bridge to sell you. A devout Christian and a staunch protector of the Constitution he would go about his work behind the scenes and avoid the limelight whenever possible. When he did give press conferences he would appear calm, cool and collected in front of the cameras.

He would also use his considerable interpersonal skills to move votes from the undecided column over to his party and give the Republicans a better chance to pass critical legislation and win more Congressional seats in 2018. Forever a forgiving figure, he is closest to Ronald Reagan in demeanor. One could see him in a contest of words with Senator Schumer, for example, on healthcare. It would go something like this: Schumer (in the Senate): "President Pence has vowed to eviscerate the middle class and take away their healthcare with the Republicans' ridiculous new bill. We will not let that happen."

Pence (in a press conference): "Senator Schumer has accused me of wanting to harm the very people that elected me and take away their healthcare. That dog just won't hunt. We pride ourselves on being good neighbors in Indiana. We help people when they're down. We don't talk down to people when they're down or make promises we can't keep. Senator Schumer might want to take some time off from preaching the gospel of division and join with me and the other 62 million Americans that voted us into office to fix things that are broken instead of breaking the tools we use to fix them."

The 'resistance' had better be careful what it wishes for. Impeachment of President Trump could turn the mid-terms into a bloodbath for the Left because Republican voters would be hyper-energized and more committed than usual to throwing even **more** Democrats out of office for removing their President. If you really want to play that card or roll those dice, I say go for it. Republicans have absolutely nothing to lose.

~

Words and phrases of the Trump Era

I've been very busy cataloguing the new phrases of the Trump era. While most of them are the media's invention, others have come from the Trump Team in the White House. They all have something in common, Donald Trump as the country's Commander-in-Chief. The mainstream media is especially good at unearthing words that were once used quite sparingly, but have now found their way into their daily lexicon. Chief among them is the word, 'unprecedented' which now describes nearly everything that comes out of the Administration's mouth.

In the old days, *unprecedented* described something that hadn't happened before, like a tsunami of epic proportions or a plague that killed millions. The nuclear destruction of two Japanese cities in August of 1945 was unprecedented as was the mass suicide of madman Jim Jones' followers in his 'People's Temple' in Jonestown, Guyana in 1978.

The Chicago fire in 1871 that burned for two days and destroyed thousands of buildings was unprecedented and so was the birth and subsequent survival of the Dionne quintuplets, born in 1938. There is one thing that is not unprecedented, however, and that is political scandals. History didn't record the first one, but I'm assuming that it probably occurred in caveman times when the first caveman king was found to have rigged his own election. We don't know about it because it was probably covered up by his caveman administration. (Had there been a lively media at the time it would have been called, 'unprecedented' I am sure.)

There are phrases that irk me, too. One of them is, "thrown under the bus." The earliest reference to that phrase that I could discover was in 1980 when English journalists wrote about the gratuitous jettisoning of a political leader (Financial Times, Dec. 10, 1980). It was used ad nauseam during our elections in 2008 and has now become a favorite of the Left that loves to use it in connection with 'disposable relationships,' usually of the right wing variety. The most often used word to demean a person of authority, like the President, for example, is to refer to him as "that guy" instead of *the President*. I shouldn't be surprised, because the word 'guy' is used to describe nearly everybody in America, even women.

I remember once having dinner with my wife in Taos at a popular watering hole when the waiter came over to our table and said, "How are you guys doing?" I looked him straight in the eye and said in my most authoritative voice, "Does this beautiful woman look like a guy to you? Think carefully. If your answer is *yes* then we are taking our business elsewhere." He looked a bit shocked and responded, sheepishly. "No, sir," but then said, "Would you guys like to order now?" I gave up and laughed out loud after which he apparently got his mistake and then turned chili red.

Words do matter, as do colloquialisms. We Americans are famous for them. I watched them play out overseas in many cultures as American tourists and even businessmen used baseball terminology in countries that have scant knowledge about our favorite pastime. 'Grand slam' was one. In one formal business meeting, a well-dressed and apparently well-educated banker I knew wanted to stand up and move about the room after sitting still for an hour and a half, so he proclaimed, "What say we all have a seventh inning stretch?"

This puzzled his foreign colleagues who looked at each other in bewilderment. Baseball metaphors have been used for eons, and every once in awhile they're dusted off like a dirty home plate and used by sarcastic politicians to describe each other, like the time former Texas Governor Anne Richards said that George H. W. Bush "was born on third base and thought he'd hit a triple." THAT'S how politicians cut the legs out from underneath their opponents when they're not calling each other 'guys,' that is.

'Fake news' is the latest entry, and it has just about taken over popular sarcasm. It is especially notable because it not only insults (the viewer/reader) but also demeans good journalism with its false reporting. It's gotten so that we don't want to give anybody the benefit of the doubt or treat them with a modicum of respect any more thanks to our skepticism.

I occasionally watch the British Prime Minister's questioning in the House of Commons on C-Span when I tire of listening to our ultra-partisan Congressional Representatives. It goes something like this when an MP is recognized to speak after listening to the PM, "The Right Honourable Prime Minister is talking rubbish. She knows that the soggy fish and chips analogy is no way to describe my district's need for more money. She is sadly misinformed or just plain daft. No amount of double-talk will erase the stain of those self-same fish and chips from her starched government jumper." (The PM responds) "The Right Honourable gentleman from the East End of South Nowhere should know better. Had he any remedial schooling at all he would have known that in my district we don't eat fish and chips!"

We might want to adopt the English ways and start addressing each other, similarly. Democrat Senator Charles Schumer could be the first to 'go British.' For example, on 'Russiagate' he could try this one for size..."The Chair recognizes the right Honourable Senator from that uber Left-leaning State of New York, Charles Schumer, for two minutes. (Senator Schumer) "Does the Right Honorable President of this Senate and this venerable body know how and when *that guy* in the White House became a stooge of the commies, and does he (the President) have any clue as to the destructive nature of his 'bromance' with Vladimir Putin?

(President of the Senate) "The Chair thanks the Right Honourable but unabashedly partisan Senator Schumer for his off the wall comments. sorry, but the Honourable Member's time has expired. The Member should now sit down with all the other Honourable dunces he calls colleagues on his side of the aisle. He'll have plenty of time later to enlighten us with his Right Honourable folderol when the general debate continues. The Chair now recognizes the Right Honourable and always right on the money Majority Leader, Senator McConnell for one hour."

On second thought, maybe we should forget about it, as it probably won't work - unless of course we thrown in a few 'guys' and some baseball metaphors along with some real balls and bats.

~

Chapter V
Post-election 2016

Most of us remember when JFK was assassinated, when Neil Armstrong walked on the moon, when the Twin Towers were viciously attacked and when Osama bin Laden was killed. On November 8th and 9th, 2016, many Hillary Clinton and Donald Trump supporters will add those dates to their mental diaries but for very different reasons.

For Democrats, their hopes of 'setting the hook' in America's culture, economy and politics were palpable. They were busy measuring the drapes in the White House for Hillary Clinton and readying the Lincoln Bedroom for her husband. For them, the possibility of a Trump win was the furthest thing from their minds. From an outdoor TV studio high above Times Square, I watched as the crowd below cheered when HRC won another state and observed total silence when Donald Trump won one. The crowd was confident that a coronation was in their future.

For eight long years Republicans felt untethered from America, adrift in a sea of Liberal extremism with no land in sight. The prospect of enduring another eight years of the same (or worse) was more than they could bear, and in the early morning hours of November 9th their worst fears were allayed. Donald J. Trump became the President-elect. Here are some articles following those history-making days in November.

Are the tactics of the Left working?

The Left is engaged in an all-out war against the Right, and they have now become the party of 'no' on steroids. This was bound to happen, and it is eerily reminiscent of the stand their Republican nemeses took after the election of Barack Obama. It was just eight short years ago that they cried 'foul' when then Senate Minority Leader, Mitch McConnell said he would oppose everything that President Obama stood for or was planning on doing.

How quickly turnabout becomes fair play and the Democrats attempt to justify their behavior by saying that it is because Donald Trump is not 'legitimate,' that he doesn't fit the mold of a President, AND because he is diametrically opposed to their big government agenda and their desire to re-make America into a socialist utopia, complete with laws protecting 'uncomfortable' un-PC speech, transgender bathrooms and sanctuary cities that would protect the rights of illegal immigrants over lawful citizens. (THAT was a mouthful.) Their anger is understandable because they are witnessing the unraveling of their nanny state, their safe spaces and their sacred cows that were created by a Progressive-inspired plan to kidnap our Constitution and social engineer our institutions.

One must give them credit for their accomplishments. They did a masterful job at turning a once-proud and vibrant, free speech-based country into one that needed permission to blow its nose. They did their best at making the rest of us feel guilty at not demanding our rights, and they rubbed our nose in our patriotism by accusing us of being gun-toting, bible-thumping bigots while they re-wrote the rules of engagement from the President on down to the corridors of the IRS. They belittled religion and religious people and accused them of being zealots and homophobes and they used the tactics of delay and of the judicial system to wear us down while sealing the deal by calling us a "basket of deplorables."

Therefore, it's no surprise that they would oppose everything and everybody associated with a move to re-right the ship of state and to give back to the states the rights that were taken from them by executive fiat. It's hypocritical that they would excoriate President Trump for issuing Executive Orders when *their man* did the same (over 1,000), often thumbing his nose at our existing laws while doing it. Hypocritical, yes, but not surprising. The all-out political warfare now playing out in DC with accusations of *Russian collusion* and the demand for resignations of any Republican in a position of power is part of the Left's playbook <u>and</u> it is transparent to anyone who follows politics for a living. Their allies - the major media outlets - have made a pact with the Devil and have promised to do their part to undermine the new Administration by a concerted and coordinated effort to search and destroy the evil Trump Team by innuendo, insults and false accusations, not to mention 'fake news.'

From CNN and the likes of Don Lemon to Lawrence O'Donnell and Chris Matthews of MSNBC to the yellow journalism of the NY Times and the Washington Post, the media ninjas are burning the midnight oil to the tune of millions of dollars in the hopes of finding any information that can be twisted and spin-dried to embarrass or discredit Republican lawmakers in the performance of their duties, often calling them traitors to 'true' American (read: liberal) ideals of fairness and compassion. Whether the topic is immigration, job creation, healthcare or the environment, the Left is livid and near apoplectic at recent White House attempts to re-forge policies that reflect traditional American values.

I cannot recall a time when so much has been done by so many to destroy so few. Protests by women, college students, immigration rights groups and just plain angry ordinary Democrats have sent shock waves throughout our major cities. The Democrats' tactics and those of the new 'Anti-Fa' hard-liners are reminiscent of those of a certain group of national socialists in the 1930s when proponents of free speech were routinely shouted down and then trampled under the heels of thousands of hob-nailed boots. Sound like our town hall gatherings?

Misinformation and propaganda, happily provided by legions of Left-wing bloggers, are their stock in trade as are 'spontaneous protests' that disrupt the lives of law-abiding citizens. Add to this their appeal to America's 'victim class' to get angry and oppose lawful government attempts to round up illegal alien felons, for example, and you can see that this is a highly coordinated attack.

The aim is to create chaos and thereby topple the new status quo of what the Left believes is comprised of a band of capitalist oligarchs and misogynist villains bent on returning our country to oppressive sweat shops and a police state. The question may not be answered in the next few weeks or months. It may take time until the country sees what the Left's actions really are...a clear manifestation of the belief that might makes right.

~

A win for the home team

Today we saw our President tell the governing board of the Paris Climate Change Accords to go pound sand by pulling the U.S. out of an agreement signed by the last President that was not ratified by the Congress (because it wasn't a treaty). Soon, probably within hours, the President will be vilified and roundly criticized as an *enemy of the environment* by the usual suspects in the media, on college campuses and by environmental special interest groups, not to mention our old friends Al Gore and Michael Moore.

This would have happened whoever engineered our exit from the Accord, but because it was Donald Trump, the vast multitude of 'Chicken Littles' will be putting an extra sinister spin on the decision and paint it as proof positive that America's CEO is nothing but a climate change denier and out to destroy our environment and all our international relationships.

This 180 degree turn is a big deal for American industry, American jobs and climatists, but it is an even bigger deal for the <u>process</u> of flattening the organization (the running of our country). I spent 20 years in the 'belly of the beast' watching the State Department do its pirouette among world organizations on trade and other issues, and it occasionally struck me that many of my colleagues occasionally forgot that it was U.S. citizens that were paying their salaries, not the European Union or some other foreign entity.

Their diplomatic ballet was frequently choreographed to a *subordinate your identity* musical score that included a 'we're all in this together' push for unity at all costs. The exception was the U.S. Trade Representative's Office and the Commerce Department who KNEW who paid their salaries when they sat at the negotiating table. American industry was fairly well-represented during the Clinton Administration but labor unions and manufacturing workers were not, especially with NAFTA, a deal that sent our companies and their investments scurrying over the southern border resulting in the loss of over a half-million well-paying manufacturing jobs.

Everything started to 'go south' (no pun intended) at a faster pace when Barack Obama brought two very destructive things together: his abiding ignorance and indifference to our economy and a slavish devotion to a one-world philosophy that subordinated America's interests in favor of a seat at the big boys international table. The buy-in on the Paris Accord on Climate was one of those bad decisions as was the Trans-Pacific Partnership (TPP).

284

Not wanting a fight with the Congress, Mr. Obama chose to end run them and treated the accord as an *agreement* instead of a treaty. This burnished his credentials as both a globalist <u>and</u> a defender of the environment, but it also showed his head of state colleagues around the world that HE was in charge and it was HIS philosophy that mattered. While this might have been good for Mr. Obama's ego, his decision to ascend to the pantheon of the supra-nationalists did little for our sovereignty or competitiveness. Rather, it told the rest of the world that we were willing to be told what to do <u>and when to do it</u> by nations who were bigger polluters than ourselves and who got an exemption from making any meaningful reductions in pollutants for another two decades while our energy sector bled jobs.

It was this flattening of the governance curve that was the big story that most of the media will probably miss as they, too, are of the belief that America needs to be taken down a peg or two, no matter if it's at the expense of a usurpation of our country's right to choose its own course. Had Mr. Obama won a third term (fortunately something the Constitution forbids) we would have seen more of our right to self-determination take a hit.

Today, President Trump effectively reversed that course with his decision to opt out of the Accord, and by doing so has sent a clear signal to our trading partners and competitors that the next item on the 'America First' agenda will be a re-structuring of our tax code and the re-shaping of another bad deal, NAFTA. The wringing of hands will surely escalate as stories about Mr. Trump's *imperial* Presidency emerge, but it's unfortunate that few in the media will look back at the last eight years to see who the real imperial President was.

~

Blame it on the Buddha

There was a time when Americans accepted that something was over when it was over. Yogi Berra pointedly said that it wasn't over until the fat lady sang, but even old Yogi knew there had to be an end in sight (even if it was the fat lady's). In golf, when an unskilled golfer makes a poor shot, he's sometimes given a *mulligan* or an extra shot. (*The Professional Golfers Association says that the term is attributed to a golfer named David Mulligan who made a bad first shot and his partners allowed him to swing again because his hands were numb after driving in the cold in an open car. The term has become synonymous with a second attempt after failing at the first.*)

Mulligan isn't the only synonym for 'another chance.' The thesaurus gives 241 of them just waiting to be used in moments like the <u>Great 2016 Presidential Election Recount</u>!

It seems that the party that garnered the smallest number of total votes - the Green Party - has decided that it would like the votes in three states re-counted. Coincidentally, those states are the key states in the Republicans' win: Wisconsin, Michigan and Pennsylvania. If all of them were overturned, they would give Mrs. Clinton the Presidency. The key word in that last sentence is 'all,' because Donald Trump has 306 electoral votes to Mrs. Clinton's 232. Overturning just two of the three states wouldn't get her into the Oval Office. She would need all three.

One can question the wisdom of trying to prove that Wisconsin's vote tally (22K+ more votes for Trump than Clinton) or Pennsylvania's (70K+ more) will be nullified by a re-count. While Michigan's could happen (10K+ more Trump votes), it's highly unlikely that the other two would be reversed in Hillary Clinton's favor. Her team has signed on to the re-count, however, citing that Democrats "have always wanted every vote to be counted."

After this exercise, that statement will probably be modified to read: "every <u>vote everywhere</u> should be re-counted." I can only guess at the Green Party's motivation in asking for the re-count, but my suspicious little mind tells me that it could be one of three things: 1. a desire to raise money for their party; 2. a wish to raise their profile with millennials and Bernie Sanders supporters; or 3. they were asked by members of Mrs. Clinton's campaign to request the re-count.

We Americans have always reserved a special place in our hearts for underdogs and for long shots. Indeed, we go out of our way to preserve and protect the appearance of a *level playing field of fairness* in many aspects of our culture. Thanks to technology, we can quickly reverse bad referee calls in sports due to the 'instant replay.' It's different in vote-counting (or re-counting). It took hundreds of people to re-count votes by hand in Florida in the Presidential Election of 2000.

While there are established minimum voting tally differences that trigger automatic re-counts, the vote margin in Pennsylvania and Wisconsin is really pushing the envelope of what is both reasonable and/or economically defensible. But, it is the Green Party's money and they can spend it however they wish.

If they think they're buying themselves respectability and credibility among the 62 million people that voted for our President-Elect with this exercise, they're hugging the wrong tree and must have been protesting somewhere and didn't get the message that the American public just wants this creature from the Black Lagoon called the election to be over, once and for all.

Actually, the do-over is not an American invention. If we're looking for a fall guy to take the rap, we might want to blame it all on the Buddha and his teachings on the subject of reincarnation and personal accountability. The Green Party would do well to read the sutras and be careful. Life is like a revolving door, and Karma has a way of slapping you in the derriere if you delay moving forward or aren't mindful of your actions.

~

Breaking the PC sound barrier

We Americans can already point to one major benefit from the election of 2016, and it's one we have to thank Donald Trump for...the loosening of the stranglehold of political correctness (PC) on American political discourse. If we take a hard look at ourselves and the way we communicated with one another a few years before the Presidential Election of 2008 B.O. (before Obama) we will see that a massive change was already taking place in the media, on university campuses and in our institutions of government. We were 'watching our ps and qs' as we used to say, carefully censoring our own speech nanoseconds after the words left our brain and long before they were being considered for release to the outside world through our reluctant lips.

Self-censorship (or self-limiting speech) has always been with us. The wisest among us have used the tactic of something similar - thinking before speaking - to great advantage, first by being aware of the sensitivities of our conversation partners and second by understanding the effect that certain words and phrases would have on the many audiences we engage throughout our lives.

America's celebration of diversity hasn't come easy, and we haven't arrived at our final destination as yet, but we are on the right path thanks to the civil rights legislation of 1968 and strangely enough by the wars we have fought since then (more soldiers of color were thrown together with those of no color and forced to protect each other in battle). When we speak of diversity and its importance to the fabric of democracy we are really celebrating integration and acceptance of one another, though the two don't always exist simultaneously or are of equal measure when they do. We're still struggling with our slave-holding past and our subjugation of Native Americans and our generationally-transmitted prejudices, but we are struggling, and that's the point.

America's Left, however, is worried that we will backslide and that the gains made by thousands of protestors and activists will be erased if we don't keep up the pressure on John Q. Public through regular media surveillance and daily reminders of which politically-correct descriptors we must use. For example, we have seen an evolution from the 1950s/early 1960s socially acceptable term for a person of the Negroid race, 'negro,' change to Afro-American, then Black, then African-American (and then back to Black). In some circles, Blacks have been lumped together with other racial and ethnic minorities and called, 'people of color' (which presupposes, I guess, that Caucasians are 'people of no color').

The above is just one example of how the terminology used to speak about America's diversity is mandated by the affected groups themselves (I have never seen any specific indentifier or requirement of reference to people's races codified in law.). It's even more confusing when people of specific ethnic groups and linguistic heritage like Hispanics or Latinos for example, insist on calling prejudice against themselves as *racism (it's actually ethnicism or just plain bigotry)*.

Those politicians who have not studied the evolution of PC have learned their lessons the hard way. Recent examples have included a 'maccaca moment' with former Virginia Governor George Allen and with our own Vice-President, Joe Biden, who alluded to the proliferation of Delaware kiosks and 7-Elevens run by East Indians. Everybody is touchy these days and for different reasons, and those near the bottom of the economic or education ladder are angry that they're not higher up where the good life resides.

Those paying the freight for America's needy at the bottom of that ladder are also angry. When engaging in a dialogue on crime or about the breakdown of the family in our inner cities, it's unacceptable to talk about specific racial or ethnic groups' roles or responsibilities, lest they be blamed for every crime or social ill. This must stop. We cannot solve America's problems if we do not discuss their root causes objectively, openly and honestly. Those believing that hopping off the PC train will result in a crash (lead to a deterioration of our racial harmony) had better take off their blinders. There is already trouble in paradise, and we desperately need leaders - and a President - that is not afraid to confront the uncomfortable and say the thinkable. I believe that all the Republican and Democrat candidates for President are basically fair-minded and compassionate people who understand that political correctness is a double-edged sword. One edge can bring them votes, but the other had better be kept in reserve for defending themselves when the long knives of the opposition are drawn.

Donald Trump is not blessed with the ability to speak in tongues that the Bible says everybody will be able to understand (Acts 2:1-13). Neither has he mastered the nuances of non-PC speech yet. Judging by past experience, he will undoubtedly have a few more setbacks as he continues his drive to enliven the political debate about America's future through plain talk. We must thank him, though, for consciously (or unwittingly) braving the attacks from people that believe that the only way to solve a thorny problem is to ignore the thorns.

~

Democrat walkabout

The Democratic Party is desperately looking for leadership and may be ready to mimic the rite of passage of the indigenous people of Australia by crossing the threshold of their ideological safe space and embarking on a intellectual 'walkabout' in search of their identity...and a new leader. This was to be expected. Every loser walks this walk to some degree. In 2012, the Republicans did an *autopsy* on themselves, hoping to find the root cause of their *death* at the polls.

Things will be different for the Democrats. At the vanguard of their walkabout will be our old friend, Barack Obama, who will be guiding their journey with the help of "Organizing for Action," a non-profit and non-partisan (really?) 501(c)4 that advocates for the agenda of guess who? Yes, Barack Obama. It's the follow-on organization to his "Organizing for America," and it is building an army of community organizers. Their manifesto? In their own words, "With more than 250 local chapters around the country, OFA volunteers are building this organization from the ground up, community by community, one conversation at a time - whether that's on a front porch or on Facebook. We're committed to finding and training the next generation of great progressive organizers, because at the end of the day, we aren't the first to fight for progressive change, and we won't be the last."

OFA was the next natural step for Mr. O who is also a very able community organizing *strategist*. Set up in 2013, OFA was pre-ordained to be the

Progressive movement's new messenger. Why? Because Mr. Obama needed a post-2016 election platform to continue preaching his sermons to us as President emeritus, sermons about his wonderfulness and how critical it is for America to continue on the path towards a utopian socialist state.

Thinking that he would have a ready-made ally in the new President (Hillary Clinton), Mr. Obama was confident that he could shoehorn his way back into the media spotlight with President HRC's help and begin to rake in mega donations to his cause. He didn't count on the 'anti-Christ' winning the election, however. So while this has made him change his approach, it will not deter him from his mission to make America, Progressive.

The principal tactic of OFA is simple...resistance. After all, isn't it resistance that won our independence from the British; that gave the Negro his freedom? Isn't it resistance that helped shorten the Vietnam War? And, perhaps, most important of all, won't it be resistance that will thwart the *dangerous* policies of the Trump Administration that are designed to bring America back into the orbit of *antiquated* American values and *save* the country from an *unhealthy* attachment to that *outdated* document, the Constitution?

I believe, that someplace in the back of his mind, Mr. Obama was actually hoping that Hillary Clinton would lose the election so that he alone could be the Democratic Party's standard bearer in the fight to slay the conservative dragon now living on Pennsylvania Avenue. After all, much is at stake for him: a possible repeal of his signature healthcare legislation, an acceleration of deportations at the border, the loss of Federal funds for 'Sanctuary Cities,' the reversal of his beloved LGBT policies, and the list goes on. Hillary Clinton proved herself incapable of mobilizing the necessary forces to take this fight to Trump.

So, borrowing heroics from the 'Lord of the Rings,' Mr. Obama is preparing to answer the people's call for help and strap on his magical sword of oratory and assault the malevolent Trumpian forces of occupation.

This kind of epic, good versus evil battle is tailor-made for an ex-President like Barack Obama whose legacy is under attack and who thinks of himself in grandiose terms. And while he may be starting out his journey to save Middle Earth as Frodo, he will quickly morph into Aragon with the help of his loyal followers. They will see to that and so will the rest of his Party when they regain their senses after their walkabout. Like the penitent man, the Democratic Party will slowly raise its head as one, gaze into the shining countenance of Mr. Obama, and embrace him as their moral compass and their William Wallace. Like the Romans at Masada and the Persians at Thermopylae, the Obamaites intend to vanquish the opposition by the sheer force of their numbers.

Counting on the support of all the angry Democrat voters, disaffected college students, the 'sisterhood' and the LGBT and minority communities, the new Progressive Obama Coalition will coalesce around OFA and '44' and use *Indivisible's* "Practical Guide for Resisting the Trump Agenda" to overthrow the illegitimate ruler of the United States. America, prepare yourself, for we are in for a very long, dark and stormy night of protests. The impending coup attempt from the Left may take awhile to reach critical mass, but Mr. Obama can wait. The only thing competing for his time is writing his memoirs (a reported $60 million book deal for his wife and himself). Not bad for a community organizer that *suffered* under the ignominious yoke of eight years of luxury in the White House.

~

Entrenched warfare

It's getting impossible to talk politics anymore without somebody going ballistic. Even the best of friends are treading on thin ice with one another when the subject of Donald Trump or the Presidential election of 2016 comes up. We must admit the fact that we have lost the war on civility and have now dug ourselves two long, parallel, deep trenches from which we are lobbing verbal grenades at each other, seemingly oblivious to the long-term effects this will have on our friendships. This parting of the ways on things political was building for a long time, but it has escalated to the point of absolute ridiculousness.

We cannot any longer discuss the important topics that affect our nation and ourselves without pulling on our partisan uniforms, wrapping ourselves in talking points and strapping on our six-guns. We have become so singularly focused on trouncing our conversation partners and beating them into submission that we have forgotten what it's like to be kind and considerate or to listen. There have already been many victims in this vicious partisan war, but perhaps the first was that old word, and necessary ingredient in any meaningful discussion, comity. Webster's defines comity as "courtesy and considerate behavior towards others," and it is absent without leave. No matter where we look, someone is taking sides and girding themselves for a rumble. It's the U.S. against

Mexico, Hispanics against the Anglos, pro or anti abortion activists against each other, internationalists against nationalists, women against men, and the list goes on.

The 'Million Women's March' of January 21st gave us a preview of coming attractions in what will become the crusade against perceived abuses of the established social order. If you are pro life you are anti woman. If you want a secure border you are a racist. If you want our government to follow the laws of our land you are a fascist. If you want lower taxes and a relaxation of job-killing regulations you are a capitalist apologist. If you support traditional marriage you are anti-homosexuals. If you say "all lives matter" you are somehow judged to be against Black America.

What we have totally forgotten is that there is a lot of space between the ends of the social and political spectrum and a huge gray area between black and white. Our conversations between friends have become sparring matches with each desperately try to gain the upper hand. The victims are ourselves and our long-standing relationships with people we have known, in some cases, all our lives. This has got to stop or we will lose the very thing that holds our society together, the free, open and civil discourse that enables us to move forward.

Acting true to form, Democrats are leading the way in our rush to the bottom of the leach fields using intransigence as their weapon of choice to slow-walk the President's cabinet nominations. Now, as of this evening, with the nomination of Judge Neil Gorsuch to be the next Supreme court Justice, the battle lines are drawn. The Democrats are intent on opposing Judge Gorsuch who was, approved, unanimously, by the Senate for his current position back in 2006! Hypocrisy rules.

It's one thing to be the 'loyal opposition' in any government, but it's quite another to oppose for opposition's sake, and in this, both parties are at fault, as Senator Mitch McConnell and Senator Charles Schumer have proven. They are both denizens of the same swamp that President Trump vowed to drain and emblematic of the destructive political war that is soon to engulf us all unless we take a different tack. It's been said that, "elections have consequences," and a truer statement is hard to find, but within that truth resides a larger truth, and it is the absolute necessity for both parties to work together for the betterment of our country as a whole. Our new President lost the popular vote by over three million votes, but won a legitimate victory with the electoral vote. While that gives him a mandate to govern, it does not give him carte blanche to ignore the 53% that <u>didn't</u> vote for him. <u>Making the same mistake as his</u>

<u>predecessor is still a mistake.</u> Leading a Constitutional republic like ours that is so divided along party and ideological lines is like walking through a minefield, but it is a journey that must be undertaken...carefully. One big misstep would be deadly for our democracy and could lead to wholesale social upheaval. We must all do our part to help President Trump sweep the field for the undetonated mines that could rip us all apart, for we are all on the same journey through the same space.

~

Failure is an orphan

There is an old saying, "Success has a thousand fathers but failure is an orphan." Nowhere is that more evident than today in that great deliberative body called the Senate. The latest attempt to redress some of the worst parts of the 'Patients Affordable Healthcare Act' aka *Obamacare* failed to pass last night. The so-called 'skinny bill' was the Republicans' last hurrah at reversing the insurance mandates unilaterally imposed by the Democrat-dominated Congress when it steam-rolled the ACA through to passage without a single Republican vote.

Remarks by then Congressional Majority Leader, Nancy Pelosi, will live on forever in the annals of boneheaded comments: "We will just have to pass the bill to know what's in it." Well, they did much to our displeasure. This set the tone for the heated healthcare debate that followed for nearly eight long years. Republicans voted repeatedly to repeal the bill, each time falling short of their goal. The government-imposed mandate was probably the straw that broke the camel's back for most Republicans who carried the fight for its nullification all the way to the Supreme Court. The result? SCOTUS said that the government had the right to tell average citizens they had to buy something they didn't want, and if they refused, they would have to pay a fine.

Even writing those words makes my blood boil. What will government demand we buy next? A faster WIFI router for our home-based business? Mandatory connectivity to a government-owned data network? A living will? An electric car? The possibilities are endless and the slope towards government intrusion into our personal lives has now been greased because of SCOTUS' ruling. We had an opportunity to turn this situation around - at least with healthcare - but the Republicans couldn't muster a majority to do so.

Democrats, predictably, all voted nay, presumably to protect their former master's legacy, proving once again that they are not the party of the jackass, but the party of the Lemming. According to the Senate Majority Leader, Mitch McConnell, Senate Republicans will now turn their focus towards tax reform and will, presumably, accept the fact that the ACA will die a painful and certain death as it collapses under its own financial weight (young healthy people would have offset the costs of insuring the unhealthy, but they have opted out). Democrats, consider yourselves warned. Your fingerprints are all over Obamacare and they cannot be erased with mere words.

President Trump is on record saying that he would have rather have saved the 'patient' than let it succumb to the terminal illness introduced to it by Democrats, but that is now in the past. It is predicted that more insurance companies will pull out of major markets leaving only one provider behind in some cases. Premiums and deductibles will continue to increase to the point that paying the penalty for having no insurance is a far better deal than owning a policy. Doctors will continue to desert their profession. Employers that purposely reduced many workers' hours so as to avoid buying expensive insurance, will not increase those hours now, thereby preserving the harm done to the same middle class that the ACA was supposed to relieve.

So, failure is now in the cards. And when Obamacare does fail there will be plenty of blame to go around...blame for the Democrats that forced an entire country to accept a 'one size fits all' insurance plan and then demanded the insurance companies offer it which created a tidal wave of confusion and uncertainty in the healthcare industry (1/6 of our economy). Republicans, too, will have their day of reckoning. Most notably, on the Republican side, they are: Senators Lisa Murkowski from Alaska, Susan Collins from Maine and John McCain from Arizona. All voted to kill a bill that would have merely opened debate. It can only be said that they preferred to a little CYA to voting for the greater good of the United States' population. Other Republicans who previously voted for ACA repeals but refused to this time will also find themselves on the receiving end of angry accusations of political 'treason' by their constituents...and justifiably so.

So much for solidarity. The coming months will see continuing tension in the insurance markets and growing frustration on the part of families forced to pay higher premiums, deductibles and co-pays. We will also witness a nasty tug of war between both political parties and especially within the Republican Party as it tries to unite its warring factions...this time on tax reform. As for America's healthcare, it has now become an orphan that may never find a good home.

~

Five stages of (political) grief

Can we all please just take a breath and accept the fact that, as former Attorney General Eric Holder said, "Elections have consequences?" A billionaire businessman won the Presidency and a multi-millionaire career politician lost. The Liberal/Progressive agenda is on hold and the Conservative agenda is in play. Under Barack Obama, Democrats lost 1,042 Federal and State seats. Democrats are now political Bedouins, wandering in the wilderness in search of a winning ideology and some new, inspiring leaders.

The intense opposition to the new Trump Administration (TA) and President Trump, himself, which includes the current *Resist movement*, 'fake news' stories and media hair-pulling is a product, I believe, of the 'Five stages of grief' (originally proposed by Elizabeth Kubler-Ross in her 1969 book, "On death and dying"). For those of you that haven't read the book or haven't suffered through the pain of losing someone close to you, here are the five stages: Stage 1: Denial and isolation, Stage 2. Anger, Stage 3. Bargaining, Stage 4. Depression and Stage 5. Acceptance. Half of America (the 65 million that voted for Hillary Clinton) is suffering from not only a profound political loss, but a loss of hope for a future that they thought would be built on an uninterrupted social compact that would continue moving America farther Left toward Progressivism.

At this point, after only fifty days in office and four months after an upset election, the TA is making good on some of its campaign promises. This much activity is unusual, and because it's unusual, it has created confusion among the opposition. They've not seen this kind of Republican activism before and don't quite know how to fight it, so they have quickly moved from stage one (denial and isolation) to stage two, anger. And they have been joined in their anger and their resistance fight by every special interest, pro social engineering group that can walk or crawl to stop anything that the Administration proposes.

This stage could last awhile before they move on to stage three, 'Bargaining,' or second-guessing themselves. While keeping their anger at a slow boil, they will begin the process of self-examination, "What could we have done, differently? Could we have seen this coming? If only, if only." This stage might actually produce some results for the Dems as they look inward and come up with some answers that will lead them to make a strategic shift. It would be nice if they put their anger on hold while making this transition, but that is not in their nature. Anger is their fuel, and they need it to keep going while they execute their battle plans.

Stage four, 'Depression' is waiting in the wings, lurking like the Grim Reaper, ready to pounce and slice your beating heart from your body and hold it up to your eyes while it destroys the real progress you have made up to this point. This is the ultimate, "Bridge out" warning sign on the road to recovery and the Democrats better be ready for it. Strangely enough, Republicans may experience stage four right along with their Democrat friends as the fact sinks in that many of candidate Trump's promises cannot be realized. Many were just too sweeping and too big to succeed, at least in the short term. This could cause some heartburn and anxiety for his supporters. It could also throw them off their game and give the Democrats a psychological advantage when it becomes apparent that the *wheels* of Congress are moving slowly on promised legislation.

This could have a positive effect on shortening the 'Depression' stage for Dems who could feel a little more wind in their sails and turn up the heat on the Republicans in the 2018 Senate and House races. The bottom line is that the normal grieving cycle could be dramatically shortened if some of the Democrats' attacks on the TA hit their target. Granted, there are some pretty big 'ifs' here, but we shouldn't forget that this is politics AND that this Administration is anything but normal. The paradigm of *business as usual* has been replaced by a chief executive who keeps his balance by throwing everyone else off theirs.

American activist, Saul Alinsky wrote extensively about tactics in his book, "Rules for Radicals," and one of the basic tenets of his philosophy was, "Power is not only what you have, but what the enemy thinks you have." There are thirteen rules for radicals that make for very interesting reading. I believe that many of them are being used by the *Resist movement* today. Ironically, some are also being used by the White House in its efforts to solidify its base and to cast doubts on media stories and the opposition's claims.

When you combine Alinsky's book with Chinese General Sun Tzu's ("The Art of War") and then throw in Donald Trump's ("Art of the Deal") you will see the current political tug of war in clearer focus. Tactical patterns are emerging, and the rules of engagement between the TA, the opposition and the media are being tweaked with every Presidential 'tweet' and with every response to a real - or fake - news story. It appears that the TA has avoided the first four stages of grief in its dealings with the *resistance*. They discovered, early on, that their defenses were better served by embracing a rapid acknowledgment of stage five, "Acceptance." By doing so, they have correctly anticipated the tactics of the Left and have been ready for them. There is one big takeaway in all of this, however. Both sides appear to be reading the same books and are using many of the same tactics. One, in particular, is Alinsky's thirteenth rule for radicals, "Pick the target, freeze it, personalize it, and polarize it."

~

Flintlock to gridlock

One hundred and fifty-six years ago our country was plunged into a Civil War which claimed the lives of 620,000 American souls in the Union North and in the Confederate South. Slavery and the economy were the principal reasons, but so was a sharply divided American society. This cultural division was rooted in the desire on the part of the South to maintain the status quo and in the North to upend the South's.

America's future hung suspended for four long agonizing years. The same was true of her economy and balance of power. It was commonly thought at the time that the country could never recover from a Confederate or Union-led government. If the South won, the way of life in the North would be destroyed, and if the North won, the South would cease to exist. So conflicted were their feelings. There was no room for compromise, though many tried before the first shots were fired at the Battle of Fort Sumter on April 12th of 1861. There was no going back. There would only be carnage until 1865.

This is what happens when people are hopelessly deadlocked and give up trying to iron out their differences. We often forget that the worst can always happen and that which we are trying to preserve can disappear, quickly and without warning. These many years later we find ourselves living in the nuclear age where a 620,000 death toll that took four years to accumulate then can be accomplished in a matter of minutes, now. Our politicians are huddled at the farthest reaches of their parties, never venturing forth into neutral territory to even consider each other's ideas or proposals. Gridlock is the new flintlock. Intransigence and the policy of personal destruction have replaced discourse.

People today say that America could never again experience another civil war, that we have become too civilized and wouldn't dream of taking up arms against our brothers and sisters. In my heart of hearts I'd like to believe that they're right. Unfortunately, today there exists the real and present danger of a major breakdown in law and order and it is leading to a political and intellectual disconnect on the part of our citizens, resulting in an unwillingness to find common ground. We needn't look any farther than our most recent Presidential election and the ascendency of Donald Trump to the Presidency to see the division among our citizens.

A seemingly unstoppable wave of protests has taken place since January 20th, protests that have found their raison d' être in a fundamental belief that America is broken and that the political Right is to blame. The loss of an election, when three million more popular votes were cast for the Democratic Party candidate, did nothing to ameliorate the growing unrest in the country. Few people calculated that the anger of the American Left was so overwhelming and so widespread that it would lead to a wholesale abdication from faith in the electoral process and the rejection of a duly elected President. The flames of this resistance have been fueled by identity politics, the media and by many Democrats in Congress and the Senate, <u>and</u> things are rapidly reaching a flash point. Giving their tacit approval to protest groups by not condemning them, these people have lost their right to be viewed as innocent bystanders. They are now unindicted co-conspirators and are guilty of courting disaster by encouraging a further loss of confidence in our country's institutions.

Those who continue to donate large sums of money in support of protests that turn violent are ignoring the dangerous consequences of their actions and the irreparable damage that can result from angry mobs. By providing the 'red meat' of financial support and the repetition of phony news stories in social media, such donors are using the First Amendment as a shield to protect themselves from criticism. Pandering is their politics, and incitement to disrupt peaceful Americans' daily lives should not be condoned or rewarded by looking the other way and ignoring our laws. It is ironic that the Left doesn't understand that by spreading dissension they are actually hurting themselves and their own causes and may move us closer to Civil War 2.0.

When order breaks down, the nightsticks invariably come out and the uniformed protective services are called in to keep the peace. We have seen this happen throughout history, and it never ends with a whimper. Now is not the time to ignore our laws. Instead, we should all be thinking of ways to make them work for everybody. The loudest voices must not be allowed to silence the thoughtful ones or we've all lost...not just the battle but the entire war.

~

Leaking and the new resistance movement

It's time to call the plumbers. All of Washington, DC is leaking! From the White House to our intelligence agencies and everything in between, there's a thousand pinhole leaks in our government's file cabinets and hard drives from which all manner of data is flowing. Some of it is classified and some of it is not, but all of it is just plain embarrassing. It's death by a thousand cuts, brought to you by a bunch of despicable characters in the 'Deep State' who've basically thumbed their noses at their oaths of office. Some may be Obama Administration holdovers and others may be Democratic Party sympathizers who flat out hate the President and all his policies and are determined to do their darndest to sabotage anything that the new Administration proposes.

They form what is now called, the *new resistance movement* (as contrasted with 'Resist') which has mobilized disparate groups into a coalition of leakers and activists who are determined to overthrow our duly elected government and return power to the 'good guys' that brought you anemic economic growth, multiple scandals, a failed healthcare law, Presidential prevarication, belligerence and character assassination. These new ideological street fighters are locked and loaded and have a battle plan that calls for public protests, a war on free speech (and a few other Amendments to our Constitution), wholesale disruption of the status quo and targeted special interest opposition like inconveniencing employers with 'days without women,' to mention just one ridiculous example.

Their plan calls for joining forces with a left-leaning media to pump out fake news stories without any real substantiation and then build on 'perception' rather than facts. The Trump Administration has decided to call them out and fight fire with fire (which may or may not be a good tactic) as was evidenced by the latest Presidential 'tweet' accusing the Obama Administration of wiretapping Trump Tower during the Presidential campaign. The resistance forces have even remade Russia into the world's biggest bogeyman (forget about China, North Korea, Iran, etc.) in an attempt to undermine the credibility of the Trump Presidential win. I can't help but feel that they must be very conflicted at the very least.

On the one hand, they're trying to portray the Russian 'bear' as nothing but a toothless political animal when it suits them, and then, later, characterize it as the ultimate villain, something akin to a Rasputin-inspired Godzilla monster. Fear and anger are driving their bus. Without the benefit of either one, they must rely on presenting a solid case <u>for something</u> rather than tilting at windmills OR they must use the 'c' word (compromise), something no Democrat is going to do. That only leaves them with one tactic... total, unequivocal resistance, and they are ready to rumble, along with their alt-Left activist friends in Anti-fa, their imbedded leaking buddies and the mainstream media. While Republican Congressional representatives are scrambling to fix the disastrous 'Affordable Healthcare Act', secure our border and kick-start the economy, the resistance movement is busy looking for new ways to oppose anything the Republicans do and knock the Administration off its feet.

'Forty-four' (ex-President Obama) is suiting up to lead a charge into the Republican-held breach through his support for "Organizing for Action" a 501(c)4 non-profit while his Congressional and Senate Democrats are using the weapons of delay and destruction in their respective houses.

The latest flurry of leaked CIA hacking tactics has shown us that none of our gadgets is safe from government's prying eyes and unwanted entry into our smart phones and Internet-connected TVs. Maybe the Resist movement should be spending more time on trying to protect our rights against illegal search and seizure of our data than agonizing over a couple meetings with Russia's Ambassador. It promises to be a long and very uncomfortable spring in D.C., one where even the famous cherry blossoms may think twice about opening up for fear of exposing themselves to a killer frost of Washington-style total annihilation politics.

~

Memo to the disgruntled

The air was crisp and the temperature was starting to drop the night after the Presidential election in New York City. I took a stroll down to Columbus Circle and Central Park to grab some of the fresh air that arrived, coincidentally, with the Trump victory. Little did I know that hundreds of disgruntled no-Trumpers would be gathering to protest his win. Most were orderly, but it was hard to fit several hundred protestors on a small space meant for a hundred or so.

Fortunately, NYC's finest were on hand to keep order and to prevent the crowd from spilling onto the street and getting hit by traffic. Walking past them, I could see that the average age was somewhere around 25, but scattered among them were middle-aged to older folk, too. The youngsters had signs and were very vocal chanting things like: "Dump

Trump" and "Not my President." Occasionally, a charged-up protestor would begin an expletive chant but was quickly shushed by one of the protest organizers that had obviously done this sort of thing many times before and was probably a merit badge holder in the art of public dissent.

It was what I expected from a very liberal New York crowd, but what did surprise me, though, was their energy level. It was high, and the crowd was definitely singing off the same sheet ("Capitalism is bad, ergo Trump is bad"). Most of the young people were experienced in sign-making and protest etiquette, recognizing when to join in the chorus of short, sound-bite like shouts just perfect for the 11:00pm news. I wondered to myself if any of these people had ever experienced an election in a third world country or oppressive regime before and had their faces photographed and used by secret police to arrest or monitor them later on.

Democracy and the right to assemble and speak your mind doesn't come cheaply if at all in many of these places, but the price of admission to America's street corners is free, and rhetoric alone won't get you thrown in jail, not even for a night. Many would probably say that these protestors should have stayed at home and licked their wounds in private instead of criticizing a fair election. I'm not one of them. It is infinitely better for us to vent than let our pain fester and consume us. In some cases it only takes a few hours to 'get it out of our system.' But that is not the case in this political rodeo.

The expectation that Hillary Clinton would win was so high that it must have seemed like an apocalyptic event when, at 4:00am the morning of November 9th, Donald Trump took the podium and announced his victory. For residents of Gotham, this was tantamount to being told they all had only a few months to live. All their plans, hopes and dreams for the first woman liberal President and a continuance of eight years of Obama policy were dashed - destroyed by a capitalist Attila the Hun. The dreamers would have to wake up; transgender bathrooms would have to wait; college tuition loans would need to be repaid, hundreds of thousands of near-term babies would now have a chance to be born into a world where air and water would be befouled through the relaxation of important environmental regulations, courtesy of the evil Trump.

One expects such exaggeration from the Left; it is what they do and do well. What surprised me was the level of their frustration and the depth of their self denial. Clintonites and Bern'ers pointed fingers at any strawman they could find to blame for Mrs. Clinton's loss. Russia and FBI Director James Comey took a hit. Then it was the election tabulating system (with recounts of Wisconsin, Michigan and Pennsylvania demanded by Dr. Jill Stein of the Green Party). Donald Trump, himself, and his campaign were supposed to have colluded with the Russians to poison the well for voters. The coup de grace came in the form of a media campaign by Hollywood malcontents to influence the Electoral College electors to change their votes and throw the election into the House of Representatives. So deep was the resentment by Tinseltown elites.

Yesterday, the Electoral College did its duty and officially voted to make Donald Trump the next President. Make no mistake, this will not deter the Left in its mission to demean, denigrate, de-legitimize and destroy Mr. Trump. We can expect the <u>next few years</u> to be an epic struggle between the forces of the 'enlightened' (the Left) and those of the 'enemies of progress' (the new Administration and its supporters).

One can only hope that our economy improves quickly so that many of the protestors can put away their poster board and Magic Markers and move out of their parents' basements into the sunlight of mainstream America. I'll even help them move if it will ease their pain and convince them to open the windows so they can breathe the fresh air of a new, more pragmatic Administration.

~

Populism a good thing?

There's a new wave of populism sweeping America (at least half of America anyway), but it's misunderstood and often confused with political pandering. That's regrettable, because populism, in its essence, is support for the concerns of ordinary people. Donald Trump knew this and that's one of the big reasons he won. Bernie Sanders knew it, too, but he lost.

Hillary Clinton knew it as well, and she lost. So what was the difference between Trump's, Sander's and Clinton's brands of populism? That's an easy one to answer. Sanders' populism was based on a socialist economic platform that appealed to an idealistic, younger demographic that wasn't going to exercise their right to vote. Instead, they howled and grumbled about the evil rich, protested and stayed home, content to be right in their hearts.

Hillary Clinton perverted her populism into identity politics by dividing the electorate into competing slices like Blacks, Hispanics and women. Her biggest mistake (other than her inability to turn around her perceived untrustworthiness) was a reliance on pursuing a populist identity politics campaign that was never going to appeal to the majority of White voters. These voters objected to being objectified and felt insulted that they were being condensed into single-issue slices of the American pie and pitted against other Americans. Then there was that *deplorables* thing that, in my opinion, sealed her fate and stiffened the opposition's spine. FBI Director Comey's comments and 'Russiagate' were just two more nails in her political coffin.

The big difference between Trump's populism and Clinton's was that voters <u>believed</u> (or wanted to believe) Trump when he spoke directly to them even when he repeated himself which he did, constantly. Though they often cringed in disbelief when he went off message and way off into the stratosphere with his controversial statements, they genuinely admired his forthrightness and forgave him for being human...like themselves. <u>The lesson for all candidates is never underestimate the power of likeability and authenticity even when that authenticity reveals human failings.</u>

Can populism possibly be a winning future strategy for other politicians, even for Democrats? A lot will depend on whether President Trump makes good on his promises to the American people. Should he backtrack too much and compromise on the basic campaign promises he made, he will not keep their support nor win re-election if he chooses to run, again. Neither will he add value to populism, in general. At this point, populism is winning the day, despite the incessant attacks on the President and his men and women by the media.

The Left-leaning media like the New York Times, Washington Post, CNN, MSNBC and others would do well to learn that by being more authentic and apologizing once in awhile for their repeated ad hominem attacks on Mr. Trump could actually earn them higher market share among a larger more diverse group of viewers.

This presumes, of course, that they could find the courage to risk losing their core demographic that is currently reveling in their wildly biased news reporting. It is doubtful that those serving up 'fake news' will find that courage as long as they are benefiting from the controversy they're stirring up. By covering protests in a continuous loop they are pandering to the millions of disgruntled anti-Trump activists. They are also burnishing their credentials as being one with the opposition as they create an upward spiral of discontent, working to help the resistance gain strength. Make no mistake, this is not a tempest in a teapot; it is a growing and soon-to-be powerful movement and will accelerate, not dissipate, over time. American politics has entered a new era, one where there are no second chances, no benefit of the doubt, no do-overs. Even apologies are suspect, no matter how sincere, especially when the <u>media</u> has decided they are not to be accepted. There is no such thing as an honest mistake in the world of Twitter and Facebook and Instagram and weblogs. So what's the alternative to admitting mistakes? Pretend that your words were taken out of context or that you were sick that day or that the Devil made you do it?

Excuses won't satisfy the populist voter, neither will smooth rhetoric à la Barack Obama. If Donald Trump wants to be loved and admired...and go beyond *governance by executive order* he will need to start mending some pretty big fences within his own party before the first strand of barbed wire is strung on our southern border. Even populism has its limits when the feelings of a populist Congress are concerned.

~

Putting country first

It's high time we put our political differences aside in favor of our country's interests. I realize that that might sound like a heretical statement to all those who are now fighting everything that the Trump Administration is doing, but it's necessary if we are to heal the deep political divide that is tearing our country apart. We have just come to the 100-day mark of the new Administration, and while half the country is smarting from a devastating election loss, the other half is intent on forcibly moving the ideological pendulum back towards the center.

To liberal or 'Progressive' Americans it may seem that the center is actually located far to the right of their political thought, but, in point of fact, it isn't. The last eight years of President Barack Obama has moved it from its historical locus and set traditional America on a radical political course towards an idealistic utopian dream resembling Marxism ("From each according to his ability to each according to his needs"). The Left has created a false narrative that <u>wealth has created poverty and inequality</u> and that meritocracy should be replaced with an autocracy built on one overarching political belief...theirs, and that achievement should not be rewarded but reviled.

Donald Trump's win in November revealed that at least 62 million voters (many of them minority voters) disagreed with the Obama course and the Left's designs for a new victim-based 'playing field.' Instead, they demanded a return to a few, time-tested and honored values. They also wanted a smaller more responsive government, straight talk, respect for the law and an acknowledgment of the reasons for America's past achievements. In addition, they wanted a more realistic and inclusive vision for the future that was based on personal accountability and civility.

Trump voters did not believe that the wealth of one person diminished the standing or opportunities of others, nor did they feel that hard work or smart investments devalued the whole. On the contrary, they wanted growth for all and not for a privileged or entitled few. They knew that the way to insure all Americans' success was through a change in our laws and attitude.

Their votes were not cast to keep our minorities from succeeding or the disadvantaged from improving their lives. If anything, the election proved that Americans would not be coerced into accepting a Trojan Horse of unworkable ideology that was rapidly being wheeled into our communities. Neither did they believe that by speaking softly to America's enemies or the enemies of freedom around the world that we would somehow turn their swords into plowshares.

The energy that is being expended today by committed opponents of the current Administration is delaying America's return to a healthy balance and preeminence. The radical Left is determined to show that our Constitution is a flawed document, and that instead of a sound blueprint for our prosperity and equality, it is an unholy covenant entered into by a bunch of old rich White slave-owning men that designed it to keep power in their own hands. Opponents of the Administration are wasting precious time, time that could be put to good use to strengthen our country and address the challenges facing all of us. Americans are strongest when we pull together.

We do not have to agree with one another all of the time in order to move ahead, but we do have to be able to discuss our disagreements to see how far apart we really are. Shouting speakers down, denying their First Amendment rights on college campuses or taking to the streets in mobs won't soften the resolve of those that would protect free speech; it will only stiffen it. This is the irony of violent dissent. We need more free speech not less, more openness not closeted opinion. It is time to be worthy of the freedom we all have by acting our age and start pulling together. If we don't, we will only be torn from our roots, split into a permanent class of warring camps and will have squandered the promise of greatness.

Sixty-two million Minutemen

Now that most of the dust has settled since the election of Donald Trump and Michael Pence as our next President and Vice President, respectively, we can all exhale and begin to speculate on what the next four years will be like in the USA.

But before we remove the cover from our crystal ball and gaze into the future we should thank the 62 million plus 'Minutemen' (and women) who left their sofas, exited their homes and exercised their civic duty by voting...in this case for the Republican ticket. These voters spoke with one powerful voice to the 'Coastalcrats' (the Democratic Party) and rejected their message, en masse, thereby throwing the conventional wisdom and the pundit/pollsters' predictions out the window. They pushed the political reset button in a way not seen since the Reagan/Carter encounter of 1980.

Like the dog that caught the car, it's now up to the Republicans to figure out what to do with all that power. Will their next four years be a Bacchanal government, drunk with power, bound on making a 180° ideological turn, or will they use a more measured, incremental approach to find the social and cultural balance most of us want? One thing I know for sure. If President-Elect Trump chooses to shove a hot poker in the eyes of the Democrats by saying, "We won, you lost, get over it" like President Obama did with Senator John McCain shortly after his election, he will find himself in a world of hurt. He will inspire more opposition and incur considerably more scar tissue on the corpus of the body politic than he ever imagined possible.

If there is any chance of healing our political wounds after such a divisive election campaign, sixty-two million Republicans must resist the impulse to lord it over their Democrat friends or neighbors. They must subordinate the pain from the wounds inflicted by the eight-year long actions of a ideological zealot at 1600 Pennsylvania Avenue.

They must suppress their urge to exact revenge on the Democrats. They must also realize that disagreements are part of politics and of life in general; that nobody ever gets 100% of what they want or even deserve; and that it does no good to fan the flames of resentment in a vanquished opponent because they may be needed, later on. What will our next four years be like then?

In a word, <u>opposition</u>. While I'd like to think we are a forgiving, compromise-seeking and reasonable people, I fear we're not because many of us are convinced that it is only through absolute power that we are able to govern ourselves in this current environment. One party, one ideology for 4-8 years and let the Devil take the hindmost. Compromise is impossible, and any deal done with the opposition must be suspect, the reason being all politicians are guilty <u>because</u> they are politicians.

The election results shouted a simple message from the rooftops. It was, "Throw the elitist, professional political class bums out!" Whether the Republicans' motivation was anger, resentment, dissatisfaction or self-preservation, there was no mistaking their actions.

So what now? Lock up Hillary Clinton? Build a north-south or bi-coastal wall to keep the Democrats where we can see them? Shout them down in public like they did to us? Co-opt the media to do OUR bidding? All unnecessary. The Democratic Party is in enough disarray that it will be spending a fair amount of time re-making and re-fashioning itself, but you can bet they will be doing so while relentlessly opposing anything Republicans or Trump propose.

The fact is that Democrats are better at multi-tasking than their Republican counterparts and they are bulldogs when it comes to keeping their focus on the *enemy*. Their ability to play defense and offense, simultaneously, is enviable and should never be underestimated. They will continue to be formidable opponents (the mid-term elections are not far away). If that's the prognosis from the 2016 election, haven't we just turned the hourglass upside down and are letting the same sand exchange places with itself?

Yes and no. True, we are the same sand, and we do flow back to the same place, together, but the sand in an hourglass is contained by the boundaries and curvature of its shape as is our politics. The difference is that our politics is constantly changing form, precisely why we must not push back with too much force at the gravitational pull of ideas, no matter how dogmatic they may appear. Sunlight is the cure for darkness, and it is not the stiffest tree that survives the onslaught of a hurricane. The flexible one will ride out the storm, successfully. The natural world has much to teach us and we ought to be listening hard these next four years. That goes for both parties.

~

The anatomy of wrong...Washington style

If we were looking for a time in recent history when the predictive wisdom of the political pundits and prognosticators was neither prescient nor wise it is now. All the big league soothsayers that had Trump trailing and Hillary Clinton climbing the heights of the electoral mountain at breakneck speed were flat out wrong. We shouldn't be too hard on them as a group. After all, it's their business to be careful, to hedge their bets and qualify their predictions and to stay reasonably close to the rest of the flock, but this year was their chance to throw off the chains of caution and be bold and trust their gut.

For many pollsters, this was apparently too risky for some reason. Why? After the Primary dust had settled it seemed that the candidates were easy to handicap. For those that wanted their polls to come down heavily for Hillary Clinton, a Donald Trump candidacy was a gift from the gods. Questions about his temperament and 'fitness to serve' were easily formulated in such a way to elicit the 'right' responses. Meanwhile, the Trump campaign was busy delivering the goods to them in the form of occasionally outlandish comments that were tied up with a bow for the 'average man' and average left-leaning media outlets' consumption.

Pollsters missed their targets on many occasions, but the biggest of all was their inaccurate assessment of the country's desire and willingness to elect a non-politician over a professional political elitist. Had the pollsters gone down <u>this</u> path of inquiry and stuck to it by formulating their questions with that one thing in mind they might have been right more often than wrong.

After the mid-terms of 2014, my co-author, Lance Tarrance and myself, decided we would write, "Breaking Republican: A campaign handbook for Third Way candidates in 2016" (BR). In it we laid out a blueprint for winning the 'new age' American election, and we accurately predicted how only a 'Third Way' (or outsider) candidate could bring the Republicans a presidential victory over one of the toughest professional politicians of our time, Hillary Clinton.

We offered five electoral vote-getting scenarios based on the outcome of the mid-terms and correctly assessed the viability of creating a 'Ruby Slipper' red axis of power that gave the Republicans an arc from the south through the mid-Atlantic states to the Midwest and beyond that would give them all the votes they needed to win. We offered up a *Third Way* candidate resumé that called for a skill set usually not found among traditional candidates. We also presented a litany of issues that we felt would be front and center in the campaign and correctly extrapolated what voter discontent would mean for each candidate.

Our book was finished on 'D-Day' and was published a few days after Donald Trump announced his candidacy in June of 2015. We rushed to add him to the chapter that talked about the Republican candidates because we felt that he just might have a chance, especially because of his 'Third Way' appeal, though most pundits had discounted his run as "pure folly." We stressed that America would see an emergence of a Nixon-style 'Silent Majority' that would come alive during the campaign.

What we didn't know was that it would take the form of a 'stealth voter' segment -- voters that wouldn't admit they were voting for Trump. We also predicted that the media would suit up and become a powerful force for the Democrats, though we hadn't anticipated such direct support from outlets like CNN and the Washington Post. On Hillary herself, we laid out, quite correctly, her two major Achilles heels: untrustworthiness and her hesitancy to commit to specific positions. We also made our case for populism and the significant role we thought it would play in the campaign...on both sides. Here is where the WASHDC crowd of prognosticators missed the boat.

They had their money on the *Democrats'* version of populism - that the income redistribution and 1% vs. 99% argument was the dominant winning formula. They hadn't counted on the Trump stealth voter and the extent of middle America's dissatisfaction with the Democrats' far left of center ideology.

In short, the entire professional pundit class was betting on the collective instead of the individual, but America simply wasn't buying what Bernie Sanders, Elizabeth Warren and Hillary Clinton were selling. Finally, many pollsters were either too timid or too unobservant to admit that a ground swell of discontent in America's rust belt could ever win over perennial 'blue' states like Wisconsin, Michigan or Pennsylvania for the Republicans! Two days before election day we predicted a significant electoral win by Donald Trump. There is no question that this election upset has been a shocker for the pollsters who should have seen it coming. These days, conventional wisdom is anything but conventional in the year of the 'Third Way' candidate.

~

309

The Capitol Hill Pirate of Penzance

DC's Capitol Hill and NYC's Great White Way have definitely traded places when it comes to entertainment. Case in point, take the laconic Senator from New York and Senate Minority Leader, Charles (Chuck) Schumer. The Senator has to be up for best dramatic actor in a docudrama if only for his statement today on the President's firing of FBI Director, James Comey. It was masterful - vintage Schumer.

Nobody but nobody can outdo *Chuck* when it comes to turning the ordinary stuff of life into the Four Horsemen of the Apocalypse. One can imagine how he would play the lead in that wonderful comic opera by Gilbert and Sullivan, the Pirates of Penzance, for example. Taking his cue as Frederic the apprentice pirate to be "light and effervescent," from the director, old Senator S. would put a head lock on the simplest five-word sentence and draw it out like a taffy pull, rolling each syllable around in his mouth, tasting every word twice, before finally giving it back to us in his best Brooklyn drawl. Yes, you have to love Chuck Schumer, a man who can turn the gayest of musical comedies into a Greek tragedy just by looking over the top of his reading glasses and staring off into space.

Charles Ellis Schumer was born on November 23, 1950 in Brooklyn, NY to an exterminating company manager and a homemaker. A graduate of Harvard, he was elected to the Senate in 1998 after defeating Alphonse (Al) D'Amato and has been in that body ever since. Prior to that, he served for 18 years in the U.S. Congress. That clearly makes him a public sector 'lifer,' and those 37 years in elected office have given him ample time to polish his stagecraft and hone his dramatic skills. And hone them he has, though taking a back seat for many years to now retired Majority Leader, Senator Harry Reid from Searchlight, Nevada wasn't easy. Both men gave new meaning to the word, *dour*, but now that Schumer has stepped out from the shadow of Reid, he's his own man and free to drone on in his own inimitable style.

One thing he isn't, however, is a method actor unless you consider his consistently singular way of speaking on any issue a 'method.' He is versatile and can play any part...as long as the part is that of Charles Schumer. As for his stance on James Comey, Schumer did a 'John Kerry' and was for him (Comey not Kerry) before he was against him, and now that Comey is unemployed and driven from the flock by the evil President Trump, he is once again for him.

Schumer is also capable of playing the villain instead of the defender of liberté, égalité, fraternité, and he does it with panache and a touch of playfulness. The result is that few of his detractors can stay mad at him or dislike him for very long. It is the Schumer charm that disarms the opposition even when he's delivering lines that he himself totally disagrees with. Republicans that know the Senator (like the President, for example) have seen him in action over the years and observed him skewer his opponents and then walk over their bleeding corpses while he plots his next appearance before the network news cameras.

Make no mistake, Charles Schumer is a consummate politician. He is like a silky smooth car salesman on a fishing vacation and has trouble stepping out of character for even a brief moment. He slowly plays out his line and takes his time reeling it in, knowing full well that whatever is on the other end will be the biggest most impressive fish ever caught.

~

The David and Goliath of governance

On January 20th, America will not only have exchanged Presidents, but also moved 180 degrees from an administration that was ideologically-driven to one rooted in pragmatism. According to many critics, we will have taken a Goliath-sized step backwards and are simply trying to re-create the bygone era of Ronald Reagan - times when tough leaders and power was something to be proud of rather than apologize for. Republicans agree about the myth but disagree about the effects.

Maybe this is what sticks in the craw of Democrats today, the fact that their own forward momentum has been halted and their pilgrimage toward the utopian politics of the collective has been stopped dead in its tracks.

After Friday, the rhetoric that characterized everything Mr. Obama touched will drift away and the clouds that have been hiding the country's real challenges will part as we embark on a journey to find the truth about who we really are and what we really need to do, together, to reclaim our birthright as Americans. These kinds of social expeditions are not for the faint of heart. Neither is there room for the spinmeisters or the obfuscators. Journeys of this sort demand the speed of a gazelle, the strength of a lion and the skin of a rhinoceros. The patience of Job and the courage of David are also required as the Goliath of big government, with all its power, pushes back. It will not go down easily, certainly not with a single slingshot of resistance. The new Administration must move, quickly, to cut off the head of the snake of special interests and entrenched single-issue oriented groups from both the Left and the Right if it is to survive and achieve its objectives. The American divide was not born yesterday, nor will it die easily.

The new President and his cabinet will be exposed to great personal and professional vilification and be opposed with every press release they issue, every utterance they make and after every decision they take. They must be prepared for relentless name-calling, innuendo, fake news and incessant propaganda. Our new leaders' resumes and experience show us that they have what it takes to do the job and that they will not be bullied nor deterred from their mission by subversion from the Left.

If history teaches us anything, it tells us that there will be times during the next four years when the new administration's forward progress will be stopped cold in its tracks. When that happens, it will need to find the courage to stay the principled course and try to achieve consensus on those aspects of their plans that will improve life for all Americans. In short, they must find new common ground both inside and outside their own party. The next four years will see our country remake itself using a new version of the Cold War era's *realpolitik*. Decisions will be based on real reality not the hypothetical reality of the last eight years.

The Obama Administration's policies have taught us one lesson of great importance: putting up impenetrable walls between the parties doesn't work for the good of the country because walls also separate the honest brokers in both parties from talking with one another.

~

The Democrats' nightmare

It's the morning of January 20th and Donald Trump has just exited Blair House and is on his way into the President's limousine that will take him to the steps of Congress to take the oath of office as America's 45th President. It's been a whirlwind 60-plus days since Trump won 306 electoral votes to become the first billionaire President in America's history. Judging by the Trump "Thank you" tour and the President-Elect's remarks about draining the swamp and making America great again by nominating other billionaires and businessmen to key cabinet positions, the first cabinet meeting might look something like this...

The Pres starts off by saying *thank you* to all that supported him but singles out a few for being a little less energetic than expected. He launches into a "Make America Great Again" speech while simultaneously tweeting a message to his millions of followers ("Got them on board. Am going to tell them they better create a million jobs each AND be ready to grab hard hats for their shift on building the wall"). The VP smiles nervously as Trump stands up and walks over to the wall and pulls down a map of the world. "See this," he says as he points to the USA. "THIS is our world. Everything else is secondary."

The cabinet claps wildly. Empowered, Trump continues. "OK, I know there are problems in the world, and I'm really sad about that, BUT just like we aren't the world's policeman, neither are we the world's Salvation Army. Mr. Secretary of Commerce, wouldn't you agree that if only these countries created a few million new jobs that many of their problems would disappear?" "Affirmative, Mr. President. Get those poor souls some work and take them off the welfare rolls." "Alright. That's the spirit," says Trump and turns to his Homeland Security head.

"How are we doing on plans for the *Friendship Wall* along the southern border?" "Bueno, el jefe. On schedule. We expect the first demolition teams to arrive next week to blow a few thousand holes in the Arizona hills to sink our concrete pilings. The new *Friendship Drones* are expected to be operational within days and will be patrolling the border 24/7 in search of illegal border crossers. By the way, we're now calling our efforts, 'Operation Fist Bump.' In February, about 75,000 National Guardsmen from Arizona and Texas will be on the move to protect the 50,000 workers who will be building the wall.

Unfortunately, Mr. President, I've been told that California will be sending about 30,000 of its National Guardsmen to harass the other Guardsmen. Governor Brown says he's doing this because he wants to make the California/Mexico border a "Sanctuary Border." "Well, we'll see about that," says Trump. "We may have to make all of California a no-fly zone and forbid commercial airlines from flying there. Can we do that Madam Secretary of Transportation?" "Absolutely, Mr. President. I've been in consultation with the Secretary of Defense on that and he thinks that we can mobilize enough fighter jets to scare the hell out of Governor Brown so that he'll back down!"

"Great. Mr. Secretary of State, will this give us problems with the international community?" "Not much, Mr. President. They're a bunch of wimps, anyway. They'll complain a bit, but I'm going to remind them of the Berlin Airlift when we saved their bacon in '48 and '49 after the Russkis rattled their sabers, and then I'll finish 'em off with the fall of the

313

Berlin Wall. They'll settle down and realize that it's better for them that we use our air power here than fly missions over their skies." "Good work, Rex. Now what about the Keystone Pipeline, Secretary Perry?"

"I've been working with Congress and the Canadians and we should get a bill passed giving us right-of-way and have the pipe-laying equipment on site in a few months and oil flowing to Exxon's refineries, oops, I meant THE refineries by the end of 2018."

"And what about our new 'Trump Dollar' Mr. Treasury Secretary?" "The presses are already churning them out, Mr. President. We expect that they will be in circulation by next week. They will be worth $1.10 to start, but we expect that they will enjoy great success and soon replace our old dollar. We have followed your instructions to the letter and have put a very nice picture of the Trump Tower on the reverse side. It's smart looking currency, I must say." "You don't think it's a bit over the top, Mr. Secretary?" "Well we have gotten some push back from the Democrats, but we have a plan 'B'. We're going to offer an alternative currency to appease them. It's the 'Hillary Dollar' - a plastic dollar that will have a face value of a quarter."

"Excellent," said Trump. The cabinet closes with the pledge of allegiance, led by San Francisco 49ers' quarterback Colin Kaepernick, who stands at attention and salutes the President when finished. Filing out, the President is overheard to say to the Vice-President, "I think that went well, Mike. Not a 'yes man' among them, right?" "Absolutely, Mr. President."

~

The last safe space

It seems that everybody is looking for a safe space these days. College students want a place   "where seldom is heard a discouraging word and the skies are not cloudy all day" (thanks go to Dr. Brewster M. Higley of Smith County Kansas for his inspirational poem, "My Western Home" that led to that great American song, "Home on the Range"). But college students aren't the only ones seeking protection from the real world.

Many non-students are also dissatisfied with the new direction the USA is taking under our new President, and they want the entire country to be declared one big safe space. Many would like that space to be one where an undergraduate degree would be free for all, a nation without borders, guaranteed minimum incomes, low or no-cost healthcare and ample legalized marijuana to smooth out all of society's rough edges.

I hasten to add that not all young people think this way, but there are a fair number of them suiting up for protest marches against the Trump Administration and all conservative Republicans who, for them, are the enemy. What is ironic with all of this is that the 'no-Trumpers' and the more militant single-issue groups are bent on turning our country's safe streets into *unsafe zones* for regular Americans! They are intent on expressing their anger by converting all our public squares, airports and stadiums into impassable human minefields, complete with 'Thunderpower Megaphones' that can put out as many as 122 decibels (for those of you unfamiliar with noise measurements, a thunderclap is 120 db and a jet takeoff is rated at 133 db).

So much for the peace and quiet of America's streets. Nearly every conceivable anti-Trump special interest group or subgroup is actively fund-raising, courting wealthy donors and recruiting new advocates for their cause. And there are plenty of willing foot-soldiers for them to choose from. They come from the ranks of the youthful unemployed, sixties counter-culture types, Hollywood celebrities, academics, women's organizations, and disgruntled Democrats. The pool is about 65 million people (the number that voted for Hillary Clinton in the General Election). All are busy cutting their teeth on smaller demonstrations and are undoubtedly reading Saul Alinsky's "Rules for Radicals" and Sun Tzu's "The Art of War" as well as watching old film footage of Abbie Hoffman, Bill Ayers, Jane Fonda and Tom Hayden, to name just a few.

By my reckoning, there is only one safe public space left where most of us can spend a few minutes alone in relative solitude...the toilet, but that, too, has been under attack by the Left. It was on the Obama Administration's hit list. The Administration also felt that the 0.3% of Americans that self-identified as transgender people (source: Williams Institute, April 2011) were being discriminated against and needed protection.

So, states were told that they had to accommodate people who were 'in transition' from one gender to the other. They were required to provide third toilets for them or allow people who 'felt' like the opposite sex to use the toilets of their chosen gender. The punishment for not complying was loss of Federal funds (13 states filed suit against the Administration which has held up the transformation). We should all have empathy with individuals going through a traumatic transformative process. It can't be easy, but when the number of affected people is 0.3% of the entire population, it hardly seems defensible to spend billions on re-purposing America's restrooms to accommodate them, not to mention upsetting the

315

other 99.7% that frequent them. What I am about to say now should not be taken as being insensitive to their plight...but this last final refuge from the cacophony of daily life should not be on our "To Do" list when we have so many other pressing problems confronting us. We, the silent majority, need to make our voices heard. That's why I suggest that on August 4th of this year (the baptism date of John Harington, the inventor of Britain's first flush toilet in 1596) that a "Million Man Toilet March" be held.

On that day, precisely at noon, men from all over the country would spontaneously self-identify as women for one hour and demand access to women's lavatories from sea to shining sea. Goodness knows the women's Johns (Jills?) will be crowded for an hour, but isn't it a small price to pay for freedom from bathroom tyranny? Remember to put the seat down, fellows.

~

The strong(man) model?

America chose its 45th President last Tuesday on the basis of a number of real or imagined notions. One of them was a perception that Donald Trump was a strong individual, both in character and in physicality. The position of President is an extremely demanding one, and it requires stamina that allows one to be on the job from morning to night with very little rest.

In that respect, I believe that the questions about Hillary Clinton's health these last few months may have definitely worked against her. While those 'problems' may have been more perception than reality, the fact is that Donald Trump just looked stronger than Mrs. Clinton and he (wisely) continued to raise doubts about her ability to go the distance. Her refusal to come clean about her dizzy spell and her pneumonia had a negative effect on the public's view of her and seemed to reaffirm the belief that she wasn't being open and transparent (again) about something of keen interest to the voters.

In my opinion, her reticence to own up to her bout with pneumonia was looked upon as a continuation of an uncomfortable and persistent pattern of deceit that kept many potential voters from casting their ballots for her. As I said, the physical demands placed on a President are enormous, and since the two candidates were almost the same age, we would be safe in assuming that both of them were judged equally on the age and stamina questions...or were they?

316

Could sexism have played a role in how Americans perceived a woman running for a "man's job"? Is there an automatic and maybe subconscious bias against women that are older when it comes to handling tough jobs? It's entirely possible and that it reared its ugly head with HRC. If that can be proven, then we need to have a public discussion about it. One of the ways to prepare ourselves for that discussion is to take a brief visit to insurance companies' actuarial tables. Let's start with mortality rates. Women live an average of nearly five years longer than men. Women are less likely to have heart attacks than men and there is no data that I could find that show that more women CEOs die on the job than their male counterparts.

Those are just a few facts that would seem to prove the assertion that we might indeed have a bias against females when it comes to strength and stamina. If it really exists then why? It could be due to a lack of awareness of health facts or a belief generated over time by circumstances or that it was a deliberate male-generated myth! America is fixated on youth and youthfulness, and while there may be a renewed emphasis on seniors and retirees in the media, that focus is largely targeted on our ailments, especially in advertisements, and it doesn't paint a very rosy picture of septuagenarians. Instead, it reinforces an image of us as decrepit and fragile.

Perhaps Mr. Trump succeeded because he understood how to market his youthfulness and stamina to *everybody* as opposed to Mrs. Clinton who chose to target her message to the millennial generation and with a decidedly un-youthful message at that! Given our recent experience, should questions about age and health be at the forefront of Presidential campaigns or should they be relegated to the 'second tier' of aspects of a person's candidacy?

If we feel they're not that important then we ought to de-couple them from the political conversation. If the candidates want to do their part, they could allay our fears by undergoing a standard health examination that is performed by the same doctors, if possible. Standardized health examinations and an effort to down-prioritize the issue of age won't work, quickly, when it comes to the media, but we have to start somewhere. Let's hope that our new 70-year-old President will shatter the 'age ceiling' by showing the rest of us, that like size, age doesn't matter as much as we once thought.

~

This whole Federalism thing

States' rights is the reason the Trump Administration gave for rescinding the Obama directive on transgender bathrooms, and while I agree that the Federal government doesn't belong in the public's bathrooms, it doesn't belong in many other places, either. The framers of our Constitution didn't take government overreach lightly, and they wisely said that those powers not enumerated as the Federal government's in Article 1. section 8 of the Constitution were vested in the states: "The powers not delegated to the United States by the Constitution, nor prohibited by it to the states, are reserved, respectively, to the people." The White House and its principal inhabitant are not 'the people' though they often act like it. The founders intended the doctrine of enumerated power to be our principal defense against a potentially overbearing and overreaching government, something the last Administration, unfortunately, proved itself to be.

This is not to say that the Obama Administration was the only administration that acted too big for its britches; many previous administrations have governed as if they possessed the reigns of legislative power and have imposed policies on citizens without legal justification or precedent.

While we always have the courts to fall back on as a means of last resort to reverse or negate such overreach, the process takes an inordinate amount of time, and while this is happening the Federal bureaucracy is able to sink its roots deep into the fine print of implementing regulations. This makes it hard to undo unwarranted power grabs.

So, what should we do to stop such executive edicts? The Ninth Circuit Court of Appeals in California showed us, recently, just how with its temporary restraining order stopping the Trump Administration's *immigrant moratorium* on seven countries that have insufficient capabilities to properly vet their would-be emigrants or visitors to the United States.

One can disagree with the court's ruling, but it is hard to ignore their power. And while they may have stayed this executive order, they will fail to stay the next one because the Administration has learned a valuable lesson; haste makes waste. A new order will exempt those foreigners who have already been issued visas to the U.S. and all Permanent Resident Card ('green card') holders.

The whole issue of the enumeration of powers goes to the heart of our Constitutional Republic and the right of the people to be free from unjustified intervention into the law-making of individual states. States must be free to enact their own laws that govern their own residents as long as those laws don't infringe on existing Constitutionally-sound Federal laws. There are several instances of U.S. Supreme Court rulings where reasonable people can disagree. The most egregious ruling, in my opinion, is the one concerning the right of the Federal government to force all Americans to purchase health insurance.

This ruling is a landmark one in that it gives sweeping power to the Federal government, allowing it to <u>force</u> people to purchase something they, in some cases, do not want nor can afford. To add insult to injury, the Obama Administration had the temerity to even decide what the product should look like, requiring seniors, for example, to have contraceptive measures as part of their insurance plans.

If we were to take that example one step further and apply it to other mandatory purchases, how would gun control advocates feel if the new Administration were to require every household to own a firearm and to qualify at a firing range once a year and pay a Federally-set fee or pay a penalty? Abuse of power is the central issue here. When the Federal government goes off the reservation and enters our private sphere it is acting as a tyrant. There is simply no other word to describe such actions.

The coming years will test the Trump Administration's resolve and its ability to resist making the same mistakes that its predecessors made. It is up to the people to remain vigilant and to call them out when and if they do exceed their power just as it is the people's responsibility to demand <u>speedy adjudication of any Constitutionally questionable overreach</u>. If we do not, we have only ourselves to blame for the consequences.

~

True confessions of a Conservative

It's become a little easier to self-identify as a conservative these days...but not everywhere and not with everybody. If you live in places like Boulder, Denver or Santa Fe you might want to think twice before proclaiming your Conservative sympathies to strangers let alone admitting that you are a Republican or *worse* a supporter of Donald Trump. But being a Conservative means not being afraid to tell truth to power <u>or to committed liberals</u>.

I think it's probably true that most people adopt their parents' political leanings, but I'm not one of them. Truth be told, I didn't know which way my parents voted, so I grew up politically agnostic. After considerable observation and reflection on the matter, I have concluded that absent that strong parental influence we tend to come to our political beliefs based on a number of things: the views of people we respect or who are important to us, from events that have affected us personally and our own life-changing experiences. I chose to follow the Conservative path in my twenties after I was married.

A few years of married life made me realize that Conservative politics resembled that holy state and was grounded in a belief of 'conserving' or protecting that which was in our mutual interest and was based on some fundamental precepts. Those were: honesty, forthrightness, open-mindedness, tolerance, compromise-seeking and forgiveness.

Conservatism meant that we needed to accept certain facts: that our beliefs were closely allied with a world view of 'let and let live,' personal responsibility and accountability, charitableness, an adherence to the concept of reward and punishment, an acknowledgement that society was made up of individuals and groups each with their own right to exist and a moral code that had the 'golden rule' at its core. Conservatism encouraged the use of our talents to realize our own potential and to enrich society as a whole. It meant never discarding anything that served us well...and that included relationships.

Conservatives used to be admired and respected because their work ethic was strong as was their patriotism and love of country. Somewhere along the way, however, Conservatives became reviled instead of revered, chastised as pariahs instead of held up as role models for our children. We have been told that our ideas are antiquated and have no place in a 'modern' society, that we are out of step or worse. Of late, we have been accused of being fascists or racists or homophobes. We have also been accused of wanting a segregated country that only has room for rich White people and for ignoring the poor because of our simple wish for a smaller more efficient government.

Today, with the election of a president that has had the courage to speak out about our problems instead of dancing a minuet of rhetoric around them like his predecessor, Conservatives find themselves on the receiving end of vile characterizations that liken us to Nazis or anti-immigrants. Our detractors would have everyone believe that *our* America is built on the establishment of rigid inflexible laws that protect the mighty while endangering the poor - restricting opportunity rather than showering it on all who would seize it.

It is painful to watch, but even more painful to experience. It saddens those of us who are working every day to heal America's wounds, through civil and constructive discourse, to have our voices drowned out by the jeers and chants from youthful protestors who would deny our right to exercise our First Amendment rights while they happily exercise theirs. The hypocrisy is staggering. It is particularly tragic that we can no longer engage our liberal friends or even family members in any meaningful dialogue, especially since this is one of the only tools we have left to find any semblance of common ground. While it is true that we can always turn to the ballot box for help, votes are only *triage* and will not heal the divide that prevents us from achieving the promise of true liberty and a country, united.

~

Truth is painful

The honeymoon is over. The gloves have come off. The guard dog has broken its leash and the President exercised his prerogative. All are perfectly fine headlines for a story about the firing of a high-ranking political appointee, but those are not the headlines that are plastered all over the airwaves this evening. Instead, today's firing of the controversial FBI Director, James Comey, is being portrayed by news outlets like CNN and others and by Senate and House Democrats as a sinister attempt to bury the truth from an ongoing FBI investigation and to whitewash the current Administration of any alleged culpability in an evil conspiracy to collude with Russia on affecting the American Presidential Election of 2016. So much for the conspiracy theory. Here are the facts...

Fact: The President has the power and authority to dismiss a political appointee, FBI Directors included. Fact: Former Director Comey departed from long-standing procedures and held a press conference in July of 2016 about his Bureau's findings in an on-going investigation of Hillary Clinton's use of a private server to send classified government materials. Fact: It was not James Comey's place to publicly announce that the FBI was re-opening the Clinton case in October of 2016, just two weeks before a Presidential election.

This situation is manna from Heaven and a lagniappe for the Democrats, many of whom were calling for Director Comey's resignation or firing months ago! It is the real 'October surprise' albeit coming in May instead of the one given by Comey with his 'Clinton reopening investigation' remarks last Fall. Democrats smell blood in the water and are now chanting "name a special prosecutor" and, if successful, would turn it into a Spanish Inquisition-type hearing or one similar to Watergate or the Bill Clinton sex-in-office scandals.

While a so-called independent prosecutor-led, public, dirty laundry airing would do wonders for the Democrats' chances to take the next giant step in the Stop Trump Movement AND improve their chances at the 2018 ballot box, it would drag all America into a deadly viper pit of hissing partisans for months to come.

The Democrats would eagerly welcome such a step and thereby prove that they could care less about the damaging effect it would have on our country. Republicans will have great difficulty in keeping that chorus silent, however, and may, in the end, be forced to give in to their demands. If that happens, it will effectively stop any forward progress the Administration and the Republicans might want to make on getting important legislation passed. It could derail tax and immigration reform, infrastructure improvements and keep a host of other vital issues from getting their day before House or Senate committees much less a vote.

In essence, a special prosecutor would be instrumental in grinding government to a halt and delay the confirmations of hundreds of unfilled positions in the new Trump Administration by stiffening the Democrats' opposition. It would be a chaotic time for all of us, Republicans and Democrats alike, and would neutralize the Administration's efforts to deliver on its promises to stimulate our economy, secure the American homeland and provide for the common good.

Democracy isn't easy, and it's made even more difficult and placed in a precarious position when those who are charged with protecting it ignore their oaths to preserve and protect the Constitution and instead choose to play political gamesmanship. This is not to say that we Americans don't deserve to know the truth about our leaders or hold them accountable for their actions. We do, and if that takes a redoubling of our efforts to find the truth through an intensified bi-partisan push in Congressional hearings, so be it. That said, a special prosecution would do nothing to heal our massive political wounds. On the contrary, it would leave those wounds susceptible to the infection of more political division through months of public flogging. To get a sense of how it would feel, just remember back to the criminal trials of O.J. Simpson and Casey Anthony. Is that what we want? I don't think so.

Cooler heads must prevail, and we must stay the course to uncover the truth about any possible Trump campaign connections with Russia that might have occurred; to see how or if the capricious attitudes and dealings of Hillary Clinton subverted long-standing government regulations on communication of classified material; to shed light on the numerous leaks of intelligence and to see who unmasked Americans caught up in intelligence surveillance. Goodness knows the press will have a field day with any proceedings, and we should allow their reporters to file their reports and even welcome their commentary on House and Senate hearings. That is the role of the Fourth Estate. It is not their role, however, to set the agenda or determine guilt before a fair hearing produces evidence to convict or acquit. As for the FBI, let this firing of its Director be a stark reminder that <u>investigation</u> not prosecution is their responsibility

~

Unbaiting the mousetrap

President Donald Trump has put a new twist on, "If you build a better mousetrap, the world will beat a path to your door," by asking Congress to fund the Mexico *Friendship Wall* (my name for the Mexican border wall). He is just fulfilling one of the campaign promises that got him elected by 62 million people or 47% of the voting population in November. Most Republicans knew it was on his 'To do' list, but those on the far Left thought the wall was just one of his many campaign slogans.

This first week in office has shown many 'doubting Thomases' that the President takes his promises, seriously. I've heard many analogies about illegal immigration. One is, "What if your daughter was getting married and a couple hundred uninvited guests turned up, insisted on consuming your expensive Salmon Fumé and drinking your champagne that cost you $40/bottle? Then they demanded to dance the first dance with the bride and when the gifts were opened grabbed a few of them for themselves, and afterwards, when the festivities ended, decided to camp out in the banquet hall and refused to pay their fair share of the costs?"

Another was, "What if you were watching the Superbowl with your family in your living room and a dozen strangers broke down your front door, plopped themselves down on your sofa and insisted you change the channel after having left their muddy footprints on your new shag carpet? Afterwards, they commandeered your bedroom and told <u>you and the missus</u> to sleep on the floor and in the morning announced they were staying on for a few years?"

Most of us would probably object, strenuously, citing our right of private property. Asserting our right to a strong national border is much the same. It's up to us to refuse entry to anyone not having an invitation (legal documents). The U.S. is one of the most generous countries in the world when it comes to accepting legal immigrants - a million a year in fact - some having waited years for the privilege of a coveted permanent resident visa. Many, I might add, are non-Caucasian immigrants from all over the world.

As I said, the process is a long one. Sometimes it takes years to complete, and while they've been waiting, hundreds of thousands have 'crashed the party' by sneaking through our southern border, after which they've thumbed their noses at our immigration laws and promptly declared themselves *asylum seekers* to our Border Patrol. During the Obama years, this was the preferred method of gaining access to the USA, as border officials were required to allow the asylum seekers to stay here while a future court date was arranged for them. Most simply ignored the court order and disappeared into the woodwork. Then there are the *visa overstayers* - people who came to the U.S. with a legal tourist visa and decided they liked it here, and stayed, permanently. They too, have gone underground. The estimated size of that group is 42% of the total illegal immigrant population, maybe five million people.

Those supporting open borders don't seem to think this is a problem. They view our country like some kind of open bar with a free smorgasbord, and that if any one of us dared to criticize these underprivileged people we are to be tagged with words like: bully, statist or racist. We are vilified for wanting law or order in our immigration system. Our new President is not going to make many friends with the 65 million people that voted for Hillary Clinton with his executive orders, nor is he going to become bosom buddies with Mexican President Nieto by building the Friendship Wall OR when he signs an executive order that cuts off U.S. aid to those countries that will not take back citizens that have committed crimes here.

The rubber will meet the road soon, and Americans will have to, once again, choose sides on the immigration debate. I can only hope that our Congress will act swiftly, in a bi-partisan fashion, to enact a new, comprehensive immigration law that will protect our borders, ensure the safety of our citizens and, yes, treat the general non-criminal illegal immigrant population with civility while we find a solution for the 11-13 million of them who have not broken any other laws and just want a chance at grabbing the brass ring of the American Dream.

~

What to do about aggression?

I've seen a few physical fights in my day, and I've even been involved in a couple. They all had two things in common...passion AND a loss of control. Matter of fact, I've never seen or been in one where passion or loss of control <u>weren't</u> the underlying ingredients.

Pacifists like the Quakers (the Society of Friends) and other religious groups would probably say that fighting is not only destructive but stupid and that there are better ways to settle disputes. While I understand the principle of non-violent problem-solving and admire historical icons like Mahatma Gandhi and Martin Luther King, Jr., I can't help but feel that there are occasions when it's necessary to put on the gloves, sound the bell and move to the center of the ring.

The situation in North Korea is a case in point. We've tried endless dialogue, sanctions, forgiveness, bribery, coalition building and all sorts of diplomatic efforts to get at least two generations of the Kim family to stop building up their military arsenal, forego nuclear testing and join up with the 'good guys.' The velvet glove approach has failed. The same is true in Iran with a group of radical Muslim clerics who see their place in history as being the one country that defeated the 'Great Satan' (us).

Granted, that for every country with a crazy dictator there are a dozen others that are moving towards democracy, but that doesn't solve the problem of what to do about the ones that aren't. America has had a spotty record of defending the truly defenseless, like the oppressed peoples of many African nations, for example. We've also looked the other way when several of our avowed allies continue to treat minorities like homosexuals and women, badly. We often ignore blatant one-sided aggression and pick our battles based on narrow national interests and geopolitics, but that doesn't erase the blemish on our collective conscience for choosing to defend one group while ignoring the others; it only makes excuses for it.

We are also fair weather friends when it comes to protecting our own people from unwanted aggression. The obvious example that comes to mind is our checkered past with our African-American population. Add the poor, illegal immigrants, those with alternative lifestyles and the elderly to the mix and you have a heap of folks suffering under one form of aggression or another.

Unfortunately, there seems to be no one universally-accepted definition of 'aggression.' Aggression comes in many guises: unfair laws, inadequate legal defense, police harassment, voter fraud, personal crime and, I would argue, general disrespect that leads to discrimination. What does a society like ours that purports to be open and equal in its treatment of its citizens do to stop aggression on all these fronts? Do we employ the North Korean example of endless dialogue, issue some sanctions and turn the other cheek? Do we keep pretending the problem isn't as bad as we think or do we start admitting it, identifying it and confronting it head-on?

Until recently, we have accepted the aggression of illegal border crossing and done little about it. We have allowed the aggression of our university administrators to refuse controversial individuals their right to speak on campuses while they carve out 'safe spaces' for sensitive students who can't seem to embrace the First Amendment. We allow Federal government employees to abuse their power and then refuse to punish them when they're caught. We plea bargain away too many offenses just to get some damning testimony on the 'bigger fish,' and when we get it we don't use it!

We have adequate metrics to determine what aggression is when it comes to war, but seem unwilling to step up and tackle it in our own backyard. We can't afford to focus our efforts solely on the many international conflicts that are brewing while our own society is in turmoil. Losing that battle on our own turf won't help us win the larger wars of aggression around the world. Like a cancer it will metastasize and consume us.

~

Chapter VI
That whole Russia thing

In the Fall of 1975, I stepped onto an SAS flight from Copenhagen and flew to Moscow via Helsinki. It was my first trip to the capital of Communism, but not my last one. I'll spare you the details, but I must tell you that my time there was something I will remember all my life, and that goes double for its people, who I found fascinating.

Anyone who has ever been in the company of or had anything to do with Russians has truly missed out. Their humor is uplifting (if not dark by our standards). Their resolve is admirable, and their survival instincts and skills (to be able to endure decades of oppressive governments) are world class. Russian emigrants to the USA have been successful here because of their desire to turn the hourglass of negative odds upside down, put their shoulders to the wheel and power on.

Like us, the Russian people choose their leaders but they don't choose their leaders' leadership styles. Most citizens cross their fingers and hope for the best - that not too much graft occurs and that not too many backroom deals are made that will hurt the average Russian. They accept human nature for what it is and don't ignore man's inherent weaknesses and vulnerabilities. They are cynical optimists that always keep one eye open...even when they sleep. The average American doesn't understand them and doesn't know their history.

That goes for the average Congressional Representative and Senator as well which may explain their push to 'roust the Reds' from our political system when the first inkling of 'Russian election interference' came to light. Since then, this connection has been so obsessively pursued that it borders on the paranoid. No, I take that back. It IS paranoid.

As of this writing, the Special Counsel, Robert Mueller has hired more staff; the House and Senate investigative committees are sharpening their knives and new potential victim lists are being drawn up. In late July, the FBI conducted a pre-dawn raid on the home of former Trump Campaign Manager Paul Manafort. The President's family is also under scrutiny. The only ones left alone (for now) are the First Lady and the President's ten year old son, Baron.

This 'Russia thing' has now escaped the gravitational pull of our physical world and is moving steadily into the outer limits of reality where it will split off like cancerous cells dividing and multiplying. When it does it will steal even more energy from America's leaders' days until it eventually winds down after the mid-term elections (the Democrats will make sure it lasts that long).

Unfortunately, there is no penalty for making wrongful accusations. The President will continue to be attacked by a carefully coordinated resistance movement - a hit squad - comprised of the anti-Trump media, university anarchists, secular Progressives, the Hollywood glitterati, feminist and alternative lifestyle groups, Democrat Congressmen and Senators and even some members of his own party.

'That Russian thing' is the Trojan Horse they're all riding in.

Adopt a Russian

Americans (at least those on the political left) are more than a little paranoid about Russia and are letting this paranoia affect their everyday lives. I suppose that's to be expected since they are convinced that Donald Trump is the Manchurian Candidate and has surrounded himself with a cadre of *Red lovers*. If you believe the mainstream media, nearly everybody associated with 'The Donald' has at one time or another been in cahoots with Vladimir Vladimirovich Putin or Ambassador Sergey Ivanovich Kislyak...or millions of other Russians.

Their beliefs are so strong that they are now demanding that the FBI launch a nationwide investigation of all of the townspeople of villages that bear Russian names. I've heard that this is pretty upsetting to the local folk of places like St. Petersburg (Florida), Sebastopol (California) and Volga (South Dakota), but the biggest offenders are those twenty states that have a town named 'Moscow' within their borders. As for the burghers of those towns, I've heard they are seriously considering renaming them to something more typically American like, *Apple Pie, North Dakota, Stand-up double, Florida,* and even *Hot Dog, Alabama.*

Another disturbing development is occurring at libraries across the U.S. It seems that many are now covering all their Russian books with brown Kraft paper and requiring anyone wishing to take out books from authors like Alexander Pushkin and Leo Tolstoy to take a lie detector test and be fingerprinted. The Russian Tea Room in New York City (in business for over eighty years) will soon be changing its name and its menu, removing any mention of 'Mother Russia' or its cuisine.

For example, Borscht has been rechristened *Yankee Doodle Soup.* Blinis have become *Don't Tread on Me Pancakes* while Blintzes are now *Shot Heard Round the World Crepes.* Even babies aren't safe from the new purge of everything Russian. Parenting class instructors will soon be encouraging new mothers and fathers to teach their offspring to say, 'ja, ja' instead of 'da,da.'

It seems that there is no end in sight, at least not until Special Counsel, Robert Mueller, is finished with his queries of Trump officials. I am told by reliable anonymous sources, however, that it won't stop there. California Congresswoman Maxine Waters, has teamed up with former Secretary of State, Hillary Clinton, to launch a nationwide *private investigation* that is expected to unearth new and damaging information about the man they call Rasputin...Donald Trump.

This just in...the Democratic National Committee has just announced that it has succeeded in getting Rand McNally and Google to remove Russia from all their printed and online maps. When an online user searches the Internet from now on for 'Russia' the search engine will take the user to three images: one of the White House, one of Trump Tower and one of the Trump Florida residence, Mar-a-Lago.

The Russians are, understandably, very worried about all the bad PR and 'fake news' that is spreading like wildfire across our country, so they have created a new strategy to combat all the vitriol and misinformation ginned up by America's mainstream media and the uber Left. Their plan is simple and ingenious.

The Russian Ministry of Cultural Collusion and Subversion is now actively looking for U.S. families that are willing to take in a Russian diplomat or a wealthy Russian oligarch for a period of one year in the hopes that the experience will help soften Americans' attitudes toward their country. The project is called, 'Adopt the Great Bear,' and when asked for his comment about the project, President of the Russian Federation, Vladimir Putin, is quoted as saying, "I support it wholeheartedly. I have my host family lined up and they already have a great space for me. It's called, 'The Lincoln Bedroom.'

~

Conspiracy theorists and other time-wasters

I think that we have finally reached our collective breaking point, the point at which we have become immune to any new revelations or information about 'Russiagate.' This 'scandal' has now surpassed that old TV series, 'Dallas,' in elevating intrigue to new heights. Because of the complexity of the story, the multitude of characters involved, and the incessant sniping by Washington, D.C. detractors at the President, many of us have completely tuned out and are thinking of other ways to pass our time than clipping news items from blogs and pasting them into a Russian conspiracy scrapbook.

We've had it. We're done. It's over for us. We either believe the Trump campaign was guilty of *something* (we don't have an actual crime as yet) or we think the whole thing is either a colossal witch hunt or as the DC pundits call it, a 'nothing burger.' If that is a factual description of where we are in this now eight-month long attack on the President and the new Administration, what are we supposed to do when confronted with 'Breaking News', turn off the TV, encourage Rover to eat the remote or

330

should we pack up our things and go for a long walk? Every time I see the 'crawler' pop up on the bottom of the CNN news screen with the word *Russia* in it, I just want to dig a big hole in the backyard and throw myself - correct that - throw THEM into it!

And CNN isn't the only one giving the scandal prime time exposure. Nearly every mainstream media outlet is bringing out their big gun Russia conspiracy experts to weigh in on the latest shocking turn of events in Trump World and spin a web of innuendo: Did the President know his son was not actually his son, but a Russian clone of his son? Was Donald Jr. a dupee or a duper? Did Trump campaign insiders actually make a pact with the Russian government to spread fake news stories about Hillary Clinton? Is Laika, the Soviet space dog still alive in a Siberian cryogenic lab? Was the Bolshoi Ballet a den of KGB agents who could dance or dancers who could spy? A thousand off-the-wall questions come to mind like: was Joseph Stalin really FDR's second cousin twice removed and that's why it took so long to realize that the Reds were dangerous to our democracy? And was it the Russians who really invented the Corvair and the Pinto and potato chips...to kill us?

My mind is now questioning everything I learned about 20th century history, and I now blame the Russians for: Pinky Lee, the collapse of Enron and the Bernie Madoff debacle, bell-bottom trousers and platform shoes, the 70s oil crisis, digital photography (to ruin Kodak), Monika Lewinsky (to ruin Bill) and political correctness (to ruin all of us).

I know that this sounds irrational, but it is every bit as rational as believing that the Trump campaign sold its soul to the devil and actively colluded with agents of a foreign power to win an election they were bound to win in the first place over a candidate that called half of America's voters, "a basket of deplorables." Another thing, do you really believe in your heart of hearts, that the Russians were willing to stoop so low as to manipulate our voters when there are so many other more enjoyable things they could be doing with their time like playing chess, vacationing in their Dachas, downing magnums of vodka and eating Beluga caviar while nuzzling hot Russki babes at all-night discos?

I met a number of ordinary (and not so ordinary) Russians when I worked in their country in the 70s and I can tell you that most of them secretly admired the USA and coveted our wealth and freedom. Destroying their own dreams of cashing in the good life was the furthest thing from their minds.

The decades since have brought them a few steps closer to their goals of achieving some modicum of personal freedom and prosperity, and I don't believe for a second that they wanted their government to kill the capitalist goose that laid the golden egg and run the risk of sowing chaos in the one country that offered them some hope.

On the contrary, I think that some of our own elected officials have been all too willing to believe that their candidate lost because of a vast conspiracy built on collusion rather than admit that an enlightened electorate chose a strong, plain-speaking, unconventional leader rather than embrace a status quo politician that espoused outmoded and unworkable policies that would have taken us down a path to creeping socialism and enormous national debt.

Back in the sixties, Nikita Khrushchev said he would bury us, but it was his 'empire' that took a dirt nap not ours. It's time we buried all the nonsensical new Russia conspiracy theories and got to work improving our economy so that we can, once again, show the world that the idea of a capitalist economy-driven constitutional republic is still bigger and stronger than the small minds that would sell us on the hobgoblins of fear and self-doubt.

~

In defense of the average Russian

Today, our President put his foot down and sent a few dozen Russian diplomats and their families packing in response to information from our intelligence agencies that they meddled into our cyberspace. Without a security briefing to confirm it, I can only assume that the President was referring to the release of hundreds of John Podesta's emails. The intrusion aside, the veracity or legitimacy of these emails has never been denied by Mr. Podesta, the Democratic National Committee or the Clinton campaign.

As much as I dislike Mr. Podesta, the breaching of the cyberwall that protected his free speech without his permission is an offence and deserving of a reprimand. What Mr. Obama did today by making Russian diplomats persona non grata appears to be justified in light of that First Amendment protection transgression. What is baffling me is the fact that the Obama Administration has known about Russian attempts to hack U.S. sites for many months, and why with just 20 days to go before he hands over the reins of power to Mr. Trump does he suddenly find the courage to act?

It smells to me like retribution to a man (Vladimir Putin) that has been a thorn in Mr. Obama's side for years rather than an action designed to protect the United States. Again, I'm not privy to the intel that may back up the President's decision, but timing in politics and geopolitics is everything. This decision, coupled with Mr. Obama's conjectural statements about his being able to have won the Presidency a third time if he had run are, unfortunately, more like comments and actions from someone trying to protect his own reputation AND one who is in denial of the truth about his party's loss in November.

It goes without saying that one of the pre-requisites to being President is having a substantially larger than average ego. Both the current President and the incumbent are uniquely qualified in the ego department. We have all heard that, "Power corrupts, but absolute power corrupts absolutely" (thanks to the quote from John Dalberg-Acton). What we don't focus on is the rest of that quote, "Great men are almost always bad men." I don't subscribe to the notion that either Mr. Obama or Mr. Trump are bad men, but it is the 'great' part and the need to be seen as great that can take good men down the wrong road and make them do things they wouldn't normally do if they weren't in possession of enormous power.

I worked in Russia in the mid-70s. These were the Leonid Brezhnev years. At that time, the country was inward-looking and distrustful of any democracy, though many secretly wanted some democracy for themselves. I'm speaking, of course, of the average Russian, the working Russian of the middle class that had to endure endless product shortages of everything from shoes to automobiles.

At the time, Gum, the Russian 'department store' that is across Red Square from the Kremlin was awash with people looking for the biggest queues. The prevailing wisdom was that the longer the line, the more important the item. I couldn't take a walk on Red Square in the evening without someone offering me money for my blue jeans, for example. The average Russian was resourceful. Western paperback novels and Western music were passed from hand to hand like the flu in a frigid Russian winter.

I remember my interpreter reading a book with a brown paper cover. I summoned up the courage to ask her what she was reading and she replied, "Shh, not too loud. It is the "Godfather" by Mario Puzo. I am almost finished and there is a long list of people that want to read it when I am done." "Okay, I said, but what is that tape you have in your purse, secret recordings of me?"

"No, you silly American. Do you think I'm with the KGB or something? It's American rock and roll!" (It was common knowledge at the time that interpreters were assigned to foreigners by the KGB to report on them.) That brings me to my favorite 'average Russian' story. At that time, our movements were limited and we were not allowed to go beyond the giant ring road that encircled Moscow. It was getting late and I asked Valentina if she and the other interpreter, Marina, would like to join me and two of my colleagues for dinner, our treat.

At once she said, "Oh, yes. I know the perfect place, too. It is a wonderful Georgian restaurant just outside the ring road." That stopped me in my tracks. Thinking that this might be a trap to ensnare me in an infraction that would send me packing, back to Denmark where I lived, I said, "But Valentina, that is out of bounds for me." She responded, "I won't tell if you won't." "Of course not," I said, so gathering up our colleagues we hopped into two taxis and made our way to the restaurant. Unfortunately, when we arrived, the line to get in was long even by Russian standards. I told her that we would never get seated, tonight.

She said, "You are rich American, and money talks," whereupon this diminutive whisp of a girl pushed her way past all her countrymen saying something like 'amerikanskje turistje' until we reached the imposing door watcher, who, to my surprise let us in (after I greased his palm with some 'thank you' rubles). Inside, we were ushered to a big table near the dance floor and proceeded to order our food. Then, wanting to impress Valentina with some fancy dance steps, I asked her to dance. We moved closer to the band that was playing 60s Beatles music, and after one dance the band started packing up their instruments.

"This can't be right," I said. It's only 8:00 o'clock!" She looked me squarely in the eyes and said, "There is a solution, IF you are brave enough to take it. We must negotiate with the band leader!" Thinking this would be a snap, I went over to him and used my fingers and said, "ten minutes, ten rubles."

The band leader then huddled with his musicians and turned to me and used his fingers, but this time, the price was twenty rubles for ten minutes. I turned to Valentina for support, but she said, "Take it. Is good deal." I forgot to tell you that while we had been negotiating, all the dancers were frozen in place, anxiously awaiting the outcome of our deal. We shook hands, money transferred ownership and the music began with, "She was just 17." Believe me, you haven't anything until you've heard a Russian band sing *that* Beatles' song.

Everyone was happy, and one-by-one couples came over to me and slapped me on the back and bought me vodka. Thirty minutes later, the band was still playing and I felt like a hero of the revolution - the new Russian-American friendship revolution! The vodka must have kicked in because the next thing I remember I was in a taxi, trying to sing 'Orchichonya' on my way back to my hotel which lay alongside the Moscow River. I woke up the next morning with a splitting headache and was supposed to meet Valentina for breakfast. I must have looked awful, but Valentina looked as if she had just stepped out of a spa. I asked her if I had behaved myself to which she responded, "It depends on who is making the assessment. You only broke a few rules that could have sent you home. Wasn't that great? THAT's how we feel when we disobey some of the stupid rules of the Soviet state."

Many things have changed since the end of the Cold War and the dissolution of the Soviet Empire, but one thing will forever remain constant...people are all pretty much the same. The average Russian is just like the average American when it comes to pushing back on unfair regulations. I'm convinced that there will always be spying. The difference today is that we have entered a new phase of it. The intrusion into people's lives is more pervasive thanks to electronic eavesdropping. If left unchecked or unpunished, it will escalate way beyond countries' borders. As for me, I will always be grateful that I saw the indomitable spirit of the average Russian at work...and play.

~

Mueller's new Russian evidence

The following dream occurred before our Presidential election of eight months ago and has been de-classified by the Russian Government. It is now in the hands of Special Prosecutor, Robert Mueller.

Vladimir Vladimirovich Putin (VP) was awakened by a loud knock at his bedroom door. It seemed that he was dreaming and shouting in his sleep. His bodyguard, Yuri Tuffski (YT), was worried and decided to check on him just to make sure that he wasn't being murdered by an American assassin. The conversation that followed was one that both Pravda and the Washington Post would have loved to print. VP: What is wrong Yuri? YT: I am sorry to wake you Comrade President, but I thought the Americans were killing you. I had to make sure you were alright. VP: I am fine. Sit down, Yuri. I need to tell you my dream.

I had dinner last night with General Syberkov, the head of our Binary Attack Team. He told me that our hack on Yahoo a few years ago had given us personal information on millions of new Americans! As you can imagine, Yuri, I was overjoyed! YT: Because you could finally influence the Americans' Presidential election? VP: No. It means that we now have a database of potential customers large enough to launch our own online buying service, *Gulagle.com*, like the Americans' amazon.com. Our market research tells us that the Americans' new Internet rules will make Amazon charge state sales tax on Internet purchases and that will kill them, clearing the field for *Gulagle*.

We will offer free shipping and no tax on anything bought through *Gulagle*, plus a free recipe for our new *Kremlin-licious* borscht. Soon, Mother Russia will dominate the Internet! YT: But I thought that we were going to interfere in the Americans' election, Comrade Leader. VP: Hah. That was a clever maneuver, something the Americans call a 'head fake' that our Secretariat of Dirty Tricks came up with. That's what we wanted THEM to believe. We purposely dropped a few digital bread crumbs like the IP address of a potato farmer near the Black Sea for their stupid CIA to follow, and bingo, they were off chasing a phony lead while Comrade Snowden was busy hacking into the Democratic National Committee's website.

He found that the largest email account was John Podesta's. It gave us thousands of emails on just about everything to just about everybody. It was the gift that keeps on giving! YT: Bravo, Comrade Leader. THAT was a great turn of a phrase. VP: I know. I'm using it next month at the annual gathering of the Congress of Evil Empires (COEE) right here in Moscow. You know, Yuri, that old cold warrior Reagan did us a big favor. He gave us the best brand any country could ask for - 'Evil Empire' - it makes me think of Star Wars and Darth Vader.

YT: You would be an excellent Darth Vader. VP: Do you really think so? YT: Oh yes. Da, da, Comrade President. VP: Excellent, then instruct my secretary to call my tailor to start work on a new Darth Vader suit for me. I can wear it when I give the opening remarks at the COEE. YT: But Comrade Leader, what were you dreaming about when I heard you yelling?

VP: Oh, that. I dreamt that I was wrestling an alligator in the United States Capitol Rotunda and the alligator had me in a headlock. American Girl Scouts were walking by, led by Hillary Clinton. I reached out to her and asked her for help. YT: What did she do? VP: She told me to wait a minute or two and she would be back after she took the girls to a safe place.

YT: So what happened? VP: Nothing, absolutely nothing. She did not come back. Instead, she sent Bernie Sanders to help me. YT: So what did <u>he</u> do? VP: He started giving me a speech, telling me that much is asked of a leader these days, especially leaders of Socialist and Communist countries, and that each should give according to his abilities and that it was my responsibility to let the alligator win! At that point, I woke up and, Yuri, I am determined to show that woman who has the <u>real</u> reset button. She is not going to sit in the Oval Office as long as I have a breath in my perfectly-sculpted body.

To quote our beloved former Premier, Comrade Khrushchev, "We will bury you." We will bury her and then dig her up and bury her again. She will wish she had not scrubbed her server in that decadent house of hers! Yuri, get my car and tell the driver I am going over to see the head of the Directorate for Sneaky Things. I need to know how he's doing with our latest weapon. YT: What is that, Comrade Leader? VP: Listen carefully. We have replaced all the electors in the American Electoral College with Communist Party members, and they have been instructed to vote a tie of 269 to 269 votes to disrupt the American election.

YT: But won't that throw the election to the Republican-dominated Congress and insure a victory for Mr. Trump? VP: Ah, ha! That's where we have them by their little capitalist pig short hairs. We have hacked into the Congress vote tabulating machine and fixed it so that the Congressmens' votes will also end up a tie! YT: Brilliant, Comrade Leader, brilliant. VP: I know, I know. It is why everybody loves me so.

~

Russian to judgment

The Kremlin must be buzzing given all the news coming out of Washington these days. I can see it all now, Vladimir Putin is feasting on Beluga caviar, swilling champagne, surrounded by balalaikas and high-stepping folk dancers, swirling like dervishes to the tune of the new U.S. media-inspired *DC Russian Two step*. He must be laughing out loud watching the Democrats sharpen their 'shaskas' (the Cossacks' weapon of choice) in the hopes of mortally wounding the new Attorney General and anyone else in the Trump Administration that has ever talked with a U.S. immigrant Russian cab driver or read a Russian novel in college.

The Republicans are saying that this whole 'Russia thing' is a tempest in a samovar, that the Democrats are engaging in a modern-day Stalin-light purge that they hope will take the entire Trump Administration down.

Were this whole hullabaloo not so serious (as it distracts from the important work that needs to be done by the new Administration), it would be a hit play on Broadway, a kind of updated version of one of Anton Chekhov's stories that revealed the seamier side of Russian life.

But it's not a play, nor is it a satire. It is, instead, a glaring example of what happens when a vanquished opponent vows to fight on and is ready to use anything at his or her disposal to strike a final blow at the victors. If I understand this melodrama correctly, the Democrats believe that the Trump campaign team actively colluded with the Russian government, so that it could insert itself into our Presidential campaign and then attack and hack the computers of the Democratic National Committee and those of Hillary Clinton and her closest aides and confidants. They did this on explicit orders from pro-Trump forces who are trying to maintain plausible deniability by 'forgetting' that some of them like the new Attorney General, Jeff Sessions and General Michael Flynn, had meetings with the Russian Ambassador.

It's all playing out like a Matryoshka doll (sometimes referred to as a 'Babushka' or grandmother doll). As one unscrews the head of the first doll it reveals another, smaller doll within it. And so it goes, yet another doll is uncovered. This is the 'drip, drip drip' that eventually killed off both the Nixon and Clinton Presidencies, and if left unchecked, will weaken the current President's ability to govern even if there is no 'there' there. In order to achieve success and take down Mr. Trump, the Democrats will need to find a 'smoking gun' to prove a link, any link, other than a chance or misremembered meeting with the Russian Ambassador or just slurping a bowl of borscht at the Russian Tea Room in New York City.

So far, the FBI and the CIA are involved as are at least two committees in the Senate and the House. The Republicans hope they can circle their wagons and avoid a special prosecutor and keep things 'in the family.' The last thing they want is to be backed into a corner and be subject to the same kind of endless hearings that Hillary Clinton endured with the Benghazi debacle or her email server. This could be disastrous to both Republicans AND Democrats as most Americans don't have the stomach for another 'Watergate.' The contentious Presidential primaries and general election drained most of our strength and left some of us bleeding on the sidelines. Even the winners don't have the patience for another round of 'Russian Roulette.'

We can only hope that any and all investigations will be undertaken, thoroughly, and impartially, and that the 'truth' will out. If it drags on, the only other alternative we have is to plop ourselves on the sofa in front of the tube with a huge bowl of popcorn and settle in for some binge watching of: Doctor Zhivago, Reds, The man who knew too little, Gorky Park and the Hunt for Red October. It could be a long night at the dacha.

~

Special prosecutor or special persecutor?

Seventy years ago last month, President Harry Truman signed Executive Order 9835 that required all Federal Civil Service employees to be screened for "loyalty." The order specified that one criterion to be used in determining that "reasonable grounds exist for belief that the person involved is disloyal" would be a finding of "membership in, affiliation with or sympathetic association" with any organization determined by the attorney general to be "totalitarian, fascist, communist or subversive" or advocating or approving the forceful denial of constitutional rights to other persons or seeking "to alter the form of Government of the United States by unconstitutional means."

As we all know, that opened the door for one Senator Joe McCarthy to begin his crusade to root out all 'subversives' in government, and the House Un-American Activities Committee (HUAC) was the principal vehicle for investigating dozens of Americans suspected of wide-ranging disloyalty to the United States.

This 'hunt for Reds' lasted several years, and many innocent people (along with a few guilty ones) were grilled about their patriotism. Later the term, *McCarthysim* became synonymous with the reckless and vicious pursuit of political opponents and demagogic attacks on individuals' character. Many have relegated the McCarthy years to the history books as a 'one-off' and don't see any parallels with our modern-day politics. I'm not one of them. While the names may have changed, the players play by the same rules: assume guilt, demean, accuse, and vilify...without evidence.

Over the last one and half centuries we've used either 'special prosecutors' (SPs) or 'independent counsels' (ICs) to investigate wrong-doing by Presidents and others. The first was in 1875 when President Ulysses S. Grant called for one to investigate something called the "Whiskey Ring Scandal" (the diversion of tax revenues by distillers and distributors). Later, other Presidents followed, like Presidents Garfield (Star Route Scandal), Coolidge (Teapot Dome Scandal), and in May 1973, President Nixon when he tapped Attorney General, Elliot Richardson, who named Archibald Cox to investigate the Watergate Scandal (we all know

339

where that led). Following Watergate, the Congress passed the 'Ethics in Government Act' which established formal rules for initiating a special prosecutor. The statute ran out, was re-instated and then ran out again. As of today, there is no Federal law governing the appointment of a special prosecutor, but there are internal Department of Justice regulations in place for naming SPs. One departmental requirement is that the special counsel must be a lawyer from outside the U.S. Government.

The decision to appoint a special prosecutor rests with the Attorney General or, historically, with the President. Congress could formally request the AG to appoint one, but the AG is only required to respond in writing with a decision. The argument cited for appointing a special prosecutor in cases like the current 'Russian election meddling' and 'Trump campaign Russia collusion' is based on the need for having a non-partisan and independent investigation, free from politics. It is thought that two-track House and Senate investigations, where both investigative committees are in the hands of Republican majorities, will not unearth the truth but only protect the Trump Administration.

Therein lies the rub. A Republican Congress will not opt for an SP as long as their investigations can proceed in both houses and be seen to be bringing material evidence to light. It is only if their investigations become bogged down and appear to be overly partisan that they will be forced to bend to the Democrats' pressure for an SP. Because Republicans are seen to be circling the wagons around the Administration and the Democrats are perceived to be waging an unholy war against President Trump that will lead to his impeachment, AND because our country is so polarized, politically, it is almost impossible to find the equivalent of Cincinnatus, the Roman protector of values, to lead such an investigation.

While there may very well be such a figure walking among us who is dedicated to God and country and to finding the truth amid all the innuendo and fake news, it is doubtful that he (or she) would be able to shield the proceedings from all the hordes of partisans who will criticize his every action and utterance, no matter how sensible or purely procedural they may be. For now, the best course may be to subordinate our partisanship for awhile and focus on the House and Senate investigations to see where they lead. Trust but verify...every step of the way.

~

The new Manchurian candidate or Fake News?

An alliance of cable and print journalists from CNN, MSNBC, the Washington Post and the New York Times have just broken what could be the story of the century. According to the coalition of news organizations that calls itself *Crusaders for Real Truth (CFRT)*, Donald Trump is really a Russian doppelganger and was installed by Russia to do its bidding. CFRT bases its claim on a super secret report that was leaked to them by outgoing CIA Director, John Brennan, who is quoted as saying, "It's taken me awhile, but I've finally got the goods on that vain commie stooge."

The report chronicles a strange and winding path to the White House for the sitting President, who is alleged to be a Russian actor and the cousin of Vladimir Putin who goes by the name of Igor Yuroxski. According to the timeline, the idea of replacing the U.S. President with a body double and rigging the American election came to President Putin when he was wrestling crocodiles in Africa. At one point, the President came face to face with croc #1 (he was wrestling three) and he saw a resemblance to Hillary Clinton. Startled by the sight, Putin thumped the croc's nose with his fist and it immediately rolled over and assumed the fetal position. Convinced that he could get even with Mrs. Clinton and the American government for its stupid 'reset' button (the translation on the button was "peregruzka" which means "overcharged" instead of "reset") he hatched his brilliant plan.

After three long years of studying Trump's, mannerisms, speech patterns and facial expressions, the Kremlin judged Yuroxski ready to make the switch. It happened on June 16, 2015 just before the now famous 'escalator ride' in Trump Tower. Needing to relieve himself (FSB agents actually spiked Trump's orange juice with a diuretic that same morning), 'The Donald' left his wife at the head of the escalator to make a quick pit stop. The switch was seamless. In went the real Trump, out came Igor. From that moment on, the Kremlin has controlled the phony candidate (now President) with instructions through a tiny earpiece which explains why the doppelganger Trump has swept his locks over his right ear to disguise the communication device.

About a month after the announcement, Mr. Yuroxski began exhibiting some speech problems. He started repeating himself and using simplistic phrases that sounded like they came from sixth graders. According to the report, the actor had suffered a minor stroke while combing his hair after a windy campaign stop and hasn't been 'himself' since. Putin is supposed to have said, "Let him be; I like his simple speech. It should appeal to those idiot American voters."

Reporters from the CFRT asked, "How did the Russians know that Trump would win the nomination and then the Presidency?" Don Lemon (CNN), Rachel Maddow and Lawrence O'Donnell (MSNBC) took turns answering. "First," said Lemon, "The Russians stacked the deck by giving lots of money to the individual Republican state chairmen and parties." "Yes," said Maddow. "That's right and they even wrote killer lines for Yuroxski to say in the debates like "Little Marco", "Lyin' Ted" and so on." "But what about the famous *bus comments* about grabbing women's (bleeped out)?" "Ah, ha," said O'Donnell. "THAT was something Putin insisted on. He thought it would make Trump seem more manly, like himself."

"Then, the election...and the hacking into the DNC and Hillary's server, that was the Russians," said Lemon. "And the Russkis stuffed the ballot boxes, electronically, in Michigan, Wisconsin and Pennsylvania, to secure a Trump win." Lemon continued, "The end game is for the *Trumposter* to suck up to Putin and eventually sign a massive trade agreement with the Russians that will give Putin access to the American market and enable them to take over the Baltic countries of Lithuania, Latvia and Estonia without U.S. objection. From there, Putin has his eyes on buying the U.S. Virgin Islands for his winter vacations."

"Where is the real Donald Trump now?," asked a reporter from Politico. Maddow replied, "We think that he is in Russia developing hotels and 'pleasure palaces' and is having the time of his life without having to get building permits, negotiate with labor unions or get bank loans." "So all this talk about Trump not being a legitimate President was true then?" asked the same reporter. "No. He is legitimate," said Lemon. "He's just not OUR legitimate President; he's Russia's!"

The press conference over, reporters rushed out to call their editors. Headlines varied from the punchy to the pusillanimous, all according to the publication. For example, the Washington Post's was, "See. We told you." CNN devoted a whole day to a panel discussion with its regular contributors that excoriated every Republican that had ever lived and blamed the whole thing on George Bush. MSNBC did much the same, but showed a graphic of Rasputin together with Trump as its backdrop for Maddow's and O'Donnell's shows. Finally, the New York Times came out with a 'second coming' (huge type) headline that simply said, "Dos Vedanya, Donald."

When asked for a comment, White House Press Secretary Sean Spicer said, "What a crock of !@#." When pressed on what the President thought about the report, Spicer said, "He can't be bothered right now; he's watching a movie." "Which one?" asked the reporter for CNN. "From Russia with Love," mumbled Spicer.

~

Voting, Moscow style

Call me crazy, but I think the James Comey hearing today was the official start of the 2018 mid-term election campaigns. As of this writing there are only 515 days to go before America once again makes the migration to the polling place (November 6th). That's actually a pretty frightening thought considering what has happened to our country since the last election day. Maybe it's my imagination, but are we holding more elections than usual? Somebody must have snuck in a few more just to liven things up a bit (as if we're bored and need more excitement)! If the Comey testimony was actually the signal for the race to begin, then what are the election talking points going to be?

For the Republicans they will be: 1. the Democrats have hijacked our Democracy by ginning up a phony scandal; 2. the Democrats are playing politics while our country is suffering with long-term unemployment and a failing health care system; 3. the Democrats are creating a toxic politically-correct environment; 4. college campuses are hotbeds of anti-democratic propaganda; 5. racial unrest; 6. rampant crime in our big cities; 7. flagrant disregard of our immigration laws; and 8. radical Islamic terrorism.

Not to be outdone, I can hear the Democrats' political consultants' computers humming away. Their election mantras will be: 1. we have an idiot in the White House that can't tell his left foot from his right unless its marked with a Sharpie; 2. we have a dictator in the White House; 3. we have a racist in the White House; 4. we have a misogynist in the White House; 5. we have a Russian spy in the White House; 6. we have a White Supremacist in the White House; 7. we have a serial liar in the White House; and 8. we have a pretender in the White House.

It's amazing to me that the Democrats have concentrated their fire solely on the President and haven't mentioned any of the things that Americans are really concerned with. In all fairness, they still have 515 days to see the light and talk about real issues.

In the meantime, however, I'm going to let you in on a little political insider's secret. Ready? The Democrats have decided to begin negotiations with the Russians for a little voter registration bump-up. Worried that President Trump may be able to pull a few rabbits out of his dunce cap, like some trade deals and a 'repeal and replace' of Obamacare, they are taking no chances. They figure on using *their* Russians against *his* Russians. The task of making the initial contacts with the Russians fell on the shoulders of an unholy troika made up of John Podestavich, Debbie Wasserman Schultzansky and Donna Brazilianov. All have been conspicuously absent from the political scene for months now. It is assumed that they are all at this very moment drinking sweet tea from silver samovars in a chic restaurant on a new side-street to the Kremlin named just for them called, 'Impossible Dreamsky Prospect.'

My sources tell me that Vladimir Putin himself is scheduled to make a hush-hush appearance in one of the Dems' first strategy sessions in Moscow AND that he will unveil the super-secret new software program to 'fix' the decadent American ballot boxes. The program is called, "Myest" (the Russian word for *revenge*).

It was developed by a group of top students from the College of Nefarious Studies of the Patrice Lamumba University and is designed specifically for the American market (it is currently being field-tested in the UK). The software injects itself into the voting machines of predominantly Republican precincts and switches every other Republican vote to the Democrats' candidate, thereby giving the Dems big wins in the 2018 elections. The program is reputed to have worked well in trials and, as mentioned, is busy vote-shifting in England. If it's successful, and Theresa May's Conservative Party loses seats, the Russians will probably up the price to the Dems' troika. A source close to Debbie Wasserman Schultzansky quotes her as saying, "Money is no object. We still have cash left over from our 'Operation Stop Bernie' campaign, and by God we'll use it. It's our turn, comrade!"

~

What you see is what you don't get...immediately

Zapping through the cable channels to escape commercials used to work pretty well. When Ron Popeil popped up with his compact fishing rod I was able to leave him in mid-sentence by changing the channel for a few minutes. No more. The networks must have made a secret pact with one another to all run commercials at the same time. Personally, I think we need a special prosecutor to investigate whether or not there was collusion going on here and, yes, maybe with the Russians, too. Permit me to explain. The scuttlebutt is that the Russians have contacted the media bigwigs and made them an offer they can't refuse - to get access to their commercials in exchange for billions of dollars.

They know that there are commercials on every channel at the same time and that we are more or less forced to listen to them. True, while some of us do leave the room for that second cup of coffee or to let the dog out, most of us stay put because we're not really sure how long it will take to return to regular programming. This exclusive information about the Russians comes to me from one of my friends who tends to be somewhat conspiratorial. He insists that the networks have allowed the Russkis to take control of our TVs during those commercials and have inserted subliminal messages (SM) into them.

Subliminal messages are actually lightning fast flashes of graphics, text or sound that appear and disappear so fast that you don't actually see or hear them on a conscious level - they are sent below our conscious threshold of perception and are stored in our subconscious for later review and actions. Think of a 'Tweet' sent at a speed so fast that you can't read it on your smart phone but is archived there, anyway.

The idea behind SM is to persuade us to buy something. That something could be a Russian product OR it could be propaganda that promotes a certain idea or point of view. For example, let's say that the Russians hacked the Democratic National Committee's (DNC) email server in order to get the names and email addresses of prominent Democrat leaders and voters. Then they created fake DNC emails which were sent to everybody on the list. In those emails, the Russians inserted SMs into the body of the message. The messages were all designed to persuade the recipients to doubt Hillary Clinton and support Bernie Sanders as their candidate...and, ultimately, swing the election in Donald Trump's favor.

A typical subliminal message would sound like this, "Hillary is crooked and can't be trusted. Only Bernie can win. Root for the coot!" There were others, too, like "Get free college, free healthcare and a free iphone - vote for Bernie!" While the messages may not have worked during the nominating process, subsequent Russian messages allegedly had an effect on the general election like this one we intercepted from a campaign speech given by Hillary Clinton, "See me. Hear me. But don't believe me. I lie for a living." If you doubt the effectiveness of SM you're probably not alone, but you do remember the old 'sleep therapy' records that we played while slumbering a few decades ago, don't you?

They purportedly helped correct bad habits or eliminate phobias like fear of flying. Or what about hypnosis that is now widely used by doctors and dentists? We know that works and has been used to replace some anesthesia, helping patients recover from procedures more quickly. Surely there's enough 'there' there on subliminal messaging to appoint a special prosecutor! If we're looking for someone above reproach with integrity and showmanship, I would recommend the mentalist, 'The Amazing Kreskin' (George Joseph Kresge). Still going strong at 82, Kreskin would be perfect for the role. He could hypnotize the witnesses and ask them questions. I can see him now questioning Susan Rice.

Kreskin: "Mrs. Rice, did you ever unmask any American?" Rice: "Yes, Timmy Feigenbaum after I took his Halloween candy in 1970." Kreskin: "Anyone else?" Rice: "A couple insignificant ones like General Michael Flynn, but nobody important." Kreskin: "Did you ever collude with the Russians yourself?" Rice: "The owner of a Russian dance studio in Washington, D.C. bought me dinner last year and afterwards asked me to dance for him in a tutu, but I told him that I had a blister on my foot."

Kreskin: "What happened then?" Rice: "He offered to sell me secret conversations between employees of the Trump campaign and a hacker named, "Kremlstilskin." Kreskin: "What did you do?" Rice turns towards Kreskin and says, "What do you think, old man? I snapped 'em up, paid him and then turned over the information to Valerie Jarrett who gave it to Huma Abedin who uploaded it onto Anthony Weiner's computer before giving it to Hillary Clinton who then gave it to James Comey. I don't know what Comey did with it."

Kreskin: "So do you think that's why the President fired Comey? Remember you're not only under hypnosis but under oath, too." Rice: "I think he was fired because he knew about poor Timmy Feigenbaum." Kreskin: "I have no further questions of you at this time. When I snap my fingers you will forget little Timmy Feigenbaum. He has forgiven you."

~

Postscript: America's social trends

America's culture is like a shark. It is constantly in motion, always prowling the waters of society's tolerance. It pushes at its boundaries, and when successful, it plants its flag in its newly-expanded territory. That's quite a mix of metaphors - sharks, flags, etc. - but I have a feeling you know what I mean. Societies and cultures are <u>always in a state of flux.</u> Sometimes they're at the cusp of a brand new curve. Sometimes they're in the middle or they're leveling out, getting ready to tackle the new challenges the next curve holds in store.

Look around you. This is not your grandfather's America. It's not even your father's, and it may not even be yours. The older most of us get the more convinced we are that the things that worked for us are the ones that will work for our children. That goes for our work ethic, attitudes on relationships like marriage, education, the fairness of our laws, our 'rightful' place in the community of nations, religion and a host of others that make up a culture and influence a society.

These days, it's getting more and more difficult to make convincing arguments for maintaining the status quo - the 'traditional America.' Our national social contract has collapsed under its own weight, partially due to neglect and a lack of commitment by previous Administrations. The Obama Administration prioritized achieving progress for some at the expense of others, the result being an alienation of a majority of Americans. By pursuing a policy of favoring some of America's communities over others, the average citizen (most notably Conservatives) felt that the change that Barack Obama was engineering was a wholesale upending of the balance between the rights of the majority and those of the minority.

His 'tail wagging the dog' policies infuriated some and stiffened the spines of many others and were, in my opinion, a contributing factor to the Democrats' loss of the 2016 Presidential election. Mainstream (read: conservative) Americans had had enough and wanted 'their' traditional America back. The Left is quick to say that what Conservatives <u>really</u> wanted was a *White* America back, but that is simply not the case, as most Americans value diversity and appreciate and respect the struggles that minorities have endured before and after the Civil Rights Acts of the sixties. Then there is the question of immigration and the part it plays in American society.

Again, the Left continues to twist the facts and has woven a false narrative that the Trump Administration - and by extension the White voter - is patently anti-immigrant simply because the Administration supports enforcing existing immigration law.

The so-called 'Muslim Ban' is a case in point. There is considerable media bias on this subject, and many in the media have become willing accomplices to and enablers of the *Resist* movement and are guilty of trying to throw the Constitution and a duly elected President under the bus in the name of 'social justice.'

As I write this, a terrible event occurred in Charlottesville, Virginia at a protest that was, according to the organizers, waged against the removal of a statue of the Confederate hero, General Robert E. Lee. Unfortunately, as so often happens in our fractured country, it escalated into violence initiated by what the media was calling, White Supremacists and neo-Nazis. Sadly, it resulted in the death of an innocent 32-year old woman who was purposely run over by an ultra-Right protestor that had traveled hundreds of miles to be at the demonstration. When mention was made of their masked, club-wielding opponents, however, the 'Anti-fa' (anti-fascists) that repeatedly beat up their opposite number, they were dubbed, "Peace Activists" by some in the media.

The President was quick to step to the microphone and issue a statement condemning the violence "on many sides." Predictably, his remarks about his disgust, sadness and anger about the violence was not enough for the mainstream media. Outlets like CNN severely criticized him for "not going far enough" in his condemnation because he didn't use the words, "White Supremacists." He did, however, two days later, but it still didn't satisfy the Left.

This showed, once again, that Mr. Trump cannot do anything right in the *fake news* mainstream media's eyes. They will continue to hold this President hostage and apply water-boarding by words to his every statement and action, no matter how honest and forthright they may be. The bottom line is that our culture is under attack by a variety of forces that hide behind the protection of the First Amendment and the anonymity of social media. The battles for America's sensibility and fairness have been joined, and it's only a matter of time before the number of casualties increase, dramatically. What about the next four years...and beyond?

We are now only eight months into Mr. Trump's presidency. If these first few months are any indication of his future in office, his chances of passing healthcare and tax reform, immigration reform or even getting an infrastructure bill through both Houses are bleak at best. This is especially likely considering the opposition from within his own party like the 'gang of three' that voted against even debating the new Republican healthcare suggestions: Senators John McCain, Susan Collins and Lisa Murkowski.

The Republican majorities in the House and Senate have not kept pace with Mr. Trump's plans to "Make America Great Again." They must realize that their majority is precarious and that they might only have one year to achieve their shared goals. Party fissures can be fixed, but time is not on their side. The Democrats sense dissension in the Republican ranks and smell blood in the political water.

Geopolitically, we are being challenged by nuclear threats from a rogue government in North Korea, intractable problems in Syria and the greater Middle East (like a nuclear Iran) and Russian adventurism. Domestically, there are the multiple investigations by the FBI, the Special Counsel and committees in both Houses of Congress. While the economy is starting to pick up, we are still suffering under Obamacare and one of the world's highest corporate tax rates. Corporations are optimistic, but they still have trillions of dollars parked offshore and will not wait forever for tax reform to bring them back.

Our major cities like Chicago are plagued by senseless gang-related murders while their mayors continue to blame 'illegal guns' instead of admitting that the root causes are more nuanced. Our *illegally here aliens* (IHA) are still being protected by sanctuary cities that refuse to cooperate with the Federal Government. Our universities have become hotbeds of anarchist teaching by seemingly untouchable professors. We continue to add hyphens between our ethnicity and our nationality and are becoming more tribal with each passing day. Our politics are driving us to leave our communities and move to towns, cities and states that share our political philosophies. Friends are frequently being *unfriended* on social media and families are breaking apart over differing political views.

Compromise and tolerance have become the new four-letter words of our times and few have the patience or endurance to listen to opposing views. So, what is in store for America? More of the same for some time to come, I'm afraid. The millennials are waiting for their parents and grandparents to die so they can re-make our country into their new sanitized politically-correct version of what they think America <u>should be</u> while the older voter is desperately clinging to *their* view of America. In addition to being tribal, we are skeptical, fearful and cynical. Some of us have chosen to retreat from bad news, fake news and ANY news.

We don't know who to believe anymore, and that deeply-rooted confusion is turning people away from information-gathering. Many are opting out of politics, and others are avoiding ideological conflict altogether. These are problems that cannot be solved by politics alone or by a strong leader. We must stay engaged. Lives lived in quiet desperation are an unacceptable alternative.

Fortunately, there are still many Americans that refuse to lower their standards or sideline their aspirations and dreams. We need these people. We must not abandon them or leave them bereft of hope. As for the future of our country, I'm reminded of Benjamin Franklin's response to a woman who was waiting to speak with him after the close of the Constitutional Convention in 1787. Her question was, "Well doctor, what have we got, a republic or a monarchy?" His response..."A republic if you can keep it." We had better keep that in mind.

www.ingramcontent.com/pod-product-compliance
Lightning Source LLC
Chambersburg PA
CBHW060835280326
41934CB00007B/787